FEDERAL PORT POLICY IN THE UNITED STATES

FEDERAL PORT POLICY IN THE UNITED STATES

Henry S. Marcus
James E. Short
John C. Kuypers
Paul O. Roberts

The MIT Press
Cambridge, Massachusetts, and London, England

387.1
F293

PUBLISHER'S NOTE

This format is intended to reduce the cost of publishing certain
works in book form and to shorten the gap between editorial preparation and final publication. Detailed editing and composition
have been avoided by photographing the text of this book directly
from the authors' typescript.

Library of Congress Cataloging in Publication Data

Main entry under title:

Federal port policy in the United States.

    Bibliography: p.
    1. Harbors--United States. 2. Harbors--
Environmental aspects--United States. 3. Transpor-
tation and state--United States. I. Marcus,
Henry S.
HE553.F37   387.1'0973   76-10853
ISBN 0-262-13125-0

Preface

Work on this book was performed for the Office of University Research of the U.S. Department of Transportation under Contract Number DOT-OS-40004 entitled "Utilizing the Existing Regulatory Structure to Influence Port Development." The authors would like to express their gratitude to DOT for making this opportunity possible and to the contract monitors, C. Peter Schumaier and John L. Craig.

A great number of people from government, industry, and academia have assisted the authors during the course of this research. While it is impractical to name each of these individuals, many of whom willingly gave much of their time, the authors wish to express their sincere appreciation for this aid. However, we would like to single out the efforts of C. Peter Schumaier who, both in terms of the amount of time devoted and the quality of his assistance, provided valuable help throughout the research.

Drafts of this manuscript were typed by Eleanor Baker, Helen Bell, and Beth Parkhurst.

The authors are solely responsible for any errors of commission or omission in this report.

To Our Parents

Table of Contents

Chapter

1. Introduction   1

2. Port Planning at the Local Level   6

3. Historical Summary of the Federal Role in Port
    Development   21

4. General Activities of Federal, State, and Local
    Organizations Involved in Port Policy and
    Development   40

5. The Federal Environmental Organizations--The
    Environmental Protection Agency and the Council
    on Environmental Quality   73

6. The U.S. Army Corps of Engineers   87

7. The Maritime Administration 126

8. The U.S. Coast Guard 139

9. The Department of Transportation 172

10. An Analysis of Key Elements of the Institutional
    Process of Port Development 202

11. Conclusions and Recommendations 215

Appendix

A. Statutory Authority for Federal Organizations
    Involved in Port Policy and Development 225

B. Principal Management and Labor Organizations 231

C. Channel and Harbor Projects with Authorized
    Depth of 25 Feet or More 239

D. Legislation Pertaining to the Port Activities
    of the Corps of Engineers 249

E. Organization and Functions of the Office of
    Ports and Intermodal Systems 263

F. Legislation Pertinent to Port and Waterways
    Activities of the U.S. Coast Guard 269

G. United States Coast Guard Planning and Programming
    Procedures 277

H. Deepwater Port Subject Areas and Licensing
    Procedures under S.1751 293

I. Federal Expenditures in the Water Resources Area . . . 301

Notes 309

Bibliography 347

Legislative Acts--Chronological 360

Index 363

List of Exhibits

1.1 Total Waterborne Commerce of the United States
     1950-1972 2

2.1 Ownership of U.S. Port Facilities 7

2.2 Berth Operating Practices at U.S. Ports 8

2.3 Comparison of Current Survey Port Development
     Expenditures with Total Outlays Since 1946 12

2.4 U.S. Container Terminal Development 13

2.5 1975 Capacity as Percentage of Demand 13

2.6 Proposed North American Port Capital Expenditures
     by Region and Facility Type (1973-1977) 15

2.7 Survey of Financial Data of 31 Ports 17

3.1 Chronology of Legislative Proposals 24

3.2 Historical Development of Federal Transportation
     Agencies 26

3.3 Discount Rates Applying to Federal Water Projects . . 33

4.1 Federal Organizations Involved in Port and Harbor
     Development 43

4.2 Matrix of the Federal Organizations Involved in
     Port and Harbor Development 45

4.3 Obligated Public Works Projects, by Type of Project . 48

4.4 Principal State Agencies Exercising Authority in
     Port and Waterway Management 67

5.1 Environmental Impact Statements Filed Annually,
     by Agency, to July 1, 1974 75

5.2 Criteria for Determining Acceptability of Dredged
     Spoil Disposal to the Nation's Waters 78

5.3 Organization Chart for the Environmental Protection
     Agency 84

6.1 Army Corps of Engineers' Civil Works Expenditures
     in Relation to Federal Government Budget, 1962-1975 . 89

6.2 Simplified Organization Chart, OCE 91

6.3 Simplified Organization Chart, Directorate of
     Civil Works 92

6.4   Work Permit Procedure, U.S. Army Corps of Engineers--
      River and Harbor Act   100

6.5   The Mechanism by Which Projects are Conceived,
      Authorized, and Constructed   102

6.6   Corps of Engineers Analysis of Average Time for
      Planning and Construction of Civil Works Projects
      (May 1971 Status)   105

6.7   Chart of Trend in Backlog of Authorized Civil
      Works Projects (Projects Unfunded for
      Construction)   106

6.8   Data Table of Corps of Engineers Trend in Backlog
      of Authorized Civil Works Projects   107

7.1   Historical Development of the Maritime
      Administration   129

7.2   Organization Chart for the U.S. Department of
      Commerce, Maritime Administration   131

8.1   U.S. Coast Guard Organization   144

8.2   Organization Chart, U.S. Coast Guard Headquarters . . 145

8.3   Digest of U.S. Coast Guard Budget Estimates by
      Activities for Fiscal Year 1975   152

9.1   Reorganization of Agencies: Proposed Organization,
      Civilian Transportation Agencies   179

9.2   Department of Transportation   181

9.3   Organization Chart for the Department of
      Transportation, Office of the Secretary   182

Appendix Exhibits

A.1   Principal Statutory Authorities for Federal
      Organizations Involved in Port Policy and
      Development   227

B.1   Principal Management and Labor Organizations   233

C.1   Channel and Harbor Projects with Authorized Depth
      of 25 Feet or More   241

D.1   Legislation Pertaining to the Port Activities
      of the Corps of Engineers   251

E.1   Text of Administrative Order to the Office of
      Ports and Intermodal Systems   265

F.1   Legislation Pertinent to Port and Waterways
      Activities of the U.S. Coast Guard 271

G.1   Program Structure--U.S.C.G. Headquarters 281

G.2   Resource Planning and Programming Procedure 283

G.3   Criteria for Inclusion of Projects under AC&I
      (Acquisition, Construction, and Improvement) 286

G.4   Resource Change Proposal Procedure 287

G.5   Planning Factors Development and Distribution 291

H.1   Deepwater Port Subject Areas 295

H.2   Department of the Interior: Deepwater Port
      Coordination Chart of Federal Agency Involvement . . . 299

I.1   Federal Outlays by Category and Agency for Water
      Resources and Related Developments 303

I.2   Comparison of Federal Outlays for Water Resources
      with Those for Other Federal Civil Public Works
      and the Total U.S. Budget 305

I.3   Estimated Historical Federal Expenditures for
      Water Resources and Related Activities 306

I.4   Total Historical Expenditures for Water Resources
      Development 307

I.5   Projection of Capital Investment Costs Based on
      Extrapolation of Needs in Framework Studies of
      WRC 308

CHAPTER 1

INTRODUCTION

The combined forces of modern technology and a growing
national environmental awareness have substantially affected the
involvement and impact of the federal government in U.S. ocean
port policy. The advent of large containerships and even larger
supertankers has revolutionized marine transportation technology
and necessitated the construction of wholly new terminal facilities to meet these modern transportation systems. Furthermore,
environmental legislation, fostered through the establishment of a
large and articulate public constituency, has also significantly
influenced port and marine transportation development.

The ocean port is at the nexus of these revolutionary changes.
As intermodal transport gateways, ports are affected by changes in
ship as well as rail and trucking technology. As major economic
entities, ports provide services which entail many types of economic costs and benefits. The magnitude of this waterborne commerce
and its concurrent national economic impact is emphasized by the
more than 1.6 billion tons of waterborne commerce that annually
flow through U.S. port facilities, as shown in Exhibit 1.1.[1]

Growing public interest in land use, coastal zone management,
and environmental and safety regulation often place port managers
in difficult and conflicting positions. Safety and environmental
regulations pertaining to ships and other transport modes affect
port operations. Terminal expansion plans may be caught up in
land use or environmental impact statement procedures. And port
development plans for intermodal transportation systems, including
highway or rail connections, may also be constrained by federal
transportation regulations.

Many of these challenges to modern ports are heavily influenced by the federal government, which has always supported port-
related activities. Traditionally, federal policy dating back to
the Constitution has been that no federal action should discriminate between ports. However, the combined factors of modern technology and environmental awareness have disturbed the traditional
port planning and development process.

Technology and Ecology

At first glance, modern technology seems to have had a paradoxical effect on U.S. ports. The United States presently does
not have a port which can handle, when fully loaded, the largest
oil tankers in international use. While lagging in this area,
however, the nation has apparently overbuilt in others. In the
words of a Maritime Administration official, "...we find the
Atlantic and Pacific coasts literally lined with container
terminals--from Boston to Jacksonville, from San Diego to
Seattle."[2] Hence, while superport development has been slowed

EXHIBIT 1.1

TOTAL WATERBORNE COMMERCE OF THE UNITED STATES 1950-1972

(in tons of 2,000 pounds)

Year	Foreign and Domestic Total	Foreign Total	Domestic Total
1950	820,583,571	169,224,695	651,358,876
1951	924,128,411	232,055,832	692,072,579
1952	887,721,984	227,326,277	660,395,707
1953	923,547,693	217,396,489	706,151,204
1954	867,640,207	213,844,290	653,795,917
1955	1,016,135,785	271,102,932	745,032,853
1956	1,092,912,924	326,689,789	766,223,135
1957	1,131,401,434	358,539,550	772,861,884
1958	1,004,515,776	308,850,798	695,664,978
1959	1,052,402,102	326,269,939	726,132,163
1960	1,099,850,431	339,277,275	760,573,156
1961	1,062,155,182	329,329,818	732,825,364
1962	1,129,404,375	358,599,030	770,805,345
1963	1,173,766,964	385,658,999	788,107,965
1964	1,238,093,573	421,925,133	816,168,440
1965	1,272,896,243	443,726,809	829,169,434
1966	1,334,116,078	471,391,083	862,724,995
1967	1,336,606,078	465,972,238	870,633,840
1968	1,395,839,450	507,950,002	887,889,448
1969	1,448,711,541	521,312,362	927,399,179
1970	1,531,696,507	580,969,133	950,727,374
1971	1,512,583,690	565,985,584	946,598,106
1972	1,618,792,605	629,980,844	986,811,761

Source: Waterborne Commerce of the United States, 1972, U.S. Army Corps of Engineers

by institutional and regulatory complexities, container terminals have continued to flourish. And federal monies, such as
those administered by the Corps of Engineers and the Economic
Development Administration, have been applied to promote such
development.

The past decade has also been one of great interest in legislation pertaining to ecology and pollution. The National Environmental Policy Act of 1969 (NEPA), which requires all federal
organizations to draft impact statements on proposed plans and
programs which significantly affect the environment, has dramatically changed the structure and balance of federal decision-
making.

As a consequence of these many concerns, federal influence in
port development is split between the special interests of a number
of federal organizations. Since individually these organizations consider only narrow conceptual boundaries, collectively
their actions relating to port development tend to be fragmented
and parochially oriented.

This report explains the genesis of this fragmented federal
system and its important effects on present-day technological
and environmental factors in ocean port development. Importantly,
the study defines a conceptual methodology for analyzing the
impact and involvement of federal organizations concerned with
port development.

The Study

The study examines U.S. federal port policy. However, since
in practice regional, state or local policy has an important influence on federal decision-making, their impacts are also discussed.

The report traces the legislation and historical accumulation of explicitly defined powers related to port activities
possessed by federal agencies. It identifies the many federal
agencies which have an impact, either directly or indirectly,
on port planning and development, and analyzes the legislative
mandates and present port activities of each of these federal
organizations. Moreover, possible bureaucratic shifts within the
existing regulatory power structure are considered in context
with the institutional pressures for change in the overall
policy-making system.

Furthermore, the study emphasizes federal port policy as it
relates to the development of ocean ports. There are 130 ports
with depths of 25 feet or greater located on the four coasts of
the United States--that is, the Atlantic, Pacific, Gulf of Mexico,
and the Great Lakes, including Alaska, Hawaii, and Puerto Rico.[3]
In many cases, the concerns of inland waterways, with depths
typically ranging between six and fourteen feet, are intertwined
with those of ocean terminals. Consequently, this study also
considers inland waterways programs and policies.

Report Format

    This report is both descriptive and analytical. In investi-
gating the role of federal organizations developing port policy,
various techniques of bureaucratic or organizational analyses
are applied. Moreover, the report develops a specific and cohesive analytical framework based on two criteria: (1) the level
of involvement in port development exercised by organizations
of the federal government; and (2) the impacts associated with
this involvement. This base provides both a straightforward
descriptive and a more subtle analytical investigation of these
actors. To further broaden the analysis, the report includes
a time, or historical, dimension.

    Public ports and port systems are components of local,
regional, and national planning frameworks. Chapters 1 and 2
consider the diverse governmental lives of ports, discuss the
concept of public ports as utilities, and describe significant
planning factors which play a role in local port development.

    Federal policy applying to ports is in one sense a captive
of historical precedent. The lengthy history of domestic port
development has given rise to a fragmentation of governmental
authority and responsibility regarding port activities. Key
planning and policy decisions affecting major port and hinterland development schemes have been traditionally left to paro-
chial localized interests--even though both direct and indirect
federal subsidies are involved. Chapters 3 and 4 of the report
discuss the historical development and the contemporary nature
of the federal port policy process.

    Chapter 3 examines the importance of precedent in federal
policy formation. In outlining the history of major federal
organizations concerned with ocean ports, the chapter focuses
on the role of Congress and its legislative activities in maritime transportation areas. Chapter 4 identifies the principal
federal actors involved in port development, and compiles information on their statutory duties and responsibilities.

    The following five chapters (Chapters 5 through 9) are
devoted to the major federal agencies and organizations involved
in port policy. The key importance of a growing national environmental awareness is emphasized in Chapter 5. Supported by an articulate and pervasive public constituency, new environmental legislation and major bureaucracies concerned with ecology have changed
the federal decision-making system. At the port level, new environmental standards and criteria have dramatically changed the
traditional port planning and development scenario.

    National environmental awareness has also been of particular
consequence to the policies and programs of the Army Corps of
Engineers. In Chapter 6, the impacts of new environmental standards and criteria on the traditional implementation of Corps
programs is examined. New technological dimensions have also
influenced Corps policy and program implementation. Advances
in intermodal transportation have made port economic analyses

more complicated. Furthermore, the uncertainties in the determination of proper criteria and standards for evaluating navigation projects comprise another area of concern for the Corps.

     The role of the Maritime Administration is examined in
Chapter 7. Under various statutory mandates, MarAd possesses
the most comprehensive legal charge of all federal organizations
in terms of port development. The degree to which MarAd has
implemented these charges, and an analysis of these actions,
are studied.

     The following two chapters (Chapters 8 and 9) consider the
Department of Transportation (DOT) and its marine component,
the United States Coast Guard (USCG). Chapter 8 discusses the
pervasive nature of Coast Guard regulatory jurisdiction at the
port level, while Chapter 9 considers the DOT's role as the
principal coordinator of national transportation policy. Importantly, these two chapters distinguish and explain the interrela-
tionship between the Office of the Secretary's strategic transportation policy role and the U.S. Coast Guard's operational
regulatory role at the port level.

     The key elements of the fragmented federal port policy
process, the inherent advantages and disadvantages of this structural system, and the possibilities for future policy development are among several issues brought forth in the concluding
two chapters of the report. Chapter 10 summarizes the principal
imperatives for policy change emphasized in the preceding chapters on specific agencies. Moreover, the chapter places these
issues in context with other maritime policy issues.

     Finally, Chapter 11 advances the conclusions and recommen-
dations of the report. Strategies for policy and program innovation are analyzed under the existing regulatory environment and
in view of potential port-related legislation.

CHAPTER 2

PORT PLANNING AT THE LOCAL LEVEL

Introduction

Before analyzing the impact of environmental concerns and technology on port development, it is useful to consider the traditional
method by which ports have developed. In the United States local
public port authorities and private terminal operators initiate
the institutional process of port development. Consequently, this
chapter will examine the process of port planning at the local level.

Port Structure in the United States[1]

The Maritime Administration (MarAd) estimates there are
2,400 marine terminals capable of accommodating U.S. world commerce and trade now in operation on all four coasts, including
Alaska, Hawaii and Puerto Rico. More than 60 percent of these
port facilities are privately owned and operated by profit-making
organizations as shown in Exhibit 2.1. These facilities are mainly used to handle single-bulk commodities such as oil, coal,
grain, iron ore, cement, salt, sugar, liquefied natural gas,
liquefied petroleum gas, etc. The port activity in this instance
is an integral part of a broader corporate function, such as coal
mining and marketing, petroleum refining and distribution, or
steel production and distribution, so that a single corporation,
such as an oil company, might own all the cargo passing through
such a terminal.

In contrast, the majority of publicly-owned port terminal
facilities handles general cargoes, typically manufactured or
semimanufactured goods, moving in break-bulk form, containers,
or other types of unitization for a multiplicity of shippers and
consignees on a "common carrier" basis. As Exhibit 2.2 shows,
the operation of these facilities varies. Most small ports with
less than 10 berths run an open public berth operation, assigning
vessels to berths on request and charging for the number of days
on berth (dockage) and tons moved (wharfage). By contrast, at
most large U.S. ports with over 40 berths, public port authorities
contract their terminal facilities through the use of such legal
means as exclusive leases or preferential permits to a specific
tenant, such as a terminal operator, stevedoring company, or steamship line. In this instance, the tenant pays an annual rental to
cover operating and fixed costs. Medium-sized ports tend to use
the operating procedures of both the large and small ports, resulting in combinations of leasing, preferential permits, and open
public berthing.

Private Terminal Development

The economic development of private terminals is similar
to the development of most other capital assets in the private
sector. When a private firm decides to buy a warehouse, a fleet
of vehicles, a machine, or a factory, it first establishes that

EXHIBIT 2.1

Ownership of U.S. Port Facilities

Type of Ownership	Number of Terminals (Estimate)	Percent of U.S. Total (Estimate)
Private (profitmaking organizations)	1,488	62.0
Local government agencies	576	24.0
State government agencies	288	12.0
U.S. government agencies (non-military)	43	1.75
Private (non-profitmaking organizations)	6	0.25
Total	2,401	100.00

Source: Estimates are extrapolated from data contained in Joint Economic Committee, the Congress of the U.S. State and Local Public Facility Needs and Financing, Volume I, Chapter 15, Marine Port Facilities, December 1966, prepared by the Maritime Administration, p. 332. Public Port Financing in the United States, U.S. Department of Commerce/Maritime Administration, June 1974, p. 3.

this purchase will fulfill an economic need to the overall corporate structure. It would be expected that similar concepts apply in the purchase of a privately-owned maritime terminal.* Consequently, on a national scale there should be neither an excessive overcapacity nor a large undercapacity of private terminals.

The development of publicly-owned port facilities differs greatly from that of private facilities. To understand the process of public port development, it is necessary to first consider the concept of the public port.

Concept of a Public Port

Ports, oftentimes referred to as "gateways," are in fact more than just gateways. With impacts on the commerce of the harbor city and its hinterland, the public port is likely viewed

---

*A private corporation moving bulk commodities may choose to acquire an exclusive lease to a maritime terminal through a port authority. By having the port authority own the terminal rather than the private corporation, the private firm enjoys some of the property and income tax exemption privileges of the port authority.

EXHIBIT 2.2

Berth Operating Practices at U.S. Ports

Small Ports	Total Berths	Leased	Preferential	Open
Buffalo, N.Y.	8	0	0	8
Providence, R.I.	8	0	1	7
Wilmington, Del.	8	0	0	8
Gulfport, Miss.	7	0	0	7
Brownsville, Texas	9	0	0	9
Vancouver, Wash.	9	0	0	9

Medium Ports				
Toledo, Ohio	11	10	0	1
Cleveland, Ohio	11	7	0	4
Philadelphia, Pa.	30	30	0	0
Baltimore, Md.	28	0	18	10
Hampton Roads, Va.	21	19	0	2
Savannah, Ga.	19	0	0	19
Jacksonville, Fla.	15	2	2	11
Galveston, Texas	37	0	20	17
Houston, Texas	29	0	3	26
Oakland, Calif.	18	11	4	3
San Diego, Calif.	16	0	0	16

Large Ports				
New York/New Jersey	90	71	0	19
New Orleans, La.	88	0	82	6
Long Beach, Calif.	45	0	45	0
Los Angeles, Calif.	86	0	86	0
San Francisco, Calif.	80	0	63	17

Source: Data compiled from Committee II, Standardization and
Special Research, American Association of Port Authorities,
Survey Questionnaire on Leasing Practices at U.S. Ports, October
1964. Published in Public Port Financing in the United States,
U.S. Department of Commerce/Maritime Administration, June 1974,
p.5.

by local communities as an important utility, serving as the focal point of a large proportion of business in the port city. Accordingly, the port is essentially a community enterprise, partly shaped by the community's conception of what the port is or should be.

Ownership and funding of a public port come in many shapes and forms, ranging from departments of municipal, county or state governments to quasi-autonomous local, state and bi-state authorities. Many have activities which go beyond strictly port matters controlling, in addition to harbor facilities, various other transportation facilities such as tunnels, bridges, airports, ferries, and so on. Thus, ports tend to assume the shape which community enterprise molds financially.

In an analysis presented in the paper "Economic Rationalization of Port Investments," the author discusses four major economic criteria considered by a typical public port in seeking a port investment:[2]

First, direct financial return--this is achieved by a variety of charges for the use of facilities or occupancy of space of a terminal, notably: wharfage--a fee levied against each ton of cargo that moves across a wharf apron; dockage--a fee levied against the vessel for the privilege of berthing alongside the terminal; demurrage--a charge levied against cargo that remains in in-transit storage in the terminal area for greater than a specified free time period; and various rental and other charges...

Second, the employment and revenue that will be generated directly within the port area as a result of the handling, transfer, and storage of cargo, and expenditures associated with the vessel while it is in port...

Third, the stimulation of local business and additional income that results from the circulation of the direct income, or the so-called "multiplier effect." The indirect income has been estimated by government agencies to be of the order of magnitude of two and one-half times the direct income.

Fourth, the savings in transportation costs to the shippers and receivers of cargo. Much of this saving is realized outside of the immediate port area and does not produce direct revenue to the area. However, the reduced costs could result in the attraction of additional cargo to the port, thereby producing the revenues and benefits noted previously.

Consequently, a public port must be concerned not only with its return on investment, similar to a private terminal, but also with its impact on the surrounding community. One port consultant has indicated that each ton of bulk cargo passing through a port brings $4 to $8 of revenue to the surrounding community, while each ton of general cargo brings in $25 to $30.[3] The Port of Seattle claims that each ton of general cargo, either containerized or in break-bulk form, passing through the port creates a gross payroll of $110.80 in the local county.[4] While analysts can argue about the exact benefit of general cargo passing through a port, there is no doubt that such commerce brings benefits to the local surrounding community. For this reason, ports have sprung up all along the coasts of the United States. Even within a major harbor or bay, two public ports may compete, such as the Ports of Los Angeles and Long Beach in San Pedro Bay, and the New York City Department of Ports and Terminals and the Port Authority of New York and New Jersey in the New York harbor area. A large coastal state like California or Texas has several major public ports competing within its boundaries.

Each public port authority is understandably interested in attracting economic benefits only for its "constituency" in the surrounding community.

Hinterland of the Port

The tributary area served by the port is sometimes known as the port's hinterland. It is characterized by the geographic extent of trade points whose economic outlet is through the port. The extent of a port's hinterland may differ for each commodity handled through the port. Factors which determine the extent of the hinterland include the demand for the commodity, the freight rates to the port, facilities located at the port, time availability and supply of vessel space at the port, the balance of general and specialized trade cargo handled at the port, and the prices charged for the port's services.[5] In addition, these factors function to divide the hinterland into competitive and noncompetitive regions.

The noncompetitive hinterland can be considered as the tributary area including the immediate port community for which the port forms a "natural" gateway. A distinct cost advantage over other ports permits the local port to attract all cargo shipments from this area.

Equal or only slightly differentiated freight rates in the competitive hinterland permits two or more ports to compete for shipping trade on the basis of factors other than rates. In this area, port cost, facilities, various port services, and frequency of vessel dockings become key factors in attracting trade.[6]

The Container Revolution

The container revolution brought serious challenges to public ports. By unitizing cargo in containers rather than handling it in break-bulk cargo form, sophisticated port facilities could maintain a cargo handling rate approximately 10 to 20 times faster than that of conventional general cargo vessels. Unitization resulted in capital-intensive operations both in vessels and terminal facilities. Operators of modern expensive containerships sought to decrease the number of port calls made so that they

could increase the productivity of their investments. In a similar
manner, public ports which had purchased new container facilities
desired to have high utilization of their equipment to obtain an
adequate economic return on their investments. Both the vessel and
terminal operations were subject to economies of scale so that,
when fully utilized, both the steamship company and port were
better off financially with their larger investments.[7]

Containerization, however, placed some ports in an awkward
situation. Port directors realized that the inevitable economic
result of containerization would be to decrease the number of port
calls per containership and bring about a transportation system
where, due to economies of scale, fewer numbers of larger containerships and larger terminals would carry an equal volume of cargo
to that which had existed earlier. A containership operator could
economically use feeder systems of truck or rail to consolidate
cargo into a major container terminal rather than making an additional port call. Consequently, large portions of what had been a
noncompetitive hinterland for one port now suddenly became part of
the competitive hinterland.

Therefore, each port director felt that, if he did not obtain
a container facility, modern containerships would discontinue service to his port, and it would simply cease to exist as a viable
general cargo port. Consequently, many public ports felt they had
no choice but to keep up with modern technology and build container
terminals.

The private interests within each port hinterland that depended on the port strongly supported this move since they did not
wish to be placed in a noncompetitive position with the decline of
their port. Labor unions, shippers, small businesses serving the
terminal facilities and vessels, and the local Chamber of Commerce
all backed the port in its attempt to modernize its facilities.

However, the extent to which a port could raise funds for new
container terminals depended partly on its ability to obtain contractual agreements with potential users. The financial resources
of the port include internal subsidies from unrelated investments
as well as subsidies from governmental bodies on a local, state
and national level.

The Rise of Container Terminals

Port expenditures for the time period 1966-1972 are compared
with the time period 1946-1972 in Exhibit 2.3. The data show U.S.
ports made more than one-third of their investments in the final
seven years of the 27-year period, reflecting the trend to more
capital-intensive facilities.

The progress of U.S. container terminal development as of
June 30, 1971, is shown in Exhibit 2.4. In February 1972, a study
sponsored by the Maritime Administration predicted a large overcapacity of container terminals by 1975, as shown by Exhibit 2.5.

EXHIBIT 2.3

COMPARISON OF CURRENT SURVEY PORT DEVELOPMENT EXPENDITURES
WITH TOTAL OUTLAYS SINCE 1946

Region	Jan. 1946–Dec. 1972	Jan. 1966–Dec. 1972	% of Total Capital Outlay	% of Total Time Interval
North Atlantic	$1,263,405,219	$ 425,210,219	33%	25%
South Atlantic	222,802,334	108,723,334	48%	25%
Gulf Coast	566,607,909	181,780,909	32%	25%
Pacific Coast	746,200,553	308,673,553	41%	25%
Alaska, Hawaii & Puerto Rico	168,435,311	66,327,311	39%	25%
U.S. Great Lakes	275,642,000	24,914,000	9%	25%
Total U.S.	3,243,093,326	1,115,629,326	34%	25%
Canada	562,761,200	134,174,200	23%	25%
North American Total	3,805,854,526	1,249,803,526	32%	25%

Source: "North American Port Expenditure Survey," U.S. Department of Commerce/
Maritime Administration, March 1974, p. 5.

EXHIBIT 2.4

U.S. Container Terminal Development

Date	6/30/67	6/30/68	6/30/69	6/30/70	6/30/71
Full Container Berths	117	132	178	202	207
Existing	50	62	69	81	90
Under Construction	40	24	41	49	51
Planned	27	46	68	72	66

Source: "MarAd 1971, Year of the Breakthrough," Annual Report of
the Maritime Administration for Fiscal Year 1971, p. 18.

EXHIBIT 2.5

1975 Capacity as Percentage of Demand

U.S. Seaboard	Container Lifts All Trades
North Atlantic	240
South Atlantic	160
Gulf Coast	90
Pacific Coast	570
Great Lakes	0
Total	250

Source: Manalytics, Inc., "Impact of Maritime
Containerization on the United States
Transportation System," Vol. I, p. 21.

The report forecast that the capacity of container terminals on
the U.S. Pacific Coast would be almost six times the demand by 1975.
It would appear that the publication of the study in 1972 predicting overcapacity had little effect on the development plans of most
port authorities. Exhibit 2.6 shows the proposed North American
port capital expenditures by region and facility type for the
time period 1973 through 1977. In comparing the data from Exhibits 2.6 and 2.3, note that each of the four coasts of the United
States plans even greater expenditures related to specialized
general cargo terminals, which include container terminals as
well as roll-on roll-off and barge-carrying ship facilities, in
the four-year time period from 1973 to 1977 than in the six-year
period from 1966 to 1972. However, these plans may be hindered
by the increased difficulty ports may experience in obtaining
sources of financing for such facility expansion and improvement.[8]

The Resulting Port Environment

Those involved in the process of port development do not necessarily share common perspectives. At the local level the director
of the port authority is concerned with developing the port in the
best interests of its constituency. However, federal officials
are typically more interested in port development on a national
scale. Therefore, competition between port authorities, which
port directors deem as necessary, may appear to be wasteful from
a national perspective.

One MarAd official describes the situation in port investment
in the following way:[9]

> In their haste to compete with others in their area,
> many ports have lost sight of what their basic purpose
> should be and have concentrated instead on imitating
> what other ports are doing. This leads to what we can
> call the "me too" syndrome, with a port building a con-
> tainer terminal, for example, not because of a basic
> need, but because a port across the bay or river has one
> and is attracting new services....

Ports also compete for other types of unitized cargo besides
containers, such as barges carried in specially constructed ships
like those of the LASH (Lighter Aboard SHip) design. A report
analyzing Texas ports points out:[10]

> ...the proposed LASH terminal at the Port of Houston
> is designed to accommodate fourteen specific vessels
> which are expected to use the facility as early as 1975.
> However, Galveston Wharves has just completed a container
> and LASH terminal facility which can accommodate these
> vessels. Since cargoes carried on LASH type vessels are
> contained in barges, the existence of two such facilities
> within fifty miles of each other and connected by a water-
> way on which the barges could be moved surely does not
> constitute the most efficient use of port development
> capital.

EXHIBIT 2.6

PROPOSED NORTH AMERICAN PORT CAPITAL EXPENDITURES BY REGION AND FACILITY TYPE
(1973-1977)

Region	Conventional General Cargo	% of Regional/ National Total	Specialized General Cargo (Container, RO/RO, Bargeship)	% of Regional/ National Total	Liquid & Dry Bulk Total	% of Regional/ National Total	Total Regional/ National	% of Grand Total
North Atlantic	$119,367,500	33%	$229,993,000	64%	$ 5,800,000	2%	$ 355,160,500	20%
South Atlantic	53,471,665	47%	55,086,665	48%	5,064,094	5%	113,622,424	7%
Gulf Coast	52,199,109	8%	45,786,233	8%	496,596,186	84%	594,581,528	34%
Pacific Coast	77,489,100	21%	219,096,600	60%	71,453,000	19%	368,038,700	21%
Alaska, Hawaii & Puerto Rico	22,323,000	62%	7,642,000	22%	5,741,000	16%	35,706,000	3%
U.S. Great Lakes	7,432,622	42%	4,066,666	24%	5,842,000	34%	17,341,288	2%
U.S. Total	332,282,996	23%	561,671,164	38%	590,496,280	39%	1,484,450,440	87%
Canada	36,038,000	16%	133,416,000	60%	51,050,000	24%	220,504,000	13%
Grand Total North America	368,320,996	21%	695,087,164	41%	641,546,280	38%	1,704,995,440	100%

Source: "North American Port Expenditure Survey," U.S. Department of Commerce/
Maritime Administration, p. 8.

The Director of Planning and Research for the Port of Los Angeles, a public port located in the same bay as the public port of Long Beach, feels that the unnecessary costs of fierce competition between Los Angeles and Long Beach extend well beyond the duplication of facilities.[11]

> The Port of Los Angeles has felt for many years that the two harbors should be joined, and the sooner the better, as additional investments are being made by both harbors in duplicate facilities, to say nothing of duplication in staff, maintenance equipment, port security, fire prevention, trade promotion trips, and other activities.
>
> It is extremely difficult for these two harbors to plan independently when they are in such a competitive position. The present situation has resulted in shipping lines merely shopping between the two harbors to see where they can get the best deal with each Harbor Department trying to accommodate them, even though there will be little or no return on investment in the required facilities.

A study by the Port Finance Committee of the American Association of Port Authorities in a survey of 31 ports indicates that little or no return on investment may be a nationwide trait of public ports, as shown in Exhibit 2.7. It would appear that the combination of fierce competition, overcapacity and low financial returns is inherent in the public port system of the United States.

Subsidies

The return on investment for ports shown in Exhibit 2.7 may be greatly overstated due to various subsidies received by the ports. That is, public ports do even worse than appears in the exhibit.

The general manager of the Port of Seattle has pointed out that almost all the ports in the world receive some type of public subsidy such as:[12]

1. Direct appropriations of national, state, and local governmental agencies;

2. Capital bonding capabilities acquired through a "de facto" subsidy of perpetual tunnel and bridge toll revenues;

3. Shorelands held in "public trust" for public harbor development;

4. In some jurisdictions (such as in the State of Washington), proportionately modest yet highly significant property taxes;

5. Provision for services (such as security, legal, accounting) at less than cost, or on a nonreimbursable basis;

EXHIBIT 2.7

Survey of Financial Data of 31 Ports

(Thousands $)

	North Atlantic	South Atlantic	Gulf	Northwest Pacific	Great Lakes	California
Gross Investments in Facilities	$25,723	26,434	45,327	50,786	27,587	97,496
Capital Funds Expended during Year	5,010	2,766	2,093	5,978	244	5,922
Capital Funds Provided from Sources outside of Net Revenues	3,916	1,873	919	5,052	38	3,650
Return on Investments						
A. Before Debt Service	1%	2%	3%	3%	3%	5%
B. After Debt Service	(-2%)	2%	1%	(-1%)	(-1%)	2%

Source: Committee VI, Port Finance, American Association of Port Authorities, made public at the 60th Annual Convention, September 1971, and published in Public Port Financing in the United States, Maritime Administration, June 1974, p. 17.

6.   And many other forms of national or local public
     subsidies--both direct and indirect.

It is difficult to determine the exact return on investment,
exclusive of subsidies, for public ports because the forms that
subsidies may take are quite varied. A recent study by MarAd,
however, shows that state subsidies account for 15 percent of
total financing for U.S. port development activities, while federal subsidies account for 7 percent.[13]   Quite often local citi-
zens have little or no idea to what extent they are subsidizing
the local port authority. In the case of a port authority which
controls a seaport as well as a toll bridge or airport, the non-
maritime facilities may make profits that outweigh losses of
the marine sector. The average citizen, unaware of this cross-
subsidization of facilities, feels that the port authority must
be running the seaport at a profit since the port is not asking
the local or state government for more funds.

Development of Superports

Segments of the country have exhibited a determination toward building offshore terminals reminiscent of the spirit that
has led to the apparent overcapacity of container terminals.
Strong forces in both Louisiana and Texas are pushing to build
offshore terminal superport facilities. Each group initially
presented a two-pronged offensive to win public support. First,
both claimed that a superport would bring valuable industrial and
economic growth to its state. Second, each group stated that
failure to build a deep-draft port facility would bring economic
disaster to its local region.

The second point is illustrated in the Texas-Louisiana
superport competition. Part of a 1971 report entitled "Work
Plan for a Study of the Feasibility of an Offshore Terminal
in the Texas Coast Region," stated:[14]

...perhaps the greatest threat to Texas ports is that
[proposed superport] taking shape in Louisiana.

Not to be outdone, an article in a New Orleans paper read:[15]

A victory of Texas in the race for a superport in the
Gulf of Mexico will not only throttle industrial expansion in Louisiana but could cause existing industries
to pack up and leave, it was predicted Monday.

Gillis Long, chairman of Governor-elect Edwin Edwards'
superport task force, told newsmen that there is going
to be only one offshore facility constructed in the Gulf
and Louisiana had better be the state to build it.

More recently the competition between Texas and Louisiana
has seemingly subsided, apparently caused by the feeling that it
is economically feasible to have offshore terminals in the form of
mono-buoys in both areas. A group of companies has formed the
Louisiana Offshore Oil Port, Inc. (LOOP) to construct a deepwater

terminal facility off the Louisiana coast, while a consortium in
Texas called Seadock has plans to build an offloading buoy facility
26.5 miles out at Freeport. Several corporations have joined both
consortia. Since investments by these firms have been proposed in
both terminal systems, this would imply there can be no great
competition between the two corsortia.*

However, there are still other parties in the Gulf of Mexico
who may yet bring about an overbuilding of deepwater terminals.
Top administration officials of Alabama, Mississippi and Tennessee
have stated that they strongly believe that a superport must be
located off the mouth of the Tennessee-Tombigbee Waterway in the
vicinity of Mobile and Pascagoula. In addition, there are parties
in Texas who want Texas superports elsewhere than the Freeport
site.

A quite different concern is that no deepwater terminals at
all will be constructed--particularly on the Atlantic and Gulf
coasts. The obstacles preventing the building of deepwater terminals are a combination of political, legal, environmental, and
procedural factors. Areas of residential housing and resort
attractions have opposed offshore terminals because of their
concern for possible oil spills and the reduction in "quality of
life" which might accompany the construction of a new refinery
in their community in conjunction with an offshore terminal.
Active environmentalist groups have championed these causes as
well as other possible ecological concerns in their legal
actions hindering deepwater terminal construction.

Ownership of Superports

While private corporations have expressed a willingness to
own and operate superports, some port authorities and state officials would prefer to see the deepwater terminals run as public
ports. Traditionally, general cargo terminals, serving a wide
variety of users, have been operated by public ports while bulk
cargo terminals, serving usually a single user, have been run by
private ports. Deepwater terminals used to serve modern huge tankers greater than 200,000 deadweight tons may be owned either privately or publicly, but in either case such superports will probably share characteristics of both types of facilities. While
such terminals would not be single-user facilities, a consortium
of oil companies could be the only users for a particular facility.
While each ton of oil or other bulk commodity passing through a
superport would not have the same economic impact as a ton of
general cargo, the huge annual throughput of cargo would have a
striking economic impact on the surrounding region.

---

*In 1973, five firms--Shell, Texaco, Amoco Pipe Line, Exxon and
Toronto Pipe Line (a Gulf Oil subsidiary)--belonged to both consortia. However, in 1976 only Shell remained in both, reflecting
rising costs and uncertainties of future oil imports.

The Federal Role

Viewing the public port as a utility does not present an unusual concept for U.S. society. Telephone companies and electric power companies are other common forms of utilities in the U.S. environment. However, public utilities do not usually compete to the extent that ports do.

A prominent characteristic of a public utility is that, in theory, it operates at its greatest efficiency as a monopoly.* This efficiency is due to the economies of scale which result in a decreasing unit cost with increasing output. Because modern port facilities are capital-intensive, the more traffic moving through the port, the lower the per-ton cost will be. From a national viewpoint, duplication of specialized facilities in ports that serve essentially the same hinterland obviously reduces the advantage gained in developing the special facilities.[16]

The following chapters will describe the historical and contemporary role of the federal government in port development. Institutionally, port policy is related to the establishment of both transportation and water resources policy at the federal level. Therefore, a discussion of the federal role in port planning and development must concern itself with the elaboration of national policies for water resources and transportation.

---

*In practice, competition may provide some protection against a poorly managed monopoly.

CHAPTER 3

HISTORICAL SUMMARY OF THE FEDERAL
ROLE IN PORT DEVELOPMENT

Introduction

The nature of technological change and its effects on patterns of social and governmental processes has, according to
Daniel Bell in The Coming of Post-Industrial Society, brought
about a new definition of functional rationality, that is, a mode
of thought which emphasizes functional relations and has as its
criteria of performance the efficient and optimal use of resources.[1]

Implicit in Bell's general argument is the gradual embrace of
this rationale by modern government. As the power of executive
agencies and officials over the direction and development of
public policy has grown, their ability to identify issues, plan
and administer programs, and generate public support has become
crucial to the broad exercise of governmental policy. In this
sense, functional rationality has become an integral component of
policy formation.

The importance of the process of formulating public policy
can be exhibited by an analysis of its effects. The broadening
policy influence of a pervasive government and administration has
resulted in governmental policy becoming the most important mechanism for administering social relations and change. As Theodore
Lowi has stated in The End of Liberalism:[2]

> Neither budgets nor bureaucrats will measure the impor-
> tance of such agencies as the Federal Reserve Board, the
> ICC and its sister public service commissions in all the
> States, the rest of the "alphabetocracy" begun in the
> 1930s, and the research, service, and fiscal components
> added largely since then. Their administrative role in
> the fate of persons and properties is important beyond
> measure.

The political power of Lowi's "alphabetocracy," embracing executive, regulatory, and independent agencies and commissions, has
been traditionally studied from two perspectives:[3] a) the ability
of executive agencies to generate constituencies supporting their
programs; and b) the technical skills and capabilities these
agencies can focus on policy issues.

This report, however, broadens this analytic framework by
considering the impacts of new policy imperatives, and the resulting implementation of federal programs on the traditional port
development scenario. Subsequent chapters consider a number of
executive organizations, linking them to both the historical
development of their port-related programs, and their present
impact on local and regional port competition and development.
The importance of precedent in congressional policy directives,

described in this chapter, is later evaluated in the light of
agency program implementation.

A History of Port Policy

Federal policies impacting on port development and operations
have historically evolved in an institutionally fragmented, patch-
work manner. Split between various federal, state, and local
policy-making and administrative structures, a unified approach
to federal port policy was difficult to generalize and problematical to implement. As a function of this multifaceted policy
process, the scope of actors involved in port development is
large indeed.[4]

Historically, the initial statement of federal port policy
began with the Constitution under Article 1, Section 9. Drafted
in response to the interstate trade rivalry under the Articles
of Confederation, and the failure of such rivalry to produce a
central authority to regulate this commerce, the section reads
as follows:[5]

> No preference shall be given by any regulation of com-
> merce on revenue to the ports of one State over those of
> another: nor shall vessels bound to, or from, one State,
> be obliged to enter, clear, or pay duties in another.

This statement, consistent with the then prevailing policy
of limiting governmental regulatory power held by both the federal and state governments, established a crucially important
policy dictum; that is, the exercise of governmental policy
affecting ports was legally mandated to be free from competitive
or discriminatory bias.* Subsequent legislation enacted by Congress reflected this spirit.

A second important determinant of federal port policy has
been its evolutionary link to transportation and national defense
policies. As a major intermodal component of land- and water-
based transportation modes, port development was shaped and influenced by enacted legislation pertinent to both. As a 1964 Operations Research, Inc., study of federal port policy noted, "Since
1789... a prime motive for merchant marine as well as port development has been military readiness."[6] Improvements in the quality
and number of marine terminal facilities has historically been
viewed by the Congress as important to national preparedness and
defense.

The passage of the first General Survey Act in 1824 established congressional appropriations for river navigation as well
as general transportation improvement.[7] The Corps of Engineers,
operating under direct Congressional oversight, was given primary
responsibility for the planning of waterways, roads and railways.[8]

---

*The definition of a discriminatory practice or activity is often
unclear. An action of the federal government which affects the
competitive status of ports may or may not be judged as discriminatory subject to court action.

In implementing these programs, the federal government tied appropriations for improvements to rivers and harbors to internal, state-initiated improvement programs. These programs were designed to facilitate intra-state cooperation in large public works projects.[9] However, since projects were often oriented towards local considerations with little regard for the overall national program, cooperation between states first became difficult, and then impossible. As one author noted:[10]

> In 1837, the national program virtually collaped as a result of state and sectional conflicts which made concerted congressional action impossible.

Faced with politically hazardous conflicts between local, state and federal constituencies, a disenchanted Congress repealed the General Survey Act in 1838. Additionally, Congress suspended appropriations for new harbor projects from 1840 to 1844 (partly due to a lack of congressional consensus regarding the constitutionality of harbor projects following the 1838 repeal) and, following a year more of bitter debate, suspended monies again from 1845 to 1852.[11] The rapidly growing sectional antagonism of this period paralyzed attempts to reinstate policy direction, and the situation continued in disjointed fashion until after the Civil War.

The first major congressional policy statement applying to a growing private development of transportation services was contained in the 1887 Act which established the Interstate Commerce Commission. Although basically a statement on the regulation of interstate commerce in general and the railroad industry in particular, the Act emphasized a developing congressional interest in national transportation policy:[12]

> It is hereby declared to be the national transportation policy of the Congress to provide for fair and impartial regulation of all modes of transportation subject to the provisions of this Act,...all to the end of developing, coordinating, and preserving a national transportation system by water, highway, and rail as well as other means adequate to meet the needs of commerce of the United States, of the Postal Service, and of the national defense.

It is important to note, however, that the 1887 Act exempted inland waterway transport services from federal regulation. So, while the formation of the Commission reflected in part a popular sentiment favoring control of the railroad industry, it also provided competitive incentives to the waterway carriers by exempting them from similar regulatory practices.

Congressional interest in national transportation policy was also seen in the number of legislative attempts to form some variant of a Federal Department of Transportation. As shown in Exhibit 3.1,[13] at least thirty-two legislative proposals were introduced in Congress between 1874 and 1966. However, most of these received only perfunctory consideration.[14]

EXHIBIT 3.1

CHRONOLOGY OF LEGISLATIVE PROPOSALS

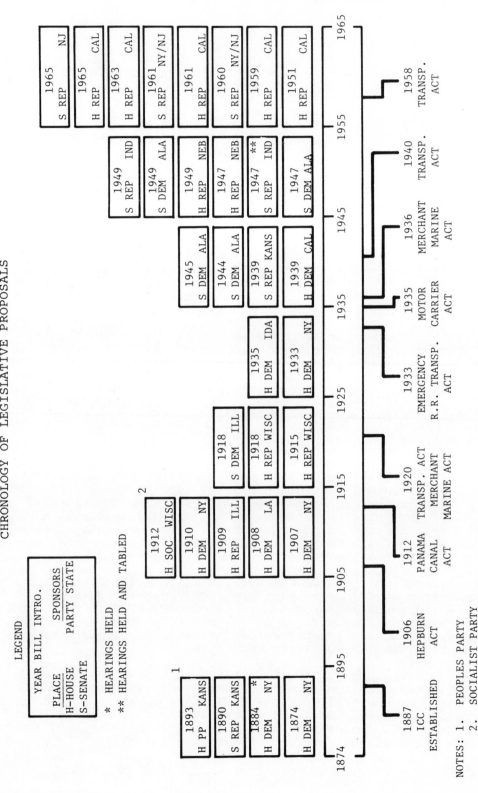

LEGEND

YEAR BILL INTRO.
          SPONSORS
PLACE   PARTY STATE
H-HOUSE
S-SENATE

* HEARINGS HELD
** HEARINGS HELD AND TABLED

NOTES: 1. PEOPLES PARTY
       2. SOCIALIST PARTY

Sources: Legislative proposals: Hearings on S.3010, Part 1, pp. 213-218, 89th Cong., 2nd Session
          Public Laws: U.S. Statutes At Large

At the turn of the century a federal program for large-scale water resources development was initiated. The Inland Waterways Commission, a federal study group created in 1907 under President Roosevelt, embraced the concept of a regional approach in planning the nation's inland waterways.[15] And more important, it recognized that port and waterway development was a component of a national system of transportation which should be developed comprehensively.

By the time of the First World War, the federal role in maritime policy, as well as transportation policy in general, had splintered to several executive and independent agencies (see Exhibit 3.2)--a pattern that was to become familiar some years later.

Within this fragmented administrative structure, government policy continued to promote port development and prohibit discrimination against ports. The Shipping Act of 1916 (Section 15) stated that all conference, pooling and related agreements concerning waterways and shipping were to be submitted to the U.S. Shipping Board, and that the board might:[16]

> ...disapprove, cancel, or modify the agreement...which it finds unjustly discriminating or unfair as between carriers, shippers, exporters, importers, or ports...

This theme of equitable treatment among ports was repeated in later legislative actions.

The strategic demands placed on port and harbor facilities during the war renewed congressional interest in the expanded development of port facilities.[17] In 1919, congressional blessings were offered to the port authority movement. The legislators wrote:[18]

> It is declared to be the policy of Congress that water terminals are essential to all cities and towns located upon harbors...and that at least one public terminal should exist...open to the use of all on public terms.

One year later, Congress passed an important piece of legislation pertaining to ocean port policy--the Merchant Marine Act of 1920.[19] Section 8 of the Act empowers the U.S. Shipping Board, predecessor of the Maritime Administration, to broad powers specifically related to port siting, development and operations (Chapter 7 will discuss this Act).

The import of congressional activity emphasized by these legislative actions and statements was to again underscore the importance of adequate port capability to the nation. However, the planning and development of this capability remained with local and state administrative organizations.

Pursuant to the Inland Waterways Commission of 1907, a series of study groups, commissions, and interagency committees were initiated in the water resources area. These study groups, such as

EXHIBIT 3.2

HISTORICAL DEVELOPMENT OF FEDERAL TRANSPORTATION AGENCIES

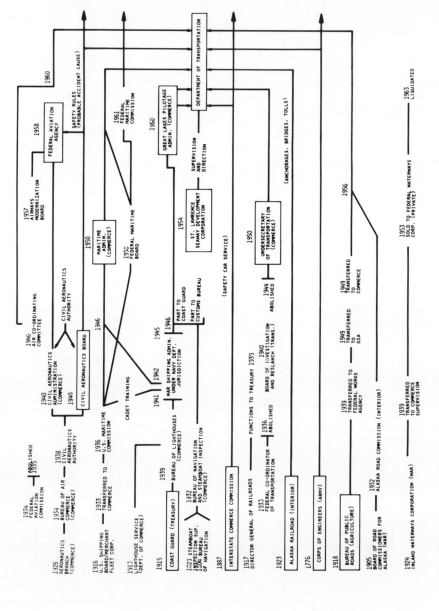

Source: Reprinted by permission of the publisher, from The Department of Transportation by Grant Miller Davis (Lexington, Mass.: Lexington Books, D. C. Heath and Company, 1970).

the Committee of Three appointed by President Roosevelt in 1938 (and subsequently during the same year, the Committee of Six), were composed of representatives ("three" or "six" from each area) from labor and management in the transportation industry, principally the railroads.[20]

The Committee of Three proposed an interim arrangement creating a temporary two-year Federal Transportation Authority with individuals appointed by the President. Less than six months later, the Committee of Six recommended the establishment of a Federal Transportation Board with powers such as the issuance of certificates of convenience and necessity, construction, operations, and so on, pertaining to the general transportation network.[21] Neither report, however, produced any legislative action in the transportation field.

In 1940, Congress passed the Transportation Act of 1940 which, in breaking with the concepts proposed by earlier Executive-level study groups, provided for the establishment of a Board of Investigation and Research to address pressing transportation problems.[22] The Board in turn recommended creating three separate federal agencies to administer transportation programs, feeling that it was not feasible to place all transportation work under one department.[23]

Another Executive study group was created in 1940 to evaluate federal expenditures on various public works projects, and to conserve natural resources.[24] The National Resources Planning Board, in complying with a Presidential directive issued in January of 1940, conducted a comprehensive assessment of the domestic transportation industry.

In reporting its findings, the Board recommended establishing a permanent government agency for transportation services, and went on to propose several organizational structures. One such recommendation was to establish a Department of Transportation, which the Board envisioned would function as follows:[25]

> These duties might be lodged in a revived Office of Federal Coordinator or in a Transportation Authority similar to the one suggested by the Committee of Three. Perhaps a more useful procedure would be to set up a Department of Transportation because of its greater prestige with the public. The direction of the work would be more concentrated and the responsibility to the Chief Executive for success or failure would be easily fixed. The quasi-judicial functions of the regulatory commissions would be left independent, so that questions of rates and discriminations would be passed upon as objectively and impartially as possible. This would leave in executive hands the research, promotion, and planning functions relative to taxes, subsidies, carrier economy and efficiency, public construction of new facilities, expansion of service, and cooperation among the modes of transport.

Criticizing the existing transportation policy, the Board singled
out public objectives and "haphazard" expenditures. They stated:[26]

> The reasons which prevented full realization of the
> possibilities of public expenditures in the transporta-
> tion field apparently derive to a large extent from the
> fact that air, water, and highway facilities have been
> furnished separately by independent government agencies
> acting as special advocates of one form of transporta-
> tion or another. The coexistence of rail facilities
> furnished by private enterprise has also introduced
> inevitable conflicts and inequalities; and it has pre-
> vented a coordinated planning of transportation as a
> whole. Additional factors contributing to an unsatis-
> factory transportation system have been the vague and
> confusing objectives of public action, ill-advised sub-
> sidies, haphazard programming of expenditures, and the
> absence of administrative coordination among units of
> government.

The differences exhibited between these various executive
commission reports and enacted congressional legislation were
based on philosophical differences over the transportation policies held by each governmental branch.

Contending that transportation was fundamentally a legislative function, Congress did not act on the majority of requests
to create a Department of Transportation. The Executive Branch,
on the other hand, was party to a series of studies which pro-
pounded exactly such a creation.

In one work concerning the legislative establishment of the
DOT, the author comments on the eventual failure before Congress
of all legislation seeking to establish one transportation agency
between 1940-1966. The analyst states:[27]

> Even though each bill submitted to Congress during the
> interval of 1940-1966 contained some fault, the major
> reasons for failing to establish a Department of Trans-
> portation were twofold. First, a majority of bills and
> recommendations sought to consolidate or alter the inde-
> pendent regulatory agencies in addition to establishing
> one executive department concerned solely with transpor-
> tation matters. Second, and more significant, no popu-
> lar support for a Department of Transportation existed
> as was the case with other executive departments such
> as Health, Education, and Welfare. Congress and indus-
> try were not interested in such an organization.

Furthermore, the author notes that in 1966, "and in 1966
alone," the proper factors were present to create a DOT:[28]

> [The factors were] a forceful President who wanted to
> consolidate executive transportation agencies, and who
> commanded a substantial influence with the Congress.

These two factors were present only during the 89th Congress.

Hence, this legislative analyst contends that the DOT was created largely because the correct political factors and balances were present between the Executive and Congress.

The pattern then of federal regulatory power over transportation, and specifically ocean port policy, has been one of fragmented authority. The gradual diffusion of responsibilities to a number of maritime-related agencies, and others in the federal government, remained unchecked throughout recent history. The resulting situation is basically a function of this lack of policy coordination.

The Commission on Marine Studies, Engineering and Resources, formed as a result of the Marine Resources and Engineering Development Act of 1966, attempted to bring about more coordination among federal agencies involved in port development. In 1969, this group, also known as the Stratton Commission, issued a report which stated:

> Because of funding procedures, it has been relatively easy to obtain harbor development projects which often exceed the real need of the community . . .

> A need exists for a National Port Survey to be conducted with the cooperation of the Departments of Transportation, Army, Commerce, and Housing and Urban Development to define the Nation's requirements in terms of major ports, offshore terminals, and other facilities for maritime commerce, on the basis of this survey, a rational scheme for port and harbor development can be established against which the real need for other harbors can be measured . . .

> Considering all factors, we recommend . . . a multi-agency study headed by the Secretary of Transportation.

While the Commission report stimulated a number of general policy movements in the maritime area, no specific Congressional action was taken on recommendations pertaining to federal port policy.*

Some progress toward federal policy coordination in water resources planning has been evidenced in recent years, however. In 1968, the Congress established the National Water Commission and charged it to complete a major long-term research study into national water resource management problems and policies. Section 3(a) of the Commission enactment summarized its duties as follows:[29]

---

*In addition, the Marine Resources and Engineering Development Act of 1966 established the National Council on Marine Resources and Engineering Development. The Council's recommendations relating to the federal role in port development also failed to result in substantive Congressional action as described in Chapter 6, pages 118-119.

The Commission shall (1) review present and anticipated water resource problems, making such projections of water requirements as may be necessary and identifying alternative ways of meeting these requirements--giving consideration, among other things, to conservation and more efficient use of existing supplies, increased usability by reduction of pollution, innovations to encourage the highest economic use of water, interbasin transfers, and technological advances including, but not limited to, desalting, weather modification, and waste water purification and reuse; (2) consider economic and social consequences of water resource development, including, for example, the impact of water resource development on recent growth, on institutional arrangements, and on esthetic values affecting the quality of life of the American people; and (3) advise on such specific water resource matters as may be referred to it by the President and the Water Resources Council.

Having a tenure of five years, the Commission produced some 50 papers on various aspects of water resource policy. The general findings and conclusions of the Commission, summarized from its final report, were as follows:[30]

In general, the Commission believes that: (1) it is necessary to plan for future water use in terms of "alternative futures" rather than to project past trends indefinitely into the future as a basis for action; (2) there is a "cultural lag" in the Nation's water institutions; they have not kept pace with the priorities and problems; (3) water is a part of the entire economic and environmental system in which we live and water resources management should be coordinated with land-use planning and water quality control; (4) water is too valuable a resource to be appropriated to meet needs such as production of food and fibre, or to be developed for water transportation at less than cost; (5) but that there are certain social purposes which justify expenditures for water resources at the expense of the general public.

Additionally, the Commission provided a series of recommendations on various aspects of the federal inland waterways program. One of these recommendations, the Commission's advocacy that user charges be established to recover federal expenditures for operation and maintenance of the inland waterway system, met with strong political opposition from both the maritime transportation industry and the Congress. Their opposition to the user charge concept was foreseeable--the barge industry would clearly oppose the imposition of additional taxes and tolls on their operations. Congress, aware that a sizable number of states maintained inland navigable water transportation systems, opposed the idea on local political constituency grounds.[31]

While the user-charges issue was not a new one (previous study groups had addressed the concept), the actors and institutions involved in the debate had increased. The Executive Office of Management and Budget (OMB) and the federal Water Resources

Council (WRC)* announced in 1973 that both organizations supported the concept. And the WRC, in establishing its institutional Principles and Objectives in October 1973, introduced substantial changes in a second, politically sensitive economic
factor in maritime operations--the discount rate to be used in
cost-benefit analyses of national public works projects. The
conceptual linking of these two issues--user charges and the
discount rate formula--by federal organizations and an independent study commission presented new water policy challenges to
the traditional marine industry lobbies, the Congress, and others
wishing to maintain the status quo.

User Charges: Recommendations and Response

The recommendations drafted by the National Water Commission
were presented to the Congress in June 1973. Those sections from
Chapter 5 pertaining to user charges and inland waterways policies
were as follows:[32]

   5-1. Any report proposing a Federal inland waterway pro-
        ject should provide an estimate of the true economic
        cost and benefit to the Nation of providing the con-
        templated transportation service, and a comparison
        thereof with the true economic cost of providing this
        service by the least-cost alternative means. This
        should be in addition to the estimate presently
        required by Section 7 of the Department of Transpor-
        tation Act of 1966.

   5-2. Legislation should be enacted to require non-Federal
        interests to bear an appropriate share of the cost
        of Federal inland waterway projects. Such legis-
        lation should require: (a) that carriers and plea-
        sure craft using inland waterways be required to
        pay user charges such that the total collections
        on all Federal waterways would be sufficient to
        cover Federal expenditures for operation and main-
        tenance of the entire system; (b) that within the
        bounds of administrative practicability the user
        charges should consist of a uniform tax on all fuels
        used by vessels operating on the inland waterways,
        plus lockage charges at rates sufficient to repay
        the cost of operating and maintaining the locks with-
        in integral segments of the total waterway system;
        (c) that charges be imposed gradually over a 10-year
        period and increased progressively so that by the
        end of that period they will be sufficient to re-
        cover annually the entire cost of operating and main-
        taining the Federal inland waterway system; and (d)
        that as a condition for Federal construction of
        future inland waterway projects responsible feder-
        ally chartered or non-Federal entities be required to
        enter into agreements to repay the construction

---

*The Office of Management and Budget and the Water Resources
Council are discussed in Chapter 4.

costs, including interest, over a specified period of years unless the Congress determines that a particular waterway will result in national defense benefits sufficient to justify assumption of a part of the cost by the Federal Government.

5-3. Any legislation requiring the payment of waterway user charges should also authorize and direct the Federal transportation regulatory agencies to regulate rates for all competing modes of transportation in such a way as to encourage the use of the waterways for any traffic that could move by that mode at the least economic cost to the Nation.

5-4. The Department of Transportation should broaden and intensify its efforts to improve national transportation policy. It should develop a plan for such administration and legislative actions as may be required to bring into being an integrated national transportation system in which all modes of transportation, including inland waterways, are utilized in such a way as to reduce to a practical minimum the cost to the Nation of meeting the demands for transportation. To prepare the way for the development of such an integrated and efficient national transportation system, the Department of Transportation should develop and submit to the President and the Congress recommendations designed to provide the data base that will be needed to achieve the objective of this recommendation.

In addition to calling for user charges to be instituted (recommendation 5-2), the Commission recommended a greater role for the Department of Transportation in the inland waterways. However, the DOT is constrained in this transport policy area. Provisions incorporated in its enabling legislation prohibit the agency from revising standards and criteria used in the economic evaluation of federal investments in water resources projects.

Consequently, recommendations by the Commission touched on two sensitive, and traditional, political areas important to Congress. Critics would argue that in 1973 and 1974 congressional inactivity on politically sensitive public works recommendations made by the Commission was the result of "pork barrel" politics.[33]

The industry case made against user charges emphasizes that such fees would "impair the position of American industry as against foreign competition."[34] The American Waterways Operators (AWO), a key barge and towing industry lobby association, argues that "waterway user charges would reduce exports, encourage imports, and put adverse pressure on the U.S. balance of payments."[35] A recent argument advanced by the AWO against user charges concerns the potential inflationary impacts of these fees on specific industrial sectors of the U.S. economy.[36]

While Congress has not enacted legislation based on recommendations presented by the National Water Commission, new institutional actors interested in user charges have entered the policy debate. Their impact will be crucially important in reassessments of present waterways policies.

The Discount Rate

A second important policy issue influencing both waterways policies and port development is the proper discount rate to be used in evaluating water projects.

The discount rate is based on the concept that capital invested in water projects would yield returns over the years if, instead, it were invested for some other purpose, and that this foregone earning potential should be taken into account by discounting those benefits of a project that do not accrue until the latter years of its life. Theoretically, the discount rate seeks to express the future benefits of a project in terms of present values.[37]

Prior to the adoption of a new discount rate structure in 1973, the old rate formula represented the average yield during the preceding fiscal year on interest-bearing marketable securities of the United States which, at the time the computation was made, had terms of 15 years or more to maturity. The rate could not be raised or lowered more than one-quarter of one percent for any year. The computation was made as of July 1 each year, and the rate thus computed was used during the succeeding 12 months. Exhibit 3.3 shows the discount rate since 1963.

The adoption of higher discount rates would mean that smaller, less costly projects having substantial benefits in the near future would be favored over large multipurpose projects having benefits slowly building up over a number of years.[38] A high rate also tends to favor projects with relatively small initial costs.

Exhibit 3.3

Discount Rates Applying to Federal Water Projects

Fiscal Year	Rate Percent
1963	3-1/4
1964	3-1/4
1965	3-1/4
1966	3-1/4
1967	3-1/4
1968	3-1/4
1969	4-5/8
1970	4-7/8
1971	5-1/8
1972	5-3/8
1973	5-1/2

Source: National Water Commission Report

In October of 1973, the Water Resources Council (WRC) initiated actions to refine the formula used to compute the yearly discount rate. Under the Principles and Standards adopted by the Council on October 30, 1973, a new rate for water projects was set at 6-7/8 percent. This substantially higher rate brought loud protests from industry, maritime organizations and lobbying groups, and members of Congress--all aware of the potential impacts of the new rate. According to the National Water Commission Report, a discount rate of nearly seven percent would likely jeopardize most river navigation projects since potential benefits from such projects do not usually reach anticipated levels until the second or third decade of project life.[39]

The accuracy of the Commission's projections was emphasized by the rapid movement of Congress to establish a new and lower discount rate. Well aware that political pressure from constituencies would be forthcoming if local civil works projects were dropped or otherwise held up, Congress speedily passed the Water Resources Development Act in March of 1974.[40] The Act set new discount rates, based on a formula promulgated in December 1968, of 5-5/8 percent for fiscal year 1974 and 5-7/8 percent for fiscal year 1975 (or about what they would have been had no action been taken by the WRC).[41]

Congressional passage of the Water Resources Development Act left water policy-makers with two "official" discount rates-- the WRC figure and the rates set by Congress. The political test of wills ended in August of 1974 when the Council decided to formally adopt the rate established by Congress.[42]

However, under Section 80 of the Act, the President was directed to "make a full and complete study and investigation" of water resources policy--one part of which includes the discount rate.[43] The investigation was subsequently assigned to the Water Resources Council.

The Council's approach to this water policy study is distinguished from previous research in two important ways: First, the study will be conducted after two Executive organizations, the Office of Management and Budget and the Water Resources Council, have given explicit support to user-charges and higher discount rates. Second, the Section 80 study will directly involve the WRC membership* in the development of major policy positions. Previously, background studies and policy recommendations were completed at the staff level and then submitted to Council members for action. Participation by Cabinet-level WRC members in the development of water policy recommendations will assure a more responsive Congress in assessing the policy impacts of the study. It may also suggest, as one inland waterways group has stated, that the study members will take a "middle ground" approach on politically sensitive issues such as cost-sharing and the discount rate.[44]

One alternative to the present controversy over discount rates is the use of different rates for different policy objec-

*The Council membership is composed of Cabinet-level officials from several federal organizations. See Chapter 4.

tives. That is, critics of present rate formulas have often
recommended using floating discount rates which reflect the
changing of relative preferences among objectives over time.
As explained by one proponent:[45]

> If we used the same discount rate for each objective,
> then we would be using constant relative weights on objec-
> tives over time, and there is no reason in general why we
> should wish to do that. Our weights on environmental
> quality benefits may increase over time, relative to their
> starting relationship to national income weights; in this
> case, we would have a lower rate of discount for environ-
> mental quality benefits than for national income benefits...
> A very useful approach is to engage in project design with
> several sets of interest rates (with appropriate opportu-
> nity cost parameters) for objectives, and then to demon-
> strate the results to decision-makers and encourage them
> to choose among the alternative designs, thus implicitly
> choosing social rates of discount.

This multiobjective approach to setting the "proper" discount rate is argued by proponents to more effectively emphasize
the design of projects in terms of all socially relevant objectives, including the national income objective.

Port Policy and the Congress: An Analysis of the Congressional Role and Some Recent Policy Imperatives

The key, historical role of the Congress in articulating
policies impacting on port development can be objectively analyzed by considering both the intrinsic policy dimensions of
enacted legislation, and the role of Congress in promoting broad
policy guidelines influencing federal port policy.

Congressional statements of policy bearing on ocean ports
can be broadly categorized under three headings:[46]

a.   National transportation policy statements;

b.   Maritime or oceans policy statements; and

c.   Policies specifically directed towards ocean ports.

In most cases no firm delimitation has existed between maritime
policy and policies specifically drafted with reference to port
issues. However, evolutionary changes in the traditional port
development scenario, resulting in part from new federal environmental legislation and advances in maritime shipping technology,
has prompted Congress to consider and enact legislation specifically directed to marine and port and harbor policy issues.
Examples of such legislation would include the Ports and Waterways Safety Act of 1971 and subsequent amendments thereto, the
Deepwater Port Act of 1974, and bills pertaining to coastal management or land use, such as the Coastal Zone Management Act.
However, consistent with historical precedent, these legislative acts deal only in general terms with a few port development issues or, in restricted cases, with specific administra-

tive regulations upon port operations. No concerted approach
to policy formation is in evidence.

The lack of a unified congressional approach to marine
policy formation can be usefully analyzed by considering both
the program implementation of enacted legislation, and the political process by which the legislation has been drafted.

Program and policy initiation by executive line agencies
is strongly dependent on the nature and content of the enacted
legislative requirement; that is, an act receiving strong congressional support and quick floor action is likely to receive
a higher policy priority in an executive agency than a relatively obscure, slow-moving piece of legislation. Constituency
groups, both internal and external, are crucially important in
implementing policies and must be nurtured carefully by policy-
making participants. Well aware of this requirement in an area
where powerful, well-entrenched maritime interest groups strongly influence marine policy formation, legislators often carefully utilize specific political techniques to build constituencies and insure orderly program implementation.

Promotion and Legislation

With an eye toward building constituencies, the language of
many congressional acts and policy directives has been promotional in content. Oftentimes legislation is couched in general
terms such as "maintaining efficient transportation," or in relation to ports, a policy of "promoting, encouraging, and developing ports and water commerce."[47] Under such legislative
provisions, it is clear that line agencies exercise the central
policy role of implementing workable programs and procedures.

A specific example of this "promotional" technique can be
found in Section 2 of the Ports and Waterways Safety Act of 1971.
This Act states that to "promote safe and efficient maritime transportation," and "to promote the safety and environmental quality of
the ports, harbors, and navigable waters of the United States,"
the Secretary of Transportation* may "prescribe standards, procedures, regulations, or other measures designed (1) to prevent
damage to, or the destruction or loss of any vessel, structure,
or facility on or in such waters, or any structure or facility
on land adjacent to such waters; and (2) to protect navigable
waters, the resources therein and adjoining land areas."[48]

Whatever the motives of Congress were in constructing the
language of this section, the crucial policy issue is the implementation and impact of the section's legislative provisions.
Since this is in part a problem of building supportive constituencies (both internal and external), the interpretive responsibility falls to the mandated line agency (agencies) and its
intrinsic political power base and technical skills.

---

*HR 867: The bill states "[to] the Secretary of the Department
in which the Coast Guard is operating."

Program implementation is therefore a two-way street. Congress must specify adequately defined, enabling legislation, and the mandated agency must interpret congressional intent and marshal the necessary resources to facilitate program development. Legislation which is heavily promotion-laden complicates this process.*

Internal Policy Constraints

With program implementation as one external constraint to congressional policy-making, the committee structure of Congress presents an internal constraint to its regulatory/administrative authority over ocean port policies. These constraints manifest themselves in two areas: (1) the potential for intercommittee rivalries and jurisdictional battles over maritime issues, and (2) the structural fragmentation of congressional committees which set policy and control budgets in the transportation and maritime areas. Generally, the former difficulty is resolved by congressional courtesies, but occasionally this system breaks down and, as one journalist noted, "Some of the heretofore behind-the-scenes hard feelings may surface."[49]

Intercommittee rivalries and "hard feelings" were present in the development of the House deepwater port bill in 1974. Three House Committees--Public Works, Merchant Marine and Fisheries, and Interior and Insular Affairs--failed to reach a consensus in the draft stages of independent deepwater port bills** (general procedure would have been that a compromise bill be reported out of joint committees).

Citing as differences issues such as public ownership and licensing authority, the Public Works and Merchant Marine Committees proceeded with separate bills during House deliberations.[50] The resultant parliamentary moves made by each committee were of great significance since the way in which a bill emerges from committee is crucially important to its legislative progress. The House decision in June 1974 concerning deepwater ports (Public Works Bill HR 10701) was affected by the outcome of these intercommittee rivalries.

The second difficulty with congressional committee structure is that it fragments national transportation planning and budgetary policy. As one author has noted:[51]

------

*For an example where promotional-political concerns dominated the legislative policy process, see the Federal Water Pollution Control Act as amended by the Water Quality Improvement Act of 1970, P.L. 91-224, which states that "The Congress hereby declares that it is the policy of the United States that there should be no discharges of oil into or upon the navigable waters of the United States."

**The respective bills were: Public Works (HR 10701), Merchant Marine (HR 5898), and Insular Affairs (HR 7501).

Government's failure to pull itself together to face the nation's transportation problems started at the top with Congress, which set national policy. In 1970 there were thirty-four separate committees of Congress through which transportation programs had to filter, piece through disorganized piece, in order to get examined and either rejected or approved and funded. There was no transportation committee in either House or the Senate.

In the House of Representatives, the Merchant Marine Committee set policy for maritime affairs but for no other part of the transportation system. In the Senate, however, maritime policy was set by the Commerce Committee, which also had jurisdiction over regulated carriers of freight and passengers as well as over airport construction.

Congress is aware that transportation policy review is highly fragmented, but meaningful reform has been slow and difficult to achieve.[52] In 1974, however, the Congress did initiate budgetary changes within committee structures and, under instigation by the Bolling Committee Report,[53] the House considered proposals for major committee reforms.

In hearings before the House Select Committee on Committees in September of 1973, Representative Lee Hamilton summarized the present congressional committee structure and called for structural reforms. He stated:[54]

The heart of congressional reform lies in restructuring the process by which Congress deals with the budget. I share the view of many Congressmen and observers of the Congress that current budgetary procedures are inefficient, outmoded, and generally inadequate.

No procedure presently exists which allows the Congress to review the President's entire budgetary program. No one committee reviews both revenue and expenditure proposals. By fragmenting its decisions on the budget, the Congress is prevented from considering the impact on the nation's economy.

Under the present system, the overall impact of the budget is established by the cumulative result of a series of separate actions. The Appropriations Committees of the House and Senate do not, as a matter of regular procedure, review the budget as a whole and determine what its impact is or should be.

As a result of the present fragmented system, Congress has no adequate method for dealing with the critical questions of priorities. Only with great difficulty does it alter the President's priorities.

Even assuming Congress fully understands the disadvantages of its present committee structures, reform attempts in 1974 and the potential for future changes in committee arrangements is seen by most to be politically improbable. Further, the con-

tinuation of the present system implies inconsistent policy
formation in both transportation and maritime areas. As one
author stated:[55]

> Until Congress is prepared to examine the nation's
> transportation policies and programs from a single per-
> spective, there is virtually no hope of weeding out the
> inconsistencies and inefficiencies that result in many
> cases from the very structure in which transportation
> decisions are made. There is no real hope that without
> incredible pressures Congress will change its ways in
> the near future. The pressures, in fact, all run in the
> other direction.

It is clear, however, that the outcome of continued pressure
for congressional committee reforms will eventually set the tone
for future action.

The National Oceans Study

Another area of congressional activity emphasizes the potential for future changes in national water policy. The February
1974 authorization of Senate Resolution 222, the National Oceans
Policy Study, may indicate that major changes in the nation's
future approach to marine affairs are forthcoming.[56] The resolution charged the Senate Commerce Committee and its ex-officio
staff with the task of studying the nation's maritime policy in
"all of its ramifications." The study's mandate anticipates that
a requirement for a centralized Federal Oceans Agency will be
established.[57] If such a requirement is proposed, one possible
administrative reorganization plan might transfer the U.S. Coast
Guard, the public works component of the Corps of Engineers, and
certain functions within the Department of the Interior to a new,
centralized oceans agency. Such a reorganization plan would of
course have profound impacts on the framework of federal port
policies of the future.

The Imperatives for Change

In summary, the historical role of the federal government
in port development and water policy generally is changing. New
maritime technology, environmental legislation, and institutional
support of administrative changes in discount rates and user-
charges concepts all constitute important incentives for policy
change.

Congress, long a proponent for status quo interests, will
be increasingly pressured to consider alternate policy futures
for water resources and ports. With the inappropriateness of
applying historical development patterns to current water policies, the present imperatives for policy change constitute the
major driving force behind the formation of new water policies.
In institutional terms, this suggests that the major determinants
of future policies for ports and waterways will be the impacts
of new governmental organizations and actors on the historical,
policy-making institutions and political processes.

CHAPTER 4

GENERAL ACTIVITIES OF FEDERAL, STATE, AND
LOCAL ORGANIZATIONS INVOLVED IN
PORT POLICY AND DEVELOPMENT

Federal

Present federal authority over ports and harbors is fragmented among more than 50 federal organizations, several more
state, federal-state or local organizations, and many quasi-
governmental or private organizations and groups.

The major federal agencies involved in port development
are the U.S. Army Corps of Engineers, the Maritime Administration,
and the U.S. Coast Guard within the Department of Transportation.
Since the port responsibilities of these federal organizations
are pervasive, separate chapters of this report are devoted
exclusively to each.*

This chapter considers the many other federal organizations
which affect, in either direct or indirect ways, port operations
and planning. Analytically, these organizations differ widely in
their internal and external activities related to ports. Their
effect on the port and maritime policy-making system is widely
different as well.

In developing descriptive and analytic measures to examine
the number of organizations involved in port operations and
development, both the internal and external processes, policies
and programs of these entities are considered. Accordingly, two
measures, one dealing with intraorganizational activities and the
second considering external or environmental dimensions, are
applied. The internal--or "focal organization"--analysis is
evaluated with respect to the policy and program implementation of
each organization. The second measure considers the "focal
organization" as a system component of related policy-making
organizations, or "organization-sets."**

Organizational Involvement

The first measure considers the extent of involvement a particular federal organization exercises in the area of port operations and development. Formally, involvement is defined as the

---

*The U.S. Army Corps of Engineers (Chapter 6); the Maritime Admin-
istration (Chapter 7); the U.S. Coast Guard (Chapter 8); and the
Department of Transportation (Chapter 9).

**In this case, "focal organization" refers to the specific
governmental entity being examined, while "organization set" considers the governmental organizations interacting with that specific entity (see A. Alan Schmid, "Federal Decisionmaking for Water
Resource Development," National Water Commission Report Number
PB 211 441).

percentage of an organization's resources which are focused on
port activities with respect to the agency's total resources
devoted to all duties and responsibilities. The measure has
both subjective and objective components.

     Objectively, this measure considers the organization's tech-
nical and administrative capability for implementing its program
responsibilities. This organizational capability was evaluated
by analyzing the number and percentage of individuals assigned to
port tasks within the agency, the budgetary (absolute and percentage of total agency) authorization sought and granted to
the organization, increases/decreases in these factors over
time, and the relative importance of the port administration*
(or group assigned to port responsibilities) within the agency's
overall administrative structure.

     Subjectively, "involvement" considers an organization's
administrative performance in implementing programs and policies
in the port area. This administrative performance was analyzed
by assessing three factors conducive to program implementation:
1) the success of the organization in building and maintaining
a supportive constituency base for policy action; 2) the history
and pervasiveness of the programs developed by the organization;
and 3) an evaluation of programs and policies relative to other
governmental organizations competing in the same policy sphere.

Policy Impact

     The second analytic measure, the impact a governmental
entity may exercise in the port area, can be defined as an action
of a governmental entity which could result in assisting one or
more ports to the detriment of competing ports. While government agencies do not objectively utilize this type of criteria,
this is a possible result of some governmental programs or
policies.

     Federal organizations can impact on the competitive balance
between ports in three ways. The first concerns the spending
of federal funds either to dredge channels, or to help finance
port facilities.

     Second, the articulation of national policies and priorities
in transportation, water resources, energy, and the environment
will have important impacts on competing ports. By influencing
how intermodal transportation will occur, how water resource
projects will be selected, how import duties on foreign energy
products are set, or how environmental factors are evaluated,
the formation of national policies will influence competition
among ports--all of which possess different natural and man-made
characteristics.

     The third impact considers how federal agencies, in inter-

---

*"Port administration" in this discussion refers to an adminis-
trative entity contained within a governmental organization which
is assigned port planning, operations, or development tasks.

preting and implementing their legislative charges, facilitate specific program designs which influence port operations and development. Actions such as setting up vessel traffic control systems, providing icebreaking operations, or determining how environmental legislation will be translated into specific operational constraints on port activities, all influence port planning and development. Since each port is unique in its geographical layout, degree of traffic, and type of weather and climatic conditions, federal actions affecting the general operation of terminals may as a byproduct put some ports at a competitive advantage or disadvantage to others.

Matrix Analysis

In summary, the two analytic measures can be considered together as follows:

a) Organizations grouped according to their level of <u>involvement</u> in port and harbor development, and

b) Organizations grouped according to their <u>impact</u> on general port and harbor development.

Further, the two measures can be thought of as defining the matrix arrangement shown below.

Level of Impact (x) vs. Level of Involvement (y)

Low (x) Hi (y)	Hi (x) Hi (y)
Low (x) Low (y)	Hi (x) Low (y)

Level of Involvement (y)

Level of Impact (x)

In practical terms, the upper left-hand corner of the matrix can be eliminated. No organization with a high involvement in port operations, but which exercised low impact in the field, was found.

Exhibit 4.1 shows the full complement of organizations identified in this chapter, in addition to the other major federal agencies outlined elsewhere in this report, arranged according to department. Appendix A outlines the principal statutory authorities for these agencies.

Exhibit 4.2 outlines these organizations in matrix fashion. The arrangement of the organizations within the matrix cells is an objective and subjective decision reached by the authors in classifying an organization within the scheme elaborated earlier.

Exhibit 4.1

Federal Organizations Involved in Port
and Harbor Development

Atomic Energy Commission (AEC)

Council on Environmental Quality (CEQ)

Department of Agriculture

- Bureau of Animal Husbandry
- Bureau of Entomology and Plant Quarantine

Department of the Army

- Army Corps of Engineers

    Board of Engineers for Rivers and Harbors

Department of Commerce

- Economic Development Administration
- Maritime Administration
- National Oceanographic and Atmospheric Administration

    Office of Coastal Zone Management
    National Ocean Survey
    National Marine Fisheries Service
    National Weather Service
    Sea Grant Program

Department of Defense (see Departments of the Army, Navy)

Department of Health, Education, and Welfare (HEW)

- Public Health Service

Department of Housing and Urban Development (HUD)

- Housing and Home Finance Agency

    Community Facilities Administration
    Urban Renewal Administration

Department of the Interior

- Geological Survey
- Bureau of Land Management
- Bureau of Sport Fisheries and Wildlife
- Office of Land Use and Water Planning
- Office of Water Resources Research

Department of Justice

- Immigration and Naturalization Service

Department of Labor

- Occupational Safety and Health Administration

Department of the Navy

- Oceanographic Office

Department of State

Department of Transportation (DOT)

- The United States Coast Guard

Department of the Treasury

- Bureau of Customs
- Internal Revenue Service

The Executive Offices of the President

- Council of Economic Advisers
- Office of Management and Budget (OMB)

Environmental Protection Agency (EPA)

Federal Communications Commission (FCC)

Federal Energy Administration (FEA)

Federal Maritime Commission (FMC)

Federal Power Commission (FPC)

Federal Trade Commission (FTC)

General Services Administration (GSA)

Interstate Commerce Commission (ICC)

National Aeronautics and Space Administration (NASA)

Smithsonian Institution

United States Congress

United States Postal Service

Water Resources Council

Exhibit 4.2

The Federal Organizations Involved in Port and Harbor Development

(P) - Potential

	High Impact	Low Impact
High Involvement	High Involvement, High Impact Maritime Administration U.S. Army Corps of Engineers U.S. Coast Guard	High Involvement, Low Impact
Low Involvement	Low Involvement, High Impact CEQ — — — — — — — — — Dept. Transportation — — — — — — Dept. Interior — — — — — — EPA — — — — — — FMC — — — — — — NOAA (OCZM) — — — — ICC OMB Water Resources Council	Low Involvement, Low Impact AEC — — — — — — Customs — — — — — — EDA — — — — — — FEA — — — — — — FTC — — — — — — HEW — — — — — — HUD — — — — — — Council of Economic Advisers Dept. Agriculture Dept. Defense Dept. Justice Dept. Labor Dept. Navy Dept. State FCC FPC GSA IRS Smithsonian Institution U.S. Postal Service

While a categorical placement of these organizations is presented here, no such firm or distinguishing arrangement exists in practice. The utility of the matrix is therefore to provide a cohesive, analytic structure for subsequent discussion and elaboration. The "p" designation in Exhibit 4.2 corresponds to those agencies which have the potential to increase their level of impact. Federal organizations are listed alphabetically within each grouping.

Finally, within each matrix subsection, organizations can be grouped according to three specific categories of port-related tasks, policies and program responsibilities. These categories of predominant agency activity are Research, Planning and Development, and Regulation and Operations.

Organizations with Low Involvement and Low Impact

Several federal organizations have only tangential or peripheral involvement in U.S. port operations. Oftentimes this involvement is derived from "spin-offs" from other organizational duties, or from general regulatory or service responsibilities which involve ports or port development.

Research Activities

The Atomic Energy Commission (AEC) and the National Aeronautics and Space Administration (NASA) both conduct research activities which have reference to port operations. The AEC develops power sources for use in navigation aids,[1] and exercises regulatory responsibility over radioactive waste discharge and disposal.[2] NASA assists in developing airborne sensor equipment (pollution detection among other uses), and transports space vehicles to launching sites by barge.[3]

The Oceanographic Office of the Department of the Navy collects and evaluates hydrographic, oceanographic, and aeronautical information.[4] This information includes nautical and aeronautical charts for distribution to the U.S. Navy and the U.S. Merchant Marine.[5] The service also maintains and improves existing Navy-controlled harbors.[6]

Additionally, the Smithsonian Institution assists in developing a technical base for predicting ocean pollution effects through its research into the nature and distribution of ocean resources.[7]

Planning and Development Activities

Related to the various research functions of these organization are planning and development activities in a range of areas.

The Economic Development Administration (EDA) under the Department of Commerce provides a combination of public works grants and loans, business loans, and technical, planning, and

research assistance for specific areas where such development
would assist in alleviating unemployment and low-income family
problems.[8]

Qualification for EDA assistance, generally based on high
unemployment or underemployment,[9] was extended to some 1,818 areas
of the country (mostly state counties) as of June 30, 1973.[10] One
component of this program is assistance for port and harbor development, contained under the Public Works Impact Program (PWIP) of
the EDA. Exhibit 4.3 shows EDA project investments for fiscal
years 1966-72. Port and harbor facilities assistance totaled
$11.459 million during fiscal year 1973. Cumulative figures for
fiscal years 1966-73 totaled $108.001 million across 84 separate
projects.[11] This level of funding represents roughly 8 percent of
the total funds allocated by the EDA during that period.

Since the EDA is specifically a grant agency, it is common
practice for it to work closely with the appropriate federal or
state agency most qualified in the particular area of development
under review.[12] Pursuant to a Memorandum of Understanding established between the EDA and the Maritime Administration in October
of 1966, the latter provides assistance and technical advice on
all projects related to port and harbor facilities assistance.[13]

Financial assistance offered by the EDA is in four forms:
(1) direct grants up to 50 percent of the total cost of qualified
projects; (2) combined direct and supplementary grants up to 80
percent of total project cost; (3) long-term loans up to 100
percent of costs for public works and development facilities; and
(4) guarantee of loans for working capital up to 90 percent of the
outstanding unpaid balance.[14]

Commenting on this fiscal assistance, a 1974 Maritime Administration report on port financing noted that these EDA grants were
not specifically directed at port needs:[15]

> EDA projects were aimed primarily at alleviating econ-
> omic distress or high rates of unemployment in desig-
> nated areas and were not predicated on the needs of the
> port industry.

However, these federal subsidies, accounting for approximately seven percent of total U.S. public port financing,[16] may
play an important role in specific port projects. If public ports
become less able to finance capital-intensive port expansion
projects, EDA assistance may be one of several factors in deciding
which projects are started.

In 1974 the EDA obtained a renewed, two-year fiscal authorization from Congress.*[17] Included within this legislation was
a provision establishing a new form of block grant monies--desig-
nated Title 9 grants. Chiefly designed to fund public works

---

*Prior to this authorization, the EDA had been operating under
various Continuing Resolutions of Congress. Administration sources
had withheld the fiscal year 1975 budget request of the agency,
placing it in jeopardy.

EXHIBIT 4.3

OBLIGATED PUBLIC WORKS PROJECTS By Type of Project

	Fiscal 1972		Cumulative FY 1966-72	
	No. of projects	EDA investment ($000)	No. of projects	EDA investment ($000)
Industrial park/site development facilities	85	$30,234	523	$191,048
General/industrial/ commercial development facilities	223	86,785	1,394	611,520
Recreation/tourism facilities	30	15,034	159	115,869
Educational facilities	20	12,733	110	75,668
Port/harbor facilities	9	10,063	72	96,149
Airport facilities	4	727	43	25,008
Health facilities	9	6,260	67	56,336
Other public facilities	92	28,133	140	55,582
Total	472	$189,969	2,508	$1,227,181

Note: detail may not add to totals due to rounding.

Source: Annual Report of the Economic Development Administration, 1972, U.S. Department of Commerce.

projects, these grant monies will maintain, and in some cases supplement, the existing public works grants.

Also included in the fiscal assistance area, the Housing and Home Finance Agency (and constituent units, Community Facilities Administration and Urban Renewal Administration) under the Department of Housing and Urban Development (HUD) makes loan and grant funds available for many functions grouped under the broad heading of urban development planning.[18] As related to port development, such monies would be available for local acquisition of blighted waterfront property, the enhancement of coastal areas, and the selection and maintenance of waste disposal lands. Often these monies are tied to general urban planning and development schemes, and hence are not available to ports.

Established pursuant to the Federal Energy Administration Act of 1974,[19] the Federal Energy Administration (FEA) has informational and energy policy coordination responsibilities with concurrent impact on the establishment of deepwater port facilities (oil transfer) in this country. Additionally, national energy policies and plans developed by the FEA may impact on ports as a function of overall maritime transportation energy utility.

The possible construction of offshore deepwater port facilities also provides for participation by the Department of State which would be responsible for ensuring that such facilities be constructed and operated in accordance with international law.[20] Under Section 11 of the Deepwater Port Act of 1974, the Secretary of State shall "seek effective international action and cooperation" in the administration and development of "appropriate international rules and regulations* relative to the construction, ownership, and operation of deepwater ports."[21] Furthermore, the Department is participating in the development of international law concerning the effect on navigation of foreign vessels using offshore ports or traversing the areas in the vicinity of such ports.[22]

Regulatory and Operations Activities

Federal organizations which conduct or are involved in the routine business of port operations include the Immigration and Naturalization Service (Department of Justice), the Occupational Safety and Health Administration of the Department of Labor, the Federal Trade Commission (FTC), the Federal Communications Commission (FCC), The Federal Power Commission (FPC), the Customs Bureau and the Internal Revenue Service within the Treasury Department, the General Services Administration (GSA), the Bureaus of Animal Husbandry, Entomology and Plant Quarantine within the Department of Agriculture, the Post Office, and the U.S. Public Health Service (within HEW).

---

*International regulations pertinent to deepwater ports are contained in the 1958 Geneva Conventions on the High Seas, the Continental Shelf, and the Territorial Sea and Contiguous Zone. Also, the International Convention for the Prevention of Pollution of the Sea by Oil, 1969 (including the 1971 amendment) is relevant.

The Immigration and Naturalization Service of the Department
of Justice administers laws and regulations relating to the
status of aliens which affect port operations and/or passenger or
merchant shipping activities.[23]

Within the Department of Labor, the Occupational Safety and
Health Administration (OSHA) prescribes safety and health regulations which affect longshoremen and other harbor workers.[24]
Additionally, OSHA maintains specific investigatory and certification powers affecting ports. OSHA investigates accidents
involving ship and harbor personnel (with the Coast Guard), and
certifies vessel cargo handling gear and shore-based material
handling devices (there is also overlap with the Coast Guard in
this area).

The Federal Trade Commission (FTC) is concerned with the
potential anticompetitive impacts which may be engendered in
the establishment of offshore deepwater port facilities.[25] Under
Section 7 of the Deepwater Port Act of 1974, the FTC and the
Attorney General of the United States are charged to consider
whether applications for deepwater port licenses would "adversely
affect competition, restrain trade, promote monopolization, or
otherwise create a situation in contravention of the anti-trust
laws."[26] License applications for deepwater terminals may not
be favorably acted upon until both the FTC and the Attorney
General file their views with the licensing authority (they must
present these opinions within 45 days of a final public hearing
on deepwater port facilities).[27]

In the maritime communications area, the Common Carrier
Bureau of the Federal Communications Commission (FCC) regulates
interstate and international communications by telephone, tele-
graph, radio and satellite.[28] Several other communications
media, such as land-line wire or cable facilities, microwave
systems, and marine and aviation radio services, are also administered by the FCC.

The Federal Power Commission (FPC) regulates the interstate
aspects of the electric power and natural gas industries.[29]
In addition to numerous specific regulatory duties under its
general charge, the FPC issues certificates for construction
and operation of interstate pipeline facilities, and, under the
National Environmental Policy Act of 1969,[30] is charged to insure
that all pipeline projects present minimum environmental disruption. The FPC also has regulatory input into the siting of
Liquefied Natural Gas (LNG) plants.

Another federal organization involved in the general regulation of ocean port services is the Bureau of Customs under the
Department of the Treasury. The Bureau is charged with assessing and collecting duties and taxes on imported merchandise,[31]
with the control of carriers and merchandise imported into or
exported from the United States,[32] and with enforcement against
smuggling and fraud.[33]

     The Secretary of the Treasury relies upon the Commissioner
of Customs for advice in matters affecting the establishment,
abolishment, or change in customs ports of entry.[34] Designated
by the Secretary, a customs "port" or "port of entry" is one
where a customs officer is assigned with authority to accept
entries of merchandise, to collect duties and administer other
Bureau responsibilities.[35] Approximately thirty applications
for "port of entry" status are filed each year. In fiscal year
1974, six applications were approved. Before designation, the
Secretary must obtain concurrent approvals from the Immigration
and Naturalization Service, the Public Health Service, and the
Animal and Plant Inspection Service of the Department of Agriculture.

     Additionally, the Internal Revenue Service (IRS) within the
Treasury Department sets regulations under which municipalities
can issue tax-exempt industrial development bonds, such as those
used by public ports for capital investments.[36]

     As a result of Executive Reorganization Plan 1 of 1973, the
Office of Emergency Preparedness (OEP) was abolished and its functions transferred to the Department of the Treasury, the Department of Housing and Urban Development, and the General Services
Administration (GSA).[37]

     The OEP had been responsible for the government-wide civil
emergency preparedness program which, in its coordination and
development of mobilization policy and plans, included an assessment of port capabilities and operations in crisis situations.
This preparedness program was transferred to the GSA under the
1973 executive reorganization plan.

     Under the new plan, the Office of Preparedness within the
General Services Administration is responsible for maintaining
(with support from all federal agencies) a national resource
evaluation capability for predicting and monitoring the status
of resources under all degrees of emergency.[38] This data base,
which includes information on port operations and facilities,
is currently being updated by the GSA with assistance from the
Maritime Administration. Plans are also to arrange for periodic
updating of this data in the future.

     Under the Department of Agriculture, the Bureau of Animal
Husbandry deals with the prevention, control, and eradication of
animal diseases and parasites.[39] In administering this charge
at the port (import/export center) level, the Bureau inspects
animal cargo for compliance with regulations upon arrival of the
vessel at the wharf.

     The Bureau of Entomology and Plant Quarantine within the
Department enforces regulations to prevent the entry into the
United States of dangerous plant pests, or plants or vegetables
likely to carry such pests.[40] Such regulations include quarantine
powers.

     The Department of Agruculture also conducts research into

the control of aquatic weeds,[41] and administers laws and regulations over pesticides and plant pest control.[42]

Additionally, the Public Health Service enforces quarantine regulations as applied to people and cargoes,[43] and administers the necessary activities to conduct such operations.

And finally, the U.S. Postal Service, through good or inclement weather, transports mail by water and administers regulations pertaining to the carriage of mail.[44]

Organizations with Low Involvement and High Impact

Federal organizations with low levels of agency involvement in port operations, but which have high impact on port policy and development, include the Office of Management and Budget (OMB), the Departments of the Interior and Transportation, and the Federal Maritime Commission, among others. The agencies included in this category do not share common grounds of technical expertise or policy or regulatory involvement in ports. However, the nature of their administrative impacts on federal port policy is important to the development of a unified federal approach to port policy.

Research Activities

The two federal environmental organizations, the Environmental Protection Agency (EPA) and the Council on Environmental Quality (CEQ), conduct research programs which, in setting air and water quality standards, affect port operations and subsequent port expansion policies. Both environmental organizations are dealt with in the next chapter.

The Department of the Interior conducts a number of port-related programs falling into several categories of involvement. The department's Geological Survey conducts research operations in several facets of geologic framework and water quality, these being listed below:

A.   Activities in Identifying Geologic Framework[45]

- Sampling
- Dredging
- Geophysics
- Drilling
- Analyses

B.   Examines and Investigates Water Resources[46]

- Quality water analyses
- Water data collection
- Salt water - fresh water interface
- Salt water intrusion
- Stream gauging
- Ground water discharge

C.   Studies Sediment Transport[47]

- Related to mineral disposition, water quality,
  salt-fresh water mixing, erosion-deposition
  of navigable waters

The Bureau of Land Management (BLM) manages and disposes
of public lands and related resources according to principles
of multiple-use management, in addition to administering mineral
resources connected with acquired and submerged lands of the
Outer Continental Shelf.[48]

The Bureau also manages the Outer Continental Shelf Mineral
Leasing Program for the development of marine reserves of oil and
gas and, under the provisions of the National Environmental
Policy Act of 1969 and others, must conduct environmental analyses and prepare impact statements on the program.[49]   In this
sense, the Geological Survey assists the bureau in its environmental research and analysis.

Additionally, the Department's Bureau of Sport Fisheries and
Wildlife conducts environmental impact assessments of such industrial concerns as hydroelectric dams, nuclear power sites, stream
channelization, and dredge and fill permits.[50]   These environmental assessments are often components of larger river basin studies
under the general review area of resource management.[51]

The Office of Land Use and Water Planning is responsible
for federal interagency communication on the use of public land
and water resources, the coordination of river basin commission
activities, and the interagency coordination of state and other
federal land use and water planning agencies.[52]   Additionally,
the Office is the Department's liaison point with the Water Resources Council.

Under Section 4(e)(3) of the Deepwater Port Act of 1974,
specific mechanical components connected with the operation of
an offshore terminal would, under certain circumstances, be
administered by the Department of the Interior under the Outer
Continental Shelf Lands Act.[53]   Ordinarily, upon the revocation
or termination of an operating license, the licensee would be
required to remove all components of an offshore terminal.[54]
However, the Secretary of Transportation, in consultation with
the Secretary of the Interior, is authorized to waive such removal if the components of the offshore terminal could be utilized in the transportation of oil, natural gas, or minerals.

Finally in the research area, the Department's Office of
Water Resources Research administers grants for research into
water quality and water resource management pertaining to estuaries, coastal rivers, and the Great Lakes.[55]   Such programs
would encompass physical, chemical, and biological research,
with the development of public investment criteria as well.

Another major federal organization involved in marine and
coastal resources research is the National Oceanographic and

Atmospheric Administration (NOAA). NOAA conducts a number of
research and planning programs related to its duties under the
Coastal Zone Management Act and other legal charges. Since these
interdependent program functions often cut across the organizational categories utilized in this section, NOAA will be dealt
with in a later, separate section of this chapter.

Planning and Development

The Office of Management and Budget (OMB), the Council of
Economic Advisers, and the Water Resources Council (WRC) all
exercise strategic, national planning and development policies
which influence the federal approach to port policy. In most
cases this impact is derived from the formation of national
policy approaches to maritime, transportation, or water resources
planning and administration. In a few cases specific port
development issues, such as deepwater terminal economics, are
addressed.

The Council of Economic Advisers (CEA), one arm of the Executive's national economic advisory groups, exerts significant
political influence in the economic assessment of federal programs and policies. In 1973, the CEA directed a collective
federal agency study into the economics of deepwater (offshore
and deep-draft) ports.

The agency study developed data on the economic benefits
and costs for a range of possible types of deepwater port facilities on the East and Gulf Coast.[56] One conclusion reached in
the study was that the deciding economic tradeoff between deepwater facilities and other terminal alternatives rested on the
expected bulk cargo throughput of the facility over its lifetime.
Further, the Council argued that the economic risks of establishing
superport facilities were not great, and stressed their development.[57]

The Office of Management and Budget (OMB), established in
the Executive Office of the President pursuant to Reorganization
Plan 2 of 1970,[58] is the more powerful successor to the old
Bureau of the Budget.[59]

OMB is oftentimes referred to as the President's "economic
watchdog," or his "budget steward." In general, OMB is charged
with the administrative supervision and control of the federal
budget, the development of an efficient and economical government service, and with conducting the necessary research to
refine the level of management and efficiency in government
service.

Formally, the OMB reviews all annual budget requests filed
by executive organizations, reviews and approves (or disapproves)
legislation drafted by agencies to file with Congress, and
clears oral testimony from agency officials to congressional
committees. It is argued that this general review process is
present to avoid interagency disputes (often OMB acts as an
agency broker), and to insure that executive agency proposals

are in accord with Presidential views.

To facilitate these duties, OMB works closely with both executive agencies and congressional committees to coordinate executive-level legislative policy. Formally then, the role of OMB is to propound Presidential policy views, and offer the President a feedback analysis in the interest of designing new or modifying old policies.

The official (or formal) statements of OMB duties and responsibilities have come under fire since their inception in 1970, however. Typical of criticisms aimed at the agency are those reported in a 1973 issue of National Journal Reports (NJR). One NJR political reporter, commenting on OMB's official charge to conduct policy analyses and offer executive legislative policy recommendations, noted:[60]

> Officially, OMB merely propounds the policy of the President and analyzes issues so that he can make new policy...
>
> But in practice, it is impossible to separate policy analysis and recommendations from policy-making decisions, and OMB frequently makes analyses and recommendations that affect the legislative policy of the executive branch.

NJR went on to cite several cases where OMB influence over certain executive agencies caused substantive policy or program shifts by those organizations.*

One example involved testimony on deepwater port legislation given by the National Oceanographic and Atmospheric Administration (NOAA) before the Senate Interior Committee in July of 1973.[61] NJR reported that a NOAA official was constrained in his testimony by OMB pressure (presumably budgetary), and in fact this constraint represented a substantive change in the desired agency policy.[62]

The resources which OMB can wield in influencing the authorizations and appropriations processes are outgrowths of the central clearance and budgeting established by the Budget and Accounting Act of 1921.[63] All legislative proposals made by executive agencies are required under central clearance to be first cleared by OMB which, in turn, decides whether the proposal is in accord with the President's program. While such a clearance does not generally constitute an absolute veto, central clearance can be used to effectively delay projects, sometimes beyond the useful lifetime of the proposal.[64] Only strong reactive pressure upon OMB to rush project approval may mitigate this tactic. However, NJR noted that OMB pressure on any agency proposal was likely

---

*The case studies deal with subsidized housing and HUD, the MAST (Military Assistance to Safety and Traffic) program in the Department of Defense, the deepwater port issue described above, health benefits for veterans, and the 1973 Federal-Aid Highway Act, among others.

to be diffuse and difficult to gauge,[65] hence compounding the difficulty of organizing any reactive political pressure.

In the water resources area, the OMB is known to be interested in user charges for waterways, and has announced that such proposals are under review. As reported in the April 19, 1974, issue of the National Waterways Conference Newsletter, Recent visitors to the...OMB were told that cost sharing for water resources projects is under active study in the Executive Branch and that imposition of navigation user changes is 'inevitable.'"[66]

Some Congressmen and maritime interests see OMB interest in recreation fees as preludes to waterway toll efforts. As Congressman James R. Jones of Oklahoma has stated, "OMB has been putting much pressure on all involved Federal agencies to raise user fees so high that an area can be self-supporting... This OMB thinking ultimately extends to getting the Corps to impose toll charges on all inland waterways."[67]

In addition to user charges, OMB has placed pressure on port improvements funding through various federal agencies. One recent casualty of fiscal austerity is the dredging budget of the Corps of Engineers, which has been held stable in obligational authority funds since fiscal year 1970 (see Chapter 6). Moreover, in the general civil works projects area, the OMB has initiated actions which in some cases resulted in local authorities being requested for voluntary contributions to large public works projects.[68]

The pressures OMB may wield are often overshadowed by the low policy profile which the Office scrupulously maintains. NJR argued that the ability of OMB to internally interrupt the policy process made the interpretation of its actions difficult to analyze.[69] As noted in the article, one Senate Labor and Public Welfare Committee staff member said of OMB, "We feel them, but we don't usually see them or hear them."[70]

The Water Resources Council (WRC), established pursuant to the Water Resources Planning Act of 1965, is an independent, interagency executive organization charged to "encourage the conservation, development and utilization of water and related land resources on a comprehensive and coordinated basis by Federal, State, local government and private enterprise."[71] The Council, composed of Cabinet-level members, includes the Secretaries of the Interior; Agriculture; the Army; Health, Education and Welfare; Transportation; and the Chairman of the Federal Power Commission. Participating agencies include Commerce, Housing and Urban Development (HUD), the Environmental Protection Agency (EPA), the Office of Management and Budget (OMB), Justice, the Council on Environmental Quality (CEQ), and the four regional River Basin Commissions.

The genesis of the Council was in 1960 with a congressional water-policy study group. Chaired by Senator Robert Kerr, the Senate Select Committee on National Water Resources

proposed five major recommendations to improve the formulation
of water resources policy at the federal level. These recommendations were:[72]

1.   the Federal Government, in cooperation with
      the States, should prepare and keep up-to-date plans
      for comprehensive water development and management
      for all major river basins in the United States.

2.   the Federal Government should stimulate more
      active participation by States in planning and under-
      taking water development and management activities
      by setting up a ten-year program of grants to the
      States for water resources planning.

3.   the Federal Government should undertake a coor-
      dinated scientific research program on water.

4.   the Federal Government should prepare bienni-
      ally an assessment of the water supply-demand out-
      look for each of the water resource regions of the
      United States.

5.   the Federal Government in cooperation with the
      states should take steps to encourage greater effi-
      ciency in water development and use.

Shortly thereafter (1961), President Kennedy transmitted
to Congress a bill incorporating the spirit of the Kerr Committee's recommendations. After four years of congressional dialog,
the Water Resources Planning Act of 1965 passed.[73]

Lengthy delays preceded the Council's adoption of organizational goals and program objectives. Jurisdictional issues
between the Congress, the Office of Management and Budget, and
the Council were the main reasons for institutional delays.

The Principles and Standards for Planning of the WRC finally went into effect on October 30, 1973.[74] The Principles
defined the organizational goals and programs of the Council,
and set a new, higher, and controversial discount rate to be
used in project evaluations of public works programs. The Council's objectives were stated as follows:[75]

The overall purposes of water and land resource planning
is to promote the quality of life, by reflecting society's
preferences for attainment of the objectives defined below:

A.   to enhance the value of the Nation's output of goods
      and services and improvement of national economic
      efficiency.

B.   to enhance the quality of the environment by the
      management, conservation, preservation, creation,
      restoration, or improvement of the quality of cer-
      tain natural and cultural resources and ecological
      systems.

The discount rate established by the Council was set at 6-7/8 percent--that figure opposed to a previous, fiscal year 1972 discount rate of 5-3/8 percent.[76] Aware that this increase would make justification of local water development projects considerably more difficult,* Congress moved quickly to override the new WRC rate through legislation.

On March 7, 1974, the Congress passed the Water Resources Development Act of 1974.[77] The Act set a new, lower rate of 5-5/8 percent--or about what the figure would have been had the WRC not set its higher rate. Until the Council formally adopted the lower congressional discount rate in August 1974, water policy-makers had faced confusion over which of the two "official" discount rates to utilize.

While quick congressional passage of the Water Resources Development Act ended the immediate, official debate over the 1974 discount rate level, it did little to settle the overall rate formula controversy. Aware of this concern during the drafting of the legislation, Congress included in Section 80 of the Act a directive to the President to complete a full investigation of the planning and evaluation of water resources projects.[78] This responsibility was subsequently given to the Water Resources Council. Wishing to develop study recommendations in time for Congressional consideration during the first session of the 94th Congress, the Council organized a special, high-level study group** and directed it to present its policy recommendations to the full Council by mid-year.[79] Recommendations made by the Council study are expected to have important water-policy impacts.

Regulatory and Operations Activities

The principal regulatory commission involved in maritime affairs is the Federal Maritime Commission (FMC). Together with the Interstate Commerce Commission (ICC), which is broadly responsible for the regulation of land transportation services as well as maritime coastal, intercoastal, and inland waterway traffic, these two regulatory commissions can exert considerable influence over port operations and development.[80]

The Federal Maritime Commission

The Federal Maritime Commission was established by Reorganization Plan 7, effective August 12, 1961, as an independent agency to administer the regulatory responsibilities outlined under the

---

*The Final Report of the National Water Commission stated that a discount rate of approximately 7 percent could jeopardize a number of existing, and planned, public works projects. See Chapter 3 for a contextual discussion of the discount rate issue.

**The special organization of the study group provides for direct involvement by Cabinet-level Council members. See Chapter 3 for a contextual discussion of the WRC study.

Shipping Act of 1916,[81] the Merchant Marine Act of 1920,[82] the Intercoastal Shipping Act of 1933,[83] and the Merchant Marine Act of 1936.[84] These laws give the FMC jurisdiction over waterborne movements between the United States and foreign countries as well as to noncontiguous ports of the United States. Additionally, the Commission administers certain provisions of the Water Quality Improvement Act (WQIA) of 1970.[85]

Collectively, these Acts empower the FMC to approve or disapprove agreements filed by common carriers, to regulate common carrier practices (and conferences of such carriers), to accept or reject tariff filings and rate alterations, to issue or deny licensing to those engaged in ocean freight activities, and to administer section 11(p)(1) of the WQIA of 1970 with respect to the financial responsibility of common carriers subject to liability for the costs of oil pollution and removal from U.S. waters.[86]

In 1974 the FMC had before it a series of cases in three areas which impact on U.S. ocean port policies: the North Atlantic Container Pool Agreement case,[87] the so-called "mini-land-bridge" cases,[88] and a number of related rate-absorption/equalization cases, such as the Intermodal Service to Portland, Oregon, case decided in 1973.[89]

The North Atlantic Pool case concerns the "pooling" of carrier services (essentially a conference system) by seven major containership lines operating on the North Atlantic Trade Routes. The carriers proposed to fix port-of-call schedules and freight rates under a joint operators commission for a period of several years. The fixing of port calls, in addition to established rate structures, is clearly a disadvantage to many smaller East Coast ports which might lose some containership service under such a plan. Hence, during the initial hearings on the case, several of these ports filed contesting briefs.

While an initial decision by FMC Judge C. W. Robinson was favorable to the Pool, a final disposition of the case may have a considerable impact on port development.[90]

In the Intermodal Service to Portland, Oregon case, the Port of Portland filed litigation because cargo originating in the Far East was being offloaded in Seattle and trucked (inland feeder system) to the Portland area at the expense of the steamship company. This practice, which involves shipping lines utilizing rate absorption or equalization to bring containers from other ports which were formerly served under the break-bulk cargo system, would allow containership operators to minimize their port time to the advantage of their capital-intensive operation.[91]

The FMC has stated in the past that the ocean carrier cannot pay the cost of the overland shipping between the port of call and the port through which the cargo would originally move. The lack of "adequate" service (defined by the FMC) in the bypassed port has been the only exception to this rule. A general FMC acceptance of the absorption and equalization practice would almost surely result in hardships to smaller port authorities.

The FMC ruling in the <u>Portland</u> case, claimed by both liti-
gants as a victory, was in fact a carefully phrased "unruling."
The Commission agreed in principle with the beneficial aspects of
saving costs through rate absorption and equalization practices,
and offered no ruling to prevent such action. But the Commission
also fully realized the detrimental effects to Portland of such a
stance, and ruled that the steamship line must stop in Portland on
every other voyage.

To be sure, the FMC decision was intended to apply only
to the Portland case, and offered no long-term policy solution
to the series of similar cases pending before the Commission.
These include the <u>Delaware River Port Authority</u> case[92] and the
<u>Intermodal Service at Philadelphia</u> case,[93] among others. In both
dockets, the controversy is similar to that of the Portland rate
absorption case.

These cases will set legal precedents for practices elsewhere when resolved. If the rate absorption practice is ruled
lawful, it might be expected that ocean carriers would expand
the practice and thereby reduce the number of ports receiving
direct containership service (to the likely detriment of smaller
ports).

If, however, the practice is ruled unlawful, ship operators
might either continue to reduce the number of ports to which
they offer direct service or, in order to use their existing
container capacity, they might be forced to serve directly those
ports at which they formerly absorbed inland transportation costs.

The final decision of the FMC on these pending rate absorption cases is made even more difficult since the United States
has neither an explicit national transportation policy nor a
national port policy which specifically addresses this issue.*

The mini-landbridge cases follow the same general pattern.
In these cases, containers are being diverted from ports on one
coast, such as Houston in the Gulf of Mexico, to ports on another
coast, such as Long Beach or Seattle on the West Coast, by the
use of unit trains specialized in carrying only containers.[94]

Proponents of the concept argue that faster service (the
alternate route would be through the Panama Canal) with equal or
lower costs would be beneficial to the overall transportation
infrastructure, while opponents argue that the mini-landbridge
would cause an imbalance of containerized freight flow. More

---

*On September 17, 1975 the Secretary of Transportation issued "A
Statement of National Transportation Policy." While a transportation policy statement issued by the head of one Federal Department does not constitute a national transportation policy, in 1976
the Secretary was moving in this direction by developing a plan to
implement this policy statement.

important, opponents argue that the concept intends to divert "naturally tributary cargo" from one port to another, thereby placing some ports in an advantageous position vis-à-vis other ports.

This latter argument is the substance of a case brought by the Port of New Orleans against Sea-Train, Inc., and presently pending before the FMC.[95] New Orleans claims that a "mini-land-bridge" operating in its hinterland area is in conflict with a series of Shipping Acts and congressional statements propounding equal shipping service opportunities between ports.

Here again, a definitive FMC decision on pending cases will establish important precedents for future actions and policies.

The Interstate Commerce Commission

The Interstate Commerce Commission was created by the Inter-State Commerce Act of February 4, 1887,[96] which empowers the Commission to regulate carriers engaged in transportation in interstate commerce and in foreign commerce to the extent that it takes place in the United States. Carriers under the Commission's jurisdiction include railroads, trucking companies, bus lines, freight forwarders, water carriers, oil pipelines, transportation brokers, and express agencies.[97]

In general, the ICC is involved in controversies over rates (including international through rates) and charges among competing and like modes of transportation, shippers, and receivers of freight, passengers, and others, and rules upon merger applications, acquisitions for control, and other types of consolidation between transport companies.[98] In transportation service, the ICC grants rights to operate to various transport media, and approves applications to construct or abandon rail lines.

Additionally, under Section 8 of the Deepwater Port Act of 1974, the ICC is the common carrier regulator of offshore ports and requisite storage facilities.[99]

The increasing transportation carrier use of international through rates--that is, shipments moving to destination via two or more transport modes under a single bill of lading, or carrier's charge--has prompted complex jurisdictional overlaps between the FMC and ICC in inland-ocean rate cases.[100] The central issue rests between the ICC's regulatory authority over domestic carrier rates and the FMC's jurisdiction over ocean carrier rates. Since through bills of lading specify a single transportation rate for a cargo movement with both a domestic and international portion, it is unclear what the role or jurisdiction of either the ICC or the FMC is in regulating international through rates.[101]

This apparent overlap in jurisdictional authority has caused institutional difficulties for the agencies in implementing their regulatory programs. As one transportation industry journal has noted:[102]

...the division in regulatory jurisdiction between the
FMC and the ICC, by which this [Federal Maritime] Commission can control only the ocean rates and practices
of the intermodal movement, adds a pervasive limitation
upon effective regulation [exercised by either agency].

Additionally, the ICC is presently involved in two further
issue areas where there are jurisdictional conflicts with the
FMC. One area of disharmony is the rate absorption or mini-
landbridge cases. Since the ICC has authority to disallow rates
on domestic cargo movements which are "noncompensatory," ports
that are being bypassed by cargo diversion actions may attempt
to stop such competition by claiming to the ICC that the overland trip to the port of export is priced at an illegally low
level.[103] Ports of the Gulf of Mexico have filed such a com-
plaint with the ICC. In this case the Gulf ports wish to stop
railroad carriers from transporting cargo which was traditionally
handled in New Orleans through South Atlantic ports for export to
Europe.

Another area of conflicting ICC and FMC jurisdictional
opinions concerns the domestic movement of barges going to or
from barge-carrying vessels as part of an international shipment.
Since the entire barge is placed upon the vessel, a domestic
movement could be construed as a pickup and delivery service
for a typical international shipment. However, since the domestic
barge voyage can be several hundred miles long, it can be thought
of as a domestic freight movement as well. Conflicting opinions
between the two regulatory agencies over the status of these shipments has caused some confusion over their regulation. The final
resolution of this conflict may have an impact on ports that are
served by barge-carrying vessels or the barges from these ships.

The National Oceanographic and Atmospheric Administration (NOAA)

Pursuant to Reorganization Plan 4 of 1970, effective October 3, 1970,[104] the establishment of the National Oceanographic
and Atmospheric Administration (NOAA) was to many a victory in
centralizing several diverse federal government functions relating to the marine environment.

With its organization and structure influenced heavily by the
1969 Report of the Commission on Marine Science, Engineering
and Resources,[105] NOAA is charged generally with effective management of its constituent units to achieve full and wise use of
the marine environment.

The establishment of NOAA combined most functions of the
following former agencies and organizations:

    Environmental Science Services Administration
    Elements of the Bureau of Commercial Fisheries
    Marine Sport Fisheries Program from the Bureau
        of Sport Fisheries
    Marine Mineral Technology Center from the Bureau of Mines

Office of Sea Grant Programs from the National Science
   Foundation
U.S. Lake Survey
National Oceanographic Data Center
National Oceanographic Instrumentation Center
National Data Buoy Project

The principal statutory functions of the agency are author-
ized by Title 15, Chapter 9, of the U.S. Code (National Ocean
Survey, formerly the U.S. Coast and Geodetic Survey); and Title
16, Chapter 9, U.S. Code (National Marine Fisheries Service).[106]
Further, the Coastal Zone Management Act of 1972,[107] the Marine
Mammals Protection Act of 1972,[108] the Marine Protection, Research,
and Sanctuaries Act of 1972,[109] and the Weather Modification
Reporting Act of 1972,[110] further define NOAA's general charge.

The various constituent elements of NOAA carry out several
activities which either deal directly with, or impact on, port
and harbor development.

The National Ocean Survey conducts oceanwide mapping and
charting operations, is responsible for the surveying and charting of U.S. waters, and conducts operations in seismic and tidal
activities.[111] As a function of these duties, the Survey compiles
and prints nautical charts, tide and current tables, provides
nautical and aeronautical charts to DOD and elsewhere, and maintains a national geodetic control network providing various types
of data to industry and government.[112]

The National Weather Service maintains a world weather
watch, issues marine weather forecasts, and maintains a comprehensive natural disaster warning system.[113] The latter includes
seismic wave, hurricane, tornado, and seismic warnings.

The National Marine Fisheries Service investigates and carries out functions relating to migratory species of game fish
and other living resources of the sea.[114]

In addition, NOAA maintains Environmental Research Laboratories (marine environment studies), conducts an Environmental
Data Service which collects and publishes environmental data
gathered on a world scale, and maintains a National Data Buoy
Project which is developing a technology for maintaining an auto-
matic ocean buoy system suitable for continuous marine environmental data.[115]

The passing of the Coastal Zone Management Act of 1972 on
October 27, 1972, codified and enlarged the statutory responsibilities of NOAA with respect to coastal planning.[116] The Act,
in establishing a "national policy providing for the management,
beneficial use, protection, and development of the land and
water resources of the nation's coastal zones, and for other
purposes," delegated to NOAA the following key functions:[117]

1. To provide incentives to states to develop coastal
    zone management programs;

2. To facilitate harmonization of local and state programs with national objectives;

3. To function as a clearinghouse for technical information relating to coastal zones; and

4. To assist state programs by suggesting other aids for evaluating coastal zone uses in economic and social terms.

Another key feature of the Act is that NOAA is authorized to make annual program development grants to states drawing up coastal zone proposals, subject to federal guidelines published in the Federal Register on June 13, 1973, and thereafter may make annual administering grants to coastal states with approved plans.[118] These grants, to be administered solely by NOAA, are on a two-thirds federal, one-third state matching basis.

The enactment of any such state coastal zone management plans would have significant impacts on the port industry. New projects initiated by port authorities would need to conform to such plans. As recent literature on seaport management has stated, the impacts of coastal zone programs on public port operations could be outlined in six ways:[119]

1. Pressure from environmental groups to delay port expansion until completion of a state's coastal zone management program, which would be a period of several years;

2. Uncertainties as to how far inland will the planning process and plan implementation extend;

3. Uncertainties as to whether port development would be included in a coastal management program as a priority use of a shoreline area;

4. Questions over whether port authorities can get adequate representation on commissions developing state plans;

5. Uncertainties as to whether a port administration can get recognition of the economic importance of port activities in the management program;

6. The significance of using the expression "Coastal Zone Management Program" instead of "Coastal Zone Plan" may indicate through the word "management" that a greater degree of control is envisioned than normally associated with the implementation of general plans.

As a result of these added responsibilities and constraints, it is clear that future port development will require additional time and will likely encounter higher costs.

To facilitate the management of the various coastal program functions, the Office of Coastal Zone Management (OCZM)
was established within NOAA in early 1973. In response to NOAA's
general charge to assist state coastal zone programs, the OCZM
issued in October 1974 a report on "State Coastal Zone Management Activities."[120] This publication comprehensively lists the
efforts at state levels to consolidate local and state planning
organizations with coastal zone activities.

While many states have some similarity in office or policy
planning structures, the OCZM report illustrates that most do
not. Coastal zone grant recipients, or those persons or offices
designated by the state Governor to work with the OCZM, range
from the Texas General Land Office to New Hampshire's Office of
Comprehensive Planning.

The salient point is that state coastal zone policy formation is being accomplished in varying office and/or organizational formats. Such a situation can only compound the difficulty
the federal OCZM faces in attempting to influence local political
machinery to develop comprehensive and workable coastal zone
management programs.

This state-initiated policy scheme also places NOAA in a
relatively weak institutional position vis-à-vis other federal
agencies in commenting on new or proposed federal legislation.
This was underscored in the July 24, 1973, testimony of Robert
Knecht, Director of the Office of Coastal Environment within
NOAA, on deepwater ports before joint Senate committees.[121] Testifying in support of the Administration's proposed deepwater
ports bill, S. 1751 (see Chapter 9), Knecht stated that NOAA
would provide "assistance" to the lead agency designated in the
proposed bill in possible facility sitings in or near coastal
areas.[122] NOAA made it clear, however, that its principal role
would be one of state-federal policy coordination--not one of
developing federal regulations to be implemented at the state
level.

The key policy importance of state-developed coastal zone
management programs is also emphasized in provisions of the
Deepwater Port Act of 1974.[123] In outlining the applications
procedures for offshore terminals, Section 4 of the Act specifies that for a facility to be licensed the adjacent coastal
state to which a deepwater port is to be connected by pipeline
must be making "reasonable progress" in developing an approved
coastal zone management program.[124] For the purposes of the Act,
a state shall be considered to be making reasonable progress if it
is receiving a planning grant pursuant to Section 305 of the
Coastal Zone Management Act.

Consequently, in cases involving both deepwater and conventional port policies and licensing procedures, NOAA exercises
potentially influential review powers over state management programs and policies. However, the role the agency will assume
in developing its policy review authority is unclear. No firm
pattern has yet emerged. To this extent, however, the case of

offshore terminal licensing presents an important institutional
policy challenge.

State Agencies Involved in Port and Harbor Development

The laws and jurisdiction affecting port authorities and
relevant marine-oriented state organizations vary widely from
state to state. Since port planning and development activities
have been traditionally concentrated at the local level, the
creation of public port authorities has taken place within a
heterogeneity of state institutional structures.

Moreover, if public port activities are considered in the
broader institutional context of maritime or transportation
policy areas, similar results are obtained. State authorities
vary widely in their jurisdictional claims over coastal areas
and resources. Some states define their limits of coastal
ownership at the High Water Mark (e.g., Hawaii); others at the
Ordinary High Tide Mark (e.g., California); one at the Mean Low
Water Mark (Massachusetts); others arrive at different formula-
tions.

Offshore ownership is likewise defined in varying ways: some
states claim a Three Mile ownership, some Three Marine Leagues,
others define their ownership rights in latitudinal degrees.
Seven states, including Alaska, hold no claims to offshore ownership. Exhibit 4.4 is a compilation of principal state agencies
exercising authority in port and harbor management, and a summary
of present state authority claims over coastal and offshore
areas.

In view of this fragmented and heterogeneous state policy
development, some states with common waterway resources and interests have recognized the need for coordination of port and water
resource development.[125] Groups of states have from time to
time petitioned Congress for approval to join together to deal
with interstate issues. In the event of an agreement, the federal government becomes a signatory to these compacts and acts
as an equal partner in all deliberations and implementing actions.*

The Changing Roles of States

The role of state governments in maritime and general transportation planning activities is increasing. New institutional
actors such as state departments of transportation, coastal zone
management, and environmental affairs are being formed in an
increasing number of states. Their creation will presumably
dislodge or modify many of the sectional agency interests which
have traditionally characterized many state governmental structures.

---

*Several compacts dealing with interstate transportation or water
problems have been formed. Examples are the New England Interstate Water Pollution Control Compact Commission, the Delaware
River Basin Compact Commission, the Great Lakes Basin Compact
Commission, and others.

Exhibit 4.4

PRINCIPAL STATE AGENCIES EXERCISING
AUTHORITY IN PORT AND WATERWAY MANAGEMENT*

	PORTS & HARBORS	WATER QUALITY
Alabama	State Docks Department	State Health Department
Alaska	No state agency	State Department of Health and Welfare
California	Department of Harbors and Watercraft	State Water Resources Control Board
Connecticut	Water Resources Commission	Water Resources Commission
Delaware	NCD**	Water and Air Resources Commission
District of Columbia	City Council	Department of Health
Florida	No state agency	Air and Water Pollution Commission and State Board of Health
Georgia	State Port Authority	NCD**
Hawaii	NCD**	Department of Health and Department of Transportation
Illinois	Department of Public Works and Chicago Regional Port District	Sanitary Water Board
Indiana	State Port Commissioner	Stream Pollution Control Board
Louisiana	No state agency	NCD**
Maine	Maine Port Authority	Air and Water Improvement Commission

*From United States Coast Guard, Ports and Waterways Administration and Management, July 1971, Appendix B-3, pp. B-3-3 to B-3-B-3-7, with some modifications.
**Not clearly defined.

	PORTS & HARBORS	WATER QUALITY
Maryland	Maryland Port Authority	Department of Water Resources
Massachusetts	NCD**	Department of Natural Resources
Michigan	State Waterways Commission	State Water Resources Commission
Minnesota	Department of Conservation	Pollution Control Agency
Mississippi	No state agency	Air and Water Commission
New Hampshire	State Port Authority	State Water Supply and Pollution Control Commission
New Jersey	No state agency	State Water Policy Commission
New York	NCD**	Water Resources Commission
North Carolina	State Port Authority	Board of Water and Air Resources
Ohio	No state agency	State Sanitary Authority
Oregon	No state authority	State Sanitary Authority
Pennsylvania	Navigation Commission and Delaware River Basin Commission	Sanitary Water Board
Rhode Island	Department of Public Works	State Health Department
South Carolina	State Port Authority	Pollution Control Authority
Texas	No state agency	Texas Water Quality and Railroad and General Land Office Commission
Virginia	State Port Authority	Water Control Board
Washington	No state agency	State Pollution Control Commission
Wisconsin	No state agency	Department of Natural Resources

LIMITS OF STATE OWNERSHIP

High Water Mark	Mean High Water Mark	Ordinary High Tide Mark	Low Water Mark	Mean Low Water Mark	None	Not Clearly Defined
Hawaii	Delaware	Alabama	Georgia	Massachusetts	Indiana	Alaska
Minnesota	Maine	California	Virginia			Connecticut
South Carolina	Maryland	Florida				District of Columbia
						Illinois
Wisconsin	New Hampshire	Michigan				Louisiana
	New Jersey	Oregon				Mississippi
	New York	Washington				Ohio
	North Carolina					Pennsylvania
	Rhode Island					Texas

OFFSHORE

Three-Mile**	One Marine League*	Three Marine Leagues*	Six Marine Leagues*	None	State Boundary	United States Current Claim
Delaware	Oregon	Texas		Georgia	Illinois	Maine
Florida[1]	North Carolina	Louisiana		New Hampshire	District of Columbia	Virginia
California	Massachusetts			Connecticut	Ohio	
Washington				Alaska	Wisconsin	
South Carolina				Rhode Island	Hawaii	
New York (Atlantic)				New Jersey	Indiana	
Maryland				Pennsylvania	Michigan	

1. Florida's jurisdiction claim is 3 miles on the Atlantic and 9 miles on the Gulf.

* Defined as 1/20th of a degree or 3.657 statute miles.

** Two distinct measures are included in this designation, a geographical mile equal to 6,280 feet and a statute mile equal to 5,280 feet.

The impetus for these changes is a point of importance.
While many new state-agency structures were created in response
to federal policy development (state offices of coastal zone
management are one example), an increasingly large grouping of
agencies are being formed in response to supportive political
constituencies and an increasing state government emphasis on
comprehensive planning methods.

As a facility embracing several modes of transportation, and
one having important impacts on local and state economics (see
Chapter 2), public port authorities are directly influenced by
these administrative changes. Moreover, port authorities are
often important elements in local, city, and state politics.
Apart from the positive economic and employment impacts they
generate in their hinterlands, port authorities may become a concern of local environmental or land use and coastal management
interests--particularly if a port has made repeated encroachments
on public land in efforts to expand and develop. Concern on the
part of local political constituencies supporting these interests
may then translate into institutional action; that is, local
groups may press for the creation of state planning or management agencies sensitive to their concerns. In the case of state
environmental and land use agencies, their creation was often
linked to a growing constituency base supporting local involvement in heretofore city, state or regional development schemes.*

Coastal Zone Management Activities

With impetus provided by the federal Coastal Zone Management
Act (discussed in the NOAA section of this chapter), thirty-one
of thirty-four coastal states and territories are participating in
the federal-state coastal zone management program. In 1974, approximately $12 million in federal and state funds have been committed
to state efforts in coastal management. As stated in a recent
NOAA summary of state efforts in this area:[126]

> This level of attention and funding reflects a nation-
> wide awareness of the problems and conflicts existing
> in the coastal zone, as well as a growing recognition
> of the need to find thoughtful solutions to the complex
> problems stemming from the sharply increasing demands
> for use of America's limited coastal resources.

One example of the institutional impact of coastal zone
efforts is its application to new legislation regarding deepwater port development. Under Section 4(b)(10) of the Deepwater
Port Act of 1974, states affected by the operation of an offshore terminal and pipeline system must be making "reasonable
progress" in developing approved coastal management programs
for the facility to be licensed by the federal government.

---

*It is important to distinguish the effects of local constitu-
ency groups on the creation of responsive state institutions with
the activities of state or federal agencies in implementing their
programs. As discussed in Chapter 4, institutions appeal to
supportive constituencies in implementing their policies and programs. The process then works both ways.

State Departments of Transportation

An important trend over the last decade in state governments has been the merging of transportation modal interests into state departments of transportation. Prior to the creation of the federal DOT in 1967, only three state departments of transportation existed. At the start of 1970, nine departments had been formed.[127] By August 1973, 20 states had established state departments of transportation, and some 12 other states were studying legislation to enhance the state's role in multimodal transportation.[128] And in 1975, at least 26 state departments of transportation had been created.

A notable consistency among the established state DOTs is the assignment of responsibility, in varying degrees, to the departments for comprehensive transportation planning and development of state transportation master plans. Where this responsibility is coupled with development authority and finance plans, the planning process provides a base for the establishment of goals and coordination in development of the total transportation system.[129]

Since state departments of transportation are essentially consolidations of several different transport modes* under one administrative roof, there is an opportunity for states to pool revenues into large general funds. The Maryland Department of Transportation, cited by MarAd as a possible model for other states to follow, pooled all revenues into two funds. The first fund covers operations of all projects initiated by the department's component parts, or pool-type** projects. These are financed by the usual revenue bonds.[130]

The second fund covers all other revenues such as port income, gasoline taxes, revenue sharing receipts, bus fares, airport income, and so on. This fund, called the Consolidated Transportation Fund, is used to back the sale of Consolidated Transportation Bonds. Receipts from the sale of these bonds, plus other revenues generated, are used for operating and construction expenses as needed by the department, according to preapproved construction master plans.[131]

By the use of this innovative financial pooling arrangement, states hope that more advantageous bond marketing benefits can be obtained.[132] In addition, the use of a master plan covering all modes can put the money to work where it can be utilized in the most efficient manner.

---

*Such as Highway, Construction and Maintenance, Motor Vehicle Administration, Airports, Mass Transit, Ports.

**The use of the word "pool" represents the component parts of the department.

Quasi-Governmental and Private Organizations Involved in
Port and Harbor Development

In addition to the numerous actors involved in port development at the federal, state, and local governmental levels, there are many quasi-governmental and private organizations which exert important policy influences on port development and operations.

Included in a listing of principal port and inland-waterways industry lobbying and management organizations would be the American Association of Port Authorities and the American Waterway Operators. Many other associations and groups in the maritime area exist, however, and a compilation and discussion of some 28 principal management and labor organizations appear in Appendix B.

The activities of industry and labor organizations are of significant importance to the federal maritime policy process. Not only do these organizations comprise a substantive lobbying and special-interest potential, their influence in representing industry views and associations constitutes potentially important, supportive policy and program constituency groups. Moreover, these organizations have important influence in opposing policy positions in congressional consideration.*

---

*Studies of the organization and workings of industry and labor groups are included in works on managerial behavior, industry associations, and public administration and policy. In the maritime policy area, a specific work which should be referenced for further information is Samuel A. Lawrence, United States Shipping Policies and Politics (Washington, D.C.: The Brookings Institution, 1966).

CHAPTER 5

THE FEDERAL ENVIRONMENTAL ORGANIZATIONS--THE ENVIRONMENTAL
PROTECTION AGENCY AND THE COUNCIL ON ENVIRONMENTAL QUALITY

Introduction

The popularization of the environmental movement in the late
1960s brought with the general citizen concern dramatic and
substantive changes in the federal bureaucracy. While in some
sense the changes in government organization, policy, and programs were a timely function of a new, ecologically-minded political constituency, the changes induced will have far-reaching,
permanent impact on our governmental policy.

The enactment of environmental legislation and the activities of supportive political constituencies have served to alter
the internal and external dimensions of policy formation and
implementation by federal water agencies. Institutionally,
the creation of new organizations has changed the structure and
powers by which the federal bureaucracy develops and implements
public policy. New institutional actors have disrupted traditional power relationships within and between federal organizations, as have the emergence and activities of strong environmental interest groups. New regulations and administrative
procedures (such as Environmental Impact Statements) complicate
the process by which policies are formed and implemented. Moreover, the time and informational requirements for policy formation consistent with environmental guidelines have been itera-
tive and supplemental in character; more time must be allotted,
and more information must be amassed, to implement policy and
programs designed under new environmental guidelines.

The Rapidly Changing Traditional Port Scenario

New environmental legislation has caused the traditional
port development scenario described in Chapter 2 to change
rapidly. Governmental policy-making institutions, actors, and
procedures are different. Ports themselves are different; new
maritime technologies, changing hinterland potentials and impacts, and new concepts of intermodal transportation all serve
to complicate the contemporary world of port planning and operations. The compressed timing of environmental changes has also
been problematical; ten years ago, few would have thought the
historical patterns of port development would so rapidly be
required to change.

The dimensions and difficulties of these institutional
changes can be illustrated by citing two examples of particular
consequence to port development--the preparation and review of
environmental impact statements, and the promulgation and implementation of dredge spoil regulations.

Environmental Impact Statements

Under Section 102 of the National Environmental Policy Act of 1969 all agencies of the federal government were directed to utilize a "systematic, interdisciplinary approach which will ensure the integrated use of the natural and social sciences and the environmental design arts in planning and in decision making which may have an impact on man's environment."[1] The provision forcing policy and program action and the heart of NEPA was Section 102(2)(c) which required each agency to "include in every recommendation or report on proposals for legislation and other major federal actions significantly affecting the quality of the human environment, a detailed statement by a responsible official on:[2]

" (i)   the environmental impact;

" (ii)   any adverse environmental effects which cannot be avoided should the proposal be implemented;

"(iii)   alternatives to the proposed action;

" (iv)   the relationship between local short-term uses of man's environment and the maintenance and enhancement of long-term productivity, and

" (v)   any irreversible and irretrievable commitments of resources which would be involved in the proposed action should it be implemented."

The Act also provides that, before a detailed EIS is made, the responsible official must consult with and obtain the comments of any federal agency which has jurisdiction by law or has special expertise with respect to any environmental impact involved.[3]

Exhibit 5.1 illustrates the comparative volume of environmental impact statements prepared by major federal agencies over the five-year history of the Act. Note that the Department of Transportation, with its large number of road projects requiring individual impact statements, represents some 25 percent of all statements filed by federal agencies.[4]

Since the adoption of NEPA, the interpretation and implementation of its provisions by federal agencies have been a topic of practical and academic concern. Time delays resulting from environmental procedures are costly to both the government and the affected project or program. In some cases, environmental procedures have delayed projects past their useful time span, or have stopped them altogether. While few would argue with the utility of environmental review, the striking of an appropriate balance between industrial development and the environment is a central government, industry, and citizen

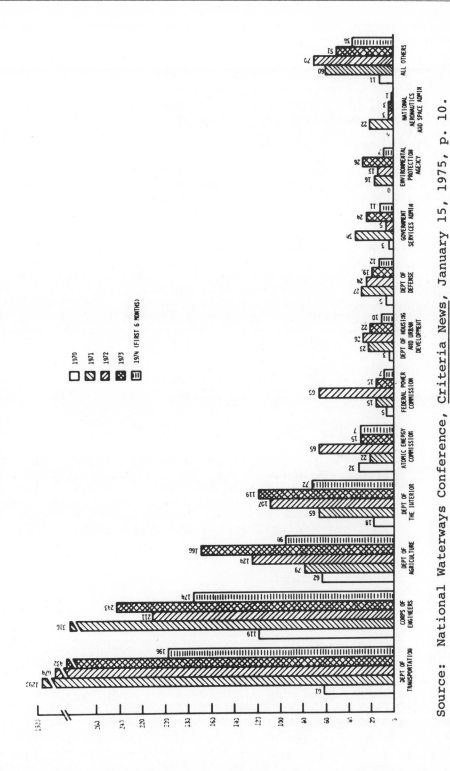

EXHIBIT 5.1

ENVIRONMENTAL IMPACT STATEMENTS FILED ANNUALLY,
BY AGENCY, TO JULY 1, 1974

Source: National Waterways Conference, Criteria News, January 15, 1975, p. 10.

concern.*

Three recent water policy cases where environmental review
and procedures have served to halt or influence the development
of proposed projects include the Mississippi River Locks and
Dam 26 case, the proposed Cross-Florida Barge Canal, and the
"mini-landbridge" case before the FMC.

The Locks and Dam 26 case concerns efforts by the Corps of
Engineers to replace a government lock facility on the Mississippi River for purposes of facilitating barge traffic.[5] Environmental groups, arguing for more complete review procedures
and additional information on environmental impacts, have effectively delayed consideration of the project.

In the Cross-Florida Barge Canal proposal, a second case
where the Corps of Engineers is considering opening up inland
water passages for barge traffic, environmental reviews and
complex procedural requirements halted the project in January
of 1971.[6] Subsequently, Congress directed the Corps to restudy
the issue and submit more detailed project assessments and
environmental impacts. The case is presently under review.

Finally, the "mini-landbridge" case before the FMC has been
delayed and complicated by legal concerns over the preparation
and handling of environmental reviews.[7] In late 1974, parties
seeking to enjoin mini-landbridge operations challenged in
federal and state courts the handling of environmental reviews
by the FMC. However, in April of 1975 the U.S. District Court
denied pleas regarding this issue, although further legal actions are expected.

Importantly, these maritime cases illustrate that environmental review procedures may be utilized as institutional obstructions by those parties wishing to prevent various marine activities.** While strategies of this type and persuasion have
seen varying degrees of success, the procedures for court action
along these lines are well known, and it is clear that the trend
will continue.

Dredge Spoil Regulations

Few environmental issues have received the degree of attention afforded to dredging operations and newly established
dredge-spoil regulations. Criteria for disposal of dredged
spoils are the principal environmental concern to ocean ports
in terms of their long-range development plans. Moreover, the

---

*A substantial literature exists on the subject. For a particu-
larly interesting account of NEPA in the courts, see Harold P.
Green, "The National Environmental Policy Act in the Courts"
(Washington, D.C.: The Conservation Foundation, May 1972).

**This "institutional delay" strategy has of course been pursued
in other areas of industrial development such as the siting of
nuclear power plants, the expansion of airport facilities, or
the development of on-land or offshore oil recovery capabilities.

scope and importance of this activity to port development is
emphasized by considering the annual national volume of new and
maintenance dredging work done. The Army Corps of Engineers,
charged by Congress to develop and maintain the nation's navigable waterway system, annually dredges some 300,000,000 cubic
yards of maintenance work and approximately 80,000,000 cubic
yards of new dredging work.

However, in recent years concern has developed over the
adverse effects on water quality and aquatic organisms entailed
in dredging operations. In order to assess the effects of
dredging and the disposal of bottom materials in open waters,
and to classify such materials as either polluted or unpolluted,
the Environmental Protection Agency (EPA)* issued in 1971
"Criteria for Determining Acceptability of Dredged Spoil Disposal to the Nation's Waters."[8] The criteria established technical standards for the evaluation of sediment pollutant levels,
and the necessary disposal technique (if allowable). Exhibit
5.2 illustrates the full text of the EPA criteria on dredging
spoils.[9]

Consistent with the criteria set out in Exhibit 5.2, approximately 31 percent (93,000,000 cu yd) of the average annual
maintenance dredging was estimated to be polluted. Of the estimated total amount of materials (250,000,000 cu yd) disposed
of annually in open water (includes "undifferentiated," "new
work," and "unconfined"), it is estimated that 30 to 35 percent
may be classified as polluted.[10] As nationwide sampling of
potential spoil disposal materials expands and the techniques
for pollutant analysis become more sophisticated, much of what
was disposed of in "open waters" may now be too polluted for this
disposal method.

The key importance of the EPA criteria is emphasized by the
impacts of new disposal procedures on Corps of Engineers civil
works projects. As reported in a recent Corps analysis of some
1,500 environmental impact studies involving 1,100 Corps projects, some 350 projects were modified, delayed or halted on the
basis of these reviews.[11] About 75 river and harbor dredging
projects were modified, many principally because of problems
in disposing of dredged materials.

One possible solution to the disposal of polluted dredged
spoils is their location behind on-land dikes. However, the
additional costs involved with such an activity might well be
several times the cost of dredging by traditional methods.
Since this incremental cost is typically borne by the port or
other non-federal parties (rather than the Corps of Engineers),
this method of dredged spoil disposal may make many dredging
projects prohibitively expensive for public port authorities.

---

*The EPA is charged generally with the protection of our nation's
environment. Setting standards for air and water quality is
one component of this charge. See the discussion on the EPA in
this chapter.

Exhibit 5.2

CRITERIA FOR DETERMINING ACCEPTABILITY OF DREDGED
SPOIL DISPOSAL TO THE NATION'S WATERS

Use of Criteria

These criteria were developed as guidelines for FWQA evaluation of proposals and applications to dredge sediments from fresh and saline waters.

Criteria

The decision whether to oppose plans for disposal of dredged spoil in United States waters must be made on a case-by-case basis after considering all appropriate factors, including the following:

(a) Volume of dredged material.

(b) Existing and potential quality and use of the water in the disposal area.

(c) Other conditions at the disposal site such as depth and currents.

(d) Time of year of disposal (in relation to fish migration and spawning, etc.).

(e) Method of disposal and alternatives.

(f) Physical, chemical, and biological characteristics of the dredged material.

(g) Likely recurrence and total number of disposal requests in a receiving water area.

(h) Predicted long and short term effects on receiving water quality. When concentrations, in sediments, of one or more of the following pollution parameters exceed the limits expressed below, the sediment will be considered polluted in all cases and, therefore, unacceptable for open water disposal.

Exhibit 5.2 (continued)

Sediments in Fresh and Marine Waters	Conc. % (dry wt. basis)
*Volatile Solids	6.0
Chemical Oxygen Demand (C.O.D.)	5.0
Total Kjeldahl Nitrogen	0.10
Oil-Grease	0.15
Mercury	0.001
Lead	0.005
Zinc	0.005

If the results show a significant deviation from this equation, additional samples should be analyzed to insure reliable measurements.

The volatile solids and C.O.D. analyses should be made first. If the maximum limits are exceeded, the sample can be characterized as polluted and the additional parameters would not have to be investigated.

Dredged sediment having concentration of constituents less than the limits stated above will not be automatically considered acceptable for disposal. A judgment must be made on a case-by-case basis after considering the factors listed in (a) through (h) above.

In addition to the analyses required to determine compliance with the stated numerical criteria, the following additional tests are recommended where appropriate and pertinent:

Total Phosphorus	Sulfides
Total Organic Carbon (T.O.C.)	Trace Metals (iron, cadmium, copper, chromium, arsenic, and nickel)
Immediate Oxygen Demand (I.O.D.)	Pesticides
Settleability	Bioassay

---

*When analyzing sediments dredged from marine waters, the following correlation between volatile solids and C.O.D. should be made:

$$T.V.S.\% \ (dry) = 1.32 + 0.98(C.O.D.\%)$$

Several ports, including the port of Baltimore, are in positions
where the added costs of dredging and disposal may cause drastic
changes to their long-range development plans.

This latter situation emphasizes the potentially important
impacts of environmental regulations on the port industry. Whether
the regulations pertain to dredge spoil disposal guidelines, or
environmental impact reviews and administrative requirements, these
regulations entail added costs and potential time delays to
ports. Since the costs entailed in meeting these regulations
and procedures are borne by the port authorities themselves or
other non-federal bodies, their expansion and development plans
are affected in the long run. The nature of this effect depends
in most respects on the extent of the planned development and
its postulated environmental impact and cost.

Other Issues

Two other governmental activities which influence the traditional port development scenario are state initiatives in establishing coastal zone management programs and offices of environmental affairs and, at the federal level, the drafting and submission to Congress of several bills incorporating direct federal subsidies and grants to assist public port authorities in
offsetting the costs of new environmental regulations.

The development of state coastal zone management programs
under the federal coastal zone act and the establishment of
state departments of environmental affairs or planning represent
a growing commitment at the state and local levels to control
the environmental impacts of industrial development in their
respective coastal regions (these issues are discussed in Chapter 4 under the National Oceanographic and Atmospheric Administration).*

Furthermore, in some cases state legislatures are being
urged to assume the financial responsibilities for providing
disposal sites for dredged materials, long a responsibility of
the Army Corps of Engineers. In the Texas Intercoastal Canal

---

*In addition to the institutional aspects of state initiatives
in creating new programs and agencies, states have the power
under federal water quality legislation to explicitly set their
own water quality standards. States may therefore elect to set
stricter guidelines than promulgated under federal law, raising
additional problems and procedural requirements for public port
operations and development. In April 1975, the Minnesota Pollution Control Agency filed suit in federal court to "clear up
a number of ambiguities" between state and federal powers in
establishing these guidelines. At the time of the suit's filing,
Minnesota state law would apparently prohibit all maintenance
dredging on the Mississippi River if the state's water quality
standards were met. See the American Waterways Operators'
"Weekly Letter" (Washington, D.C.: American Waterways Operators,
Inc, April 19, 1975), p. 6.

case, fears by the state legislature that federal environmental laws could force closing of the canal have led the state to consider funding operations and maintenance on its own.[12] In the future, states may become increasingly drawn into similar federal regulatory constraints regarding the maintenance dredging of their inland waterways and harbors.

Implications of Environmental Regulations

Environmental and related safety and facility regulations established by the federal government have resulted in sharply increased costs to public ports. In some cases, public port authorities or port associations have implied that environmental regulations have the potential for creating competitive disequilibriums between nominally competing ports.[13] This disequilibrium might occur since each port's long-range development plan will likely reflect varying environmental costs, thereby placing intrinsic regulatory cost advantages or disadvantages to each port's development scheme.

Partly in consequence to these concerns, the American Association of Port Authorities (AAPA) has called for federal funding assistance to public ports in connection with environmental and related regulatory costs.[14] Three resolutions enacted at the 1973 AAPA Annual Meeting urged the Congress to consider types of funding assistance which would permit public port authorities to meet "without financial burden" new worker occupational safety and health regulations, cargo security procedures, and environmental regulations.[15] Five bills have been submitted in Congress to this effect.*

The Environmental Agencies

Having dealt with several issues and policy imperatives which affect all federal, state and local environmental activities, the two major federal organizations concerned with the environment will be discussed. The Council on Environmental Quality (CEQ), an organization within the Executive Office of the President, principally coordinates and develops national environmental policies and programs.

The Environmental Protection Agency (EPA), a line executive agency, is concerned primarily with the regulation and enforcement of environmental protection criteria and standards.

The Council on Environmental Quality (CEQ)

The Council on Environmental Quality was established by the National Environmental Policy Act of 1969[16] (NEPA) to "formulate and recommend national policies to promote the improvement of the quality of the environment."[17] The Office of Environmental Quality, which provides staff support for the Council, was later

---

*The five "port aid" bills will be discussed in Chapter 10.

established by Title II of the Environmental Quality Improvement
Act of 1970.[18] Located within the Executive Office of the
President, the Council is composed of three members appointed
by the President and approved by the Senate.

Under NEPA, the Council is charged to report to the President at least once each year on the state and condition of the
environment, to develop and recommend to the President national
policies to foster the improvement of the environment, to gather
and analyze authoritative information concerning the trends and
conditions affecting environmental quality, and to review and
appraise various federal programs with respect to the environment.[19]

Additionally, under the Water Quality Improvement Act of
1970,[20] the CEQ was charged with the publication of a National
Contingency Plan for Oil and Hazardous Materials Pollution Control. Pursuant to this charge, the CEQ published in June of
1970 the National Oil and Hazardous Materials Pollution Contingency Plan. The plan is "to provide for efficient, coordinated,
and effective action to minimize damage from oil discharge,
including containment, dispersal, and removal of oil."[21] The CEQ
plan provides for a National Inter-Agency Committee (planning
phase), a National Response Team, Regional Response Teams, and
Strike Force capabilities.

Pursuant to these general legislative charges, the Council
compiled several types of environmental information for the
summer 1973 joint Senate hearings on deepwater port facilities.
Among the information collected and developed was a major interagency study of the environmental effects of deepwater ports.[22]
Importantly, the study included an assessment of landside environmental implications of deepwater port development.

As indicated by the director of the CEQ at that time, the
Council would provide consultative services to the lead agency
involved in deepwater port regulation, mainly in an informational
role.[23]

This position was consistent with the Council's overall
responsibility as a coordinating organization for environmental
policy design and implementation.

The Environmental Protection Agency

The Environmental Protection Agency (EPA) was established
as an independent agency in the Executive Branch pursuant to
Reorganization Plan No. 3 of 1970, effective December 2, 1970.[24]

Created to accomplish effective governmental action with
respect to the environment, the EPA maintains and coordinates
a variety of research, monitoring, standard setting, and enforcement activities. Additionally, the EPA supports research and
antipollution activities by state and local governments, educational institutions, and public and private groups.

The organization of the EPA, shown in Exhibit 5.3, consists of an Administrator and his Staff Offices, five Assistant Administrators designated by program area, and the requisite number of office structures under each program area. The EPA's ten regional offices represent the local program development of the Agency.

The Administrator of the EPA is charged with administering, among others, the Federal Water Pollution Control Act (FWPCA),[25] the Clean Air Act,[26] and amendments thereto. This administration involves reviewing state programs establishing effluent and emission standards, issuing federal standards, and ruling on discharge, dumping, or other factors affecting water or air quality.[27]

All civil works projects affecting the marine environment must receive a water quality certificate and EPA approval before work can be commenced if they are sponsored by a federal agency, and unless the agency can otherwise justify the project without violating CEQ guidelines or the requirements of NEPA.[28]

The EPA is responsible for all air and water quality programs including oil pollution control, and works in conjunction with other state and federal agencies to promulgate, implement, and enforce standards in this area.

Additionally, the EPA may assist in the preparation of Environmental Impact Statements required under NEPA, but reviews and comments on all such statements prepared by other federal agencies on major federal actions and legislation.

The passing of the FWPCA Amendments of 1972 provided a new and comprehensive program of pollution control. As stated in the Act, it is the national goal that the discharge of pollutants into navigable waters be eliminated by 1985.[29] Pursuant to Section 402 of this Act, the EPA established a new federal-state nationwide water permit program--the National Pollutant Discharge Elimination System (NPDES).[30] NPDES will require, through new, specific effluent limitations, that a point source pollutant discharger meet certain effluent standards and, in some cases, monitor continuously the source, nature, and amount of discharge.[31] Permit standards are set with the 1983 and 1985 water quality goals of the FWPCA Amendments in mind.

NPDES is based on effective federal-state participation, the eventual objective being a state-administered permit program with federal review. Since full implementation of the program by states is anticipated to take some time, either a limited life interim state program, or a federal permit program, is in effect.[32] The procedures to be followed by EPA in processing and issuing permits were published in the Federal Register on May 22, 1973.

The provisions of the NPDES program place certain requirements on port authorities and other port-related groups in terms

EXHIBIT 5.3

ORGANIZATION CHART FOR THE ENVIRONMENTAL PROTECTION AGENCY

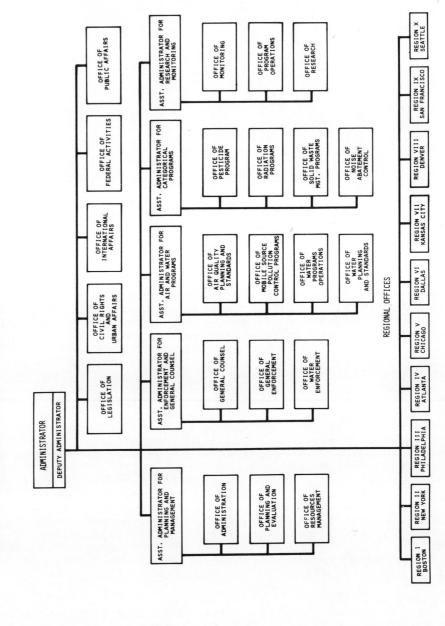

Source: U.S. Government Manual, p. 431.

of their environmental (water quality) impacts. While state-
permit programs are to be the local permit authorities, the EPA,
under the 1972 Amendment and others, holds review and monitoring
powers. Final review authority for any permit granted rests with
the federal government, specifically the Administrator of the
EPA.[33]

Also impacting on port and harbor affairs, the EPA works
in coordination with the U.S. Coast Guard on research and development of pollution ("spill") abatement systems, and has some
overlapping authority with the Coast Guard in the enforcement of
marine pollution laws.[34] Such statutory overlaps, in this case
and others, are handled through interagency agreements.

The Superport Dilemma

As a nation which has become increasingly reliant on imported petroleum to meet national energy needs, the United States
is presently confronted with a number of major policy decisions
regarding current oil import and energy policies. One major component of this overall situation is the present world use of Very
Large Crude Carriers (VLCCs), or supertankers, and the feasibility of establishing deepwater ports serving this country.[35]
The essential dilemma will be the economic versus the environmental tradeoffs in establishing these facilities.[36]

The CEQ, which is concerned with overall environmental
quality, and the EPA, which is responsible for air and water
quality, oil pollution control, and enforcing the Federal Water
Pollution Control Act and the Clean Air Act, are thus intimately
involved in this overall policy process.

Chief among the various environmental concerns are oil spill
problems, operational pollution, and secondary impacts of the
requisite materials and people needed to build and maintain any
site. The latter issue was one part of a major multiagency
study commissioned by the CEQ.[37]

The study, "Potential Onshore Effects of Deepwater Oil Terminal-Related Industrial Development," focused on the potential
economic and environmental impacts of a deepwater facility off
specific coastal areas.[38] The CEQ found that, although predic-
tions could be made in regional impact studies, generally insufficient data and methodological difficulties left room for contest
over secondary impact assessments.[39]

One component of this interagency study, in addition to
other regional environmental studies conducted with support from
the CEQ, (such as the "Preliminary Assessment of the Environmental
Vulnerability of Machias Bay, Maine, to Oil Supertankers") was
the argument that to reduce potential oil pollution hazards,
deepwater facilities should be moved far offshore.[40]

The idea here is that crude oil, when spilled into seawater,
releases most of its toxic properties within 24 to 72 hours by
evaporation and dissolution.[41] If spilled oil does not reach

biologically productive shore areas (such as estuaries or coastal wetlands) within this time period, major ecological damage can be generally averted. Naturally, wind and current conditions play a major role here.

Given these points, the Council indicated in 1973 Senate hearings on deepwater ports that it would favor the establishment of deepwater facilities far offshore.[42] Such a recommendation may have an impact on the design of offshore terminals; as the site moves farther from shore and water depths increase, construction costs of a fixed platform increase much faster than the relative costs of a floating mono-buoy system. Such economic/ environmental constraints pose additional tradeoff questions not addressed by economic analysis alone.

Additionally, the CEQ secondary impacts study focused attention on whether deepwater facilities would be constructed offshore of "new" areas, i.e., residential or recreational sites, versus their construction offshore from already established industrial or petrochemical development areas. Both environmental organizations will have a significant impact on the resolution of this particular issue.

CHAPTER 6

THE U.S. ARMY CORPS OF ENGINEERS

Introduction and Overview

Historically, a major factor in the development of the U.S. port industry has been the dredging operations of the Army Corps of Engineers.* The navigation budget of the Corps has provided the great majority of federal funds and technical assistance related to port planning and development. Moreover, the dredging of channels and harbors by the Corps has traditionally been performed without cost to the ports.**

Initially charged with broad public works responsibilities in the early 1800s, the Corps of Engineers currently operates under a pervasive mix of legal authorities gained from historical jurisdiction and contemporary legislative adaptation to the newer problems brought about by technological change and environmental awareness.

Technology and ecology have facilitated institutional changes in the organization of the Corps as well as placing pressure on the traditional implementation of its program and policy responsibilities. Changes in maritime transportation technology have engendered greater economic impacts on local and regional port hinterland areas. Moreover, these changes have pointed out that the Corps should move towards utilizing a regional approach to cost/benefit analyses of water resource projects. Traditionally, the organization has been concerned with studies on an individual port project basis.

The growing national environmental awareness has also been of particular consequence to the implementation of Corps policies and programs. New environmental constituencies have emerged to challenge Corps operations in areas such as dredging and the construction of dams for hydroelectric power and flood control.

Specifically, the setting of federal and state criteria for the disposal of dredged spoils has seriously affected the Corps' traditional pattern of operations in the port area. With the advent of larger and deeper-draft containerships and bulk carriers, many U.S. ports have filed applications with the Corps for the dredging of deeper harbors. However, under new environmental guidelines pertaining to spoil disposal techniques, dredging operations are now considerably more costly.

The technological necessity of acquiring deeper-dredged harbors versus the increased dredging costs associated with new environmental criteria places the activities of the Corps under two paradoxical, institutional constraints. On one hand, the

---

*See Chapters 2 and 3.

**The cost of dredging in berthing areas is typically paid for by the port. In addition, many ports are now paying for the disposal of polluted dredged spoils.

Corps is being asked to deepen many channels and harbors, while on the other it is being restrained by new environmental legislation and regulations. The strategy for resolving these conflicting forces on the implementation of Corps policies and programs constitutes a principal contemporary problem area of the Corps. Moreover, two additional issues which impact on the dredging dilemma are the discount rate to be used in justifying public works projects, and the possibility of user charges being levied on the inland waterways carriers.*

As a consequence of these concerns, the Corps of Engineers represents an illustrative case of a traditional organization experiencing the dilemma of change. This chapter will outline these concerns as they relate to and affect the traditional organization and program implementation of the Corps.

The Role and Organization of the Corps of Engineers in Port Development

The Department of the Army and the Corps of Engineers are charged by Congress with a major federal role in water resources development encompassing both ocean ports and inland waterways. Since the inception of the Corps of Engineers in 1779, this role has been the outgrowth of legislative and administrative activity.

Non-military activities of the Corps, including the navigation program, are contained within the federal civil works program. Exhibit 6.1 illustrates the Corps' civil works expenditures compared with the total budget authority of the federal government for the years 1962 to 1975. Although fiscal year 1974 expenditures of $1.886 billion comprise a more than 70 percent increase over budget expenditures in 1964, when annual civil works expenditures are expressed as a percentage of total federal budget authority, this ratio has decreased from .827 percent to .614 percent over the decade.

Furthermore, of the fiscal year 1974 budget request, $413 million was for "Operation and Maintenance--General," of which approximately one-third of the total was applied to dredging activities to maintain federal channel and harbor projects in the interests of navigation.[1] In the case of waterways and harbors, the Corps normally must perform maintenance in any one year on approximately 300 out of the 1,000 total projects.[2] Appendix C compiles a list of allotments of Corps funds to rivers and channels over 25 feet in depth for the years 1970-1973.

Corps of Engineers Regulation 1165-2-1 sets forth a comprehensive organizational listing of civil works water resource policies and activities.[3] The Corps' civil works responsibility started as a result of an Act of Congress in 1824 for the improvement of rivers and harbors for navigation. Subsequently, a num-

*See Chapters 3 and 4.

Exhibit 6.1

ARMY CORPS OF ENGINEERS' CIVIL WORKS EXPENDITURES
IN RELATION TO FEDERAL GOVERNMENT BUDGET, 1962-1975

Fiscal Year	Budget Authority, Federal Budget (Millions)	Budget Authority Corps' Civil Works (Millions)	Percentage
1962	$ 118,814	$ 975	0.821
1963	130,882	1,046	0.799
1964	132,636	1,097	0.827
1965	171,944	1,286	0.748
1966	163,123	1,330	0.815
1967	182,562	1,293	0.708
1968	190,649	1,305	0.685
1969	196,167	1,245	0.635
1970	212,973	1,156	0.543
1971	236,406	1,310	0.554
1972	248,097	1,589	0.640
1973	276,417	1,836	0.664
1974	307,400	1,886	0.614
1975	324,500 (est.)	1,706	0.526

Note: Except for Fiscal Years 1973 and 1974, the above figures
represent actual budget authority. In FY 1973, an additional
$116 million was appropriated for civil works programs, resulting
in a total budget authority of $1,952,000. However, $116 million
was subsequently deferred until Fiscal Year 1974, allowing a program of $1,886,000--in contrast with the budget authority in that
year of $1,770,000. Figures for Fiscal Year 1975 are estimated.

Sources: Corps of Engineers, U.S. Army
           U.S. Department of Commerce

ber of congressional River and Harbor Acts in the late 1880s and 1890s broadened the authority of the Corps in navigation control. Since then, the Corps' functional responsibilities have been expanded by major legislation and now include the following:

1. Hydroelectric power in navigation dams

2. Flood control

3. Recreational navigation

4. Recreation

5. Irrigation (limited)

6. Water supply

7. Shore and beach erosion protection

8. Hurricane protection

9. Water quality

10. Environmental emphasis

The organization of the Office of Chief of Engineers is shown in Exhibit 6.2. The Director of Civil Works is responsible to the Chief of Engineers for the supervision of all matters relating to the planning, design, construction, operation, and maintenance of the Corps' Civil Works Program. The organization of the Civil Works Directorate is shown in Exhibit 6.3. There are in excess of 28,055 permanent, 1,585 temporary, and 339 officers in the Corps' Civil Works Program.[4]

The majority of work assigned to the Chief of Engineers is accomplished through delegation to several field officers and their staffs, under the supervision of the Office of the Chief of Engineers.

U.S. Army Engineer Divisions have jurisdiction over eleven specified geographical areas of the nation. The Division Engineer's responsibilities include:

1. Administering the mission of the Chief of Engineers involving civil works planning, engineering, construction, operation and maintenance of facilities and related real estate matters;

2. Commanding and supervising districts assigned to their control. This supervisory responsibility includes review and approval of the major plans and programs of the districts, implementation of plans and policies of the Chief of Engineers, and review and control of district operations;

EXHIBIT 6.2

SIMPLIFIED ORGANIZATION CHART, OCE

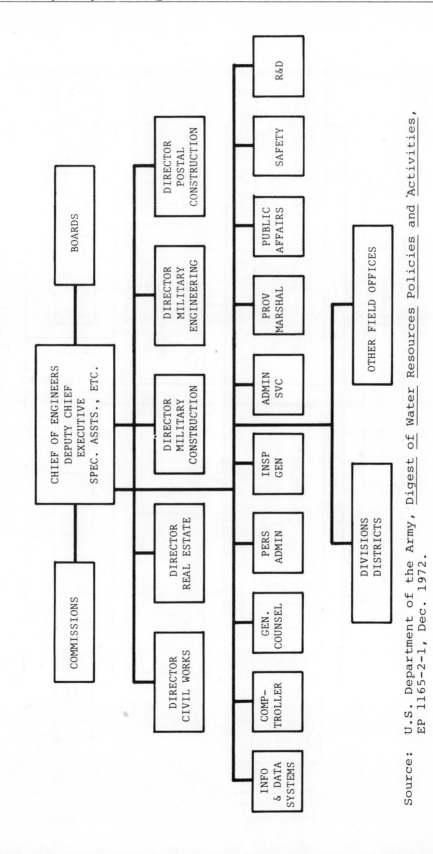

Source: U.S. Department of the Army, *Digest of Water Resources Policies and Activities*, EP 1165-2-1, Dec. 1972.

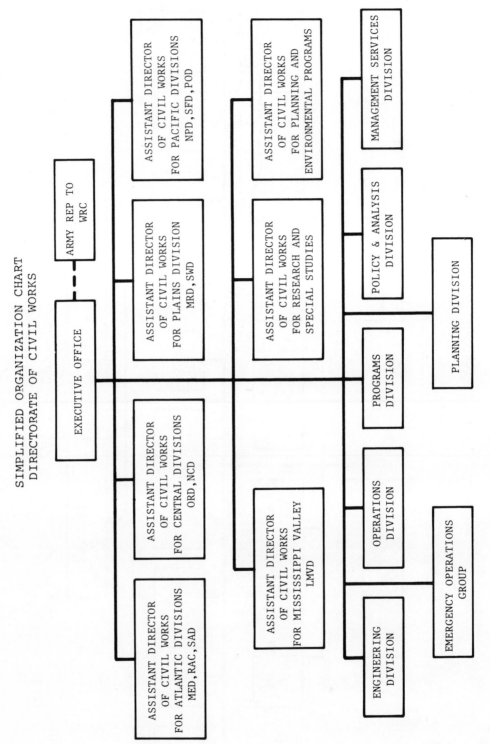

EXHIBIT 6.3

SIMPLIFIED ORGANIZATION CHART
DIRECTORATE OF CIVIL WORKS

Source: U.S. Department of the Army, Digest of Water Resources Policies and Activities,
EP 1165-2-1, December 1972.

3.   Assigning missions to the districts, coordinating, executing, developing cooperative interests, and representing the division as a whole.

The 36 U.S. Army Engineer Districts are the principal state and local planning and project implementation offices of the Corps. District Engineers are responsible for:

1.   Preparing and submitting water resource needs and development studies in response to specific congressional resolutions;

2.   Preparing engineering studies and developing the design for facilities;

3.   Constructing civil works facilities;

4.   Operating and maintaining major water resource projects and river and harbor projects;

5.   Administering the laws for the protection and preservation of the navigable waters of the United States;

6.   Acquiring, managing, and disposing of real estate.

The field offices include research, development, and investigation activities as well.

In addition to the major institutional components of the Corps' civil works program, there exist several specialized elements of the organization which conduct numerous, specific activities. The U.S. Army Engineer Waterways Experiment Station (WES) conducts engineering research, development and investigations in the fields of hydraulics, pavements, soils (except seasonal frost and permafrost), concrete (except rigid pavements), and dredging spoils.

Through its research and development activities in the field of coastal engineering, the U.S. Army Coastal Engineering Research Center (CERC) develops plans on coastal winds, waves, tides, and currents and materials as they apply to navigation, recreation, flood and storm protection, shore and beach erosion, shore structures and offshore islands and structures. CERC also conducts research on the effects of Corps of Engineers activities on the ecology of the coastal zone.

The U.S. Army Construction Engineering Research Laboratory (CERL) develops methods of advancing the concepts and technology of the design, construction, operation, and maintenance of all types of Federal structures and facilities through research, investigation and analytical studies.

The U.S. Army Engineer Institute of Water Resources (IWR) develops and coordinates planning guidance for water resource developments which involve new institutional, physical or socioeconomic concepts in meeting long-range or regional objectives. The IWR develops, coordinates, and performs studies and research in the general fields of water resources and related socioeconomics. The IWR also provides consultive and problem solving services in water resource development planning to the Corps' field offices and other government agencies.

Additionally, since its establishment in 1902 by Congress, the Board of Engineers for Rivers and Harbors (BERH) has played an important part in the overall Corps role in water resource management. This board conducts independent reviews of planning documents and special reports as requested by Acts of Congress or resolutions of congressional committees, or as directed by the Chief of Engineers. These reviews are for the purpose of determining the advisability of authorizing the construction of works for water resource development. The Board also reviews post-authorization reports, small project reports, and Phase I General Design Memoranda.

The Policies, Procedures, and Authorization Process of the Corps' Navigation Program

The pervasive number of marine and port-related responsibilities of the Corps of Engineers is reflected in the structure of the organization's policies, program design, and procedures in the civil works area. There are at least two dimensions to this organizational complexity. The first is the internal complexity of the Corps' civil works administration and its large number of organizational units responsible for specific water or port-related tasks. The second dimension is the external bureaucratic role of the Corps within a large group of federal organizations comprising the marine policy-making system.

The following section is a detailed look at the priorities, policies and programs of the Corps in the civil works and port and harbor development area. The extent to which Corps responsibilities interface with the port-related concerns of other federal organizations is also highlighted. Further, Appendix D sets forth a chronological listing of legislative Acts pertinent to the Corps' role in port planning and development.

Overall Program Objectives: The Setting of Priorities and the Annual Budget Submission

Consistent with the functional legislative responsibilities delegated to the civil works program,* the Corps' Chief of Engineers formulates a Civil Works Investment Program to meet regional needs on a priority basis through the programming of new public works surveys and projects. Long-range civil works program objectives are developed by the Division Engineers. In turn, the Division Engineers formulate estimates of their respective regions' needs which the overall Corps program can fulfill. These estimates are then referred to as the Corps' program objectives.

---

*These responsibilities are outlined in the previous section.

In arriving at these objectives, time estimates are projected for periods of 10, 15, and 20 years forward. From these
projections, five-year investment programs for new project starts
are developed. The five-year investment programs serve as the
principal basis for selecting and recommending new pre-construction planning and construction starts for the President's budget.

The criteria for selection of fiscal year 1974 new starts:[5]

...began with development of a list of projects in the
fiscal years 1974-78 investment program that would be
ready to proceed to the construction stage in fiscal
year 1974. These projects had to have the required
non-Federal local cooperation assured and had to have
sufficient funds appropriated through fiscal year 1973
to complete pre-construction planning. In addition, to
be considered ready for construction, the final environmental impact statement had to be on file with the Council on Environmental Quality or scheduled for filing
with CEQ by March 1973. In the selection of these projects...priority was generally given to projects in
those regions which, after four years of new start decisions by the Congress and the President (fiscal years
1970-73), were furthest away from fulfilling their
fiscal years' 1970-74 investment allocation....

In order that projects will be available to meet the
needs of each region, priority was generally given to
new planning starts in those regions which now have a
backlog of planned projects. In the final selection,
emphasis was given to projects which would satisfy the
needs for existing urban flood control, municipal and
industrial water supply and harbors for commercial
navigation.... [Underlining supplied by authors]

Finally, we compared needs between regions...to select
new starts that were judged most relevant for the
Nation as a whole.

Once program-level objectives and specific project priorities are established, the Corps submits its annual budget recommendation through the Secretary of the Army for review by the
Office of Management and Budget. OMB may place a specific ceil-
ing on the overall Civil Works budget recommendation (it has frequently done so). When a cut is ordered from the overall request,
it is the Corps which decides through its priority system which
projects will be cut.[6] The amended budget is then defended by
the Corps before the House and Senate Appropriations Committees.

Once funding for a specific program or project has been
authorized, the Corps can transfer funds among projects in the
construction category of up to 15 percent of the amount available
for obligation to a project for any fiscal year. The exceptions
permit the transfer of up to 25 percent for projects on which the
amount available for the year is ₄500,000 or less.[7] For trans-

fers above these amounts, approval must be obtained from the
Appropriation Committees. It is the Corps' policy to transfer
funds only to those surveys or projects which have previously
received approved allocation through the budgeting process.[8]

Corps Civil Works Program Procedures: Evaluating
Navigation Projects

The Corps has established specific organizational procedures
for the formulation and evaluation of feasibility and authorization studies for navigation projects. The Chief of Engineers
makes the determination as to whether a waterbody is a "navigable
water of the United States." This term is used to distinguish
those waters over which certain federal powers may be exercised.

The Corps has set forth the following definition of navigable
water of the United States:[9]

...water bodies which are presently, or have been in
the past, or may be in the future, susceptible for use
for purposes of interstate or foreign commerce.

The geographic and jurisdictional limit of rivers for federal regulatory jurisdiction extends laterally to the entire
water surface and bed of a navigable water body, which includes
all the land and water below the ordinary high watermark. For
ocean and tidal waters, the Federal Water Pollution Act of 1972
extended the definition of navigable waters beyond the three-
nautical-mile limit to include the territorial seas.[10]

According to the stated policy of the Corps, an important
procedure in the formulation and evaluation of Corps studies is
that alternate means of satisfying the needs of each project must
be considered. The policy states that a program, project, or segment of a project should not be undertaken if it would preclude
development of any other means of accomplishing the same results
at a lower net resource investment.[11] This limitation would
apply to alternative possibilities which would be displaced or
precluded from development if the project is undertaken. Part
of the measurements of the project's costs are the adverse impacts
or effects. These associated costs are deducted from the benefit
estimates.

However, the apparent loss of traffic by existing carriers
from diversion of traffic to a waterway is not applied as a reduction of benefit. The Chief of Engineers[12]

...considers that there is an overall economic gain to
the nation when transportation is made available to the
public at lower cost and that, as has happened in most
such cases, benefits to overland carriers from feeder
and transfer traffic developing as a result of the
waterway will in the long run offset losses by overland carriers of shipments suited to water movement.

Monetary cost estimates involve determining the costs necessary to establish and operate the project, interest charges, amortization of investments during the specified period, salvage value, and similar factors. This estimated economic cost is expressed in equivalent average annual terms to permit direct comparison with estimated benefits similarly expressed. An estimate is made of the life of the project. It is Corps policy to assume a useful life of 50 years for such port improvements.[13]

After the monetary cost estimates are computed, then the benefits of the project are measured. This is done by first determining the physical output of the projects. The objective of such measurement is to determine increases, net of associated or indirect cost, in the value of goods and services which result from conditions with the project as compared with conditions without the project. The value of the outputs is either the market value (demand price) or, in the absence thereof, the expected costs of production by the most likely alternative source that would be utilized in the absence of the project. In this national income evaluation, normally no monetary values are placed on the extended benefits of a project--such as stimulation of business activity.

The ratio of benefit to cost is then used as an indicator of the project's efficiency. Tangible benefits, as they are expected to occur, then are brought back to present worth by a given interest rate (which is currently specified by the Water Resources Council)* and then amortized to obtain average annual benefits. The ratio derived from dividing the average annual benefits by average annual costs is referred to as the "benefitcost" ratio. Projects are seldom authorized unless the benefitcost ratio exceeds one.

It is the policy of the Corps to coordinate programs among local, state and federal agencies. Several laws such as the National Environmental Protection Act, formal and informal agreements with other agencies, as well as a Coordination Directory for Federal Agencies issued by the Water Resources Council have become a part of the integrated planning and development process. These coordination efforts take the form of written communications as well as public meetings. In the selection of the recommended plan it is the policy of the Corps to have the selection directed toward achieving the best possible use of the resources employed, taking all pertinent factors, tangible and intangible, into account.[14]

Cost allocation must be made among purposes served by the project on multi-purpose construction where reimbursable functions such as recreation are involved. At the present time, there is no uniform cost allocation method established by law. The practice appears to be that the agency responsible for planning, constructing, operating, and maintaining the project is responsible for cost allocation. Some headway has been made in this area in that in 1954 the Departments of the Army and the

---

*See discussions on the discount rate included in Chapters 3 and 4.

Interior, and the Federal Power Commission entered into an interagency agreement recognizing three methods of allocation as
acceptable: "Separable Cost--Remaining Benefits," the "Alternative
Justifiable Expenditure," and the "Use of Facilities" methods.
The Corps considers the "Separable Costs--Remaining Benefits"
method as preferable for general application. The principle is
that all project costs are distributed among the purposes on the
basis of the alternative costs that could justifiably be incurred
to achieve equivalent benefits by alternative means.[15]

The cost allocated to specific project purposes is shared
generally in accordance with pertinent congressional laws, the
specific requirements of Acts authorizing the projects in some
cases, and the administrative instructions of the Office of Management and Budget, the Water Resources Council, and the Secretary
of the Army. Assessments made by the latter federal organizations are based on their interpretation of general law or discretionary authority (where the rules for cost-sharing in particular
cases are not specified by law).[16]

Completed Corps reports follow procedures for processing
and review. After the report is completed by the District Engineer, the Division reviews it to insure compliance with required
regulations, principles and procedures to include public notice
of the conclusions and recommendations. Upon completion by the
Division Engineer, the report is then reviewed by the Board of
Engineers for Rivers and Harbors. Review is concurrently undertaken by the Civil Works Directorate of the Office of the Chief
of Engineers to insure its overall conformity to engineering,
economic principles and established policies.

The proposed report of the Chief of Engineers, together with
the reports of the District, Division Engineer, and the Board of
Engineers for Rivers and Harbors are submitted to the governors of
affected states and to federal agencies having an interest
in the investigation for their formal review and comment. Federal agencies are given 90 days to address their comments.[17]
The report with comments, along with a copy of the Secretary of
the Army's proposed letter of transmittal to Congress, is submitted to OMB for determination of the relationship to the program of the President. The report is then transmitted to Congress as final compliance with the authorizing act or resolution.

The completed reports are normally accumulated and are considered by the Committee on Public Works for inclusion in an
omnibus authorization bill, usually at two-year intervals. However, projects of less than $10 million cost may be approved by
resolution of the Committee.[18]

The Planning Permit, Authorization, and Construction Process of Civil Works Projects

The process by which civil works projects are conceived,
authorized, and constructed by Congress through Corps of Engineers review is complicated. In recent years, the permit and
authorization process for these projects has been marked by

steadily increasing costs in terms of time, energy, and conflict between congressional committees, environmental groups, local interests, and the Corps.[19]

The Corps is responsible for the construction of all structures and all work including dredging in the navigable waters of the United States--except for the building of bridges and causeways, and the placement of aids to navigation by the U.S. Coast Guard. The decision whether to issue a permit is based on the public interest and its intended use under authorities primarily derived from Sections 9, 10, 11 and 14 of the River and Harbor Act of 1899.[20] The public interest in a proposal is determined by its consistency with state plans and interests; by its effect on navigation, fish and wildlife, water quality, economics, conservation, aesthetics, recreation, water supply, flood damage prevention; impact on ecosystems; and, in general, the needs and welfare of the people.[21] In determining the public interest, the District Engineer will seek comments, suggestions or objections on the proposed work by public notices. Usually, then, a period of 30 days is allotted for public comment. Public hearings may also be held if appropriate.

Section 103 of P.L. 92-532, the Marine Protection, Research and Sanctuaries Act of 1972, provides the Corps with permit authority over the transportation of dredged material for the purpose of dumping in ocean waters. The Corps may issue permits when it is assured that such dredged spoil disposal will not unreasonably degrade or endanger human health, welfare or amenities, or the marine environment, ecological systems, or economic potentialities. In reaching its determination, the Corps applies criteria established by the EPA to define whether dredged spoils are polluted.*

Furthermore, the Marine Protection and Sanctuaries Act requires that permits set out at a minimum the amount, type, and location of the material to be dumped, and the length of time for the dumping and, after consultation with the Coast Guard, provide for any special monitoring or surveillance provisions.

Exhibit 6.4 details the work permit procedure of the Corps relative to navigable waters projects. Note that this procedure is required to authorize any work planned in the navigable waters of the United States where federal appropriations for dredging or other construction are not included.

Exhibit 6.5 describes the overall mechanism by which water projects are planned, appropriations for dredging and other construction are requested and authorized by Congress, and funding is secured for engineering and construction phases. Note that in several "time frames" (indicated by each independent box), federal environmental review procedures and regulations could substantially influence the course of the proposed project. Opposition from local environmental constituency groups might

---

*See Chapter 5.

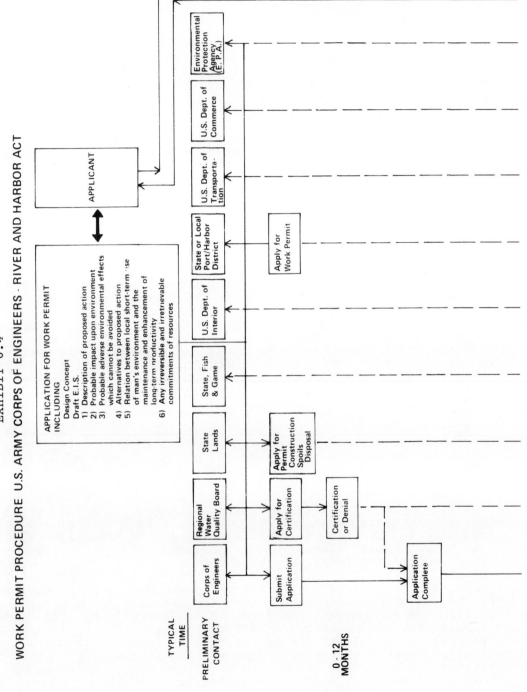

EXHIBIT 6.4

WORK PERMIT PROCEDURE U.S. ARMY CORPS OF ENGINEERS - RIVER AND HARBOR ACT

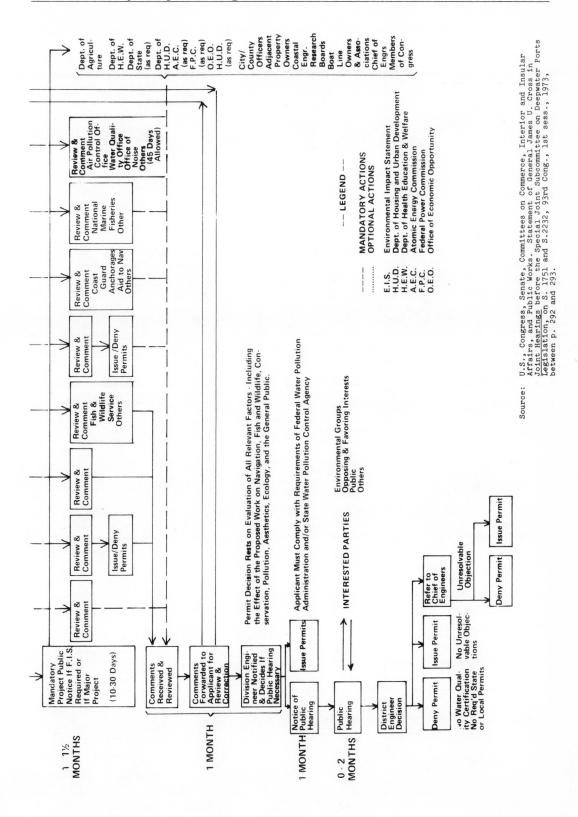

Source: U.S., Congress, Senate, Committees on Commerce, Interior and Insular Affairs, and Public Works. Statement of General James U. Cross in Joint Hearings before the Special Joint Subcommittee on Deepwater Ports Legislation, on S. 1751 and S.2232, 93rd Cong., 1st sess., 1973, between p. 292 and 293.

EXHIBIT 6.5

**THE MECHANISM BY WHICH PROJECTS ARE
CONCEIVED AUTHORIZED AND CONSTRUCTED**

* The Mississippi River Commission Functions in Lieu of the Board on Projects in the Alluvial Valley

Source: U.S. Department of the Army, Corps of Engineers

EXHIBIT 6.5--continued

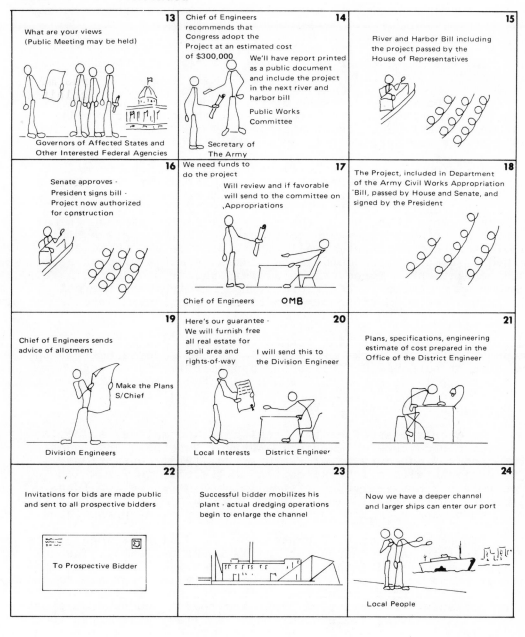

13 What are your views (Public Meeting may be held)

Governors of Affected States and Other Interested Federal Agencies

14 Chief of Engineers recommends that Congress adopt the Project at an estimated cost of $300,000

We'll have report printed as a public document and include the project in the next river and harbor bill

Public Works Committee

Secretary of The Army

15 River and Harbor Bill including the project passed by the House of Representatives

16 Senate approves - President signs bill - Project now authorized for construction

17 We need funds to do the project

Will review and if favorable will send to the committee on Appropriations

Chief of Engineers   OMB

18 The Project, included in Department of the Army Civil Works Appropriation Bill, passed by House and Senate, and signed by the President

19 Chief of Engineers sends advice of allotment

Make the Plans S/Chief

Division Engineers

20 Here's our guarantee - We will furnish free all real estate for spoil area and rights-of-way

I will send this to the Division Engineer

Local Interests   District Engineer

21 Plans, specifications, engineering estimate of cost prepared in the Office of the District Engineer

22 Invitations for bids are made public and sent to all prospective bidders

To Prospective Bidder

23 Successful bidder mobilizes his plant - actual dredging operations begin to enlarge the channel

24 Now we have a deeper channel and larger ships can enter our port

Local People

effectively delay, or halt, proposed projects. Specific criteria
and standards applying to dredged spoil disposal methods or air
and water quality would most likely entail higher project costs and time delays. Moreover, in some states projects
would need to comply with stricter state environmental standards
and regulations--further confounding the permit authorization
process.*

     As a consequence of many of these potential institutional
obstructions, the time involved in each phase of the permit
authorization process is substantial. Testifying in June of
1971 before the Subcommittee on Investigations and Oversight
of the House Public Works Committee, Major General Frank Koisch
estimated that it would take 17 years and 11 months from the
initial authorization of a study to completion of construction
in a civil works project.[22] Exhibit 6.6 shows the breakdown of
time required for each phase of the overall project approval
process. Note that, while environmental review procedures may
lengthen approval times and raise project costs, this exhibit
indicates that substantial allotments of time are being con-
sumed by complex bureaucratic and administrative procedures
and regulations. Moreover, as administrative procedures have
become more complex, the informational requirements for policy
decisions based on these organizational functions have enlarged as
well. This in turn has added its own time dimension.

     With such substantial segments of time required to gain
approval of civil works projects, it is not surprising that the
backlog of authorized civil works projects is increasing.
Exhibit 6.7 illustrates this trend as a function of the number
of projects, project cost, and fiscal year authorized. Exhibit
6.8 organizes the data in table form.

     The Corps classifies the backlog of uncompleted authorized
projects into three categories: Active, Deferred, and Inactive.
The "Active" category as of February 28, 1973, consisted of
386 projects with a federal cost of $11.4 billion for which
Congress has not yet appropriated initial construction funds.
Included in the total backlog were seven projects costing $439
million on which only acquisition funds had been appropriated.[23]

     Congress has not been unaware of the rising national costs
of authorizing and constructing civil works projects. The policy
dilemma, as phrased in congressional directives and outside administrative analyses, is the striking of an appropriate balance
between public works development, environmental legislation, and
the increasing complexity of state and federal bureaucratic procedures. Moreover, it is clear that legislative attempts to
facilitate faster project authorization procedures must be cognizant of the changed policy-making system and bureaucratic environment. As summarized in a 1972 report prepared for the National Water Commission, Authorization and Appropriation Processes
for Water Resource Development:[24]

---

*See Chapter 5.

EXHIBIT 6.6

CORPS OF ENGINEERS ANALYSIS OF AVERAGE TIME FOR PLANNING AND CONSTRUCTION OF CIVIL WORKS PROJECTS (MAY, 1971 STATUS)

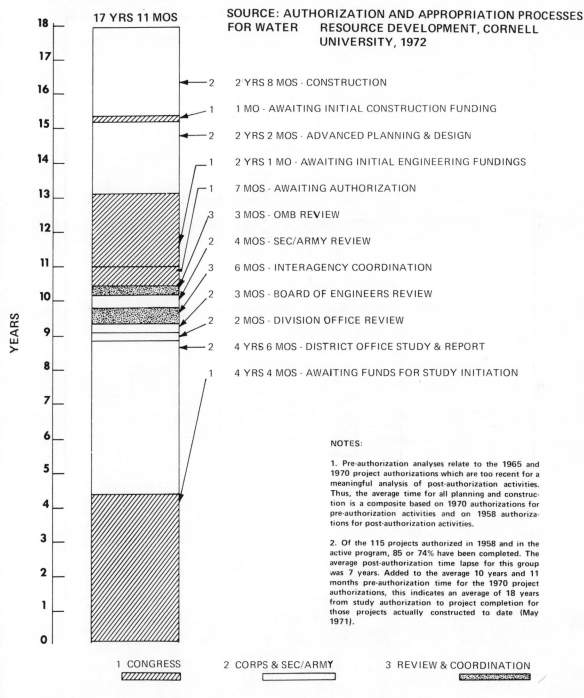

SOURCE: AUTHORIZATION AND APPROPRIATION PROCESSES FOR WATER   RESOURCE DEVELOPMENT, CORNELL UNIVERSITY, 1972

17 YRS 11 MOS

YEARS

2 2 YRS 8 MOS - CONSTRUCTION

1 1 MO - AWAITING INITIAL CONSTRUCTION FUNDING

2 2 YRS 2 MOS - ADVANCED PLANNING & DESIGN

1 2 YRS 1 MO - AWAITING INITIAL ENGINEERING FUNDINGS

1 7 MOS - AWAITING AUTHORIZATION

3 3 MOS - OMB REVIEW

2 4 MOS - SEC/ARMY REVIEW

3 6 MOS - INTERAGENCY COORDINATION

2 3 MOS - BOARD OF ENGINEERS REVIEW

2 2 MOS - DIVISION OFFICE REVIEW

2 4 YRS 6 MOS - DISTRICT OFFICE STUDY & REPORT

1 4 YRS 4 MOS - AWAITING FUNDS FOR STUDY INITIATION

NOTES:

1. Pre-authorization analyses relate to the 1965 and 1970 project authorizations which are too recent for a meaningful analysis of post-authorization activities. Thus, the average time for all planning and construction is a composite based on 1970 authorizations for pre-authorization activities and on 1958 authorizations for post-authorization activities.

2. Of the 115 projects authorized in 1958 and in the active program, 85 or 74% have been completed. The average post-authorization time lapse for this group was 7 years. Added to the average 10 years and 11 months pre-authorization time for the 1970 project authorizations, this indicates an average of 18 years from study authorization to project completion for those projects actually constructed to date (May 1971).

1 CONGRESS   2 CORPS & SEC/ARMY   3 REVIEW & COORDINATION

EXHIBIT 6.7

TREND IN BACKLOG OF AUTHORIZED CIVIL WORKS PROJECTS
(PROJECTS UNFUNDED FOR CONSTRUCTION*)

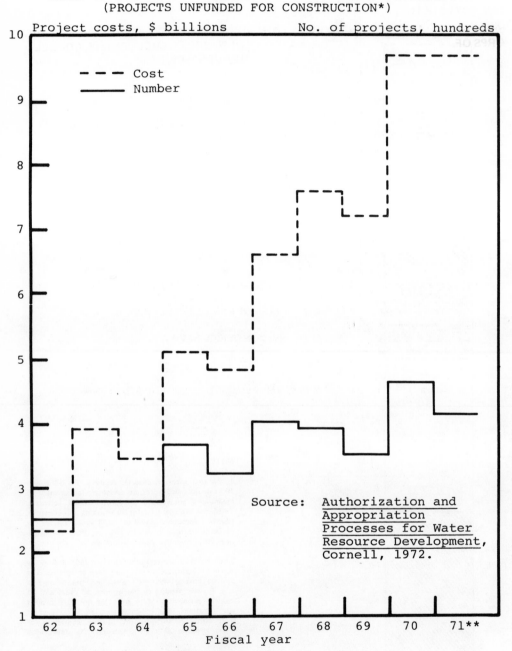

*Excludes Mississippi River and tributaries projects
 (i.e. alluvial valley of the Mississippi)
**Excludes Dec. 1970 Authorizations which will be reflected
 in FY 1972 figures.

Exhibit 6.8

Corps of Engineers

Trend in Backlog of Authorized Civil Works Projects

Fiscal Year	No. of Active Projects Unfunded for Construction,* #	Cost in Millions
1971	408	$9,670
1970	452	9,675
1969	361	7,198
1968	388	7,614
1967	399	6,519
1966	312	4,854
1965	377	5,198
1964	273	3,468
1963	279	3,941
1962	245	2,332

*Excludes Mississippi River and Tributaries projects
(i.e., alluvial valley of the Mississippi).

#The projects authorized in various omnibus acts are reflected
in the unfunded project figures for the following FY years.

Source: Authorization and Appropriation Processes for Water
Resource Development, Cornell University, 1972.

Backers of current water projects must be ready to tole-
rate and overcome conflict. The traditional rules of
the game in authorizing and funding projects have operated
to maintain low levels of controversy. These old rules
no longer operate with regularity, and conflict cannot
be avoided.

Further, the report notes that the time span between initiation and final construction, exacerbated by the factors discussed
above, is "likely to become longer than shorter in the future."[25]

The Operation and Maintenance of Completed Civil Works Projects

The responsibility of the Corps for the maintenance and
operation of completed civil works projects is derived from
river and harbor and flood control law and administrative policy.
For fiscal year 1971, operations and maintenance expenses for
U.S. ports in excess of 25 feet were set at $73.8 million.
Eighty-four percent of these funds were spent on dredging activities.[26]

Specific Corps responsibilities in this area are defined as
follows:

1. For most existing navigation improvements, the
    maintenance and operation responsibilities are
    assumed by the federal government.

2. For commercial navigation, the same scenario
    applies.

3. Recreational navigation in many instances is sub-
    ject to federal, state, and local cost-sharing.
    However, to date projects which were originally
    authorized by Congress have been federally main-
    tained.

4. Emergency clearing is provided on a limited basis
    under Section 3 of the 1945 River and Harbor Act,
    but it is local responsibility to maintain work
    done under Section 3.

The capability of each harbor project to serve current
navigation requirements is determined at least once every year.
The District and Division Engineers take necessary action, including requests for required authority and funds, to perform
justified maintenance dredging. Corps criteria specifies that
the actual requirements of existing commerce and the economies
obtainable by advance maintenance dredging operations govern the
extent of the maintenance work undertaken.[27]

For maintenance dredging operations the 10-, 15-, 20-year
program and five-year investment programs designed to meet the
priority objectives of the Water Resource Council are not prepared. Neither is the cost-benefit ratio used again to justify

maintenance projects. On maintenance projects required each
year, a written justification is submitted from the District
Engineer to the Office of the Chief of Engineers where allocations are made for each region.

    The Corps is also responsible for recommending to Congress
the abandonment of projects which no longer serve commercial
traffic.[28]

    In the recreational navigation and maintenance area, govern-
mental interest in cost-sharing approaches has been increasing.
The Office of Management and Budget (OMB)* has pointed out in the
past that Section 107 of the 1960 River and Harbor Act, as amended
(33 U.S.C. 577), contains authority for the Corps to institute
cost-sharing on recreational boat survey reports submitted to
Congress for authorization.[29] Moreover, additional legal authority has been granted in the relevant case of charter fishing
craft. Section 119 of the River and Harbor act of 1970 (P.L.
91-611) specifies that:

    The Chief of Engineers, for the purpose of determining
    Federal and non-Federal cost-sharing relating to
    proposed construction of small-boat navigation proj-
    ects, shall consider charter fishing craft as commer-
    cial vessels.

    Further discussion on cost-sharing policies will be pursued
in Chapters 10 and 11.

    In terms of waterways and harbor channel operations and
maintenance, the River and Harbor Act of 1917 authorizes the
Corps to set forth regulations for the use and administration of
U.S. navigable waters. This general authority allows the Corps
to establish speed limits to prevent damage to federal or public property, or to exercise control in the general public interest over the movement of vessels in a restricted channel.
Similarly, the Coast Guard is also authorized to set speed limits
for the safe operation of vessels in channels and harbors in
accordance with the Ports and Waterways Safety Act of 1972.
The Corps may also establish restricted areas and danger zones
where required for the protection of life or property, or set
aside areas for defense operations.[30] The Corps is also responsible for Aids to Navigation that are temporarily required because of construction operations.[31]

    Additionally, under Section 111 of the River and Harbor Act
of 1968 the Corps has authority to:[32]

    ...investigate, study and construct projects for the
    prevention or mitigation of shore damages attributable
    to Federal navigation works.

Projects under $1 million do not require congressional approval.

---

*See Chapter 4 for a contextual discussion of the cost-sharing
issue.

Navigation Program Assessments, Informational Roles, and
Research and Development Activities

A major role the Corps undertakes in navigation and port
planning and development is that it acts as an engineering consultant to Congress. The Corps may undertake investigations of
port projects under Congressional authorization in the form of
resolutions of the Committee on Public Works from either the
House or Senate, or legislative actions by Congress. Continuing
authorities for small studies permit the Corps to undertake
investigations and construction of projects without being specifically adopted into law.

In terms of actual project construction based on study
results, Section 201 of the 1965 Flood Control Act authorizes
the Corps to issue permits for water resources development projects (permit authorizations are not limited to navigation and
shore protection if funding requests are less than $10 million).
Approval by the Public Works Committee is required prior to
project implementation.

The 1960 River and Harbor Act, Section 107, authorizes the
Corps to construct small harbor improvement projects not specifically authorized by Congress if such projects do not exceed
$500,000. These projects must be complete in themselves and
not commit the federal government to any additional improvement
to ensure successful operation.

The Flood Control Acts of 1937, 1954, and the River and
Harbor Act of 1945 authorize emergency clearing of snags and
unreasonable obstructions to navigation in varying amounts from
$100,000 to $300,000 under continuing statutory authority.
Other legislation allows the Corps to undertake investigations
for modifying completed projects (Section 216 of the 1970 Flood
Control Act), and for the mitigation of shore damage due to
navigation projects (Section 111 of the 1968 River and Harbor Act).

Furthermore, as a result of the River and Harbor Acts of
1960 and 1970, Congress granted continuing statutory authorization for limited improvement projects on rivers and harbors not
to exceed $2 million for one fiscal year with not more than
$200,000 to be allotted for construction of a project at any
single locality.

In addition to the Corps' role as the principal engineering
consultant to Congress, the organization serves as a major con-
duit of information on port and harbor transportation services.
Under the River and Harbor Act of 1918, Congress directed the
Chief of Engineers to submit an annual report to Congress indi-
cating..."the character of the terminal and transfer facilities
existing on every harbor or waterway under maintenance or improvement by the United States, and whether they are considered
adequate for existing commerce." However, no criteria for commercial adequacy was set out in the Act. Also, the report only
requires information on the character of terminal and transfer
facilities, and not of the condition of the channel or jetties
in relation to maintenance requirements or commercial adequacy.

The types of program or project assessments or investigations that the Corps performs vary. Framework Studies and Assessment (Level A) are directed by the Water Resources Council and
are of a regional and national scope.[33] These studies deal with
very broad questions such as "should there be more growth in the
Northwest." Level C, Implementation Studies of the Water Resources
Council, applies to Corps projects. These include the detailed
program or project feasibility studies which Congress has required for authorization. The implementation studies are also
made to determine appropriate Corps action under continuing
authorities. Post-authorization studies (Advanced Engineering
and Design) are also included in Level C studies.

The post-authorization studies consist of Phase I and
Phase II studies. Phase I studies are an extension of the pre-
authorization studies and update the basic plan, making it conform
to physical, environmental, social and economic changes that have
subsequently occurred. Phase II is the functional design memorandum concerned chiefly with the technical design of the structures
necessary to achieve the objectives of Phase I. There are no
Phase I or Phase II studies for projects under Special Continuing
Authorizations.

In performing these assessment studies for Congress, the
Corps is influenced by a number of policies in water resource
management enacted by Congress and the Executive Branch. Two
congressional actions, contained in the 1970 River and Harbor and
Flood Control Act, are important in defining study objectives:[34]

(1) Section 122 directed the Secretary of the Army,
acting through the Chief of Engineers, to promulgate
guidelines for consideration of significant economic,
environmental and social effects of proposed water
resources development, so that project decisions are
made in the best overall public interest. These guidelines were issued by ER 1105-2-105.

(2) Section 209 expressed the intent of Congress that
the objectives of enhancing regional economic development, quality of the total environment, well-being of
people, and national economic development are to be
included in the formulation and evaluation of Federally
financed water resource projects.

Additionally, Section 7(a) of the Department of Transportation Act of 1966 provides that:[35]

The standards and criteria for economic evaluation of
water resource projects shall be developed by the Water
Resources Council established by Public Law 89-80.
For the purposes of such standards and criteria, the
primary direct navigation benefits of a water resource
project are defined as the product of the savings to
shippers using the waterway and the estimated traffic
that would use the waterway; where the savings to shippers shall be construed to mean the differences between

(a) the freight rates or charges prevailing at the
time of the study for the movement by the alternative
means and (b) those which would be charged on the proposed waterway; and where the estimate of traffic that
would use the waterway will be based on such freight
rates, taking into account projections of the economic
growth of the area.

However, this section of the DOT Act creates a certain bias
toward navigation projects. In actuality, the appearance of
water carrier competition normally causes railroads (a competing
mode) to lower their rates--producing what is known as "water-
impelled" rates. By using the prevailing railroad rates before
project construction in the economic evaluation, Section 7(a)
results in biasing the evaluation in favor of the water carriers.

Furthermore, the National Environmental Policy Act of 1969
requires the Corps to consider environmental impacts.* However,
Corps policy to date has been that only programs and projects that
demonstrate economic feasibility will be recommended unless
there are overriding social impacts warranting a departure from
economic decisions.[36]

A review of current Corps feasibility studies indicates
that the Corps has considered the objectives of enhancing regional economic development and social effects as required by the
1970 River and Harbor and Flood Control Act.[37] In compliance
with the law, no dollar amounts are computed for these factors.

The Corps is also involved in the collection of specific
waterborne commerce information. Authorized under the 1942
Federal Reports Act, the 1950 Accounting Procedures Act, and an
1891 statute (26 Stat. 766, 46 U.S.C. 48), the Corps collects and
compiles data on domestic waterborne commerce pursuant to its
navigation policy responsibilities.

In addition to civil works program and project assessments
and studies, the Corps' functional research, development and
investigation bodies, such as the Institute for Water Resources
and the Waterways Experiment Station, have actively engaged in
strategic policy studies covering several maritime topics.

In 1970, the Institute for Water Resources (IWR) contracted
with the consulting firm of Arthur D. Little, Inc. for a study
entitled "Foreign Deep Water Port Developments." The purpose of
the study was:[38]

...to analyze selected foreign harbors (and off-shore
loading and unloading facilities) where the experience
was judged to be relevant to the U.S. situation. Specifically, the study seeks to explain (for the nations
studied) how the decision to deepen or enlarge ports
was arrived at; the approaches considered and the
actual adjustments made to accommodate deep-draft ships,

*See later discussion in this chapter as well as in Chapter 5.

including the difficulties met and solved in construction and operation; and the character of future plans.
Assessment of the social disruptions and environmental
impact of port development was an additional important
objective of the investigations.

Additionally, the IWR later contracted with Robert R. Nathan
Associates to conduct a related deepwater port study which was
published in five volumes in August of 1972. The purpose of the
second study was:[39]

> ...to provide an overall appraisal of the U.S. deep-
> water port needs. It is not intended that the study
> concentrate on the specific needs of any port area
> but rather on the basic element of an overall plan and
> upon (1) identification (and whenever possible quanti-
> fication) of the factors critical to the U.S. deep-
> water port decisions; (2) development of the criteria
> (engineering, economic, and environmental) appropriate
> to the evaluation of deepwater port needs policies;
> (3) analyses of the development options available at
> this time and the critical issues surrounding each;
> and (4) identification of the critical issues which
> need further analysis.

Other studies pertaining to port planning developed by
the Institute for Water Resources include:

1. IWR Report 72-7, Planning for Coastal Ports on a
    Systems Basis: Preliminary Methodological Design,
    May 72. This report develops the preliminary speci-
    fications for an integrated system of models which
    would permit the planning of multiple ports on a
    systems basis.

2. IWR Report 73-4, Institutional Implications of
    U.S. Deepwater Port Development for Crude Oil
    Imports, June 73. This report provides an over-
    all appraisal of the institutional problems asso-
    ciated with the planning, construction, and opera-
    tion of deep-draft port facilities in the United
    States and adjacent waters for the reception and
    transshipment of imported crude petroleum.

3. IWR Report 70-5, Environmental Guidelines for
    the Civil Works Program of the Corps of Engineers,
    Nov. 70. This report presents the Chief of Engi-
    neers' policy on environmental aspects of the Corps
    of Engineers' mission in Civil Works.

Additionally, the IWR, the Corps' Office of Systems Analysis
and Information, and the North Central Division of the Corps of
Engineers participated in a jointly-sponsored survey with the
U.S. Department of Transportation and the U.S. Department of
Commerce on the Domestic and International Transportation of
U.S. Foreign Trade for 1970.

The primary purpose of the jointly-conducted survey was:[40]

...to obtain new data on the domestic leg of U.S.
foreign trade and to link those new facts with already
available information on the international segment of
"liner-type" commodity flows...the coupling of the
domestic and the international legs of each. Shipment in the survey creates a new set of data for use
in the systematic analysis of commodity flows between
the interior of the United States and foreign countries.

The Corps had been involved in a similar joint study in
1956 on a smaller scale.[41]

The Corps has also been active in the evaluation of the San
Francisco Bay area. In October 1967, the Corps received authori-
zation by the House Committee on Public Works to conduct a San
Francisco Bay Area In-Depth Study, the purpose of which was the[42]

...investigation of current shipping problems, adequacy
of facilities, delays in intermodal transfers, channel
dimensions, storage locations, and capacities, and other
physical aspects...

affecting the San Francisco Bay area. However, the extent of this
analysis has been limited by a lack of funds.

In July of 1973, at an estimated cost of $1.28 million, the
Corps completed detailed studies of the environmental, engineering, economic and sociological aspects of deepwater port development on the Atlantic, Gulf and West Coasts of the United
States.[43] The authorization for each of these studies was by
separate resolution by one of the Committees of Public Works
in the Senate or the House pursuant to Section 2 of the River
and Harbors Act of 1902.

An example of the congressional mandate given the Corps
was the Senate's Committee on Public Works resolution of 27 October 1971 which requested review of the commercial navigation
channels and harbors along the Atlantic Coast:

...with a view to determining the most efficient, economic and logical means of developing facilities to accommodate very large bulk cargo carriers including, but not
limited to, offshore facilities. In carrying out this
study, consideration shall be given to a governing organization and financing methods to construct, operate and
maintain such regional facilities serving more than one
of these areas as may be found desirable, to ensure equitable benefits to such areas. Further, in carrying out
this study, the Corps of Engineers shall cooperate with
and coordinate its efforts with all affected Federal
departments, agencies, and instrumentalities, including
the President's Council on Environmental Quality, the
Environmental Protection Agency, and all other interested parties, public and private, and, in addition,

shall ensure that any project proposals include appropriate measures for the protection and/or enhancement
of the environment.

Another major research study which the Corps has been
charged with is the five-year Dredged Material Study Program
which was authorized by Congress under Section 123(i) of Public
Law 91-611. This $30 million program is being administered by
the U.S. Army Engineer Waterways Experiment Station in Vicksburg,
Mississippi. The purpose of this study is to carry out a comprehensive program of research, study and experimentation related
to dredging and the disposal of dredged material.

The Corps has also been directed by Congress to perform a
$600,000 National Dredging Study. This study is being conducted
by Arthur D. Little, Inc., and will review in depth the dredging
policies and practices of the Corps and how the agency can accomplish its dredging requirements in the most efficient, economical
and timely manner.

Port Policy and the Corps: An Analysis of Its Changing Role and Some Recent Policy Imperatives

The combined effects of a changing maritime technological
base and a growing national environmental awareness have placed
paradoxical pressures on the traditional implementation of Corps
policies and programs. On one hand, the use of larger ships,
combined with technological changes in port terminal capacities
and hinterland effects, have facilitated greater pressures on
Corps operations in dredging and navigation areas. However,
new environmental legislation and supportive political constituencies have worked to restrict, or in some cases to halt, the
industrial development pattern which might normally be assumed
to have progressed in the absence of ecological controls. The
institutional problem for the Corps is its implementation of
agency policies and programs within the constraints afforded by
these conflicting forces.

The following cases exhibit several quandaries in the strategy of Corps program implementation. Sections on containerization,
and superport development focus on the changes in maritime technology, while a discussion on environmental issues outlines the
effects of new ecological controls. Furthermore, a final section on cost-benefit analysis and discount rates emphasizes the
importance of economic criteria and standards on port planning
and development.

Technological Imperatives: Containerization and Superports

Containerization has placed added pressure on the traditional
navigation and dredging operations of the Corps of Engineers.
New laws regarding dredging spoils have increased costs (making
it a budgetary problem) as well as made program implementation

subject to greater institutional opposition.* While the Corps
has dredged most containerport channels to depths of approximately 35 or 40 feet, some modern containerships would prefer
to use channels of 45-foot depth. Consequently, if the next
decade sees a general increase in the size of containerhips,
there may be a nationwide containerport cry for dredging to
45 feet (Los Angeles has already made such a request).

The budget limitations of the Corps of Engineers would prohibit dredging all containerport channels to 45 feet. However,
if the cry for deeper-dredged harbors continues to materialize,
the Corps will have to decide on a priority basis which channel
or harbor will be dredged first. In this way, the Corps would
actually be placing some ports in favorable positions relative
to others and, in consequence, would then be setting national
port policy by its actions--even if it did not wish to do so.

To add to the budgetary problems of the Corps, U.S. Representatives from Texas have recommended the dredging of channels
into bay systems for the construction of "superharbors." Such
a channel from the end of the Galveston jetties south to the Gulf
would be 92 feet deep, 1,000 feet wide, and 45 miles long.[44]
According to testimony presented by Texas Representative Brooks
before joint Senate committee hearings on July 25, 1973, a
dredging project of this magnitude would require removal of 340
million cubic yards of dredge spoils.[45] (More recently, revised
plans proposed a dredged channel 67 feet deep.)

Additionally, the Port of Corpus Christi would also like to
undertake a major dredging project 9.6 nautical miles long
and 72 feet deep (requiring a dredge spoil removal of 62 million
cubic yards).[46]

These huge dredging projects, however, stand in contrast to
the majority of plans to establish deepwater port terminals--**
most proposed facilities for handling supertankers are offshore
terminals (principally mono-buoy systems) which probably will
be constructed without federal aid. It is not therefore obvious,
even if the dredging plans advanced by the two Texas Congressmen were approved, that the Corps would pay the entire dredging
cost of such a project.

However, even in the more likely event that offshore mono-
buoy terminals will be constructed without federal funds, deepwater ports will cause indirect problems for the Corps. A large
number of channels and harbors are presently being maintained
at relatively constant depths by the Corps--these justified by
savings accruing to tankers using the ports. Once a deepwater
terminal capable of serving an entire region is built, the Corps
must decide whether it need maintain the depth of channels at
nearby onshore terminals for the use of smaller tankers. Since
maintenance dredging is performed by the Corps without charge
to the ports, it is likely that ports will continue to request
such dredging even after the construction of deepwater ports.

_____

*See discussion in Chapter 5.

**See Chapter 9.

The Impact of Technology on Corps Planning

New maritime technology has also made port economic analysis performed by the Corps more complicated. Advances in both the technology and practice of intermodal transportation services have created port facilities with regional rather than local hinterlands. The ability of the Corps to adequately revolve these changing hinterland potentials will in part depend on the extent to which they perform regional planning* studies rather than traditional analyses of individual port projects. Furthermore, such regional studies are already called for by the stated policy of the Corps as well as other federal criteria and regulations.

Pursuant to the National Environmental Policy Act of 1969 (NEPA),[47] the Council on Environmental Quality published in the Federal Register guidelines for the preparation of environmental impact statements applicable to all federal departments and agencies.[48] Under Section 1500.2 of these guidelines, federal agencies are charged with the following responsibilities:[49]

> In particular, agencies should use the environmental impact statement process to explore alternative actions that will avoid or minimize adverse impacts and to evaluate both the long- and short-range implications of proposed actions to man, his physical and social surroundings, and to nature. Agencies should consider the results of their environmental assessments along with their assessments of the net economic, technical and other benefits of proposed actions and use all practicable means, consistent with other essential considerations of national policy, to restore environmental quality as well as to avoid or minimize undesirable consequences for the environment...
>
> A rigorous exploration and objective evaluation of the environmental impacts of all reasonable alternative actions, particularly those that might enhance environmental effects, is essential.

Furthermore, the Corps of Engineers Digest of Water Resources Policies and Activities states that:[50]

> A program, project, or segment of a project should not be undertaken if it would preclude development of any other means of accomplishing the same results at a lower net resource investment. This limitation applies to alternative possibilities which would be displaced or precluded from development if the project is undertaken.
>
> Other means of obtaining similar benefits which would not be precluded from development are not limitations on project justification but are, in effect, additional projects

---

*Sometimes the phrase "load-center concept planning" is used instead of "regional planning." The meanings here are the same.

which may be compared in an array of alternatives to
determine which should be given prior consideration from
the standpoint of resource efficiency. The general environmental impact of alternatives must also be described
and evaluated to the fullest extent. Alternatives must
be identified as to their beneficial and detrimental effects
on existing economic, social and environmental conditions
specifically accounting for the alternative of no action.
This last alternative requires a projection of future conditions if the project is not undertaken.

The salient point to these legislative charges is the requirement for the consideration of alternatives with the goal of mini-
mizing net resource investment. Such a charge comprises a
strong policy statement towards the consideration of all alternatives in the authorization process for civil works projects.
However, in practice the Corps has narrowly interpreted the consideration of alternatives to essentially include only variations
within a port or harbor area, rather than looking at the needs of
a multi-port region.

A Corps of Engineers official recently summarized the status
of federal activity related to regional port studies as follows:[51]

In 1968 the Marine Science Council, that was the predecessor of the present Interagency Committee on Marine
Science and Engineering, established a "Committee on
Multiple Use of the Coastal Zone." It was made up of
representatives from 19 agencies, including some of the
top people in resources management and covered all the
principal agencies concerned with ports and harbors. The
Committee requested the Corps of Engineers, in cooperation with the Department of Transportation and the Maritime Administration, to develop a conceptual approach and
procedure by which proposed regional harbor and port development studies could be coordinated, managed, and conducted.

An ad hoc task force consisting of the three agencies
named above undertook and completed the requested plan in
April 1968 and submitted it for committee consideration.
At the same time, the Corps of Engineers and the Department of Transportation submitted draft legislation "to
authorize a nationwide study of deep-draft ports and the
preparation of harbor plans." No action was taken by
Congress due principally to heavy opposition by local interests of ports and harbors and the industry.

It was envisioned that the studies, if authorized, would
focus on transportation requirements including the "super-
ship" problem, and that the relationship between transportation, urban renewal, and estuarine resource development
would be identified. Such a concentrated effort at the
ports would involve local governments, regional planning
groups, private interests, and the several Federal agencies.
An effective program would embrace a range of activities,

from the possible creation of entirely new port or waterfront complexes to rehabilitation and conversion of existing waterfront land and facilities.

After the initial rebuff from local port interests, the ad
hoc task force restricted the transportation study proposal and,
on recommendation from the Marine Council's Committee on Multiple
Use of the Coastal Zone, proposed the following three alternate
study phases:[52]

(a) the report "Conceptual Plan for Harbor and Port Development Studies" prepared by the Committee on Multiple Use
of the Coastal Zone will serve as a planning guide for Federal
agency programs concerning harbor and port development;

(b) the Committee encourages the necessary consultations
with private interests which will facilitate Congresssional
support for draft legislation to authorize such studies;
and

(c) the Committee report to the Council by June 1, 1969,
on steps that have been taken to advance the study proposal.

Continued heavy opposition from local port interests, however, again terminated the proposed study.[53]

Consequently, in both cases local port interests were successful at blocking attempts at regional port planning--even
though such planning appears to be required by law. Moreover,
Corps of Engineers project analyses seem to exhibit similar
patterns.

A recent report issued by the Corps, "Interim Review Report
on Los Angeles-Long Beach Harbors," illustrates how the agency's
narrow interpretation of its statutory mandates has precluded
regional study analyses.[54] The report, which investigates the
economics of dredging in conjunction with expanding the container
terminal facilities at the Port of Los Angeles, does not adequately assess alternatives outside the port.

The alternatives considered take the form of the economics
of different dredging depths and variations within the port itself. However, no calculations are presented assessing alternatives related to placing the new terminal facilities at another
port within the same geographic region--or even in another port
within the same bay. In brief, the report does not consider the
alternative of allocating assistance to another port(s) in lieu
of performing this project. A study which considered these
alternatives and tradeoffs would be a regional port analysis,
but the limited considerations of the Los Angeles-Long Beach
study do not place it in this category.

The challenge then for the Corps is to develop a framework
for regional port development studies consistent with its statutory mandates. Such an effort would mean an end to the present

Corps policy of appeasing the port industry by not doing regional port development studies.

Environmental Imperatives: New Institutional Roles and Regulations

New environmental legislation has initiated changes in both the institutional bureaucratic structure of the Corps as well as its implementation of policy and program responsibilities. In organizational terms, the Corps adapted to meet new environmental responsibilities in a variety of ways, ranging from increases in staff capacity to handle impact statements to the expansion of the Corps' laboratories for environmental research.

Bureaucratic transfers of power or responsibilities, in addition to increases in these factors as a result of new enabling legislation, have also occurred. Pursuant to the Federal Water Pollution Control Act of 1972 (Public Law 92-500), the Corps transferred certain water permit activities to the Environmental Protection Agency (EPA). Under the 1972 law, the EPA is responsible for the issuance of permits for discharges of pollutants into navigable waters, except for dredge and fill material for which the Corps retained responsibility. Furthermore, the Corps is still required under the Act to review each applicant for an EPA permit to ensure that the anchorage and navigation of any navigable waters would not be substantially impaired by a proposed discharge. Prior to PL 92-500, the Corps had responsibility for review of permit applications for all discharges into navigable water.*

Additionally, the Federal Water Pollution Act of 1972 assigned responsibility to the Corps for issuance of permits for the discharge of dredge and fill material into navigable waters. The term "navigable waters" under this Act was extended by definition to include "waters of the United States and territorial seas." The additional regulatory jurisdiction encompasses waters beyond those which are tidal or used in interstate commerce.

Another legislative action charging the Corps with new environmental responsibilities was the Marine Protection, Research, and Sanctuaries Act of 1972. This Act extended the Corps' regulatory jurisdiction to include the transportation of dredged material for dumping in ocean waters.

An important factor required in both Acts is that the Corps offer an opportunity for public hearings in connection with the processing of permit applications. Although the discretionary use

---

*It should be noted, however, that Section 402 of PL 92-500 replaced the Corps' Refuse Act Permit Program under the Act of 1899 without repealing that Act. As such, all permits that the Corps has already issued are considered valid under the EPA program.

of informal hearings has always been provided for in Corps permit proceedings, in the future hearings must be held if requested by a person having an interest that may be adversely affected by the activity.

Furthermore, an additional area the Corps is becoming involved in is local cost sharing of recreation projects where the federal government has provided a significant part of the investment cost. This responsibility resulted from passage of Public Law 92-347 on July 11, 1972.

In addition to the agency's structural responses to new legislation, the policy and program implementation of traditional Corps activities has changed in several ways. The magnitude of these alterations can be illustrated by examining the effects of the National Environmental Policy Act of 1969* on overall Corps program operations:[55]

1.   For projects the Corps was planning, delay on the
      average of about a year and an increase in plan-
      ning cost from 25 to 50 percent.

2.   For projects from conception until completion of
      construction, delay from two to three years. The
      increase in cost up until the time the project
      goes under construction ranges from 25 to 50 per-
      cent.

Moreover, a recent Corps of Engineers analysis performed on 1,500 environmental impact studies involving 1,100 Corps projects indicated that approximately 350 of them were modified, delayed or halted by environmental review.[56] The Corps survey also found that one out of every four projects under study or construction was changed, and that the operation procedures at one out of every two completed projects were modified to improve their social and ecological impact. Thirty-three studies or projects were halted.[57]

In each study, the greatest number of changes in projects and procedures were made in dredging operations and particularly in the disposal of dredged material.

Varying bureaucratic interpretation and program implementation of new environmental regulations has also created jurisdictional issues and differences of opinion between the EPA and the Corps. For example, under the Federal Water Pollution Control Act of 1972, the EPA is charged with promulgating guidelines for the selection of sites for disposal of dredged materials. The Corps of Engineers is participating in the formulation of new disposal guidelines, yet differences of opinion and approach exist. EPA's approach is based on analysis of the material in place, while the Corps advocates an approach based

_____

*See Chapter 5.

on the impact of the material's discharge on the quality of
receiving waters. Clearly, the way in which these differences
are settled will influence future discourse between the agencies.

Frustration at both the type of environmental criteria and
standards enacted in recent years, and the rapidity in bureaucratic application of these regulations, has often been expressed
by elements of the port industry. Typical of many criticisms is
the following statement by an industry observer:[58]

> The momentum of the current ecological interest has
> forced federal, state, and local agencies to promul-
> gate criteria in pollution control programs without
> adequate time, staff, or budget to determine whether
> the criteria are valid or not.

Resolution of these conflicting industry and government
views on the environment will likely be a lengthy bureaucratic
process.

Navigation Planning Criteria and Cost-Benefit Analysis

A major challenge confronting the Corps is the program
application of criteria and standards to be used for navigation
and port planning and development. As discussed in Chapter 4,
the Principles and Standards for Planning of the Water Resources
Council went into effect on October 30, 1973. The standards
set down a twofold criterion consisting of national economic
development and environmental quality. However, two additional
factors, or accounts--the beneficial and adverse effects on
regional development and social well-being--are to be considered by the decision-maker where appropriate. This formulation
is referred to as the "2 Objectives - 4 Accounts" framework.*

According to some critics, however, the emphasis of using
national income as the only quantifiable objective is inconsistent with the needs of today and the intent of the "public
interest." Multiobjective analyses could be defined and performed. This analysis emphasizes the design of projects and
programs in terms of all socially relevant objectives, including
the national income objective. The distinction between tangible
and intangible (and the related distinction between monetary
and nonmonetary) as it is presently used, some critics argue,
is not a useful one. System contributions to all relevant objectives should be measured in one or another metric, and, when
this is effectively accomplished, then systems can be designed
to effectively reflect all objectives--rather than simply the
national income objective.[59] Unfortunately, multiobjective
analysis, if improperly implemented, could also provide a guise
by which uneconomic and unnecessary projects could be justified.

---

*For more information, see Warren D. Fairchild, Director, U.S.
Water Resources Council, "2 Objectives - 4 Accounts," in U.S.
Army Corps of Engineers, "Water Spectrum," (Washington, D.C.:
Department of the Army, Vol. 5, No. 4, 1973).

A related economic issue confronting the Corps of Engineers is the proper discount rate formula to be used in cost-benefit evaluations of water resources projects.* A high rate level would make justification of many existing civil works programs or projects tenuous--a point both the Corps and Congress have been acutely aware of.** When the Water Resources Council promulgated a higher discount rate under its Principles and Standards for Planning in October 1973, Congress took less than six months to legislate through the Water Resources Development Act of 1974--a provision of which set a new and substantially lower rate.

Furthermore, under the 1974 Act the Congress called for a complete study and reevaluation of all major components of the water evaluation process. That is, the Act specified the following water policy areas for examination and policy review:

a.   Planning objectives;

b.   Project evaluation (discount rates); and

c.   Cost-sharing approaches.

The study was subsequently assigned to the Water Resources Council in early 1975.

Another provision of the Water Resources Development Act of 1974 which will affect the evaluation procedures and program implementation of the Corps is the new mechanism for deauthorizing certain civil works projects.*** Under the Act, the Chief of Engineers is charged to annually review projects which have been authorized for eight or more years without receiving congressional funding and, based on that review, to recommend deauthorization of certain projects subject to new criteria and standards. As of January 1975, the Corps had recommended the deauthorization of 370 civil works projects.[60]

The Politics of Administration

The ability of governmental organizations to adjust themselves to their administrative environment, and their relations

---

*See Chapters 3 and 4 for extended discussions on this issue.

**According to the National Water Commission Report of 1973, a discount rate of near 7 percent would likely jeopardize most river navigation projects.

***This deauthorization mechanism is in addition to a requirement for project reevaluation promulgated under the Principles and Standards adopted by the Water Resources Council in 1973. These standards state that, if a civil works project is not funded within five years of authorization, it must be reevaluated under present criteria and standards.

with competing and other organizations, with Congress, and with
their public constituencies, are adjustments and relations of
political dimension and character.[61] Oftentimes referred to
as the "politics of administration," these organizational relations are important in the understanding of the structure and
policy of the Corps of Engineers.

Politically, the Corps is an unique institution. Although
technically an executive organization, the Corps has traditionally maintained a strong relationship with Congress and its
public constituencies. As one political scientist has stated:[62]

> The Corps is perhaps the classic example of an agency
> which has secured effective independence from its hier-
> archical superiors in the Executive Branch through its
> network of congenial relationships with the private
> groups and congressional committees most interested
> in its work.

The Corps' extensive use of public hearings, contacts with
private groups, and its strong relationship with Congress has
facilitated a greater administrative sensitivity to local public
concerns than exhibited by other federal organizations. More
important, bureaucratic power held and exercised by the Corps
is based on its traditional pattern of organizational relations
and adjustments. Administrative politics at this level is of
course substantively influenced by industry trade associations,
lobbying groups, and other special-interest organizations.

While allowing the organization unusual flexibility and
independence in its organizational responsibilities, the Corps'
close relationship with Congress has brought about criticism as
well as praise. Oftentimes cited for the degree of political
influence it exerts in the determination of public works and
water resources appropriations, Corps funding procedures have
been criticized by observers both within and outside government.

In the book Uncle Sam - The Last of the Big Time Spenders
by Senator William Proxmire, the author refers to several major
Corps of Engineers programs or projects as "public works boon-
doggles."[63] Citing faulty economic planning caused in part by
sectional political interests, Proxmire notes that "three or
four bad ones (public-works projects) are included for every
one justified on its economic merits."[64]

Political influence in water resources appropriations was
also the subject of concern in a 1973 study by Schenker and
Bunamo, "A Study of the Corps of Engineers' Regional Pattern
of Investments."[65] In this paper the authors conducted a quantitative analysis of Corps regional investments utilizing a time-
series, cross-sectional data array, and employing multiple
regression techniques. Those variables found significant when
tested against Corps expenditures included several political
factors, such as congressional committee membership and length
of years in Congress, and certain regional biases in allocations.
Their conclusions state in part:[66]

...this study examines the macro-implications of the
Corps' investment activity and indicates that the
Corps' expenditures have a very significant relation
to political influence. This would imply that water-
works programs are, in some sense, pork barrel legislation and helps explain the inefficiency of cost-
benefit technique as applied to project selection.

The bureaucratic political pressure found by Schenker and
Bunamo can be largely explained by the activities of industry
lobbying groups and other politicized special-interest organizations focusing on narrow, partisan concerns. As stated by the
Association of American Railroads:[67]

...Navigation projects should not only be evaluated from
an economic standpoint, but they should be evaluated to
determine if they would provide a transportation service
which is required from the public viewpoint, and not
merely from that of waterway carriers and shippers who
seek improved facilities to enhance their profits.

Consequently, while the administrative structure and traditional mode of policy and program implementation of the Corps
has facilitated a certain political uniqueness in its organizational role, the Corps is also peculiarly sensitive to those
public constituencies and organizations interested in its work.
To the extent that this political environment has been managable
in the past, recent changes in the role and program orientation
of the Corps have complicated the process. Furthermore, since
the combined effects of technology and ecology have their own
intrinsic political dimensions, new and emerging constituencies
and policy opinions have changed the traditional political
structure within which the Corps operates.

In institutional terms these factors suggest that the major
determinants for future changes in Corps of Engineers policies
and programs will result from the impacts of new governmental
and private-interest organizations on the traditional policy-
making structure and process of the Corps.

CHAPTER 7

THE MARITIME ADMINISTRATION

Introduction

The Maritime Administration of the Department of Commerce is charged with a major role in the promotion and development of federal policies and goals regarding U.S. ocean ports. Broadly, MarAd administers programs to aid in the development, promotion, and operation of the U.S. merchant marine and its constituent elements.[1] It is also charged with the organization and direction of emergency merchant ship operations.

The central role of the Maritime Administration is the administration of the merchant marine subsidy program which had its beginning in 1936.[2] Under the Maritime Subsidy Board, this program provides for construction and operating differential subsidies to the U.S. merchant marine. Characteristically, these subsidies comprise 75 to 80 percent of the budget requests made by the Administration.[3]

As a component of the Department of Commerce, MarAd has responsibility for the promotion and development of waterborne transportation for the domestic and foreign commerce of the United States. Such a charge, including more specific statutory authorizations to be detailed, provides broad mandates for MarAd involvement in port operations and development.

Organizational History

The Maritime Administration traces its roots back to the establishment of the U.S. Shipping Board pursuant to the Shipping Act of 1916.[4] The purposes of this Act were to:[5]

> establish a United States Shipping Board for the purpose of encouraging, developing, and creating a naval auxiliary and naval reserve and a merchant marine to meet the requirements of the commerce of the United States with its Territories and possessions and with foreign countries; to regulate carriers by water engaged in the foreign and interstate commerce of the United States, and for other purposes.

Created at a point where a prime motive for merchant marine as well as port development was military readiness,[6] the developmental authority over port matters granted by Congress was to both military departments (Corps of Engineers) and the U.S. Shipping Board.

Accordingly, at the end of the First World War, the Congress charged the U.S. Shipping Board with broad, comprehensive powers relating to ocean port development. Under Section 8 of the Merchant Marine Act of 1920:[7]

...it shall be the duty of the board, in cooperation with the Secretary of War, with the object of promoting, encouraging, and developing ports and transportation facilities in connection with water commerce over which it has jurisdiction, to investigate territorial regions and zones tributary to such ports, taking into consideration the economies of transportation by rail, water, and highway and the natural direction of the flow of commerce; to investigate the causes of the congestion of commerce at ports and the remedies applicable thereto; to investigate the subject of water terminals, including the necessary docks, warehouses, apparatus, equipment, and appliances in connection therewith, with a view to devising and suggesting the types most appropriate for different locations and for the most expeditious and economical transfer or interchange of passengers or property between carriers by water and carriers by rail; to advise with communities regarding the appropriate location and plan of construction of wharves, piers, and water terminals; to investigate the practicability and advantages of harbor, river, and port improvements in connection with foreign and coastwise trade; and to investigate any other matter that may tend to promote and encourage the use by vessels of ports adequate to care for the freight which would naturally pass through such ports: Provided, That if after such investigation the board shall be of the opinion that rates, charges, rules, or regulations of common carriers by rail subject to the jurisdiction of the Interstate Commerce Commission are detrimental to the declared object of this section, or that new rates, charges, rules, or regulations, new or additional port terminal facilities, or affirmative action on the part of such common carriers by rail is necessary to promote the objects of this section, the board may submit its findings to the Interstate Commerce Commission for such action as such commission may consider proper under existing law.

This section, in seeking to establish a strong port development plan to facilitate both expanded commerce and military readiness, laid the statutory groundwork for later MarAd involvement in the port development process.*

In 1933, the Board was transferred to the Department of Commerce to facilitate more broadly its functions in promoting maritime commerce.[8] Shortly thereafter, a major organizational change took place. Pursuant to Title II of the Merchant Marine Act of 1936, the U.S. Maritime Commission was established--a forerunner to both the Maritime Administration and the Federal Maritime Board.[9]

Under the Act, the Commission was charged to:[10]

---

*The Merchant Marine Act of 1920 has remained in force through subsequent administrative reorganizations and transfers of responsibility leading up to the Maritime Administration.

further the development and maintenance of an adequate
and well-balanced American merchant marine, to promote
the commerce of the United States, to aid in the national defense, to repeal certain former legislation, and
for other purposes.

Section 212 of the Act specifically authorized the Commission
to "study all maritime problems arising in the carrying out of
the policy set forth in Title I of this act,"[11] which included
the development of a "shipping service essential for maintaining
the flow of domestic and foreign waterborne commerce."[12]

The 1964 Operations Research study,[13] in noting that "administration development to date has concentrated in equipment
(vessels) rather than facilities," saw no reason that would preclude MarAd "from participating in port development functions
concurrently with the Corps"[14] under Section 212.

Pursuant to Reorganization Plan 21 of 1950 (effective May 24,
1950), the modern composition of the Maritime Administration was
initially set down.[15] The Plan, in abolishing the U.S. Maritime
Commission, created the Federal Maritime Board and the Maritime
Administration. The Maritime Board was given responsibility for
supervision and control of rates, fares, discriminatory practices,
subsidy awards, and so on.[16] These functions were primarily
regulatory in nature.

The Maritime Administration, whose Administrator also served
as chairman of the Federal Maritime Board, was charged with the
responsibility for administering subsidy contracts in addition
to acquiring generally the operational and developmental function of the former Maritime Commission.

In recognizing that the functional breakdowns of responsibility between the Maritime Board and the Maritime Administration
were not sufficiently defined, the Congress passed (under Executive instigation) Reorganization Plan No. 7 of 1961, effective
August 12, 1961.[17] The Plan segregated the functions of the
Maritime Administration and established the Federal Maritime
Commission (FMC), replacing the former Maritime Board. In effect,
the reorganization separated the promotional, developmental, and
assistance functions, placing them in the Maritime Administration,
while centralizing the regulatory and policing functions in the
new FMC. Exhibit 7.1 shows the development of these governmental
changes.

Accordingly, the Maritime Administration is charged with the
following major statutory responsibilities and duties:[18]

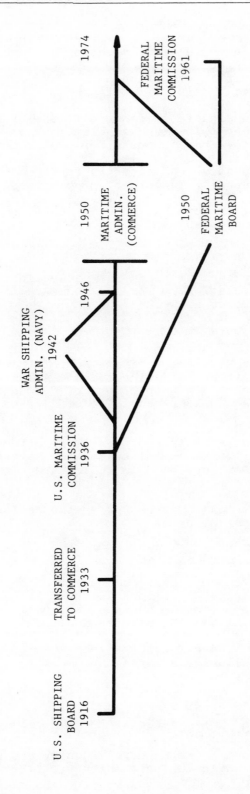

EXHIBIT 7.1

HISTORICAL DEVELOPMENT OF THE MARITIME ADMINISTRATION

- the administration of maritime laws pertaining to
  construction-differential and operating-differential
  subsidies to the American merchant marine; financing
  guarantees for ship construction and other financial
  needs to shipping;

- maintaining national defense reserve fleets of govern-
  ment-owned merchant ships; and acquisition, allocation,
  and operation of merchant ships under emergency conditions;

- determining ocean services necessary for the development and maintenance of U.S. foreign commerce;

- the investigation of foreign and U.S. vessel construction and operating costs; and

- the training of merchant marine officers.

These functions are basically administrative in nature; however, because of their relation to foreign commerce, several functions are developmental ones as well.[19]

Administrative Organization

As shown in Exhibit 7.2, the Maritime Administration is organized about a head Administrator (designated the Assistant Secretary for Maritime Affairs of the Department of Commerce), four
Assistant Administrators, and the requisite office and field
structure.

The Assistant Administrator structure is functionally organized: Office of the Assistant Administrator for Maritime Aids,
Operations, Commercial Development, and Policy and Administration.

The port functions and policies of MarAd are handled in the
Office of Ports and Intermodal Systems under the Assistant Administrator for Commercial Development.

Port Planning and Development Program

Under Section 8 of the Merchant Marine Act of 1920 (previously cited), the Maritime Administration has maintained a
formal organizational component to handle these port development
functions since the Administration's inception in 1950.

Albeit low level,[20] these functions from 1950 to 1965 basically encompassed the following areas:[21]

- conducting developmental activities with respect to
  ports and port facilities;

- the maintenance of domestic and foreign port data;

- maintaining liaison with the port industry and providing technical advice on port matters;

EXHIBIT 7.2

ORGANIZATION CHART FOR THE U.S. DEPARTMENT OF COMMERCE, MARITIME ADMINISTRATION

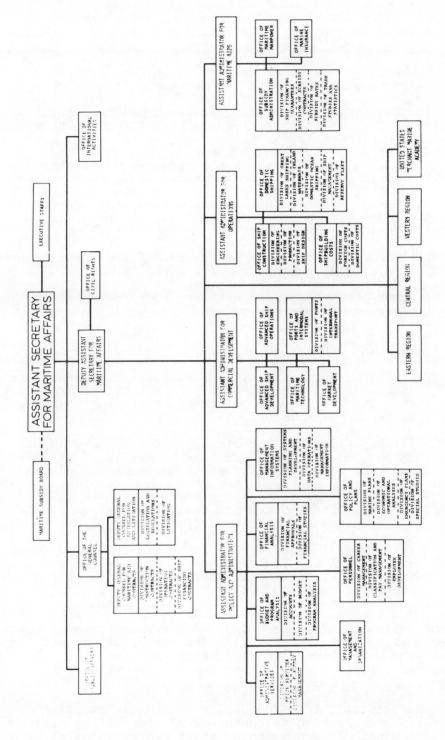

Source: U.S. Department of Commerce.

- issuing Port Series publications jointly with the
  Corps of Engineers, providing statistical and economic
  data on U.S. ocean ports;

- providing technical assistance in foreign port development under the Foreign Assistance Program.

In addition, in 1957 MarAd was assigned responsibility for
conducting defense mobilization planning functions relating to
ports and port facilities.[22]

Since 1965, MarAd has taken a number of initiatives designed
to give increased emphasis to its port development responsibilities. In 1966, the Office of Maritime Promotion was established
and within that Office, three Divisions relating to ports were
set up: the Division of Ports and Systems, the Division of
Cargo Promotion, and the Division of Trade Studies.

According to the Manual of Orders for the Division of Ports
and Systems, the division was charged to:[23]

- formulate and conduct programs to promote integrated
  transportation systems;

- implement certain provisions of Section 8 of the
  Merchant Marine Act of 1920, including developing
  "estimates of National needs and (the) preparation
  (of) long-range plans, as required, to the end that
  adequate port facilities may be established for handling the foreign and domestic water-borne commerce
  of the United States";

- develop plans for coordinated efforts among agencies
  of the federal government for promotion, development and utilization of ports and port facilities;

- conduct emergency preparation plans for ports and
  port facilities under national mobilization conditions, pursuant to Executive Order 10999;

- gather and interpret certain types of data on foreign
  and U.S. ports, and represent the Department of Commerce
  and the U.S. Government in the international field of
  ports, as requested.

To facilitate these and further directives, the port development program was expanded in 1969. A new Office of Ports and
Intermodal Systems was established under the Assistant Administrator for Operations. Two further breakdowns: the Division of
Ports and the Division of Intermodal Transport were added in
1970.

Additionally, in 1970 the Maritime Administration expanded
its field organization to encompass all 50 states, divided into
three regions. A port planning staff was established in each

region to concentrate on port activities at the field level.

And finally, the Office of Ports and Intermodal Systems (OPIS)* was placed under the Assistant Administrator for Commercial Development in 1973 to facilitate closer coordination between port development and promotional activities (market development, etc.) as well as research and development activities.[24]

The following table shows the number of positions (headquarters and field components) allocated to the ports and intermodal systems program from 1970 to 1974 in the Maritime Administration.

	HQ	Field	Total
April '70	15	5	20
July '70	20	5	25
July '71	20	10	30
July '72	22	11	33
July '73	23	12	35
April '74	23	13	36

Total MarAd employment - April 30, 1974 - 1539

As shown, the port staff component of MarAd is small, but has been increasing.

The duties and responsibilities of the new Office are manifold: The Manual of Orders directing the Office lists broad responsibilities in the coordination, promotion, and development of port policies within the federal government. Appendix E contains relevant portions of this Manual, the salient points of which are summarized below.

Comparable in many respects to the duties authorized under the earlier 1965 Manual of Orders for the Division of Ports and Systems, the new Manual (1973) extends those responsibilities.

The Office (OPIS) is charged to formulate national policies and plans for the development and utilization of ports and port facilities; to study and survey a broad spectrum of operations relating to ports (the section is based on Section 8 of the Merchant Marine Act of 1920), including the recommendation of "new locations and new types of terminal construction including off-shore installations, and shore equipment required for modern ships,"[25] to assist in more effective coordination between agencies of the federal government with respect to ports, and to "compile information and publish information listed...including the economic impact of United States ports; port development expenditures by United States ports; marine containerization and port development; and systems criteria for future terminal facilities reflecting advances in container, LASH, general cargo and bulk cargo operations."[26]

---

*Hereafter referred to as the "Office."

Additionally, the Office has the responsibility to "serve as a port consultant to the Economic Development Administration providing comments and recommendations on applications for grants and loans for port technical assistance and public works projects received from economically distressed communities,"[27] in addition to several other promotional and operational duties relating to ports.

Clearly then, the broad responsibilities outlined in the Manual, based on Section 8 of the Merchant Marine Act of 1920, comprise the most extensive, specific planning duties held by any federal agency relating to U.S. ocean ports.

Recent Initiatives

In implementing these duties and responsibilities, the Maritime Administration, through its Office of Ports and Intermodal Systems and others, has initiated several role-broadening activities.

One such activity is the Administration's early and continuing interest in deepwater port development. Under contract from MarAd, Soros Associates completed in 1972 a major study on deepwater port development, "Offshore Terminal Systems Concepts."[28] The Soros study prompted a number of working arrangements to be initiated between MarAd, agencies of the federal government, and port and oil industry interests as well.[29]

Another early activity initiated by MarAd was assistance to the shipping and port industries in developing the knowledge and technology to meet new environmental requirements.

As has been stated by a MarAd official:[30]

We in the Maritime Administration fully recognize the need to establish safeguards that will protect the marine environment. In this connection, we have made and released environmental impact statements on each class of American-flag tankers that are being built with governmental assistance. On the international scene, the United States also has been the most vigorous proponent of marine pollution-abatement measures.

Accordingly, MarAd has offered technical services and assistance toward the development of pollution abatement equipment.[31]

Along similar lines, an economics and safety analysis of the transportation of hazardous substances in bulk was released by MarAd in June 1974.[32] The study, prepared for MarAd by A. D. Little, Inc., under a $99,800 contract, was undertaken to assess the impact of the Federal Water Pollution Control Act Amendments of 1972[33] on the domestic waterborne commerce of the United States.[34] In summary, the analysis showed that bulk transportation of hazardous materials was most economical by barge, with barge transportation also found to be generally safer than overland modes.[35]

Additionally, two joint MarAd-Coast Guard studies are underway in this area. One study will assess tank barge designs and
the incremental life-cycle costs of providing various levels of
environmental protection. The second study will evaluate temporary repair materials and their application to tank barges.[36]

Two research and development activities pursued by the
Administration which impact on the general pollution area are
ship-collision avoidance techniques and associated control systems, and ship communication hardware.

With reference to the former, MarAd has been experimenting
with radar transponder techniques and other ship collision avoidance systems.[37]

In ship communications, MarAd, in cooperation with NASA,
has been experimenting with the efficiency and dependability of
communications between vessels at sea and their headquarters via
the recently-launched Applications Technology Satellite-F. Since
1970, MarAd has invested approximately $9.8 million in applying
space technology to improving the operations and management of
American-flag merchant vessels.[38]

In January 1973, MarAd released a study conducted by the
University of Michigan on extending the season of Great Lakes
shipping operations. Entitled the "Economics of Great Lakes
Shipping in an Extended Season," the report developed a computer-
ized model to assess the potential benefits to shipowners who
might engage in extended season operations.[39]

In terms of waterborne shipping forecasts and port facilities studies, MarAd has compiled and released several reports
this year. In February of 1974, the Administration published an
analysis of the markets for domestic waterborne shipping. The
study, entitled "Domestic Waterborne Shipping--Market Analysis,"
concentrates on developing market aids and strategies to assist
domestic marine carriers in assessing transportation needs.[40]
The study includes an analysis of expected commerce flow to the
year 2000.[41]

In March, MarAd released a survey analysis of North American
port expenditures for new and improved facilities through 1977.
The report, "North American Port Development Expenditure Survey,"
based on 127 responding ports, notes that between 1973 and 1977
continental U.S. ports will spend $1,484,450,000 on facilities
improvements.[42]

Additionally, in June of 1974 the Maritime Administration
published a management analysis of the port industry and its
emerging financial problems. The report, "Public Port Financing
in the United States,"[43] was prepared "specifically in response
to a Congressional inquiry on the subject of the absence of
federal financial aid to the U.S. port industry."[44]

The study examines the financial problems facing U.S. public port facilities such as the costs of new marine technology, environmental legislation, and added cargo security, and surveys the existing port financing methods (generally some type of bonding mechanism). The report then pursues selected federal assistance programs (mentioned are the DOT, MarAd, the EDA, and NOAA) and concludes by discussing alternative sources of port financing.[45] Implicit within the study is the recognition by both the federal government and the ports that some form of direct assistance may be necessary in the near future.

In August 1974, MarAd released the "Neobulk Shipping Study," examining neobulk cargo and detailing methods for U.S.-flag penetration of that market. Neobulk cargo is defined as "that portion of the trade which, by virtue of its cargo characteristics, is beginning to show an increasing trend towards movement by irregular service in less than hold-size lots up to shipload lots."[46]

MarAd is also participating since 1974 in a cost-shared master planning program with the Washington Public Ports Association. The study will determine the role of the ports in the State of Washington in handling the state's and nation's export/import cargo needs to the year 2000.[47]

Additionally, as noted in Chapter 4, the Maritime Administration is collecting the data necessary for the General Services Administration to develop a national port emergency mobilization plan.

Finally, MarAd is seeking to serve in the role of ombudsman for the port industry when it encounters difficulties in dealing with other government agencies.[48] As an example of this role, MarAd recently filed its opposition to HR-12891 with the House Interstate and Foreign Commerce Committee.[49] The bill, which would amend the Interstate Commerce Act to permit the railroads to establish variable freight rates, is opposed by MarAd on the grounds that it could adversely affect the water carriers.

Potential Impacts

To be sure, strong Maritime Administration initiatives in port planning and development functions are a recent phenomenon. While formal organizational components to perform port-related duties existed before 1972, overall activities were limited. The reason for this, in light of the very broad mandate contained in the Merchant Marine Act of 1920, was explained by a MarAd official in December of 1972 before the North Atlantic Ports Association:[50]

> The U.S. port industry has grown to its current state of development and sophistication through vigorous competition and with very little participation, assistance or guidance from the Federal Government. While the Maritime Administration has had broad statutory responsibilities in the promotion and development of U.S.

ports since the Merchant Marine Act of 1920, a successful
dialogue of mutual support and cooperation with the
port industry has never been brought to full bloom.

The reason for this lack of a meaningful MarAd port
program rests with both parties. MarAd's traditional
preoccupation with its shipping role has completely over-
whelmed its port functions, resulting in a low level
of port consciousness within the Agency. At the same
time, the steadfast opposition of the port industry to
any Federal Government involvement has not afforded an
atmosphere to encourage MarAd to develop meaningful port
initiatives.

Too, as explained earlier in this chapter, the 1920 Act
can be received as _prima facie_ promotional in nature, designed to
foster military preparedness by increasing the number and size
of port facilities across the nation.

The lack of MarAd initiatives in the very early stages subsequent to the 1920 Act established a pattern of relationships between the burgeoning port industry and the federal maritime organizations, a pattern which essentially left to the Maritime Administration, established in 1950, a historically low-level, promotional role. Given that, MarAd interest itself was limited until
the late 1960s, when a series of technological, environmental
and safety issues allowed federal organizations with statutory
authorizations in the port area to initiate moves themselves.

Challenges to the Maritime Administration

The ability of the Maritime Administration to influence port
activities is limited since it has little or no power to allo-
cate federal port-related funds, set national policy impacting
on ports, or regulate port operations. Recent MarAd initiatives
in the port policy area have focused on the potential financial,
operational, and regulatory problems that public port facilities
will likely encounter in the future; however, these studies and
reports are primarily informational or promotional in character.

The public port financing study conducted by MarAd discusses
various types of federal subsidies for port facilities. However,
in 1972 a MarAd study conducted by Manalytics Inc. on the
impact of marine containerization argued that by 1975 the ratio
of container lift capacity to demand would equal 250 percent
nationwide (570 percent on the West Coast).[51] Clearly, the consideration of federal subsidies for ports would necessarily require related consideration of fiscal allocations by public port
facilities--and, of course, the reasons for overcapacity in container lifts.

Additionally, it may be difficult for MarAd to continue what
are primarily promotional activities when container terminal overcapacity has been shown--while at the same time, under various
federal statutes and regulations, MarAd is charged with the consideration of national needs related to ports and marine commerce.

Accordingly, a major challenge to the Maritime Administration is the blending of its responsibilities outlined under the Merchant Marine Act of 1920, but never implemented with related legislation, with its recent initiatives in the port policy area. However, the prima facie interpretation of the 1920 Act as promotional by the Administration limits MarAd moves into related policy areas as well.

Since the research interests and concerns of MarAd in the port area overlap with those of other federal agencies, a vehicle for greater communication between MarAd and these agencies would be joint research in common areas to the greatest extent possible. This process has already begun in some study areas.

CHAPTER 8

THE U.S. COAST GUARD

Introduction

The United States Coast Guard is charged with a major administrative role in the operation of U.S. ports and harbors.
Traditionally, the Coast Guard involvement in domestic port
development has been in the operations regulatory area. The
agency enforces regulations and standards pertaining to the
safety of port and vessel operations, the safe transport of
dangerous or hazardous cargoes, the control or abatement of
marine pollution, and a number of other maritime regulatory
tasks.

However, institutional changes in the traditional port development scenario have engendered new policy challenges and different administrative roles for the Coast Guard in its port and
harbor affairs. New environmental legislation has added many
policy and program responsibilities to traditional Coast Guard
operations, while advances in maritime technology have placed
administrative pressures on many traditional regulatory duties
as well as requiring new policy approaches.

This chapter will identify these recent policy imperatives
in light of the traditional operations of the Coast Guard in the
port area. As a modal component of the Department of Transportation, the overall policy and program challenges to the Coast
Guard will be discussed in the following DOT chapter.

The Beginnings

The beginnings of the Coast Guard are replete with stories
of United States history. Originally conceived as a "Revenue
Marine" or "Revenue Cutter Service," the infant agency was authorized by Congress on August 4, 1790, to construct "ten boats
for the collection of revenue."[1] This action was the result of
an ongoing smuggling practice, chiefly occurring in the Gulf
Coast, begun by profiteers under British rule to avoid duties.
Continued after the end of the Revolutionary War, the practice
was seriously depleting tax monies from the new Treasury Department. Secretary of the Treasury Alexander Hamilton posed as a
cure the establishment of a waterborne customs enforcement service. Congress agreed, and monies were secured.

Almost immediately the duties of the new service were expanded. Since the Revolutionary Navy had been disbanded in 1790,
Hamilton knew that the small fleet would serve as the nation's
naval arm until a regular Navy was constructed. Accordingly,
Hamilton argued that the Cutter Service's officers be commissioned, and hold the same rank as those held formerly in the
Navy. Under the Act of 1799[2] this was accomplished, and the
military character of the young service was established.

An inkling of one of the Coast Guard's major contemporary
roles came in 1836 when cutters were charged "to aid persons at
sea, in distress, who may be taken aboard,"[3] and again in 1843
when the preservation of property and cargoes at sea were included in the charge.

Several contemporary aspects of the modern Coast Guard
emerged in the 1840s. One analyst has written:[4]

In the 1840's a new era dawned for the Revenue Marine
under the able direction of Secretary of the Treasury
John C. Spencer. Spencer set out to reorganize the
service along more efficient and modern lines. For the
first time since its founding, the Revenue Marine was
established as a bureau in the Department of the Treasury. It had accounting, engineering, personnel, operations, intelligence, and legal branches, and a captain
was selected to head the bureau.

Also during this time, the Lighthouse Establishment, which
had been part of the Revenue Marine, was detached and set up as
a separate administrative unit under the Treasury Department.[5]

The birth of the modern era of the Coast Guard came as the
result of controversy. During his administration President Taft
appointed a Presidential commission to investigate possible avenues
to governmental reorganization. After finding many Cutter Service
duties obsolete under examination, the Commission recommended
that the service be abolished and its duties taken over by the
Navy. The President agreed, and a report was sent on to Congress.[6]

The recommendations of the Taft Commission relating to the
Revenue Cutter Service were not initiated, but the debate over
the report raised some critical issues. Apart from the questions
of whether specific Revenue Cutter Service duties were obsolete,
the larger question was whether important duties fulfilled by
the Cutter Service were of necessity based in an organization
separate from the Navy and, if so, what then should be the character and composition of such a service.

In dealing with the Taft Commission report, the Congress
had argued that the duties carried out by the Cutter Service
were specialized in nature, and that to assign them to the Navy
would burden the latter and possibly reduce military effectiveness. But the Congress also realized that in the marine services
area there were several smaller agencies with overlapping roles
operating independently of each other. Two of these, the Revenue
Cutter Service and the Lifesaving Service, were both concerned
with safety of life at sea. Accordingly, on January 20, 1915,
the Congress decided to combine them into a new agency to be
known as the United States Coast Guard.[7]

Since the establishment of the service, the Coast Guard has
gradually been given additional duties and responsibilities.
These include law enforcement powers on the high seas and navigable waters in 1936,[8] the transfer of the Lighthouse Service

in 1939,[9] and the transfer of the Bureau of Marine Inspection
and Navigation in 1942.[10] Existing along with these duties has
been that of maintaining a state of readiness as a specialized
service prepared for active participation with the Navy in time
of war.

A year before the United States formally entered World War I,
the Congress enacted the Espionage Act of 1917,[11] which authorized the President to delegate to the Coast Guard the protection of ports and waterfront areas. The Act defined the protection of ports as "to safeguard (the port) against destruction, loss, or injury resulting from sabotage or other subver-
sive acts, accidents, or other causes of similar nature,"[12] Port
security has continued to be a major Coast Guard mission.

Prior to the outbreak of the Second World War, the Coast
Guard comprised 267 cutters, 199 picket boats from 34 to 65
feet long, 39 lightships, and numerous auxiliary craft for
various services.[13] It was this force which was directed to
defend the coastline after hostilities broke out for the second
time in World War II.

In each case up to and including the Second World War, the
Coast Guard's statutory mandate for its military operations was
derived from the Act of 1799, which stated:[14]

Revenue Cutters shall, whenever the President of the
United States shall so direct, cooperate with the
Navy of the United States.

In 1949, under a general reorganization and codification of
Coast Guard responsibilities and statutory mandates, the wording
of the old Act was revised to state:[15]

The Coast Guard as established January 28, 1915, shall
be a military service and a branch of the armed forces
of the United States at all times. The Coast Guard
shall be a service in the Treasury Department except
when operating as a service in the Navy.

Consequently, though originally charged with a public service
role, in time of war the Coast Guard has served as a supportive
military force. The effect of these institutional transfers
has prompted the Service to assume a dual capacity in public
service and military roles. And, to the extent the Coast Guard
has operated in these dual capacities, the experiences gained
have shaped both the Coast Guard's conception of itself, and the
conception of the public it serves.

Congressional recognition of this special public role of the
Service was underscored by the transfer of the Coast Guard to the
new Department of Transportation in 1967. In April of that year,
after 177 years in the Treasury Department, the Coast Guard moved
to the new department pursuant to the Department of Transportation Act of 1966.[16] Transferred as an indivisible unit, the Coast

Guard retained all functions, powers, and duties it held previously under the Treasury Department.

The Overall Policies and Programs of the U.S. Coast Guard

The various interdependent functions of the Coast Guard
had not been expressed collectively in any legal statute prior
to the Second World War. The Service had been gradually given
additional duties and responsibilities since its inception in
1799. During the summer of 1949, the Congress expressed a desire
to revise Title 14 of the United States Code in order to have
outlined in one section the broad scope of the functions of the
Coast Guard.[17] On August 4, 1949, a revised Title 14 set out
the primary duties of the Coast Guard as follows:[18]

> The Coast Guard shall enforce or assist in the enforce-
> ment of all applicable Federal laws on or under the high
> seas and waters subject to the jurisdiction of the United
> States; shall administer laws and promulgate and enforce
> regulations for the promotion of safety of life and
> property on and under the high seas and waters subject
> to the jurisdiction of the United States covering all
> matters not specifically delegated by law to some other
> executive department; shall develop, establish, main-
> tain, and operate, with due regard to the require-
> ments of national defense, aids to maritime navigation,
> icebreaking facilities, and rescue facilities for the
> promotion of safety on, under, and over the high seas
> and waters subject to the jurisdiction of the United
> States; shall engage in oceanographic research of the
> high seas and in waters subject to the jurisdiction of
> the United States; and shall maintain a state of readi-
> ness of function as a specialized service in the Navy
> in time of war.

Administrative Organization with Emphasis on Ports and Waterways

The operation or program areas of the Coast Guard are organized along functional, or "mission-oriented," lines. Navigational Aids, Search and Rescue, and Merchant Marine Safety (among
others) are program duties which have developed through legislative action or the transfer of functions. Program development
has largely been Coast Guard action.

In general terms, these program areas include:[19]

a. Maritime law enforcement;

b. Saving and protecting life and property;

c. Safeguarding navigation on the high seas and
    navigable waters of the United States;

d. The lead agency in the enforcement of pollution
    laws regarding navigable waters of the United
    States;

   e.   Preparedness for military operations.

   These responsibilities are delegated to the District Commander in each of 12 Coast Guard districts in the United States.

   Exhibit 8.1 is an organization chart of general Coast Guard
staff and field structure. Coast Guard operations at the regional
and local levels are handled by either the two area offices, the
12 district offices mentioned earlier, or delegation to the 15
headquarters units around the country.

   The establishment of regional and local offices to accomplish specific duties has been tied to the gradual accumulation
of duties and responsibilities acquired by the Coast Guard since
its inception.

   The modern organization and composition of the Service is
defined in Title 14 of the United States Code, "The United States
Coast Guard."[20] Contained in Title 14 is a summary of legal
acts and statutes specifying the powers of the Service, its
staffing and organization structure, and its relationship to
other federal agencies.

   Headquarters organization at the Coast Guard is defined
along functional mission areas. Exhibit 8.2 is an organizational
chart of Coast Guard headquarters.

   The establishment in 1970 of the Office of Marine Environment and Systems (W) was based largely on the need for a concerted Coast Guard response to new environmental and technological challenges affecting U.S. ocean ports. The new office, made
up of law enforcement, port safety, and aids to navigation duties
from the Office of Operations, and the Bridge Administration Program, was a major organizational shift to centralize a number of
interdependent Coast Guard functions with respect to port safety
and environmental protection responsibilities. Incorporated into
this office was the Ports and Waterways Planning Staff, a new
staff function with specific responsibilities in studying and
developing the Coast Guard role in port and waterway management.
Appendix F is a compilation of present legislation pertinent to
the port and waterways activities of the Coast Guard.

Regional and Local Administration

   At the regional and local level, Coast Guard operations are
accomplished by the Captain of the Port (COTP) and the Officer in
Charge, Marine Inspection (OCMI).[21] These two organizational
entities carry out the major duties of the Coast Guard at the
port level--that of vessel safety and inspection, and port and
harbor safety.

   Administratively, the COTP and the OCMI are the Coast Guard's
field representatives at the port. Each is charged with a variety
of interrelated program area responsibilities, and each operates
respectively with broad statutory duties in both regulatory and

EXHIBIT 8.1

U.S. COAST GUARD ORGANIZATION

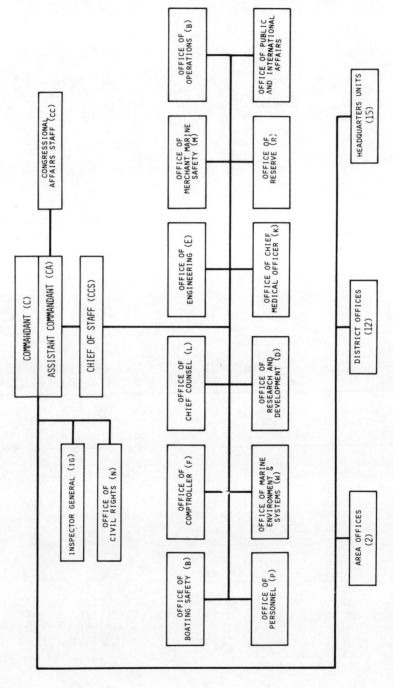

Source: U.S. Department of Transportation.

EXHIBIT 8.2

ORGANIZATION CHART, U.S. COAST GUARD HEADQUARTERS

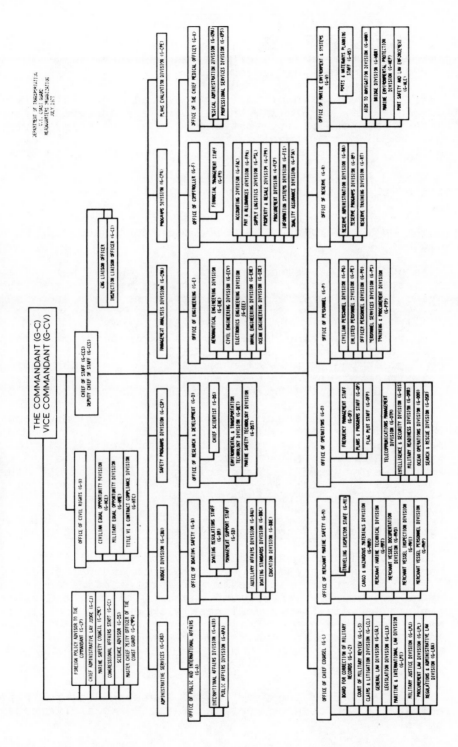

planning phases. It is characteristic of the Coast Guard planning
process that field and regional levels have direct impact on headquarters planning; hence, the COTP and OCMI have important influence over the duties they accomplish.

Fifty-four Captain of the Port offices presently serve the
United States.[22] Generally, these COTPs are assigned a geographical area of responsibility that encompasses one major port and a
group of small or intermediate ports. In the largest ports, such
as New York, the area of responsibility is confined to that port.

Command responsibility for direct administration of the
Captain of the Port duties and responsibilities has been delegated to the District Commander by the Commandant. The Operations Division within each District Office is responsible for
the day-to-day supervision of COTP operations occurring within
the District.

The OCMI is the commanding officer of one of many designated
Marine Inspection Zones, which in turn are components of the
49 Marine Inspection Offices which implement the responsibilities of Merchant Marine Safety at Coast Guard Headquarters.[23]

The total operating, training and administrative personnel
allocated to the Commercial Vessel Safety program implemented
by the OCMI at the port level numbers 1,446 (includes officers,
warrant officers, enlisted men, and civilians). Authorized
personnel, which include general detail, total 1,577.[24]

In some regional areas, the COTP and the OCMI are combined
under one port (or ports) supervisor. In these cases the supervisor carries dual statutory duties and responsibilities. Currently, 24 OCMIs also serve as the COTP. Moreover, a recent trend
within the Coast Guard is the combining of COTP and OCMI functions
into one position which represents the role of the control administrator of Coast Guard operations at the port level.

A Review of Specific Coast Guard Missions Relating to Ports

The initial statement of Coast Guard responsibility in port
and harbor operations came under the Rivers and Harbor Act of
1915, which directed the Secretary of War to define and establish
anchorage grounds for vessels and harbors, rivers, and other such
waterways.[25] As is the general case with overall administrative
duties, Coast Guard responsibilities in port operations have
developed along functional mission-oriented lines.

Port Safety/Security

The objective of the Coast Guard Ports and Waterways programs
is included in the opening section of the Ports and Waterways
Safety Act of 1970:[26]

To promote safe and efficient maritime transportation
and to promote the safety and environmental quality of
the ports, harbors and navigable waters of the United
States.

Interpretations of the language of this objective have been
stated by Coast Guard planning materials in this fashion: the
wording "safe and efficient maritime transportation" is interpreted to mean an "orderly flow of commodities and passengers
via waterborne carriers in and out of U.S. ports and on U.S.
navigable waters, with minimum danger to persons or property and
minimum interruption of this flow from accidents, incidents or
other occurrences of an unusual or abnormal character." "Safety
and environmental quality of the ports, harbors and navigable
waters" is interpreted to mean "a condition of minimum danger to
persons, property and the natural ecology of the port and waterway environment from activities associated with waterborne commerce or recreation."[27]

The legal basis for the Port Safety/Security program area is
Executive Order 10173 issued in 1950 pursuant to the Espionage Act
of 1917.[28] This order established, among other things, the Captain
of the Port (COTP). The authority and regulations regarding the
COTP are set forth in 33 CFR 6. Basically these regulations
designate the COTP to enforce the Espionage Act by controlling
vessel movements, dangerous cargo operations on vessels and waterfront facilities, and access to vessels or facilities.

The duties and responsibilities of the COTP in this area
have been an evolutionary process. Originally, the Espionage
Act dealt with port security functions, but gradually this function has evolved into a combined safety/security mission.

The Functions of the COTP in the Port Safety Program

Generally, the following duties have evolved as COTP
responsibilities:[29]

(1) Safeguarding of vessels, harbors, ports and water-
     front facilities of the United States;

(2) Carriage of explosives and other dangerous articles
     on vessels;

(3) Vessels having on board inflammable or combustible
     liquids in bulk;

(4) Inspection of foreign vessels of novel design or
     construction, or whose operation involves potential
     unusual risks;

(5) Anchorage grounds and special anchorage areas for
     vessels in all harbors, rivers, bays and other
     navigable waters of the United States;

(6)   Movement and anchorage of vessels in the St. Mary's
      River;

(7)   Control of anchorage and movement of vessels to
      ensure safety of Naval vessels;

(8)   Loadlines for vessels making domestic and foreign
      voyages;

(9)   Oil pollution of coastal waters and pollution of
      the sea by oil;

(10) Deposit of refuse in navigable waters of the United
      States;

(11) Inquiries, examinations, inspections, searches,
      seizures, and arrests upon the high seas and waters
      over which the United States has jurisdiction, for
      the prevention, detection, and suppression of viola-
      tions of laws of the United States;

(12) Cooperation with any Federal agency, State, Terri-
      tory, possession, or political subdivision thereof,
      or the District of Columbia;

(13) Render aid to distressed persons, vessels, and air-
      craft on the high seas and in water areas over which
      the United States has jurisdiction.

These functions are carried out by approximately 1,415
Coast Guard personnel staffing the 54 COTP offices across the
country.[30]

Present COTP Activities in Port Safety

As the chief organizational entity in port and harbor enforcement, the COTP accomplishes a range of day-to-day tasks.
These tasks can be briefly stated to include: (A) protection
and security functions; (B) functions involving the handling of
explosives; (C) the enforcement of the Dangerous Cargo Regulation; (D) the enforcement of Tank Vessel Regulations; and (E)
miscellaneous functions.[31] Each of these tasks will be discussed separately.

A.   The Protection and Security of Vessels, Harbors and
      Waterfront Facilities

The enforcement responsibilities in this area are aimed at
the prevention of accidental or intentional loss or destruction
of vessels or harbor facilities. Under federal law, the responsibilities encompass the following areas:[32]

(a)   Preventing access of persons, articles or things
      to vessels or waterfront facilities;

(b)   Establishing security zones;

(c)   Patrolling harbor areas;

(d)   Visiting and searching vessels or waterfront
      facilities;

(e)   Controlling the movement of vessels in port;

(f)   Conducting a port security card program;

(g)   Supervising the handling of explosives and other
      dangerous cargo;

(h)   Inspecting vessels and waterfront facilities for
      compliance with applicable safety regulations;

(i)   Conducting a public and industry educational program
      to enlist the cooperation of other governmental and
      private agencies to enhance compliance with these
      regulations.

In carrying out these functions, the COTP has authority
only to issue orders; regulations are established by the Commandant. Additionally, the COTP's authority to issue orders is
restricted solely to the safeguarding of port areas and the
included vessels and facilities.[33]

B.   The Handling of Explosives or Other Dangerous Cargoes
     Within Areas Contiguous to Waterfront Facilities

Federal laws and supplementary Coast Guard regulations specify detailed procedures to be followed when handling, storing,
loading or discharging explosives, flammable or combustible
liquids in bulk or other dangerous articles or cargo.[34] The
COTP has authority to issue permits or waivers authorizing particular actions, in addition to basic inspection of vessels and
harbor facilities.

The following functions, Dangerous Cargo Regulation and
Tank Vessel Regulations, are specific functions relating to the
general transport of these hazardous cargoes.

C.   The Enforcement of Dangerous Cargo Regulations

Under the Dangerous Cargo Act of 1970, regulations classifying dangerous cargoes and their stowage aboard vessels were
established, and these regulations apply to all vessels in the
navigable waters of the United States.[35] Basically, Coast Guard
functions involve the identification and classification of hazardous cargoes, supervision of handling and stowage, and under
the Coast Guard's Explosive Loading Details (ELD), the supervision of commercial vessels offloading military explosives.[36]

D.   The Enforcement of Tank Vessel Regulations

    In order to regulate the transport and storage of these
hazardous cargoes, the COTP has enforcement powers concerning
tank vessels, or liquid bulk vessels or barges.[37] Two categories
of vessels are subject to inspection:

    a)   Foreign tank vessels ("compliance vessels") carry-
         ing cargoes of particular hazard (LPG, LNG ships);

    b)   All other foreign or domestic tank vessels or barges
         carrying combustible liquids in bulk.

    The area of hazardous cargo operations and regulation is
a major and difficult role of the Coast Guard. In fiscal year
1969, some 45,168 waterfront facilities were inspected; 5,535
port safety/security violations (of varying types) were detected;
1,218 port security advisory warnings were issued; some 74,734
hours of harbor pollution or anchorage patrols were conducted
in addition to 13,633 hours of port safety promotion; and, in
terms of vessel regulations and hazardous cargo operations,
some 30,909 vessels were boarded, 2,621 vessel violations were
found; and some 40,382 hours were invested by Coast Guard personnel in dangerous cargo supervision.[38]

E.   Miscellaneous Functions of the COTP

    The COTP conducts several other miscellaneous functions at
infrequent intervals. These functions involve disaster control
planning, prevention and detection of illegal entry, and various
anchorage regulations transferred from the Secretary of the Army.

    Disaster control and recovery planning specifies contingency
steps to be taken in the event of an unusual or infrequent occurrence or disaster. Although no specific law or regulation clearly defines these functions, the basic authority is derived from
Title 14 of the U.S.C.[39] and has been subsequently amended by
the Water Quality Act of 1970 and the Ports and Waterways Act
of 1971. The basic areas of interest are:

    a)   Nuclear accidents;

    b)   Pollution incidents (subsequently amended and expanded);

    c)   Hazardous cargo accidents;

    d)   Civil disturbances;

    e)   Emergency utilization of ports.

    Planning is generally done by each District Commander suited
to that district.

    The recent inclusion of pollution control within the sphere
of COTP authority has dominated recent budget improvement requests

in the port safety/security area, traditionally a lower-priority budget item than other mission areas.[40] The estimated 1975 fiscal requests stipulate improvements to be made in cargo security and certain provisions of the Ports and Waterways Safety Act of 1972, to be carried out under the auspices of marine environmental protection activities. Exhibit 8.3 shows the overall Coast Guard budget requests for fiscal year 1975 and the spent appropriations figures for fiscal years 1973 and 1974.

Another COTP function is the Prevention and Detection of Illegal Entry program, or PADIE, an interagency coordinated program to establish a network of government agents to detect attempts of illegal entry and smuggling over the beach.[41] Chiefly, the program is a coordination device.

The Coast Guard, upon transfer to the Department of Transportation in 1967, was given the authority to establish and regulate anchorage grounds for vessels in navigable waters.[42] This duty is carried out by the COTP.

The Merchant Marine Safety Program

The general objective of the Merchant Marine Safety Program is to reduce the loss of life, personal injury and property damage in marine transportation.[43] The program consists of two broad categories under the general headings of construction standards and the enforcement of safety regulations:

1)   The development of construction, operating and repair standards; and

2)   The enforcement of regulations pertaining to ship operations, including the licensing of marine transportation personnel.

The development of construction standards is concerned primarily with assuring that the vessel and shipboard equipment are safe for their intended use, while the regulatory component is to promote vessel and port safety by insuring that the operating vessels, personnel, and so forth, meet various safety standards.[44]

The Office of Merchant Marine Safety is comprised of five divisions, their chief duties being to organize and implement the Marine Safety Program. The Merchant Vessel Personnel division exercises control over the technical competence and licensing of personnel.[45]

Operating expenses for the Office of Merchant Marine Safety have been increasing at roughly 10 percent a year since 1972. Actual fiscal year 1973 funds appropriated were $38.554 million, with estimates for fiscal years 1974 and 1975 at $41.894 million and $47.745 million respectively.[46] These figures are roughly 7 percent of the Total Operating Expenses of the U.S. Coast

EXHIBIT 8.3

DIGEST OF U.S. COAST GUARD BUDGET ESTIMATES BY ACTIVITIES
FOR FISCAL YEAR 1975

Appropriation: Operating Expenses

Program by activities:	1973 Actual		1974 Estimate [1/]		1975 Estimate		Increase or decrease (-) for 1975	
	Full-time perm. pos.	Appropriation	Full-time perm. pos.	Appropriation	Full-time perm. pos.	Appropriation	Full-time perm. pos.	Amount
1. Search and rescue............	12,900	$177,019	13,225	$189,139	13,764	$204,588	539	$15,449
2. Aids to navigation..........	8,441	105,924	8,259	108,666	8,279	113,967	20	5,301
3. Marine safety..............	3,294	38,554	3,388	41,894	3,494	47,745	106	5,851
4. Marine environmental protection..	2,455	22,857	2,764	25,964	3,181	34,888	417	8,924
5. Ocean operations...........	5,691	88,855	5,105	78,890	4,544	78,181	-561	-709
6. Military readiness.........	2,678	26,947	2,564	27,887	2,578	28,307	14	420
7. General support...........	6,209	88,744	6,201	96,954	6,188	104,324	-13	7,370
Total............	41,668	548,900	41,506	569,394	42,028	612,000	522	42,606
(Military)..............	(36,538)	xxx	(36,387)	xxx	(36,910)	xxx	(523)	xxx
(Civilian).............	(5,130)	xxx	(5,119)	xxx	(5,118)	xxx	(-1)	xxx

1/ Includes proposed supplemental of $2,058 thousand for classified pay increase costs (E.O. 11691), $1,706 thousand for wage board pay increase, and $20,230 thousand for military pay increase costs (E.O. 11692).

Summary Explanation of Changes Requested for Fiscal Year 1975

	POSITIONS				AMOUNT BY ACTIVITY							
	Military	Classified	Un-graded	Total	Total	SAR No. 1	AN No. 2	MS No. 3	MEP No. 4	OO No. 5	MR No. 6	GS No. 7
1. Adjustments to base and built-in changes..	...	...	...	...	$42,977	$12,431	$7,424	$4,185	$3,559	$5,540	$2,547	$7,291
2. Operate newly acquired facilities........	652	25	...	677	7,015	2,146	341	54	1,633	2,512	25	304
3. Increase operations................	911	56	...	967	11,347	3,278	757	2,153	4,043	457	275	384
4. Maintain capability of physical plant....	42	52	...	94	1,185	272	230	26	124	251	97	185
5. Recruit, train, and maintain service in all-volunteer environment.............	59	11	...	70	962	249	152	56	52	96	50	307
6. Improve management effectiveness.........	27	16	...	43	662	102	62	23	23	39	20	393
7. Program decreases	-1,168	-161	...	-1,329	-21,542	-3,029	-3,665	-646	-510	-9,604	-2,594	-1,494
TOTAL INCREASE FOR 1975 OVER 1974 APPROPRIATION OR ESTIMATE..................	523	-1	...	522	42,606	15,449	5,301	5,851	8,924	-709	420	7,370

Source: U.S. Coast Guard, OMB Stage Budget, Fiscal Year 1975.

Guard ($570 million for fiscal year 1974) for the fiscal year given.[47]

Control over the development and enforcement of standards is jointly exercised by the other four divisions: Merchant Vessel Inspection, Merchant Marine Technical, Merchant Vessel Documentation, and Cargo and Hazardous Materials. The functions or field implementation of the program (under the two broad categories of inspection and personnel) are carried out by 49 Marine Inspection offices in the United States. These inspection offices are headed by the Officer in Charge, Marine Inspection (OCMI) at each port. Oftentimes, OCMI functions are combined with COTP functions.

The OCMI offices perform the following tasks:[48]

a)   Vessel inspection;

b)   Casualty and personnel investigation;

c)   Licensing and certification of merchant seamen;

d)   Shipment and discharge of seamen; and

e)   Vessel documentation.

Several technical field offices exist under the Office of Merchant Marine Safety to provide review and technical guidance for the OCMI within their respective geographical areas. Additionally, there is a Marine Safety Division in each of the 12 District Offices.[49]

The vessel inspection or "Commercial Vessel Safety Program" of the Marine Safety program begins before the keel of a U.S. flag vessel is laid, and continues through its operating life. Basically, Coast Guard functions are to establish standards of ship design, institute vessel design reviews, inspect during the construction and service of the vessel, initially license ship personnel, and investigate marine casualties.

Design reviews (or "Plan Reviews") are instituted by the Coast Guard to ensure that all designs and alterations are in order before the keel is laid, and subsequently the construction and operation of the vessel is subject to a periodic inspection which comprehensively covers hull, machinery and equipment.

Certificates are issued to all vessels in conformity to these regulations. A vessel must then meet ongoing stability tests (or "seaworthiness"), contingency tests performed when any repair, alteration, or drydocking of the vessel occurs, and, should any casualty occur, the Coast Guard is empowered to investigate and recommend measures to prevent another occurrence of such a case.[50]

The Office of Merchant Marine Safety also licenses maritime

personnel and inspects foreign vessels carrying passengers for
compliance with applicable laws. Additionally, the Coast Guard
inspects foreign vessels carrying hazardous cargoes.[51]

And, as the main maritime enforcement agency, the Office of
Merchant Marine Safety in the Coast Guard is responsible for
investigations of marine casualties, personnel injuries, and
death on board vessels and on platforms in the continental shelf.[52]

Control of Hazardous Materials

Related to vessel transport safety is the regulation of movements of dangerous materials and industrial products in U.S.
waters.[53] Most hazardous cargoes shipped by water in the United
States are products of either the chemical or petroleum industries. The former industry is one of the fastest growing in
the country; the average increase of chemical industry shipments
for the period 1963-1968 was 8 percent compared to an industry
average of 6 percent for the same period.[54]

Petroleum and petrochemical production have also experienced strong growth. The greater annual increases have occurred
in the demand for certain petroleum byproducts, such as liquid
petroleum gas (LPG). For example, LPG experienced a 10 percent
annual increase in demand between 1960 and 1969 (from 620,000
barrels/day in 1960 to 1.5 million barrels/day in 1969).[55]

The Cargo and Hazardous Materials Division of the Office of
Merchant Marine Safety is the principal Coast Guard organization
charged to identify and develop appropriate regulations with
respect to dangerous material transport.

General Authority

General authority for the Coast Guard in hazardous cargo
transport is derived from several sources. The Ports and Waterways Safety Act of 1972 authorizes the Coast Guard through the
Secretary of the Department of Transportation to "establish or
approve procedures, measures, and standards for handling, loading, discharge, storage, stowage, and movement, including the
emergency removal, control, and disposition of...explosives or
other dangerous articles."[56]

The Water Quality Act of 1970 designates specific responsibilities to the President relative to the control of hazardous
polluting substances.[57] Excerpts of relevant parts of this Act
state:[58]

Sec. 12(a) The President shall...develop, promulgate
and revise, as may be appropriate, regulations (1)
designating as hazardous materials, other than oil...
such elements and compounds which when discharged in
any quantity into or upon the navigable waters of the
United States...present an imminent and substantial

danger to the public health or welfare...; and (2)
establishing, if appropriate, recommended methods and
means for removal of such substances.

Sec. 12(d) Whenever any hazardous substance is discharged into or upon the navigable waters of the United
States...unless removal is immediately undertaken by
the owner or operator of the vessel or facility from
which the discharge occurs...the President, if appropriate, shall remove or arrange thereof...

And, under the general duties of the Coast Guard specified
in Title 14 of the U.S.C., the service is charged to protect
life and property in the event of marine disasters, floods and
other natural disasters, or national emergencies.[59]

The Hazardous Materials Transportation Control Act of 1970
delegates responsibility to the Secretary of Transportation for
the safe transportation of dangerous cargoes.[60] Under this general legislative authority, the Coast Guard has participated in
several department-wide projects begun in accordance with this
overall directive. Specifically, one such project involves the
development of new definitions and classifications for all materials that present hazards in transportation, and another involves a similar reassessment and development of standards for
packaging of dangerous cargoes.[61]

Specific Authority

   The specific legal authorization to implement the general
policy directives contained in Title 14 of the U.S.C., the Ports
and Waterways Safety Act of 1972, and the Water Quality Act of
1970, is scattered. Under Coast Guard initiative, extensive
regulations applying to specific cargoes have been issued by the
Commandant and incorporated in Title 46 of the Code of Federal
Regulations.* The Captain of the Port's responsibilities in the
area of hazardous cargo transport are specified in Title 33 of the
Code of Federal Regulations; basically these regulations are
general in nature and apply to the handling and storage of dangerous cargoes. And, under a general program in DOT to implement the
Hazardous Materials Transportation Control Act of 1970, the Coast
Guard is reviewing and updating regulations and special permits to
embrace improving technologies and recent safety information.[62]

---

*Coast Guard regulations pertaining to specific bulk liquid car-
goes carried by foreign vessels are contained in "Navigation
and Vessel Inspection Circular No. 13-65," 30 Sept. 1965 (46
CFR 2.01-13), as updated by "Navigation and Vessel Inspection
Circular No. 6-73," 13 June 1973. These circulars identify
certain liquid bulk cargoes as dangerous, as establish procedures
for plan review and vessel inspection for foreign vessels carrying such cargoes.

Additionally, the control and movement of such vessels in U.S.
waters is subject to certain regulations in accordance with
33 CFR, Part 6.

The Office of Merchant Marine Safety periodically publishes safety information on dangerous materials. A comprehensive Chemical Data Guide for bulk shipment of hazardous materials was recently updated (the previous addition was published in 1969) and distributed.

The Chemical Transportation Industry Advisory Committee, an industry group with representatives appointed by the Commandant of the Coast Guard, was restructured in 1971 (it had been the "Chemical Transportation Advisory Panel") to facilitate greater industry assistance to the Coast Guard in developing regulations for hazardous vessels and waterfront facilities.[63]

In the international field, Coast Guard representation on the Inter-Governmental Maritime Consultative Organization (IMCO) and its various committees has brought about greater dialogue and technical information exchange on a world scale.* Several improvements, among them international regulations for portable tanks carrying dangerous materials and the instigation of ongoing studies into the properties of Liquefied Natural Gas (LNG) under transport and storage, have resulted.

Vessel Traffic Control Systems

Interrelated in both discussions of Port Safety/Security and Merchant Marine Safety is the control of marine traffic in America's oftentimes congested waterways and harbors. While it is obvious that some type of marine traffic control would be a useful tool in reducing accidents and collisions, traffic systems are new to the marine industry. Until early 1970 there were minimal marine traffic systems operating at only select ports in United States waters.[64] In view of the economic value of the ships, the cargo carried, and the potential risk to life, it is

---

*Under the Subcommittee on Ship Design and Equipment, IMCO, the two basic bulk liquid cargo regulations (developed with U.S. Coast Guard assistance) are:

Chemical:

 "Code for the Construction and Equipment of Ships
 Carrying Dangerous Chemicals in Bulk," A VIII/
 Res. 212, 29 Oct. 1971.

Gas:

 "Code for the Construction and Equipment of Ships
 Carrying Liquefied Gases in Bulk," DE/92,
 20 Sept. 1973, Working Paper.

(Note: Gas Code to be fully completed by 1975)

difficult to understand why the maritime industry has not in-
stalled systems, or developed regulations to accomplish the
former, themselves. A study conducted by the Coast Guard outlines one problem as industry bureaucracy:[65]

> ...the variety and number of recognizable interests
> involved in this area of the maritime scene are numer-
> ous, diverse, political, and bureaucratic. The mari-
> time industry, the oldest in the movement of bulk mate-
> rials, is quite conservative. Significant changes in
> this industry are costly and take years to accomplish.
> Furthermore, the industry is one of the most non-
> standardized industries in the transportation field.
> Only with the recent advent of containerized cargo has
> there been any attempt at standardization of facilities,
> equipment or procedures. Standardized Marine Traffic
> Systems for this mode of transportation will for these
> reasons be unique in this country.

The Coast Guard went on to note that the goal of an efficient traffic control system should be "to integrate the ports
and waterways components in order to provide fast, safe, efficient and convenient movement of traffic...without stifling the
flow of commerce or infringing upon the rights of users through
unnecessary controls, rules or regulations.[66]

Objectives of a Marine Traffic System

The steps toward accomplishing the goal of "safe and efficient movement of traffic" have been stated by the Coast Guard
in the following manner:[67]

a.   Identify the ports and waterways where a high acci-
     dent potential exists;

b.   Measure or quantify the potential magnitude of
     that accident hazard;

c.   Determine the most cost-effective method(s) for
     reducing the hazard(s).

Accordingly, the planning of Coast Guard efforts in vessel
traffic control systems might be stated as to include both an
educational function and an operational function. The policy
instigation of other functions, although there have been some
exceptions, is a recent phenomenon.

New Administrative Frameworks

Alerted to a growing public concern over the potential for
increased numbers of vessel casualties occurring in U.S. waters,
the Congress enacted the Ports and Waterways Safety Act of 1972
on July 10, 1972.[68] This Act, among other things, authorizes
the Secretary of the Department in which the Coast Guard operates to "establish, operate and maintain vessel traffic services

and systems for ports, harbors, and other waters subject to
congested vessel traffic."[69]

Since 1972, Congress has authorized $1.68 million (through
fiscal year 1974 estimates) to implement various Titles of the
Act, and the program has a Coast Guard officer commitment of
64 personnel.[70] Anticipating the passage of this bill, the Coast
Guard developed in July of 1971 preliminary concepts to guide the
implementation of vessel traffic services and systems.[71]

A Major VTS Study

In February 1972, a broad-based Vessel Traffic System Study
was initiated by the Coast Guard.[72] The objectives of this study
were stated as follows:[73]

1. Identify specific VTS program goals, anticipated
    benefits, and alternatives.

2. Analyze the potential VTS roles of federal, state
    and local authorities, and private enterprise; and
    recommend the most beneficial role for the Coast
    Guard.

3. Analyze the quantitative and qualitative factors
    to be considered in the determination of the needs
    for various levels of VTS in U.S. ports.

4. Prepare short- and long-range staffing and funding
    plans.

5. Prepare a management plan to use as a guide in plan-
    ning, development, and implementing new systems.

The study was initiated in two stages. The first was to
seek contractual assistance for three specific tasks:[74]

a) develop a conceptual framework for VTS;

b) identify the potential roles of participants;

c) develop an algorithm to determine the need for
    various levels of vessel traffic system in U.S.
    ports and waterways.

The second stage was the formation of a Coast Guard study
group to "manage the contract study, to respond to the issues
not covered by the contract, and to develop a management plan
for the VTS program."[75]

Completed in March of 1973, the systems study concluded
that the need for vessel traffic systems was based on three major
facts: that the incidence and severity of marine casualties
and loss of life associated with these casualties was rising,
but could be alleviated in part by collision avoidance systems;
that the estimated 2.35 million gallons of pollutants spilled in

U.S. waters in 1971 could be substantially controlled by avoiding collisions and groundings; and that a positive consensus existed in the maritime community towards improving marine traffic management and safety.[76]

Additionally, the Coast Guard study noted that to facilitate interport and intraport movements at an acceptable cost, automated communications procedures should be more fully developed and implemented. The study states:[77]

> The best way to meet anticipated future demands on vessel traffic systems lies in automation and high precision navigation systems. In the most congested sectors of a busy port or waterway sophisticated control procedures based on automation will be needed...

In view of the number of ports and waterways serving the United States, and the differences in vessels using those ports, the implementation of any vessel traffic program on a broad scale is a massive undertaking. The practical solution proposed by the study group is to designate "priority ports," or ports with high accident potential, selected on the basis of a mathematical model utilizing cost-benefit criteria.*

Initially, two pilot programs were developed in San Francisco Bay and Puget Sound in 1972, and tentative schedules call for three additional systems to become operational in the near future.[78] These pilot programs, and several less extensive systems,[79] were selected on the basis of suitability for experimental programs before a more formalized implementation schedule was set up. Accordingly, the quantitative modeling structure applies to decisions made for fiscal year 1976 and beyond.[80]

---

*The model uses recent empirical data to estimate expected casualty losses by vessel type, and then uses a combination of empirical data and judgment to determine the expected reduction in losses if a VTS is implemented or improved. The four quantifiable loss categories included in the model are:

a)   Vessel and cargo damage in dollars;

b)   Property damage in dollars;

c)   Pollution in incidents or gallons; and

d)   Deaths and injuries by number.

The latter component of the model, a combination of empirical data and judgment, is based on varied statistics for each port, together with operating experience in the harbor area. As such, this component is being updated and refined by upgrading statistical measures and refining criteria for judging operational experience (see U.S.C.G. Study Report, "Vessel Traffic Systems Study," Final Report, Vol. 1, Executive Summary, March 1973, pp. 12-17).

Included in the determination of a VTS for any specific site are the various options for funding, operation and manning of such systems.[81] User charges have been considered, and are presently under review by the Office of the Secretary of Transportation.

A Management Proposal

The vessel traffic program, administered by the Marine Traffic Management Branch of the Office of Marine Environment and Systems, is presently combined with the Port Safety/Security program. As such, a high degree of coordination is required with related programs such as commercial vessel safety, and environmental protection.

The VTS study also recommended that marine traffic management "be established as a separate and distinct entity within the Coast Guard program's structure," and that it be organized under the "cognizant Captain of the Port, either as a sub-command or an integral section."[82]

Fire Fighting and Fire Prevention

There is no nationwide policy setting forth fire prevention or fire fighting standards for the ports and waterways of the United States.[83] Fire prevention codes vary greatly throughout the country, and as a result many ports in the United States are poorly equipped to combat fires. Moreover, it is not the smaller ports which most frequently dominate the fire response listing kept by the Coast Guard: a recent Coast Guard study noted that the geographical areas in which the Coast Guard responded to fire alarms most frequently included Boston, Massachusetts; New York, New York; Norfolk, Virginia; New Orleans, Louisiana; and San Francisco, California.[84]

The inclusion of these major ports suggests that the problem lies less in the fiscal resources area than in the education and regulation area. Accordingly, Coast Guard efforts in this area have focused to some extent on airing the problems and possible solutions in an overall attempt to improve fire fighting capabilities.[85]

General Authority

No specific statutory authority delegates to the Coast Guard responsibility for fire fighting. Under generalized legislative mandates and duties, the Coast Guard assists in fire fighting and prevention. However, as noted before, oftentimes Coast Guard facilities comprise the major fire fighting hardware in port areas and, in some cases, such fire fighting hardware is the only system available.[86]

Under Title 14 of the U.S.C., the Coast Guard "may render aid to persons and property at any time and at any place at which

Coast Guard facilities and personnel are available and can be
effectively utilized."[87] Additionally, federal law authorizes
federal agency heads charged with the duty of providing fire
protection for any property of the United States "to enter into
reciprocal agreements with fire organizations maintaining fire
protection facilities in the vicinity of such property, for
mutual aid in furnishing fire protection for such property and
for other property for which such organization normally provides
fire protection."[88]

The Ports and Waterways Safety Act of 1971 authorizes the
Secretary of the Department in which the Coast Guard is operating
to "prescribe minimum equipment requirements for structures and
facilities to assure adequate protection from fire, explosion,
natural disasters, and other serious accidents or casualities."[89]
Accordingly, the implementation of the provisions of this Act,
and the responsibilities authorized under the various Titles of
the U.S.C., are incorporated into the existing field operations
of the U.S. Coast Guard, specifically the Captain of the Port.

Additionally, the Commandant may prescribe "conditions and
restrictions relating to the safety of waterfront facilities and
vessels in port including, but not limited to, inspection, operation, maintenance, guarding, and manning of, and fire prevention
measures, as he finds necessary under the circumstances."[90]

Budget Limitations on the Merchant Marine Safety Program

Thus, the marine safety mission, incorporating these related,
technically complex areas of hazardous materials regulation,
vessel inspection, fire fighting and fire prevention, and others,
is tied together under the general designation of Merchant
Marine Safety. Taken in relationship with other program areas
in the Coast Guard, marine safety has not received the measure
of funding and manpower accorded to other mission areas such as
Search and Rescue, Operations, and so forth.

Recent indications point to higher percentage increases in
the appropriations requests for the program, however. For fiscal
year 1975, request estimates are set at $47.7 million versus a
fiscal year 1974 estimate of $41.8 million, up $5.9 million or
12 percent. Search and Rescue budget figures for the same time
period were $204.588 million (fiscal year 1975 estimate) and
$189.13 million (fiscal year 1974 estimate), up $5.49 million
or 7.5 percent.[91]

Marine Pollution

The public and governmental interest in the marine environment has prompted the establishment of the Coast Guard as the
lead agency in the regulation and enforcement of marine pollution
abatement and control. A myriad of complementary projects and
programs to deal with environmental problems are presently underway throughout the federal government, and specifically the

Coast Guard. (In addition to the marine pollution control efforts
within the federal government, the international movement of tankers has also required greater ongoing international cooperation.)

Statutory Authority in the Marine Pollution Area

Coast Guard involvement in the enforcement of marine pollution laws specifically rests with four major Acts and their
amendments:[92]

   a)   The Refuse Act of 1899;

   b)   The Oil Pollution Act of 1961, as amended;

   c)   The Federal Water Pollution Control Act (FWPCA),
        as amended by the Water Quality Improvement
        Act of 1970; and

   d)   The International Convention for the Prevention
        of Pollution of the Sea by Oil, 1954, as amended.

Additionally, the National Environmental Policy Act of 1969
directs each federal agency to prepare a detailed statement of
the environmental impact of any proposed major action.[93]

Under the Water Quality Improvement Act of 1970 (WQIA),
the Congress stated that "it is the policy of the United States
that there should be no discharge of oil into or upon the navigable waters of the United States."[94] Pursuant to this policy
statement, the Congress charged the President, and specifically
the Council on Environmental Quality, with the preparation and
publication of a National Oil Pollution Contingency Plan.[95]

Published by the Council in June 1970, the National Oil and
Hazardous Materials Pollution Contingency Plan is "to provide for
efficient, coordinated, and effective action to minimize damage
from oil discharge, including containment, dispersal, and removal
of oil."[96] Coast Guard responsibilities under the plan are
numerous. These duties include membership on the National Inter-
Agency Committee (planning committee), membership on the National Response Team (and Regional Response Teams), On-Scene Commander responsibilities and Strike Force responsibilities.[97] These
committees are charged with the responsibility for the coordination and administration of cleaning up oil spills on the high
seas, coastal and contiguous zone waters, and coastal and Great
Lakes port and harbor areas.[98]

Administrative Framework: The Marine Environmental Protection
Program

The Maritime Pollution Control Branch of the Law Enforcement Division was created in 1969 within the Office of Operations
to assist in developing and administering the Marine Environmental Protection Program. The objectives of this program, in
response to Coast Guard responsibilities under the various environmental acts cited, were basically fivefold:[99]

a)   General responsibilities in implementing a program
     to respond to the President's call for environmen-
     tal protective measures;

b)   The enforcement of anti-pollution laws, i.e., the
     detecting, investigating, and reporting of marine
     pollution violations under their basic statutory
     authority;

c)   Responsibility for responding to polluting spills
     in both a preventative and curative way;

d)   The abatement of pollution by Coast Guard vessels
     and shore stations; and

e)   Regulatory functions essentially directing the
     Coast Guard to issue and enforce subsequent regu-
     lations pertaining to pollution from vessels and
     harbor facilities.

In 1970, the Pollution Control Branch became part of the
newly established Office of Marine Environment and Systems (W).
Under this Office, the Branch directed its efforts toward coordinating a national response to pollution spills and other incidents.

The Coast Guard's antipollution efforts at the local level
are administered through the Port Safety/Security program.[100]
Approximately 1,300 men assigned to the 54 COTPs throughout the
country enforce, in addition to other responsibilities, pollution
laws.[101] This group provides the curative and preventative aspects of the program. That is, the former involves on-scene assistance to local authorities during cleanup operations, and the
latter, or preventative component, involves routine harbor patrols
to prevent unlawful discharges of oil cited under federal law.[102]

Under the WQIA as implemented by Executive Order 11507,
the Coast Guard is required to take steps to prevent air and
water pollution from its vessels and facilities.[103] And, as an
enforcement agency for federal antipollution laws, it is highly
important that the Service implement a strong program to stress
leadership in this area.

Funding support for pollution activities by the Coast Guard
has been expanding rapidly. Appropriations in fiscal year 1972
for the marine environmental protection program were set at
$27.19 million, and have risen to a request of $41.26 million in
fiscal year 1974 estimates.[104] These funds are directed heavily
toward research and development in hardware (pollution abatement
systems) items to be described in the following section.

Additionally, since 1965 the Coast Guard has spent on the
order of $100,000 per year of either Operations or Research and
Development funds towards the installation of pollution abatement
equipment on its vessels and facilities.[105] Present planning

anticipates compliance with all existing air and water quality standards by Coast Guard vessels in 1975.[106]

Research and Development

A major part of Coast Guard efforts in the marine pollution field is directed towards continuing research in the design and operation of marine pollution abatement equipment. These abatement activities are centered in five general areas:[107]

a)   Sewage Pollution;

b)   Oil Pollution;

c)   Air Pollution;

d)   General Marine Pollution; and

e)   Hazardous Materials Control.

Since 1968, the Environmental Protection Agency and the U.S. Coast Guard have coordinated their efforts in the research and development field.[108] Generally, EPA efforts have concentrated on techniques for oil pollution abatement suitable for sheltered water, and the Coast Guard has concentrated on rough water equipment.

Three supportive systems are necessary to effectively combat offshore spills. These are:[109]

a)   Systems to reduce the quantity of oil released
     in a tanker accident;

b)   An oil containment system effective on the high
     seas;

c)   Oil harvesting equipment which can be operated
     at sea.

Several types of systems are presently under development in these general categories. One such system is the Air-Delivered Anti-Pollution Transfer System (ADAPTS).

Consisting of pumping and parachute delivery subsystems, ADAPTS is an emergency system designed to unload oil from undamaged cargo tanks in high-risk situations, as that of a grounded tanker in danger of breaking up due to heavy sea conditions. A technical discussion of this, and other pollution control and abatement systems, is contained in a February 1973 Technology Review article entitled "Marine Oil Pollution Control."[110]

In implicitly arguing that the level of technology in marine pollution control is still in its primacy, the article concludes by offering a status report on the general field of marine pollution control:[111]

Since the "Torrey Canyon" episode significant progress
has been made in improving our capability to cope with
oil spills. New regulations, vessel traffic systems,
shipboard oil/water separation equipment, and sensor
equipment for improved law enforcement should all foster reductions in the number of pollutant incidents...
Though this article emphasizes activities of the U.S.
Coast Guard, readers should recognize that a considerable worldwide effort is underway...

But much remains to be done. Systems now under development must be completed, and new prevention and law
enforcement procedures must be implemented. Spill
response systems effective in high currents still are
lacking. And specialized equipment and procedures to
cope with oil spills in cold climates remain to be
studied.   The forces which man can bring to bear often
prove puny beside those of nature against which they
are arrayed.

Additional Duties and Responsibilities of the U.S. Coast Guard

The previous discussion has identified the major programs
of the Coast Guard with respect to ports and waterways policy,
operations and management. A discussion of two additional program areas with indirect impacts on ports and waterways policy
follows.*

Emergency Preparedness

Under Executive Order 11490, "Assigning Emergency Preparedness Functions to Federal Departments and Agencies," the Department of Transportation is charged with several safety and enforcement powers relative to the marine field.[112] Section 1303,
Departmental Emergency Transportation Preparedness, states that
the department's responsibilities include:

(5) Maritime safety and law enforcement over, upon,
and under the high seas and waters, subject to the
jurisdiction of the United States, in the following
specific programs:

(a) Safeguarding vessels, harbors, ports, and waterfront facilities from destruction, loss or injury,
accidents, or other causes of a similar nature.

(b) Safe passage over, upon, and under the high seas
and United States waters through effective and reliable systems of aids to navigation and ocean stations.

---

*This report specifically treats those program and policy areas
related to port operations and development. Several general
sources on the Coast Guard, such as Kaplan, This Is The Coast
Guard, give a broad account of all duties of the agency.

(c) Waterborne access to ice-bound locations in fur-
therance of national economic, scientific, defense,
and consumer needs.

(e) Safety of life and property through regulation of
commercial vessels, their officers and crew, and
administration of maritime safety law.

(f) Knowledge of the sea, its boundaries, and its resources through collection and analysis of data in
support of the national interest.

These duties and responsibilities have been delegated to
the Coast Guard in time of emergency by the Secretary of Transportation.

Bridge Administration Program

The Bridge Administration Program of the U.S. Coast Guard
is charged with insuring the "safe and unencumbered passage of
marine traffic on the Nation's waterways; and to insure, in
cooperation with other modal administrations, that the needs of
all using surface transportation are met without unduly impeding
marine transportation."[113]

Statutory authority for this program is derived from the
Department of Transportation Act[114] which transferred from the
Department of Defense the duties of the Secretary of the Army
and the Corps of Engineers relating to bridges.[115] Under the
Coast Guard program, applications for bridge permits are reviewed
to insure that unreasonable obstructions to navigation in U.S.
waterways are avoided. The Commandant may declare certain
bridges to be unreasonable obstructions to navigation subsequent
to investigations and public hearings.[116] The bridge is then
either redesigned, or an alternate site is proposed.

Coast Guard Planning and Programming - An Overview

The planning and programming process of the Coast Guard is
subject to continued administrative change and refinement. The
following section is a summary discussion of the general structure and concepts inherent in the development of Coast Guard
plans and programs. A detailed treatment on the subject is contained in Appendix G.

Plans and Programming Definitions

Prior to the transfer of the Coast Guard to the Department
of Transportation, marine transportation programs administered
by the organization were broadly categorized under two major
subject headings: (a) assistance to marine commerce, and (b)
military readiness.[117]

Upon transfer to the Department, active programs of the
Coast Guard were classified into 22 categories.[118] These pro-

gram definitions were expanded because of the utilization of
the Planning-Programming-Budgeting-System by the Department of
Transportation in 1967.

Although the basic programs of the Coast Guard remained
unaltered, internal planning techniques adopted by the Service
in response to PPBS increased the number of program classifications. As originally set down, the concept of the PPB system
called for:[119]

1. Designing for each government agency an output-
    oriented program structure under which data on
    all operations and activities can be presented
    in categories that reflect the agency's purpose
    or objectives.

2. Making analyses, in terms of costs, effectiveness
    and benefits of possible alternatives for meeting
    agency program objectives.

3. Translating decisions on programs into financial
    budgets for consideration and action by the Presi-
    dent and the Congress with subsequent devising of
    operating budgets for management control purposes.

The major intent of this process was that documented objectives, criteria, and benefits became a significant part of the
analytical process in arriving at an informed judgment. Additionally, this reporting format also facilitated measuring the
efficiency of the organization. Before the application of PPBS,
the Coast Guard reported output only.[120]

While newer managerial techniques of analysis have replaced
PPBS (Management by Objective, "MBO"), the practical and theoretical genesis of measuring administrative efficiencies in quantitative terms was initiated in the PPB system.

Planning and Program Structure

Program objectives and the planning system needed to implement such objectives are basically formulated at two levels
within the Coast Guard. The overall objectives for all program
areas within the Service are the responsibility of the Commandant of the Coast Guard and his headquarters staff.[121] At the
headquarters level, plans and program objectives are evaluated,
program budgets are developed and finalized, and plans and program recommendations from the second policy level, the Field
or Operations level, are evaluated for possible implementation.

At the Field level, District Commanders and District Division
Chiefs formulate objectives consistent with the general principles
and goals set down by the Commandant, towards the implementation
of their respective responsibilities. Consequently, the field
commanders may exercise a strong influence on the overall policies
of the Coast Guard.

This dual Headquarters-Field-level planning (within overall objectives set down by the Commandant) promotes a direct cross-fertilization of planning and program opinions between the field representatives of the organization and the administrative hierarchy of the Service.

Plans Implementation

Headquarters-level planning is facilitated through the Program Director who is responsible for translating overall policy guidelines into plans and program development. The Program Manager assisting the Director is then responsible for the continuous review and implementation of these programs. Symmetrical implementation structures have been set up at the Field level.

Budget Preparation

Preparation of the annual budget is closely tied to the program area emphasis of the Coast Guard. An OMB stage budget is prepared in the fall of each year by Coast Guard Headquarters and, after required adjustments, is transmitted to Congress. In February (of the budget year) the Programs Division at Coast Guard Headquarters supplies field commanders with budget information necessary for the submission of their respective budget requests. Budget changes, reallocations of resources, and so forth, are accomplished through a variety of formal and informal methods (see Appendix G).

Long-Range View

In addition to the regularized planning and programming processes, the Coast Guard prepares a long-range policy statement which attempts to forecast where the Service will be in ten years.

Port Policy and the U.S. Coast Guard: An Analysis of Its Changing Role and Some Recent Policy Imperatives

The combined effects of a changing maritime technological base and a growing rational environmental awareness have placed additional pressures and responsibilities on the implementation of Coast Guard policies and programs. Technological imperatives for policy change can be seen in the adoption of regulatory legislation for deepwater port development and in the increasingly voluminous transport of hazardous cargoes in U.S. waters. New environmental protection responsibilities have supplemented traditional Coast Guard duties and have placed additional demands on existing agency resources. Furthermore, as a consequence of its participation and activities in these policy areas, the visibility and administrative role of the Coast Guard in the marine policy-making system has been heightened.

However, the movement of the agency into these policy areas
will engender certain organizational dilemmas for the Coast Guard.
Traditionally the agency has not devoted a large percentage of its
resources to activities which will now require such support. This
emphasis will place added demands on the resources of the organization, and thereby raise administrative questions over the allocation of personnel and material.

In view of these new and added responsibilities, the Commandant of the Coast Guard has urged sizable expansions to the organization. As reported in August 1974:[122]

The Commandant of the U.S. Coast Guard says that this
often overlook^d service is about to take on a new importance, and must expand.

Adm. Owen W. Siler said Thursday the extension of the
3-mile limit off U.S. shores, the construction of deep
water ports and the starting of tanker traffic to bring
Alaska oil south will all add to the Coast Guard's
mission.

He pointed out that the replacement of the 3-mile limit
with a 12-mile limit, supplemented by a 200-mile
"economic zone" offshore, is now being discussed at
the Law of the Sea Conference in Caracas, Venezuela.
Bills have been introduced in both the House and Senate
to make the same changes unilaterally.

...He estimated that to handle this and other new enforcement duties, the Coast Guard needs an increase in its
present $800 million annual budget by about $14 million.
He said the Coast Guard also needs six more ships and
would like to acquire 40 new jet patrol planes. They
would be its first jet planes. Additional manpower
requirements have not yet been determined.

The Coast Guard currently has 38,000 military personnel,
7,000 civilians, 300 ships and about 180 aircraft.

Moreover, the Coast Guard has received some implicit support
for its expansion aims from those groups or organizations which
point out the difficulties the agency faces in implementing its
regulatory responsibilities consistent with new legislative guidelines. For example, a recent committee report to the President
and the Congress states:[123]

The recent passage of significant environmental legislation impacts the USCG--to the point that the laws
may not be adequately enforced or enforceable because
of the limited manpower and material to do the job.

To the extent that new regulatory responsibilities will
require additional enforcement capability, expansion of the organization in both field and administrative components appears
inevitable.

Technological Imperatives for Policy Change

Under the Deepwater Port Act of 1974,[124] the Secretary of
the Department of Transportation was charged with overall licensing authority for the development of superport terminal facilities.* The Coast Guard was delegated the task of regulating the
operations of these facilities.

Prior to the January 1975 signing of the Act and in anticipation of its expected regulatory role, the Coast Guard established a Deepwater Ports Project within the organization in July
of 1974.[125] This project investigated the ongoing port safety,
navigation, and environmental responsibilities anticipated under
new deepwater port legislation.

Several elements of Coast Guard vessel and port safety
duties and responsibilities may have direct economic effects
on deepwater port operators. Under the Ports and Waterways
Safety Act of 1972,[126] the Coast Guard may legally determine
maximum wave heights, or minimal climatic conditions, under
which supertankers can moor to offshore ports and terminal systems. In being able to establish regulations in this area,
Coast Guard actions will clearly impact on the economics of specific deepwater port sites, in addition to exerting possible influence over the types of facilities envisioned

Furthermore, numerous Coast Guard regulations and services
will impact on the economics of transporting Alaskan oil to the
mainland. In the services area, the amount of icebreaker service will affect ship operator schedules and port-of-calls,
hence directly influencing the economics of the transportation
operations. In the case of regulations, possible Coast Guard
requirements for vessel design features such as double bottoms
on tankers, in addition to other possible safety and pollution
equipment requirements, will also have important economic impacts.

In the hazardous cargo transport area, Coast Guard regulations, such as those promulgated for LNG and LPG ship construction, have important economic impacts. Moreover, some legislative thought has recently been given to charging the Coast
Guard with a major role in determining acceptable sites for
LNG terminal facilities--again with obvious, important economic
implications.[127]

As a consequence of these policy imperatives, the Coast
Guard is being administratively drawn into the area of considering the economic implications of its regulatory policies and
programs. The agency's strategy for incorporation of the new
dimensions into its traditional mechanisms for policy formation
constitutes a major short- and long-term challenge to the
organization.

---

*A discussion of the Act and its legislative provisions is con-
tained in Chapter 9.

Environmental Imperatives for Policy Change

New environmental legislation has added many policy and
program responsibilities to the traditional operations of the
Coast Guard. As the lead maritime pollution control organization, the Coast Guard enforces a myriad of antipollution laws
and regulations (both preventative and curative) pertaining to
vessel containment systems, pollution identification and recovery techniques and hardware, harbor pollution patrols and facility inspections, and so forth.

As a pervasive addition to Coast Guard policy and program
formation and development, environmental duties comprise major
challenges to Coast Guard implementation of its operational
regulatory responsibilities.

CHAPTER 9

THE DEPARTMENT OF TRANSPORTATION

Introduction

Since its inception in 1966, the Office of the Secretary of the Department of Transportation (DOT) has not been substantively involved in maritime transportation activities. This area was characteristically left to its marine operational regulatory component, the U.S. Coast Guard. However, recent policy events have thrust the Office of the Secretary (OST) into a more direct and important role in the maritime transportation area.

Under the Deepwater Port Act of 1974, the Secretary of Transportation is charged with the overall licensing authority for the development of offshore superport facilities.* In the administrative licensing process for these facilities, the Secretary must consider the "economic, social and environmental effects of the construction and operation of a deepwater port" with other competing terminal facilities (including deep-dredged harbors). As a consequence of this legislation, the Secretary must therefore require an increased OST effort in developing and coordinating the appropriate technical and administrative capabilities to facilitate these new marine transportation responsibilities.

In its role of presenting testimony before legal proceedings concerning transportation issues and controversies, the DOT is also being drawn into a more active policy role regarding port and maritime activities. The "mini-landbridge" and related rate-absorption cases pending before the Federal Maritime Commission will have important policy impacts on the role of DOT in water transportation policy.** Since decisions in these cases affect the movement of commodities by rail across the country to port load centers, the intermodal character of any FMC decision will pose questions of strategic transportation policy importance to the DOT. As a function of these concerns, the department is participating in these FMC proceedings.

Furthermore, the current policy debate over user taxes*** and the introduction of legislation in Congress to create a new Inland Waterways Administration within DOT has focused attention on the role of the department in water transportation policy. While the DOT currently has modal administrations for aviation, highway, railway and mass transit systems, the department has traditionally resisted suggestions to move into a more active role in developing maritime transportation policy. However, the policy imperatives for change exhibited in these and other maritime areas will institutionally move the department into a more active water policy role. The administrative effects of these policy changes will be discussed as a component of this chapter's

---

*See later discussion in this chapter.

**See Chapter 4 discussion.

***See Chapter 4 discussion.

treatment of the history, organization, and program implementation
of the department.

Transportation Concepts and the "Power of the Past"

The five major modes of transport in this country have
emerged at different times, and the regulatory policies affecting
them have likewise been developed and intertwined with policy
considerations of the past and present. The steamboat, our first
mode of transport services by mechanical power, was soon followed
by the steam locomotive and the development of railroads. These
two modes of transportation dominated until after World War I
when the evolution of automobiles, trucks, airplanes, and pipelines
began to occur. The importance of the railroads on our nation's
overall transportation thinking cannot be stressed enough. One
author has stated:[1]

> The history of transportation in the United States for
> the last three-quarters of the 19th century, particular-
> ly the last half, and the first quarter of the 20th
> century was the history of railroads. From 1860 to
> 1920 the railroad was literally the sole supplier of
> inland transport except for the limited and restricted
> role of water. Public policy, especially with regard
> to regulation, was confined almost exclusively to the
> railroads, while transport economics and railroad econ-
> omics were practically synonymous terms. The develop-
> ment of the program of regulation around the idea of
> railroads as natural monopolies led to the belief that
> all transport needed to be regulated in this fashion,
> with the result that the extension of regulation to
> the other agencies after 1920 was patterned in this
> mold. Thus the history of transportation in the modern
> industrial world has been until very recently the history
> of railroads, and the shaping of public policy with
> regard to transport for the past 150 years has been the
> result of the problems connected with the railroads.

This "power of the past" in many phases of federal involvement in planning for transportation continues to exert a strong
influence in the present. As one author notes, one "need but
examine the lasting influences of early economic commitments, laws,
administrative actions, and political decisions to sense the
"layered" quality of present-day transportation development."[2]

This "layering" of development has brought with it a broadening context of the role transportation plays in modern community
life. In its narrowest sense, transportation provides for the
movement of people and goods. But in the broader context, it is
instrumental in organizing and maintaining community life.

In this sense, analysts have argued that the nature of
transportation problems encompasses not merely one sector of the
economy, but a link between sectors. To improve transportation
for its own sake, they argue, is erroneous unless such improvement
serves other objectives as well. Central to this argument is

the institutional avoidance of planning and managing transport
in isolation from the rest of the economy.[3]

National leaders in both the private and public spheres
generally interpret transportation systems as a means for accomplishing other objectives[4] and, as such, policy development has
usually been linked to the need and functionality of transport
service. As such, the historical pattern of public policy and
transportation is that the policy aspects came into focus after
the emergence of the transport system.

Such a pattern of development suggests that the modes of
governmental control over such an enterprise would necessarily
fall into a regulatory, as distinguished from a planning, sphere.
The notion of transportation planning necessitates the defining
of transportation objectives, system alternatives, facility and
system construction plans, and so on. While the need for the
development of such definitions was recognized by government
leaders, the notion of a national transportation policy did not
advance significantly until after the Second World War. And it
was not until the establishment of the Department of Transportation in 1966 that the Congress created under one roof an agency
with a mandate to coordinate transportation planning.[5]

Accordingly, the Department of Transportation is to some
extent a brokerage house for a variety of specialized regulatory
functions which had traditionally operated apart from each other.[6]
Its effectiveness in the strategic planning of transportation
objectives and policies thus lies to an important degree in the
department's ability to coordinate a variety of specialized
interest groups while redefining transportation objectives along
national policy guidelines.

As such, the functions of the DOT could be viewed as consisting of two somewhat competing interests: a) that of defining
and solving overall national transportation problems; and b) that
of dealing with traditional transportation interest groups and
constituencies in politically acceptable ways. This situation
is complicated by the limited control the DOT may exercise in the
implementation of transportation solutions, and the limitations
on the capital allocation powers of the department.

The development of national transportation policies must
therefore be accomplished by careful applications of rules, regulations and programs which are carried out under a coordinated
development plan. As a function of these interests, this chapter of the report will discuss the Department of Transportation
in four ways: 1) the early proposals calling for a transportation department; 2) the establishment of the Department of Transportation and its organizational structure; 3) programs, goals,
and national transportation policies of the DOT relating to waterways, ports and harbors, and shipping; and 4) future transportation issues.

The Beginnings

Early interest in nationwide planning for transportation
was at best a paradoxical pursuit when judged against the early
American tradition of local self-government and indulgence in
sectional and state interests.[7] The author of one such paradoxical proposal was an early Secretary of the Treasury, Albert
Gallatin.

The Gallatin Plan, presented in 1808 by the Secretary, proposed the development of projects linking sections of the country
through an extensive scheme of highways and waterways. The
projects involved were as follows:[8]

1. Great canals along the Atlantic seacoast to unite
    New England with the South;

2. Development of links between the Atlantic and
    western waters;

3. Transportation between the Atlantic, St. Lawrence,
    and the Great Lakes;

4. Interior canals and roads.

Gallatin's plan was based upon two crucial factors which
largely guided federal interest in transportation development
until the end of the 19th century: 1) Development capital in the
early days of the Republic was scarce, and proponents of major
public works programs necessarily looked to the federal government for funds; 2) the country's population at this time was
sparsely distributed, leaving large gaps of territory between
population centers, thus making the need for efficient transport
more crucial.[9]

The Gallatin proposal did not win congressional approval,
but it did stimulate interest in the federal funding of public
works programs. And in one sense this outcome had a major impact on future transportation development--that which one transport analyst has termed "development-bartering."[10]

Waterways and shipping policies were initially drawn up by
the States, but eventually the difficulty of implementing river
improvements and the resulting expenses led to congressional
interest in providing direct federal monies. The Rivers and
Harbors Act of 1823 authorized limited federal expenditures for
improvements to waterways navigation--these funds approved by the
Congress upon recommendation of the Secretary of War. Although
the Act has since been refined and altered, its basic import has
remained.[11] The Army Corps of Engineers is today responsible for
authorizing any changes or improvements in the navigable waterways
of the United States.[12]

The building of the country's railroad network dominated
governmental interest in the mid-1800s. After a series of committee reports citing rate improprieties and other rail service

abuses,[13] the Interstate Commerce Commission (ICC) was established in 1887 by Congress.[14]

Thirteen years earlier, the first proposal to establish a
Department of Transportation was presented in Congress by Ohio
Representative Lourin Woodworth.[15] Woodworth proposed that a
Bureau of Transportation be set up to regulate the railroad
companies.

Dating from the Ohio Representative's first proposal in
1874 until the successful establishment of the Department almost
100 years later, some 32 separate plans advocating the creation of
a Federal Department of Transportation were presented to Congress.
Additionally, congressional and private study groups from time
to time recommended the creation of a Transportation Department
or some variant thereof. (In 1874 Mr. Woodworth's bid had gained
House, but not Senate, approval.)[16]

Immediately following the First World War, the railroads
still dominated national transportation policy and regulatory
interest. The industry was responsible for carrying 84 percent
of intercity freight and 85 percent of all passenger miles traveled
by public carriers.[17] Partly as a result of interest generated
when the railroads were placed under the Railroad War Board in
1918, extensive congressional hearings on the industry were held
following the war. Conducted largely to secure information on the
return of the railroads to private control, the subject of coordinated transportation systems was injected several times into the
proceedings. In a memorandum filed by Major General W. B. Black,
Chief of the U.S. Army Corps of Engineers, and sent to the House
Committee on Interstate and Foreign Commerce during the hearings,
the General examined the need to establish a Department of Transportation. He stated:[18]

> The greatest efficiency in transportation can be ob-
> tained only when all of the agencies of transportation
> are coordinated and each is used to its full economic
> value. These agencies are railroads, coast and trans-
> atlantic shipping, inland waterways, trolley roads,
> and highways. At present each of these agencies is
> considered and operated, if at all, by a separate and
> independent agency of the United States. Coordinated
> action is difficult if not impossible. In general it
> does not exist....All of the transportation agencies
> should be considered together under a single responsi-
> bility and operated together insofar as public policy
> demands national operation.

Other support came from various quarters, but the Congress
chose to enact a more narrowly construed act, the Transportation
Act of 1920.[19] Chiefly drawn up to give a positive effect from
ICC regulation on railroad problems, a pertinent provision of
the Act related to transportation planning. Basically, the
provision required the ICC to devise a national plan for railroad
consolidation.[20] The development of this plan in turn necessi-

tated national planning and policy guidance by the ICC, and thus represented a new relationship between government and the transportation industry.[21]

Furthermore, the Transportation Act of 1940[22] contained in the preamble to the Act a general statement on national transportation policy, again related to the ICC. Since a preamble statement does not embody any specific rule of law, it was a general expression by the Congress of the policy which it expected the ICC to follow. The declaration stated:[23]

It is hereby declared to be the national transportation policy of the Congress to provide for fair and impartial regulation of all modes of transportation subject to the provisions of this Act, so administered as to recognize and preserve the inherent advantages of each; to promote safe, adequate, economical and efficient service and foster sound economic conditions in transportation and among the several carriers; to encourage the establishment and maintenance of reasonable charges for transportation services, without unjust discriminations, undue preferences or advantages, or unfair or destructive competitive practices; to encourage fair wages and equitable working conditions; all to the end of developing, coordinating and preserving a national transportation system by water, highways, and rail, as well as other means, adequate to meet the commerce of the United States, of the Postal Service, and of the national defense. All of the provisions of this Act shall be administered and enforced with a view of carrying out the above declaration of policy.

This declaration was, in the general sense, the nation's first attempt at written transportation policy.[24] As a general policy statement, the language of the declaration was criticized by some for being vague and in conflict. Specific criticisms noted that the Act called for balance among conflicting transportation practices, but that it neither defined this balance nor explained how it was to be achieved.[25] Further, the Act caused little, if any, effect on the Commission in its resolution of the issues that came before it.[26] Accordingly, the Act of 1940 contained a general policy statement, but broke no new functional policy ground.

Two years later, a group created by President Roosevelt to investigate the domestic transportation industry issued a report calling for a Federal Department of Transportation.[27] Citing the diffuse and uncoordinated planning done in the transportation field, the National Resources Planning Board reported in May of 1942 that the problems of transportation were "too complex" for intermittent attention, and that a permanent government agency excluding the ICC should be created to analyze and deal with the problems of transportation continuously.[28]

     While the Board's recommendations were not adopted by the
Congress, support continued for coordinating federal transportation programs. In March 1949, the Commission on Organization of
the Executive Branch of Government, known as the "Hoover Commission," published a comprehensive transportation study.[29] Chaired
by former President Hoover and sponsored by the Department of
Commerce, the Commission recommended consolidating homogeneous
activities in the Department of Commerce and establishing a
departmental organization structured to assist transportation
and industry.[30] A specific commission task force, however, split
with the major Commission's recommendation and advocated the
establishment of a central Department of Transportation.

     The same year (1949) saw the completion of a major Brookings
analysis of national transportation policy completed by Charles
Dearing and Wilfred Owen.[31] Criticizing the Hoover Commission
report for failure to think in terms of overall transportation
requirements, Dearing and Owen recommended incorporating all
transportation-related promotional activities into a Department
of Transportation while simultaneously consolidating the independent regulatory agencies into a National Transport Regulatory
Commission.[32] An organization chart depicting the authors' proposed Department of Transportation is illustrated in Exhibit 7.1.
Dearing and Owen's basic argument was that the preservation of
workable competition in the transport industry represented the
foundation for economic regulation, and the promotional and subsidy programs aimed at encouraging national transportation planning were executive phenomena.

     Early in 1961, a penetrating analysis of the government's
relationship to transportation was submitted to the Senate Committee on Interstate and Foreign Commerce. Chaired by Major
General Thomas Doyle, the "Doyle Report" proposed two important
recommendations: 1) the consolidation of all executive promotional functions into a Department of Transportation; and 2) the
establishment of a Federal Transportation Commission for consolidating all independent regulatory agencies dealing with transportation.[33] Both recommendations were directed toward achieving
federal consistency and coordination in transportation matters.

     In delivering his proposal for a Department of Transporta-
tion before Congress in 1966, President Johnson drew from a long
series of governmental studies and reports when he emphasized
that a lack of coordination in existing transportation programs
inhibited the progress of the general transportation system.[34]
In recommending that the Congress establish a cabinet-level DOT,
the President proposed the consolidation of transportation promotional activities managed by competitive executive agencies.

     Responding to Presidential request, two bills were sub-
mitted in Congress.[35] Following legislative hearings, a new
bill, H.R. 15963, was drafted, and on October 13, 1966, the bill
became law. The Department of Transportation Act incorporated
many of the executive transfer requests made by the President
and, moreover, aligned the principal operating divisions modally
under the four administrative heads.[36]

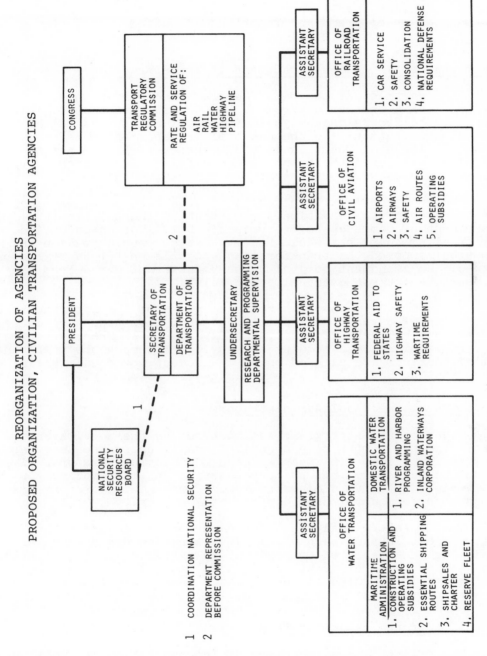

EXHIBIT 9.1

REORGANIZATION OF AGENCIES
PROPOSED ORGANIZATION, CIVILIAN TRANSPORTATION AGENCIES

Source: Charles L. Dearing and Wilfred Owen, National Transportation Policy, (Washington, D.C.: The Brookings Institution, © 1949), p. 353.

Hence, after over 100 years of proposals and considerations, a cabinet-level Department of Transportation was established. Major programs and functions conducted by DOT are analyzed in the following section.

The Organization of the Department of Transportation

The enactment of the Department of Transportation Act
created within the new department the Federal Aviation Administration, the Federal Highways Administration, the Federal Railroad Administration, and the National Transportation Safety
Board.[37] The U.S. Coast Guard was transferred by the Act to
the Department, and the Saint Lawrence Seaway Development Corporation was placed under the Secretary of Transportation.[38]

The President's original bill to establish a DOT had included
the transfer of the Maritime Administration (MarAd) from the
Department of Commerce to the proposed DOT. The maritime industry (feeling that they would receive better representation in
Commerce) opposed the transfer, and a battle on the House floor
ensued. An amendment to strike the transfer of MarAd from the
proposed Department eventually won 261-117.[39]

Exhibit 7.2 is an organizational chart of the Department.
Consisting of seven modal administrations, five Assistant Secretaries, and a General Counsel, the Department of Transportation
is organizationally a holding company.[40] Although the operating
administrations are aligned on an in-product, or modal, basis,
the Assistant Secretaries are organized functionally.

Functions of the Modal Administrators

Transportation programs administered by the modal agencies
within the Department come organizationally under the Secretary
of Transportation. Inasmuch as each administrator reports directly to the Secretary, his primary function is to promote vigor-
ously his respective administration. These administrators are
prohibited from developing departmental policy.[41]

The Secretary analyzes under departmental criteria the
optimum contribution each modal administration can make toward
achieving an integrated transportation system which is, in effect,
the statutory objective of the agency,[42] and authorizes program
assignments predicated on that format. He is constrained, however,
by the funding available and authorized by Congress.

Functions of the Assistant Secretaries

The Office of the Secretary of Transportation is functionally organized. Exhibit 7.3, an organizational chart of the office,
illustrates the components of the assistant secretarial levels
and their functional alignment. Following is a summary discussion of these administrative levels and the duties thereof.

EXHIBIT 9.2

DEPARTMENT OF TRANSPORTATION

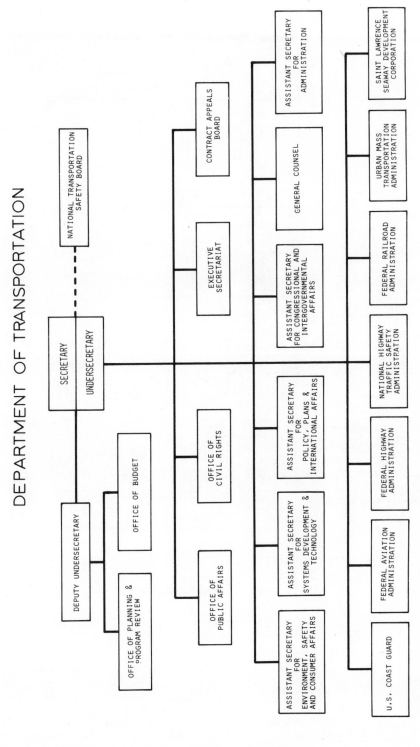

Source: U.S. Department of Transportation.

EXHIBIT 9.3

ORGANIZATION CHART FOR THE DEPARTMENT OF TRANSPORTATION, OFFICE OF THE SECRETARY

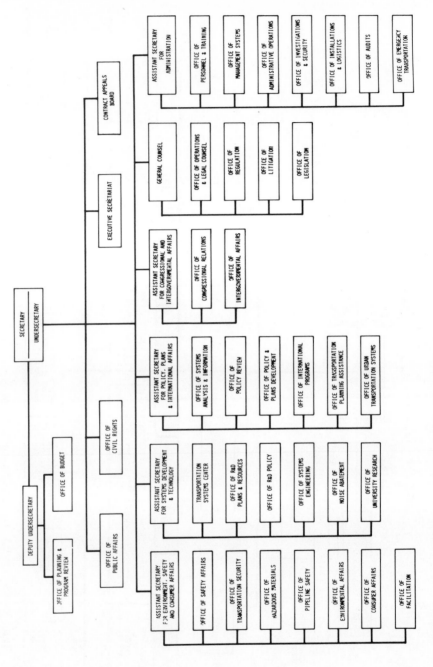

Source: U.S. Department of Transportation.

The Secretary

The Secretary and the Under Secretary are responsible for the overall planning, direction, and control of departmental affairs. The Deputy Under Secretary is specifically responsible for programming and budgeting, and is authorized to act for the Secretary and Under Secretary with respect to the immediate Office of the Secretary.[43] It is the Deputy Under Secretary who reviews the budgets of the modal agencies and meets with them annually in the program budget stages.[44]

Policy, Plans and International Affairs

The Office of the Assistant Secretary for Policy, Plans and International Affairs performs functions which include the analysis, development, and articulation of new and revised policies, plans, and programs for urban domestic and international transportation; analysis of the interplay between transport systems operations and established policies; the development of a comprehensive transportation data and information system; and transportation planning assistance and coordination among federal, state, and local governments, among other duties.[45]

Environment, Safety, and Consumer Affairs

Under the Assistant Secretary for Environment, Safety, and Consumer Affairs, this program area is responsible for broad functions which include the safety of passengers and cargo in transit, the regulation of hazardous materials transport, the implementation within the Department of the National Environmental Policy Act (NEPA),[46] and additionally serves as the department's contact point in relations with public and private organizations directed to consumer interests.[47]

Specifically, the office performs the functions of the Secretary under the Natural Gas Pipeline Safety Act of 1968[48] and under the Transportation of Explosives Act as amended by the Department of Transportation Act.[49] Under these statutes, DOT has authority to establish regulations for the safe transportation of petroleum, petroleum products, and other hazardous materials by pipeline within the United States, including pipelines operating from offshore areas. Insofar as proposed deepwater terminals involve the use of pipelines connecting offshore facilities with landed installations, the Office of Pipeline Safety within DOT would have responsibility over them.[50] These tasks would be administered by the Offices of Hazardous Materials and Pipeline Safety within the secretariat level Office of the Assistant Secretary for Environment, Safety and Consumer Affairs.

With reference to marine applications, the Hazardous Materials and Pipeline Safety Offices within DOT draw on Coast Guard personnel and expertise. Additionally, the Coast Guard has within its Office of Merchant Marine Safety separate programs concerned with hazardous cargo transport and pollution from offshore systems (including pipelines). These programs are separate but interrelated.

Furthermore, DOT is currently working with the Environmental Protection Agency to develop regulations required under the Water Pollution Control Act of 1972.[51] These regulations pertain to the prevention of oil discharges into the navigable waters of the United States.

Systems Development and Technology

Transportation research and technology is essential to the development of a safe and efficient national transportation system. The Office of Systems Development and Technology conducts research directed to improve the effectiveness, safety, and economy of transportation systems. Included in this area would be noise abatement hardware, telecommunications systems and technology, and high-speed ground transportation vehicles.

Additionally, the Assistant Secretary for Systems Development and Technology is responsible for providing to the Secretary a technological input into the development of general transportation policy and programs.

Congressional and Intergovernmental Affairs

The Office of the Assistant Secretary for Congressional and Intergovernmental Affairs performs functions which include the coordination of legislative matters within the Department and the direction of the Department's legislative program to Congress. The office also works to ensure a continuing program of communication and coordination with other federal agencies, and with state and local governments.[52]

General Counsel

The General Counsel is the chief legal officer of the Department. Accordingly, the Counsel is the legal adviser to the Secretary and his support staff, and holds final authority within the Department on questions of law. The Counsel (and his staff) represents the Department in proceedings before regulatory agencies, and under the Uniform Code of Military Justice[53] exercises the functions and powers as a Judge Advocate General with respect to the U.S. Coast Guard.

Administration

The Office of Administration runs the organizational aspects of the Department of Transportation. The functions of the office include management studies, delegations of authority, training, management information, installations and logistics policies, and numerous other support activities for the Office of the Secretary and other components of the Department.

     As in the case with the General Counsel's office, the Assis-
tant Secretary for Administration is not directly concerned with
the policy-making process of the agency.

Regional Representatives

     Another major organizational entity of DOT is the Regional
Representatives appointed by the Secretary. Located in the
headquarters city of each of the 10 standard federal regions,
a field representative of the Department is present to assure
effective administration of federal transportation programs.
The Regional Representative works with state and local agencies,
public interest groups, and other federal agencies on matters
involving the Department.[54]

Summary

     The organizational structure of the DOT is defined on two
levels: the operating administrations are organized on a modal
basis, while the assistant secretariat level is functionally
arranged. The strength of this bureaucratic structure rests
with the fact that it promotes the cross-fertilization of ideas
and concepts with a minimization of modal influences.[55] However,
while in theory the structure of the department is organizationally ideal in that the functional Assistant Secretaries oversee
the modal agencies, in fact the Secretary must derive a substantial portion of his bureaucratic power base from the backing he
receives from the President and the Office of Management and
Budget.

     The bureaucratic position of the Secretary results from
several structural differences in the organization of DOT in
comparison with other executive agencies. Modal organizations
within the department, while submitting their annual budget
requests through OST for approval, receive separate budgetary
authorizations from Congress. Moreover, the policy and program
framing of these budgets generally occurs within the modal
agency itself. As such, these bureaucratic constraints complicate the process by which the Secretary administers the
policies and programs of the department.

Programs, Goals, and National Transportation Policies of the Department of Transportation with Reference to Ports and Waterways

     A principal goal of the Department of Transportation con-
cerns the attainment of an integrated national transportation
system developed through the use of economic criteria. Under
Title 49 of the United States Code, the Department of Transportation is charged with broad planning and coordination functions.[56] In the Department of Transportation Act, the Congress
defined the purposes of the newly-created department as follows:[57]

     The Congress hereby declares that the general welfare,
     the economic growth and stability of the Nation and

its security require the development of national transportation policies and programs conducive to the provision of fast, safe, efficient, and convenient transportation at the lowest cost consistent therewith and
with other national objectives...

The Congress therefore finds that the establishment
of a Department of Transportation is necessary...

- to assure the coordinated, effective administration of the transportation programs of the Federal
  Government;

- to facilitate the development and improvement of
  coordinated transportation service, to be provided
  by private enterprise to the maximum extent feasible;

- to encourage cooperation of Federal, State, and
  local governments, carriers, labor, and other interested parties toward the achievement of national
  transportation objectives;

- to provide general leadership in the identification
  and solution of transportation problems;

- and to develop and recommend to the President and
  the Congress for approval national transportation
  policies and programs to accomplish these objectives
  with full and appropriate consideration of the needs
  of the public, users, carriers, industry, labor, and
  national defense.

Accordingly, the department has sought to define general
objectives in the area of transportation coordination and planning.
And since the passage of the Department of Transportation Act in
1966, several developments in the field have expanded the scope
of these objectives and responsibilities: the increasing intermodal character of transportation and its impact on planning
operations; the need for federal investment in the transportation infrastructure; and the responsibility to minimize the
harmful effects of transportation systems and facilities on the
environment.[58]

The policy development within the Department, in view of
these general responsibilities, has been directed toward several
goals consistent with the duties and functions delegated by the
Congress. These general objectives can be outlined as follows:[59]

- economic efficiency in transportation - to provide
  the mix of transportation alternatives, including
  modal systems, related facilities and manpower,
  research and development, which results in attaining the maximum benefits for a given cost (where
  benefits are stated as service, convenience, safety,
  comfort, and speed);

- optimal use of environmental resources - to increase
  the benefits derived from the preservation of the
  environment and the quality of life;

- safety - to minimize the loss of human life, property,
  and human suffering through injury from transportation-related accidents;

- support of other national interests - to further
  other objectives of the Federal government which
  impact on transportation or expertise possessed by
  the Department.

Operationally, the program development within DOT is intermodal in character, and is derived from the use of PPBS.*[60]
The system identifies the modes of transportation which are
involved, and facilitates within the departmental structure
a range of intermodal solutions to the problem.[61]

The Integration of Ports into the Total Transportation System

While the Department of Transportation has very broad transportation policy responsibilities, it has traditionally maintained only limited authority in the area of ports and waterways.** Specifically, under Section 7(a) of the DOT Act, the
department is constrained in conducting economic evaluations of
proposals for the investment of federal funds in transportation
facilities or equipment in water resources projects.*** Moreover,
traditionally the department has not chosen to assume an active
policy role in the maritime area--even in the light of its administrative participation on the Water Resources Council (WRC).****
DOT is represented on the WRC by a member of the Coast Guard
rather than by personnel from the policy-making branch of the
Office of the Secretary. As one analyst has noted, the "inadequate
role of the Department of Transportation in water resources planning and evaluation" constitutes a substantive "deficiency" in
the current principles and standards of the WRC.[62]

However, even though specific operational constraints have
influenced the DOT in its policy decisions regarding the port
area, several general transportation responsibilities have facilitated a departmental role in port development. Under DOT's
pervasive charge to "coordinate all transportation policy" and to
provide for the safe transport of people and goods within the
country, general departmental responsibilities in the port area
can be broken down into five topic areas:[63]

---

*Planning-Programming-Budgeting System. See discussion in Chapter
8.

**Exclusive of statutory mandates applying to the U.S. Coast Guard
and the recent January 1975 passage of the Deepwater Port Act.
This Act will be discussed later in the chapter.

***A specific discussion on Section 7(a) is pursued later in this
chapter.

****See Chapter 4.

1. The promotion of carrier safety and efficiency;

2. The protection of environmental, recreational,
    and other resource claims;

3. Facilitating the movement of passengers and cargo
    through the land/water interface;

4. Insuring that the inherent advantages of ocean
    transportation are fully utilized in conjunction
    with other modes to provide an economical and
    convenient transportation system; and

5. Helping to coordinate and balance port investment
    with other transportation investments.

Under these general headings, the Department has specifically pursued three functional programs and has other approaches
under review. The three programs involve transportation facilitation, the study of national transportation needs, and transportation regulation.[64]

Transportation Facilitation

Under the Assistant Secretary for Environment, Safety and
Consumer Affairs, the Office of Facilitation has had for several
years an active program to smooth out institutional obstructions
to transportation efficiency.[65] Such obstructions would include
unnecessarily complex customs clearance, transportation equipment
procedures and interchanges, and problems arising from cargo
losses and security procedures,* among others.

The departmental projects designed to accomplish this objective include the incorporation of a standardized form for bills
of lading (international), support for the development of uniform
commodity description codes, promulgation of various cargo security provisions and regulations, and a negotiated agreement
on the interchange of shipping containers and related equipment,
presently called the Uniform Intermodal Interchange Agreement.[66]

Projects in the area of facilitation seek to increase the
efficient service level which all modes of transportation can
provide while reducing overhead costs.

National Transportation Needs

The initial National Transportation Study was completed by
the Department in 1972. Containing the first full description
of the existing transportation system and its place in the
national economy, the report discussed projections of future
transportation demands, a delineation of current and emerging

---

*The Secretary of Transportation has been directed by the President
to investigate and develop a program to eliminate cargo losses in
all modes of transportation.

problems, and the transportation needs and capital improvement
programs as seen and reported by the States.[67]   A principal
finding of the report was the need for increased flexibility in
federal aid programs.   Traditionally, state and local officials
have been restricted in their freedom to use funds earmarked
for specific projects, such as highways.   (Recently a small degree of flexibility has been achieved in the use of earmarked
funds, specifically highway trust funds for urban mass transportation.)

     The report also recommended that planning for transportation
at all levels of government should be based on a periodic reporting system of which the 1972 report was the first part.[68] Pursuant
to this recommendation, the second of a series of National Transportation Studies was instituted during fiscal year 1972.   While
the first study was essentially a descriptive document, the second study was designed to concentrate on the performance of
transportation systems throughout the country.

Transportation Regulation

     The department annually participates in a number of cases
before the transportation regulatory agencies--the Interstate
Commerce Commission (ICC), the Civil Aeronautics Board (CAB),
and the Federal Maritime Commission (FMC).   Generally, this
participation is limited to cases of major policy importance
affecting broad spectrums of the transportation industry, shippers, and the interests of consumers.

     Two examples of regulatory cases of importance to the port
industry and the Department of Transportation are the Portland
cargo diversion case[69] and the mini-landbridge case.[70]

     In Intermodal Service to Portland, Oregon,[71] the complaint
presented to the FMC was that shipping lines formerly using
Portland facilities were calling at Seattle, and absorbing the
cost of moving overland freight originating in or destined to
the Portland area.

     Although not participating in the case, DOT was most inter-
ested in Portland's argument that cargo which was "naturally
tributary" to its port was being illegally diverted to Seattle.
With restrictions, the FMC held that carriers could use the
Seattle port and absorb inland freight charges.   Accordingly,
the decision indicates that the concept of "naturally tributary"
is being reevaluated and may be no longer available as a re-
striction against economic competition.[72]

     The Department is also currently involved in the mini-land-
bridge case.[73] This case involves the overland movement from a
U.S. seaport on one coast to another coast, as part of cargo movements to foreign ports, rather than all-water movements from a
U.S. coastal port directly to the foreign port.[74] The issues
which have arisen concern traffic diversion, discriminatory
pricing, and port discrimination or preference, and thus have

an influential impact on several modes of transportation and
regulatory policies which affect these systems.

In addition, at the request of the Senate Commerce Committee,
DOT has studied another multi-modal issue, the controversy concerning the proposal to replace Locks and Dam 26 at Alton, Illinois.
In September 1975 the Department published "The Replacement of
Alton Locks and Dam 26, An Advisory Report of the Department of
Transportation to the Senate Commerce Committee." The report
provides an overall assessment of existing transportation facilities in the area of the proposed project, identifies potential
effects of expanding the upper Mississippi and Illinois waterway
systems, and comments on the information necessary to make cost-
effective decisions on the investment of public dollars in transportation to meet future demands in this area. The outcome of the
court decision concerning Locks and Dam 26 may have a significant
effect on the future development of the inland waterway system.

The Deepwater Port Act of 1974: New Responsibilities in Transportation and Energy Policy

The passage of the Deepwater Port Act of 1974 established
the Department of Transportation as the lead licensing authority
for the development of offshore, deepwater terminal facilities.[75]
As the maritime component of the DOT, the U.S. Coast Guard was
delegated the task of regulating the operations of these facilities.*

The executive signing of the House-Senate conference bill
culminated nearly two years of congressional dialog and dis-
agreement over major provisions of the enabling legislation.
Initial House and Senate versions of the bill had provided for
lead licensing authority to be held by the Secretary of the
Interior, with operational regulatory authority being vested in
the U.S. Coast Guard.** However, the final decision to place
licensing authority with DOT resulted in part from extensive
compromises worked out between affected committees of Congress
and the results of the final House-Senate conference agreements.

---

*The Secretary of Transportation delegated certain responsibili-
ties received under the Deepwater Port Act of 1974 to the Commandant of the Coast Guard and the Assistant Secretary for Environment, Safety and Consumer Affairs (40 FR 20088-9).

**Initial Senate versions of the bill (including S.1751) specified
the Interior Department, which oversees offshore drilling operations and other energy-related activities, as the licensing authority for deepwater facilities. See U.S. Senate, Special Joint
Subcommittee on Deepwater Ports Legislation composed of the Committees on Commerce, Interior and Insular Affairs, and Public
Works, "Deepwater Port Act of 1973," Hearings, 93rd Congress,
First Session, Parts I and II (Washington, D.C.: U.S. Government
Printing Office, August, 1973). Appendix H describes federal
agency authorities related to deepwater port subject areas and
illustrates the licensing procedures proposed under S.1751.

The legislative consideration of the Act was complicated by the number of congressional committees exerting jurisdictional claims in the proceedings. Fully six committees of Congress--three (Commerce, Public Works, and Merchant Marine) on the House side and three more (Commerce, Interior, and Public Works) from the Senate--participated in the drafting of legislation. Jurisdictional differences of opinion became particularly acute in the House (which at the time was also considering major committee reorganization proposals), and their effect on the legislative passage of the final House bill had a doubtless impact on the conference agreements between the two congressional bodies.* These jurisdictional issues also largely explain the lengthy time consideration afforded to the legislation.

In summary, the legislation--which does not apply to offshore port facilities proposed to be built within territorial waters**--provides for the following major legislative provisions:[76]

A. Licensing Agency. The legislation authorizes the Department of Transportation as the licensing authority for the development and operation of deepwater port facilities. Furthermore, under Section 5(a) of the Act, the DOT must also provide for the "full consultation and cooperation with all other interested Federal agencies and departments and with any potentially affected coastal State, and for consideration of the views of any interested members of the general public."

B. Adjacent State Veto. The legislation provides coastal states adjacent to the proposed develop ment of a deepwater port the right of veto. An "adjacent coastal State" is broadly defined and includes (1) a state which is directly connected to the port by pipelines; (2) a state located with in 15 miles of the proposed port; and (3) a state threatened with a possible oil spill from the port.

C. Licensing Procedures. The Act establishes an eleven-month approval timetable for administrative action on a license. The procedures involved in clude: a) an application by a qualified ownership interest; b) state and federal environmental impact reviews and considerations; c) public hearings; d) review and administrative action by all inter ested federal, state or public interests; and e) final action by the Secretary of Transportation. Applications to build ports in the same location are handled by a procedure designed to consider all

---

*See Chapter 3 for a contextual discussion of these jurisdictional issues.

**Port facilities within three miles will be licensed in the usual manner by the Corps of Engineers.

applications for any one location. If all applicants qualify, the Secretary is directed to issue
licenses according to the following priorities--
(1) a state application; (2) an application by an
independent terminal company; and (3) any other
application.

D.   Environmental Review Criteria. The DOT, in accor
      dance with recommendations from the EPA and NOAA,
      is directed to establish environmental review crite-
      ria for the evaluation of applications to construct
      deepwater port facilities. The criteria are di-
      rected to be consistent with NEPA and comprehen-
      sive in design.

E.   Antitrust Review. Section 7 of the Act provides
      for the antitrust review of facility applications.
      The U.S. Attorney General and the Federal Trade
      Commission are directed to offer recommendations
      to the Secretary as to whether issuance of any
      facility license would adversely affect competi-
      tion, restrain trade, further monopolization, or
      otherwise create or maintain a situation in contra-
      vention of existing antitrust laws.*

F.   Common Carrier Status. Existing statutes regula-
      ting the transportation of oil and natural gas in
      interstate commerce are made specifically appli-
      cable to deepwater ports.

G.   Navigational Safety. The Act authorizes the DOT
      to establish regulations to ensure navigational
      safety around or near a deepwater port, and to
      further designate a safety zone about any such
      facility within which no incompatible uses or
      developments are to be permitted (these responsi-
      bilities have been delegated to the Coast Guard).

H.   Liability Provisions.** Strict liability for pol-
      lution damage caused by a discharge from the port
      itself or from a vessel within the safety zone is
      provided for under the legislation. The Act
      allocates liability among the following interests:
      (1) the licensee up to $50 million; (2) the owner
      and operator of a vessel up to $20 million; and
      (3) a Deepwater Port Liability Fund for all other
      proven damages (including clean-up costs) not actu-
      ally compensated for by the licensee or the owner
      or operator. The fund, administered by the Secre-
      tary, is created by a 2¢ per barrel charge on oil
      until the fund has reached $100 million.

---

*See the discussion on the FTC in Chapter 4.

**The exact liability provisions account for acts of war, negli-
gence on the part of the Federal Government or other parties, etc.

I.   Economic Evaluation. A further provision of the
Deepwater Port Act authorizes the Department of
Transportation to compare the "economic, social,
and environmental effects of the construction and
operation of a deepwater port" with the same effects
of the "construction, expansion, deepening and
operation" of a planned onshore deepwater terminal.[77] Consequently, this provision authorizes
the comparison of economic benefits accruing from
dredging an onshore deepwater port with those of
building an offshore terminal facility. Such an
economic evaluation would be quite complex since
an onshore deepwater port may be handling break-
bulk cargo, containers, and dry bulk, as well as
the petroleum products which would be handled at
the offshore terminal.

While the DOT as a department has had little experience in
the economic analysis of ports, administrative efforts have been
made to facilitate and develop the agency's technical expertise in
this area. In anticipation of the transportation and energy
policy impacts of deepwater port development, the Office of
Assistant Secretary for Policy, Plans and International Affairs
(TPI) developed in May 1974 an econometric model to study the
impact of inland transportation costs of petroleum products on the
least-cost location of deepwater ports.[78] The heuristic DOT model
is presented in a five-volume TPI report entitled "Economic Aspects
of Refinery and Deep-Water Port Location in the United States."[79]
Results of this report pertaining to offshore facilities indicate
that a) "markets determine where the refineries should be;" b)
"refinery locations dictate where deep-water ports should be;" and
c) "deep-water port locations are only partially influenced by the
overseas crude oil sources and supertanker economies."[80]

However, while DOT efforts in this area have added to the
information decision-makers will utilize in determining licensing
and other deep-water port policies and programs, other federal
agencies are currently involved in such activities as well. The
Corps of Engineers* performs benefit/cost analyses on all proposed
dredging projects using federal funds. The Maritime Administration** has partially funded a regional port study of the Pacific
Northwest and tentatively plans such studies for other areas of
the United States. Unfortunately, the obvious conceptual overlaps
in these studies and analyses has not stimulated the participating
agencies to formally adopt common data bases, criteria, and methodological approaches to be applied in their respective reports.

New Administrative Structures and Program Design

Pursuant to the legislative passage of the Deepwater Port
Act, the Department of Transportation established in early January

---

*See Chapter 6.

**See Chapter 7.

1975 the Office of Deepwater Ports (ODP).[81] This new office will
serve as the central administrative machinery for the processing
of licenses to construct and operate deepwater offshore terminal
facilities. To the extent that deepwater port development will
likely bring about conflicting activities among industrial applicants for licenses and environmental and recreational groups and
interests, ODP will have to "referee" private, state and federal
rivalries and jurisdictional differences of opinion.

Regulatory Impacts on Transportation Safety Responsibilities of the DOT

In addition to the new responsibilities and policy imperatives engendered in the Deepwater Port Act, several traditional
areas of DOT involvement in transportation safety will also be
affected. Under the Assistant Secretary for Environment, Safety,
and Consumer Affairs, the Office of Pipeline Safety has responsibility for insuring the reliability of pipeline systems from the
deepwater terminal to the shore, to the refinery, and ultimately
to the consumer. This jurisdiction over offshore liquid pipelines
derives essentially from the Transportation of Explosives Act[82] as
amended by the Department of Transportation Act of 1966.[83] Under
these statutes, DOT has authority to establish regulations for the
safe transportation of hazardous materials, petroleum, and petroleum products by pipeline in offshore areas. Such regulations
relate to carriers engaged in interstate or foreign commerce.
Moreover, to the extent that deepwater ports in the future will be
involved with handling liquefied natural gas (LNG),* DOT has
jurisdiction over the transportation of such gas by pipeline under
authority of the Natural Gas Pipeline Safety Act of 1968.[84] DOT
is also authorized to establish regulations for the safe transport
of this commodity.

And finally, laws pertaining to the land-based activities of
operating administrations of the DOT and related to deepwater port
development must be coordinated within the agency to facilitate
the efficient licensing of these facilities.[85]

Port Policy and the DOT: An Analysis of Its Changing Role and Some Recent Policy Imperatives

The duties and responsibilities of the Department of Transportation (exclusive of specific mandates to the Coast Guard) in
the area of ports and waterways policy basically encompasses two
administrative areas: a) general powers resting with the Secretary
concerning the coordination and facilitation of national transportation systems and infrastructure; and b) specific regulatory
responsibilities pertaining to the licensing of deepwater ports,
the safety of pipeline systems operations, and the safe transport
of hazardous materials and cargoes across the United States.

---

*An earlier version of the Deepwater Port Act of 1974 specifically
authorized the licensing of offshore terminals handling LNG, but
this feature was removed from the final bill.

The administrative breadth of these responsibilities is
largely dependent on the course the Department seeks in operation-
alizing its broad legislative mandate to coordinate and develop
national transportation systems and policies. Moreover, the
manner in which the Department implements its functional programs
assumes substantive policy importance in at least two areas: a)
the bureaucratic character of the regulations implemented by the
Department defines the way in which the organization perceives its
own role in the overall planning of ports and waterways development;
and b) the extent to which these regulatory responsibilities are
continually reinforced with explicit planning and development
objectives belies the organization's conceptual approach to policy
and program integration at the field level.

The analysis of policy and program design must also take
account of the bureaucratic and issue environment. The combined
effects of a changing maritime technological base and a growing
national environmental awareness have placed added policy and
program responsibilities on the DOT and its modal administrations.
In the most direct sense, technology has broadened DOT responsibilities in the port area while ecological controls have placed
certain structural restrictions on its program implementation.
The strategy of organizational activity within these institutional
constraints constitutes a principal administrative dilemma for
the DOT in the port and waterway area.

In terms of policy and program design and administration,
a major structural challenge to the Department of Transportation
is the integration of new departmental policy and planning roles
(emphasized by agency duties under the Deepwater Port Act) in
the maritime area with the traditional regulatory functions and
responsibilities of the U.S. Coast Guard. To the extent the
DOT is administratively charged with the general "development
and improvement of coordinated transportation services," and
"leadership in the identification and solution of transportation
problems," these broad responsibilities outline what can be termed
the strategic functions of transportation planning and development.[86] Operationally, the overall policy decisions of the Department are funneled through the Assistant Secretariat levels and
the modal organizations which comprise the Department's policy
instrumentalities.

However, as a separate modal agency operating within the
DOT, the Coast Guard assumes an advocate bureaucratic position
for program development consistent with its conception of its
role in the marine transportation field. While internally the
activities and emphasis of the organization are set by the policy
and program design of the Coast Guard, as a modally organized
agency within the DOT its external policy guidance is influenced
by broad departmental policies, goals and responsibilities.

Accordingly, a major bureaucratic challenge to the DOT is
the administrative integration of two essentially dissimilar
planning roles into the implementation of complementary program
objectives. Issue areas where elements of this organizational
challenge manifest themselves include the rate-absorption and

mini-landbridge cases pending before the Federal Maritime Commission (FMC),* deepwater port development, administrative responsibilities pertaining to hazardous cargo transport, and environmental policy and program duties.

In the case of rate-absorption and mini-landbridge dockets pending before the FMC, the interests of the DOT and the Coast Guard are different. The Department's concern with the cases focuses on the strategic effects of their impact on the general movement of commerce into and from U.S. port facilities. This would include secondary effects such as impacts on other transportation modes (trucks and rail) as well as intermodal transfer and design. However, Coast Guard planning and program interest in the cases largely pertains to the agency's traditional port functions in the regulation of vessel and terminal operations, including its responsibility related to vessel traffic systems.

The strategic policy and operational regulatory differences in administrative outlooks emphasized in the FMC dockets are also found when considering the relative responsibilities mandated under the Deepwater Port Act of 1974. As the lead licensing authority for offshore deepwater facilities, the DOT is concerned with the strategic transportation, energy, and environmental consequences of deepwater port development. However, as a component of these overall policy areas, the Coast Guard will have ongoing operational regulatory authority pertaining to offshore facilities. Furthermore, to the extent that Coast Guard regulatory activities may impact in substantive terms on the economics of any specific deepwater port site, the effects of these differing administrative outlooks will have economic as well as administrative/bureaucratic incentives to coordinate policy and program design between the Department and its modal agency component.

Additionally, a related safety-oriented area of administrative and regulatory concern for both the DOT and the Coast Guard is hazardous cargo transportation. Under the Assistant Secretary for Environment, Safety, and Consumer Affairs, the DOT maintains certain statutory responsibilities regarding the transportation of hazardous materials. Furthermore, the Coast Guard has within its Office of Merchant Marine Safety separate programs operating in hazardous cargo transport regulation, and pollution from offshore systems (including pipelines).

New Institutional Structures or Changes in Policy and Program Emphasis

To facilitate the proper integration of policy and planning roles between the DOT and the Coast Guard with respect to the maritime issues discussed above, it is necessary for both organizations to pursue policies which, in expanding their actions, complement their respective administrative roles. To the extent that each of these issues comprises important institutional imperatives for policy changes and coordination of bureaucratic out-

---

*See Chapter 4.

looks, pressures from both outside interest groups and internal
interests wishing to reorient agency resources will be reflected
in changes in either administrative structure or the reordering of
program emphasis within existing agency components.

In institutional terms, one set of alternatives for policy
integration is the creation of new bureaucratic or administrative
entities designed to interface between sectional agency interests.
In this sense, the creation of the Office of Deepwater Ports (ODP)
can be regarded as an internal agency attempt at facilitating
policy and program development concerning offshore terminal facilities. Presumably, one element of the duties of the Office will
be the coordination of internal agency policy and programs regarding these facilities.

In addition to the ODP, other types of bureaucratic structures or entities can be envisioned. Internally, the Department
could establish different types of agency bureaucratic structures
which would interface between maritime issues and sectional
agency interests more broadly than in the case of the ODP.*
Externally, the Department could seek to develop a supportive
political constituency base with which to conduct certain types
of integrated policies or programs.

Supportive constituencies or other interested political
parties may also directly call for institutional or bureaucratic
changes in an agency. Legislation introduced by Senator Humphrey
calling for the establishment within DOT of a new Inland Waterways Administration is one example (discussed earlier). A second case would be the possible creation of a new "Assistant
Secretary for Waterways" within DOT--an idea supported by an
industry trade association and some waterways conference officials.[87] The probability of success for either bureaucratic
reorganization proposal is, however, more likely connected with
extraneous political factors and balances rather than with the
theoretical, administrative advantages of a new bureaucratic
structure.

Economic Evaluation and the Intent of Congress

Apart from the bureaucratic political factors which play
an important role in how an executive agency administers new or
added responsibilities, a federal bureaucracy must also be cognizant of the legislative role and intent of Congress in formulating policies and programs. In the case of Congress and water
resources policy, however, this may not be easy.**

Under Section 7(a) of the Department of Transportation Act
of 1966,[88] the Secretary shall "develop and from time to time...
revise standards and criteria consistent with national transportation policies, for the formulation and economic evaluation

---

*See Chapter 11.

**See Chapter 3.

of all proposals for the investment of Federal funds in transportation facilities or equipment, except such proposals as are
concerned with...(5) water resource projects."[89] The section
goes on to state that the standards and criteria for evaluation
of water resource projects shall be developed by the Water Resources Council (WRC), subject to final approval by the Congress.
Accordingly, the legislative import of this section was to restrain the Secretary from evaluating the expenditure of federal
funds in transportation systems pertaining to ports and waterways transport and, more generally, water resource projects
(such as those operated by the Army Corps of Engineers).

    However, more recent legislative actions and the institu-
tional effects of new maritime technologies and environmental
awareness have caused apparent shifts in the expressed intent
of Congress in this area. For example, under the Ports and
Waterways Safety Act of 1972, the Secretary of Transportation
is charged with the responsibility to consider the economic
impact and effects of the agency's regulatory activities on
maritime commerce. As Section (e) of the Act states:[90]

> (e) In carrying out his duties and responsibilities
> under this title to promote the safe and efficient con-
> duct of maritime commerce the Secretary shall consider
> fully the wide variety of interests which may be affected
> by the exercise of his authority hereunder. In deter-
> mining the need for, and the substance of any rule or
> regulation or the exercise of other authority here-
> under the Secretary shall, among other things, consider--
>
> (1) the scope and degree of the hazards;
>
> (2) vessel traffic characteristics including
>   minimum interference with the flow of com-
>   mercial traffic, traffic volume, the sizes
>   and types of vessels, the usual nature of
>   local cargoes, and similar factors;
>
> (3) port and waterway configurations and the
>   differences in geographic, climatic, and
>   other conditions and circumstances;
>
> (4) environmental factors;
>
> (5) economic impact and effects;
>
> (6) existing vessel traffic control systems,
>   services, and schemes; and
>
> (7) local practices and customs, including vol-
>   untary arrangements and agreements within
>   the maritime community.

Furthermore, in addition to subsection (5), note also that section (e) uses the words "safe and efficient conduct of maritime
commerce instead of the phrase "maritime transportation." The

use of the term "commerce" was presumably made to include other
impacts of transportation services. Accordingly, this broadens
the scope and intent of the section.

Additionally, under the Deepwater Port Act of 1974, the
Congress charged the Department of Transportation with certain
powers regarding the economic evaluation of offshore versus
onshore deepwater port facilities. Consequently, while traditionally the Congress has restrained DOT from performing economic analysis concerning federal expenditures in the water
resources area (including dredging), the Department is now charged
with conducting economic analysis related to maritime transportation and certain port facilities.

While these recent policy initiatives underscore congressional recognition and acceptance of DOT economic evaluations,
Section 7(a) of the 1966 Act has not been revised or recon-
structed. However, since national water resources and maritime
transportation policies are interrelated, DOT is confronted
with an administrative dilemma in dealing with economic evaluations in one area, but not the other.* Nevertheless, legislative encroachment on the restrictive provisions of Section 7(a)
is likely an easier political task than calling for congressional
review and legislative change.

Future National Transportation Issues and Strategy

As an industry transportation presents a unique problem for
national policy-making because of its intimate relation with community and business life. The public-private mixture of enter-
prises and policy-making actors involved in transportation planning obscures clear definitions of how transportation infra-
structures affect communities, and complicates the division of
responsibility for the quality of national transportation.

Additionally, the role of precedent and tradition in the
development of national transportation policy has left indelible
marks on the character of planning affecting all modes of transportation. As one analyst has noted: "Precedent has not only
provided the basis for attempts at the national level to apply
patterns of policy cross-modally; more basically it has routin-
ized the practice of developing policy on an ad hoc basis."[91]

In this sense, some analysts have argued that major governmental policy-makers have therefore confined themselves to largely an operational type of influence rather than undertaking a
strategic planning role in shaping national transportation
policy.[92]

Accordingly, a major future concern for the Department of
Transportation is the issue of developing national transporta-

---

*This issue is exacerbated in that no common denominator exists as
a criterion for public expenditures for both the water resources
and transportation areas.

tion policies for the long run consistent with the short run
need for increased and improved information and data for making
present policy decisions. The 1972 and 1974 National Transportation Needs Studies completed by the Department work toward
the establishment of the basic framework of needed information,
data, and conceptual methodologies for the development of coordinated national transportation policies and programs.

In terms of altering the present institutional structure
of transportation development to facilitate greater policy integration, the potentialities of technological progress constitute
one of the most influential imperatives for changes in traditional transportation policy-making.[93] The costs implicit in
technological system progress have in one sense brought about
an increasing federal role in the underwriting of research costs.
The short-term startup costs of most complex transportation
systems are so enormous that private enterprise, even with increased capacities for capital investment, cannot meet the
expense alone. The inputs of large amounts of federal monies
in transportation will thus bring about an intensification of
planning interest at the federal level.

Related to this issue of technological innovation and the
new institutional arrangements it will bring is the present
extent of federal power and control. As one transportation
analyst has noted:[94]

At this point, it is obvious that federal policy has
inexorably moved towards securing a greater degree of
domination over virtually all aspects of national transportation. Numerous examples of this growing control
exist: detailed standards for improvement of inland
waterways; control over virtually all standards of aircraft performance and maintenance, pilot training, schedules, fare structures, navigation; safety specifications
and standards for federally assisted highway construction and for the manufacture of autos, trucks, and buses;
design and operation characteristics of shipping constructed with MARAD subsidies; detailed specifications
for the qualification of UMTA capital grants. These
represent but a sampling of the totality of federal
controls.

But in the long run even their influence may prove
insufficient to meet the enormous transporation challenges of the future. We may be approaching the point
at which national population growth and demand for
greater transportation capacity will mandate control
over the quantities of transportation conveyances produced and their usages. Such a possibility does not
appear too remote when viewed against the background of
a motor vehicle output growing at a much faster pace
than the general population.

Furthermore, the choosing of alternatives between competing
modes of transportation systems as well as intermodal facilities
is a necessary function of federal planning influence.

In essence, then, the foci of future federal transportation policies will necessarily extend beyond the present regulation of quality control and mixed federal planning efforts at federal, state and local levels. These policies will need to deal with conscious selection and financial support of different types and modes of transportation systems for the future, and the coordinated social and community planning necessary for the integration of such systems into American life.[95] As a component of this transportation framework, ports and waterways policy and development will need to be integrated into the more general sphere of national transportation policy.

CHAPTER 10

AN ANALYSIS OF KEY ELEMENTS OF THE INSTITUTIONAL
PROCESS OF PORT DEVELOPMENT

A public port has many pressures on it to expand with the
purchase of modern capital-intensive facilities. U.S. domestic
and international commerce continues to increase. Private interests economically depending on the port demand modern facilities
and excellent customer services. The port itself constantly
strives to maintain competitive advantages it may have over other
ports or moves to acquire such advantages. Finally, the entire
future of the port and the job security of its management and
labor may depend on acquiring new modern facilities.

Once a port has decided to acquire new facilities, it enters
a framework of institutional procedures and paper work. This
chapter will describe the key elements in this process and discuss
the advantages and disadvantages of the system. Within this
framework, conflicts occur between the economic benefits of modern
technology and environmental considerations. Local business
interests may support port expansion, while others may oppose it
on the basis of the environmental harm they perceive resulting
from such undertakings. The degree to which these conflicts are
resolved--for better or worse--is a function of the dynamics of
the port development process.

Federal Influence

Within the process of port development, federal agencies
influence the port in three basic ways: (1) through allocation of
federal funds for port-related projects; (2) through implementation
of existing regulations as they pertain to the siting and operation
of terminal facilities and their vessel movements; and (3) through
formulation of policy which directly or indirectly affects ports.
While a myriad of government agencies are involved in port activities, many in a peripheral way (i.e., Postal Service, Weather
Bureau, etc.), only those federal agencies that fit one of the
three basic criteria above, and have a substantive impact on the
process of port development, will be mentioned in this chapter.
In addition, a port may be influenced by actions of the state or
local municipality in its activities.

Allocation of Federal Funds

The key federal agency providing funds for port projects is
the Corps of Engineers. In response to requests for aid from
local port interests, and following congressional authorization,
the Corps of Engineers evaluates, plans and constructs federal
navigation, flood control, shore protection, and other related
projects under the civil works program.

Since its inception, the Corps through fiscal year 1971 has
spent approximately $5.5 billion on navigation projects, including

advanced engineering, design and construction, and about $8.0 billion on flood control including the alteration of bridges obstructing navigation.[1] In 1973 the allotment of federal funds to the Corps for navigation projects relating to ocean port operations was approximately $141 million, consisting of almost $60 million for 23 new construction projects and about $81 million for 98 maintenance projects.[2] Dredging activities comprise the main segment of these funds. The dredging of channels and harbors is performed by the Corps without cost to the port. However, the port may have to pay for the dredging of berthing areas and the disposal of polluted dredged spoils.

The Economic Development Administration also provides financial assistance to aid in the building of port facilities. Since 1965, EDA has spent more than $100 million in port and port-related projects. These funds make up approximately 7 percent of capital investments by public ports. While these funds are small in comparison with Corps allocations, an EDA grant may make the difference as to whether a particular port project will be undertaken or not.

Formulation of Federal Policy

While there is no agency in charge of formulating or coordinating the development of a national port policy, several agencies set policy guidelines in areas which directly or indirectly influence port development. Each of these federal organizations bodies has the potential to have a significant impact on port development.

The Water Resources Council is charged with setting guidelines and criteria for evaluation of water resource projects which include the dredging activities of the Corps of Engineers. These criteria play a major role in what types of dredging projects get approved. However, the actions of the WRC have been challenged by Congress in recent years.

The Department of Transportation is charged with formulating national transportation policy in the 1966 Act. However, the powers of DOT are limited in that it cannot evaluate federal grants-in-aid programs such as the navigation program of the Corps. To the extent that policy activities of the DOT affect maritime transportation, port development is influenced. Moreover, the role of DOT in licensing deepwater ports may have an impact on the number and location of these terminals.

By formulating environmental policies, the Council on Environmental Quality affects port development in several ways. Where dredging is involved, CEQ is concerned with the environmental implications of depositing dredged spoils. Concerning the siting of offshore terminals, CEQ is interested in the probability and impact of oil spills as well as the secondary onshore effects including the building of refineries, employment levels, pollution, etc.

     As part of its overall agency responsibilities towards devel-
oping national energy strategies, the Federal Energy Administration
recommends actions which affect port operations and development.
For example, FEA is involved in setting import duties to influence
the importation of foreign energy products, and also recommends
actions to encourage the use of various domestic sources of energy.
In this way, the FEA affects the quantity and types of bulk commodities imported (i.e., crude oil versus refined). Consequently,
these actions have an impact on the number and type of bulk commodity terminals built.

Regulations and Operations

     Federal agencies not traditionally in policy-setting institu-
tional roles may still carry out actions that have strong policy
implications. For example, the FMC and the ICC, transportation
regulatory bodies, base their decisions on existing laws. However, using these laws calls for an interpretation of what is
meant by such terms as the "public interest," "discriminatory
practices," and the "inherent advantages" of each mode. These
legal actions affect commercial transportation interests involved
in port operations such as steamship lines and railroads.

     The operations of the Environmental Protection Agency and the
Department of the Interior have an influence on port development
primarily through their review of Environmental Impact Statements
on proposed port projects. EPA, in interpreting the ecological
aspects of projects as well as setting and enforcing various
environmental standards, can cause modification or cancellation of
a proposed project. The Department of the Interior may have the
same impact in its review of a project as to its effect on such
natural resources as wildlife, estuaries, or fish. The actions of
EPA and DOI result in policy implications as to what types of port
projects are acceptable.

     Many of the decisions of the Coast Guard have policy impli-
cations such as the following: determining the level of icebreaking service to various ports; evaluating whether domestic
tankers carrying oil from Alaska should be required to have double
bottoms with the additional required capital cost; deciding whether
technical standards for liquefied gas carriers coming into U.S.
ports should be more stringent than the standards of other countries; determining which ports should receive vessel traffic
systems; and deciding under what conditions offshore terminals
should curtail operations because of pollution considerations.
While these decisions are related mainly to aspects of port safety
and marine pollution, there are definite economic impacts from
each decision which will influence vessels and port facilities,
and consequently port development interests.[3]

     The Maritime Administration conducts and sponsors research
which has policy implications for port development. Studies on
topics such as deepwater terminals, regional port analysis, and
public port financing may directly or indirectly influence legislation or policy changes in these areas.

At the executive policy-making level, the Office of Management and Budget may initiate budgetary actions which affect the implementation of port-related programs by federal agencies--thus directly influencing the conduct of marine or port-related policies and programs. When considering the allocation of federal funds to dredge a particular port project, OMB may take action to request from the port a voluntary contribution for the project or can delay final action of the project. These actions obviously have an impact on the types of projects that will receive federal funds most easily.

The Office of Coastal Zone Management within NOAA is involved in preparing guidelines for CZM plans, issuing grants to states to prepare such plans, and reviewing these plans for approval. In theory, the OCZM has the potential for having a major impact on CZM policies) however, federal actions to date suggest that coastal zone management policy is basically formulated at a state rather than at a national level.

Impact of State Actions

Actions of state agencies also influence port development. In setting up a CZM plan, a state must recognize that any piece of land in the coastal zone may serve more than one function. The land desired by a port for a new terminal facility can also have alternative uses. Once a state has established an approved CZM plan, any proposed port project must conform to stated guidelines.

The creation of state departments of transportation in more than half the states of the nation also has an impact on port development. While the federal DOT is limited in its powers to compare and evaluate investments in different modes of transportation, a state agency has no such institutional or policy constraints. Consequently, a state can assess the overall transportation system within its boundaries, striving for the proper balance between investments in the various modes. A proposed public port facility now has to fit within the framework of the overall transportation system rather than as an independent mode.

Advantages and Disadvantages of the Present Institutional Process

The present approach to port development can be analyzed by considering the results of the process. Inherent in this process is the conflict between national and local interests. Looking at the situation economically from the national viewpoint, if federal funds contribute to overcapacity, they bring no benefit to the nation as a whole. As long as the building of one more container terminal simply aids the competitive position of a public port authority rather than actually increasing the national flow of cargo or decreasing the overall costs of the national transportation system, the federal government is in the role of subsidizing public utilities to compete with each other. While a particular port community can derive great benefits from diversion of cargo, from a national perspective public ports, like other utilities, will theoretically operate most efficiently when run as monopolies rather than as competing entities.

The Concept of National Port Overcapacity

It now appears that an overcapacity of container terminals exists in the United States. This would imply that the present network of many container terminals geographically dispersed is less efficient than a smaller number of larger terminals located as regional facilities at key load centers.

Conceptually, one can think of the optimum container terminal capacity as that capacity which minimizes cost. However, container cost may be interpreted to mean simply the cost of cargo moving between the dock and the gate of the terminal, or in addition the seaward portion from the dock to the open sea, including costs of port congestion and queueing for dock space. A more general approach would view the port as one part of an overall transportation system carrying cargo from origin to destination. In theory, one should define a criterion in terms of national income, where the objective would be to minimize the cost to the nation of moving a given volume of cargo through U.S. ports. An elaborate analysis could include all social costs, such as the increased air pollution caused by overland feeder transportation systems serving centralized facilities. Needless to say, performing the analysis related to the objective referred to above is an extremely difficult task.

The MarAd sponsored study, The Impact of Maritime Containerization on the United States Transportation System, that predicted great container terminal overcapacity assumed that 100 percent capacity of a container terminal occurred when each container crane averaged 16 hours of work per day, five days per week, 50 weeks per year, or 4,000 hours per year. Each container crane was assumed to make 20 lifts or 10 "round trips" per hour. While this may be a reasonable estimate, it does not explain the complexity of determining terminal capacity.

While in some instances the capacity of a terminal may be constrained or defined by the number of container cranes, that is certainly not always the case. The bottleneck in a particular terminal which limits capacity may be such factors as access roads, ability to handle paper work at the terminal, storage space for containers inside the terminal, or amount of dock space. Consider the simple example of two terminals which each handle 4,200 containers per week consisting of 2,100 containers in each direction. One terminal is served once a week by a single ship that unloads and loads 2,100 containers. The other terminal is served daily by a vessel that loads and unloads 300 containers. While both terminals handle the same amount of cargo, the demands on each terminal are quite different. The terminal serving one huge ship per week needs space for approximately 4,200 containers and a good deal of equipment in the terminal to efficiently serve this vessel. On the other hand, the terminal handling one small vessel per day needs much less storage space and probably a lower investment in terminal equipment. This simple example shows that the optimal configuration of a terminal will be dependent on the size of vessels and their frequency and pattern of arrivals.

Furthermore, the size and mix of containers, the imbalance and seasonality of trade, and the amount of "stuffing" and "stripping" to be performed in the terminal must also be considered.

Besides the difficulty in defining and measuring overcapacity, it should be pointed out that there may be advantages to having more terminals than the capacity considered theoretically optimal to move a specific pattern of cargo at a given point in time. Because of future uncertainties, terminal overcapacity could be helpful in the event of a sudden increase in commerce. Note also that the lead time required to build a new facility may make it desirable always to have a certain amount of extra terminal capacity available for such contingencies. Consequently, to define that optimum capacity that would minimize national cost, one would have to predict the cargo flow many years into the future to be able to minimize cost over the life of the investment in terminal facilities. In this way, what appears to be an overcapacity today may not be in the longer run.

In addition to strictly economic arguments, there may be other advantages to having terminal overcapacity. In the instance that a major harbor was immobilized either by an enemy attack or a civil emergency such as a collision involving vessels with toxic contents that caused the surrounding area to be temporarily evacuated, terminal overcapacity spread out among other harbors would be desirable. Likewise, in the instance of a labor strike closing down a major port or one particular region of the country, overcapacity in other ports or other regions would be very useful.

If the United States had the optimal capacity of terminals, there would be considerably less competition among ports than with the present apparent overcapacity. Consequently, it would be necessary to insure that the ports did not raise their prices to unreasonable rates. While this type of regulation now exists, as it does for all utilities, more effort would probably be needed in this area.

A subtle benefit of terminal overcapacity concerns conferences, the price-fixing cartels which operate on major liner routes.[4] Economists generally agree that such cartels charge higher rates than necessary, responding to the needs of the more inefficient carriers in the group. One of the restraints on conferences in the U.S. trade are small liner companies that operate outside the conferences. To the extent that terminal overcapacity helps these carriers to exist, and to the extent that their existence helps to hold down conference rates, or provide lower rates for U.S. shippers on non-conference vessels, terminal overcapacity provides benefits to the United States.[5]

The Theoretical Costs of Overcapacity

While what can appear to be an overcapacity of container terminals may provide certain benefits to the nation, there are also definite costs involved. However, these costs are diverse and difficult to measure because the information presently available is inadequate to allow a precise determination of the optimal national container terminal capacity.

The most straightforward cost of overcapacity is the amount of funds spent to construct unnecessary facilities. Other costs include the opportunity lost in terms of utilizing the waterfront property for unnecessary terminals rather than more productive uses. In addition, the unnecessary duplication of personnel and services from competing ports means that these resources could be better employed elsewhere.

Since there are economies of scale in the operation of port facilities, overcapacity results in underutilization and higher unit costs. That is, if the United States had a smaller number of larger container terminals, the cost per ton would be lower. To the extent that this higher-than-necessary terminal cost is passed on to the shipper, the cost of shipping and receiving goods is higher than need be. The ultimate result of this higher-than-necessary shipping cost is that some commerce that would pass through U.S. ports at the lower cost is presently economically prohibited from moving.

Impact of Federal Spending

Surprisingly little is known about the impact of federal funds to pay for essentially 100 percent of the dredging of U.S. ocean ports and approximately 7 percent of capital investment in public port facilities. There appear to be instances where the spending of federal funds is clearly not in the national interest, as shown by the following statement of Senator William Proxmire:[6]

The government spent $70 million dredging the Delaware River from Philadelphia to Trenton to a depth of forty feet...

Since completion, the Delaware River project has cost a great deal to maintain and in some years has been little used by vessels with forty-foot drafts. In the two most recent years, maintenance of the Philadelphia-Trenton stretch of the river has cost between $1.25 and $1.4 million annually. In one year only ten vessels with forty-foot drafts, carrying only seventy thousand tons, made the trip.

However, there is little knowledge as to the economic impact of federal port-related spending at the local, state and national levels. No research exists that clearly explains the effect at the local, state and national level of reducing federal port-related funding. In some instances, the lack of federal spending may have little impact on overall port development. In an analysis of the Port of Los Angeles, the Corps of Engineers recently stated:[7]

If the Federal project of deepening the inner channel is not realized, the Port of Los Angeles would in all

probability deepen the inner channel in order for the
flow of commerce to continue and to be competitive with
the Port of Long Beach and other west coast ports and to
maintain its world trade.

This statement may imply that the benefits of the proposed
project are local in nature rather than national. While the
enactment of this project with local rather than federal money
would have no impact on the overall national allocation of resources, it may mean that local funds rather than national general
tax funds would be used to derive largely local benefits.

Fragmentation of Federal Power

The fragmentation of agencies associated with port policy at
the federal level has basic disadvantages. Since the Corps of
Engineers, MarAd, and DOT all play a role in the planning of
maritime or overall transportation policy and development, the
task of setting up a national port policy or a national transportation policy must take account of considerable variation in
agency views, jurisdictions and program designs. Without a clearly
stated port or transportation policy, federal agencies within this
fragmented institutional structure may implement programs which
conflict. Consider, for example, a case where the Corps of Engineers would be dredging a small port while a decision of the FMC
would result in vessels bypassing that port and absorbing the
inland feeder costs of bringing the cargo to a larger port of
call. Another example is an instance where the Corps of Engineers
would refuse to perform a dredging project which it deemed uneco-
nomical due to small volumes of cargo, while the EDA would provide
funds to help construct new terminal facilities to aid the growth
of the port.

Resulting Federal Institutional Environment

The factors of technology and ecology have placed many federal agencies in the position where their actions have an impact
on the competitive status among ports. However, no analysis is
underway to determine the overall economic impacts of federal
actions on the national port network. This situation results, in
part, because no one agency has the proper combination of congressional mandates, resources, and administrative willingness to
perform a comprehensive national port study. In addition, some
agencies are not thoroughly analyzing the economic input of their
own activities on ports, much less considering the economic impact
of other federal bodies.

A further problem exists in that no attempt has been made to
determine in a quantitative manner an optimal national port network
for the United States. In fact, there is not even a consensus of
what an optimal national port structure means in conceptual terms.
Consequently, while federal agencies are having an impact on the
competitive status among ports, it is not obvious whether specific
federal actions are improving or worsening the national port
network since there is no agreement on what is the optimal national
port structure.

Pressures for Immediate Legislative Changes

The fragmentation of federal power, the lack of a comprehensive national port study, and an ignorance of the impact on ports would all appear to be institutional pressures leading to legislative changes concerning the federal role in port planning and development.

Elements of various institutional pressures can be seen in government, industry and public constituencies supporting specific policy orientations. Governmental constituent groups include Congress, national commissions and federal agencies. Steamship companies, freight shippers and labor unions are part of the industrial constituencies. In order to determine whether interest group politics will pressure Congress to enact legislative change, the potential forces calling for such action must be considered. Several candidates will be studied including the steamship companies, the reports of various commissions, the executive branch, the Congress, and the ports.

The steamship companies support the present system with its apparent overcapacity and competitive prices; they resist a strengthening of the planning role at the federal level. Shippers and receivers of cargo in general also wish to maintain the apparent overcapacity and competitive prices of the present system. Longshoring unions have their members geographically dispersed in relation to the competitive status among ports. Any change in the federal structure which results in the altering of cargo flows through the U.S. port network will upset those union members who lose part of their normal workloads. In addition, to the extent that federal actions reduce the apparent terminal overcapacity, less work for longshoremen will result on a national scale. Consequently, longshoring unions oppose any changes in the status quo.

However, the National Water Commission report and the Water Resources Council have implicitly called for changes in the status quo by recommending modifications of the criteria used to evaluate dredging projects and for user charges. The many transportation studies of previous years recommended a Department of Transportation which would include the maritime mode in a greater degree than has been enacted. The fulfillment of these various recommendations would affect the process of port development.

Although no serious legislative attempt has been made to administratively transfer MarAd into DOT since the failure of enacting such a change at the time of the passing of the DOT Act, Senator Humphrey has recently introduced legislation to increase the powers of DOT in the inland waterways area.* The proposed

---

*One possible motivation for this proposed legislative action is that it traditionally has been easier to add new bureaucratic power to an agency rather than simply reorganize existing authorities among agencies.

legislation (S. 671) would establish within DOT a Federal Inland
Waterways Administration which would perform (Sec. 4) such functions of the Maritime Administration of the Department of Commerce,
the Federal Maritime Commission, the Corps of Engineers of the
Department of the Army, the Tennessee Valley Authority, and The
Interstate Commerce Commission as the Director of the Office of
Management and Budget determines relates to inland waterways. The
enactment of this legislation could set a precedent for increasing
the bureaucratic power of DOT in ocean port activities.

Some smaller public ports, in danger of being economically
squeezed out of existence by the container revolution and various
government regulations, would support direct government aid for
the building of port facilities. However, it is questionable
whether such a new type of federal subsidy could be granted without
any strings attached. It is the feeling of the Maritime Administration that:[8]

Any federal financial aid program that might be developed and legislated for the port industry would undoubted-
ly have to incorporate some sort of master plan feature.
It would make no sense for the national government to
participate in a financial aid program that would have
the capability of creating redundant and competing facilities. That, obviously, would not be a wise use of
capital.

Consequently, smaller ports would only support legislation for
such a program to the extent that they felt the financial benefits
would outweigh the possible costs resulting from a greater federal
voice. While some larger ports might be in favor of a federal
financial aid program for port facilities, in order to gain the
economic benefits, others would probably oppose such legislation
to minimize the federal role in port development and to maintain
their competitive advantage of greater financial strength over
some of their weaker competitors.

The Congress, of course, is the body that must pass new
legislation. Past actions of the Congress show that commercial
maritime interests are well represented in this legislative body.
The decision to keep MarAd out of DOT, the passage of the Merchant
Marine Act of 1970 with its maritime subsidies, the action not to
implement the recommendations of the Bolling Committee to reduce
the bureaucratic power of the House Committee on Merchant Marine
and Fisheries, the quick response to lower the discount rate used
in evaluation criteria, and the prevention of introduction of user
charges for water resource projects, even when restricted to
recreation aspects, seem to make it clear that federal control of
maritime affairs will not be greatly increased by legislative
action in the near future. Since the majority of states, and
therefore Congressmen, are located adjacent to bodies of water, it
is politically disadvantageous for a Congressmen to take legislative action that could hurt industries or other constituent groups
back in his home state.

Moreover, local constituencies have traditionally exerted little political pressure on Congressmen to change this basic approach. Each state is anxious to get the benefit of federal funds, with no matching funds required, and there appears to be no general public concern pertaining to the misallocation of federal funds in port development.

One reason for this congressional position of generally maintaining the status quo is that traditionally Congress has not considered port development to be a major issue. The level of federal funding in this area partially reflects this low priority; federal funds involved in port development do not consume an inordinate amount of money when viewed in the overall framework of federal expenditures in either the water resources area or the transportation area. Exhibits in Appendix I from the National Water Commission report show that, whether viewed in terms of recent past, present or predicted expenditures, federal funds for navigation projects have only accounted for roughly five to ten percent of federal outlays for water resources and related developments. In addition, federal water resources expenditures as a whole have only made up 20 to 35 percent of federal civil public works funds and less than two percent of the federal budget.

When viewing federal expenditures in a transportation framework, the federal port-related funds appear small compared to the Highway Trust Fund which spends on the order of $5 billion per year. However, it should be pointed out that the Highway Trust Fund gets its money from user charges by such devices as gasoline taxes, etc. While some persons in the maritime field feel the U.S. Customs revenues related to marine shipments of more than $3 billion per year act as a type of user charge for international waterborne shippers, it is questionable whether customs and import duties, established mainly to protect U.S. industries from foreign exports, should be interpreted in this manner.

While there appears to be little chance of direct legislative action in the near future to reduce the fragmentation of federal power in the port development area, pending legislation may entail subtle changes having long-range administrative impacts on the federal role in port planning.

Pending Port Aid Legislation

In May 1975 five "port aid" bills were pending before committees of Congress.* The purpose of all five bills, which were

---

*H.R. 4964 was introduced March 14, 1975, by Merchant Marine and Fisheries Committee Chairman, Mrs. Sullivan, with the following co-sponsors: Dingell (Mich.) Downing (Va.), Daniels (Va.), Murphy (N.Y.), Jones (N.C.), Anderson (Cal.), de la Garza (Tex.) Metcalfe (Ill.), Breaux (La.), Rooney (N.Y.), Studds (Mass.), Bowen (Miss.), Eilberg (Pa.), de Lugo (R.I.), Zeferetti (N.Y.)

introduced by a total of 20 sponsors and co-sponsors, is identical
in its twofold purpose; the proposed legislation would establish a
grant program to enable public ports to comply with certain federal
standards and would direct the Secretary of Commerce to undertake
a comprehensive national port study.

The grant program would allow any state, local government, or
interstate agency, or other public port authority to apply to the
Secretary of Commerce for financial assistance. This financial
aid could be used to assist the port agency in making such improvements as may be required to any port operated by it in order to
bring such port into compliance with any requirements which may be
imposed by federal law. These regulations relate to environmental
protection, the public health and safety, or port or cargo security. Such improvements include the construction, repair, or
rehabilitation of port structures and areas, the training of
employees, and the hiring of additional personnel. Thirty million
dollars in the form of grants is authorized to aid these improvements for fiscal year 1975, and each fiscal year thereafter.

The proposed legislation also directs the Secretary of Commerce to undertake a comprehensive study to determine the immediate
and long-range requirements of public ports for expansion and
modernization. Such public port investment will be necessary in
order to meet adequately the economic and defense needs of the
United States and to meet such standards as may be imposed by law
for purposes of environmental protection and port safety and
security. The study will also include a comprehensive evaluation
and analysis of the amount and kinds of funding which public ports
have available to them for purposes of implementing current and
projected expansion and modernization. If the Secretary of Commerce finds that public ports do not, or will not, have adequate
funding capability for such implementation, he will include in the
study his recommendations for achieving such a capability. However, if the Secretary makes any recommendation for federal participation in achieving such a capability, such recommendation may
not propose any action which would disrupt the existing competitive
relationship among public ports or in any manner discriminate
between such ports.
In carrying out the required study, the Secretary of Commerce
will solicit the views of appropriate federal, state, interstate,
and local agencies, as well as of representatives of shipping,
cargo handling, land transportation, and other interested indus-

---

Oberstar (Minn.), Au Coin (Ore.), and Foresythe (N.J.).

Mrs. Sullivan's earlier port aid bill (H.R. 1084) was co-sponsored
by Messrs. Downing, Anderson, de la Garza, Breaux, and Daniel
above, plus Congressman Ashley (Ohio). Mr. Breaux also sponsored
his own bill (H.R. 2380). Mr. Whitehurst (Va.) separately sponsored H.R. 3364, and Mr. Edwards (Cal.) separately sponsored
H.R. 4613.

tries. To the extent necessary, the Secretary will consider the requirements of public ports on a regional basis in order that problems common to public ports in any region may be given particular attention. One million dollars is authorized for each of the fiscal years 1975 and 1976 to carry out this study.

The American Association of Port Authorities has for several years supported the idea of a grant program similar to that expressed in the port aid bills. The idea of a comprehensive national port study is disliked by many AAPA members; however, a $2 million study which cannot propose any action disrupting the competitive relationship among public ports is likely viewed as a small price to pay for perpetual annual grants of $30 million to public ports. Consequently, AAPA has come out in favor of the port aid bills.

Many congressmen apparently feel that the inclusion of a comprehensive national port study provides justification for the grant program in that the study may conclude that the federal funding is necessary. While it may be more economically logical to delay the start of the grant program until after hearing the results of the national port study, congressmen seem to feel that it is politically advantageous to start the grant program and the study at the same time. The large number of congressmen involved in sponsoring port aid bills is in part a reflection of the strong industry support for such legislation.

However, a comprehensive national port study would represent a radical shift in the congressional approach to the economic investigation of the nation's ports. A thorough analysis of the needs of public ports nationwide has never been performed, nor has the concept ever been supported in Congress. This traditional attitude is reflected in the legislative requirement that forthcoming recommendations specifically do not disrupt the competitive relationship among ports. Nevertheless, such a comprehensive study, if conducted, could provide an informative data base on the implications of federal funds on port development.

CHAPTER 11

CONCLUSIONS AND RECOMMENDATIONS

The Conditions for Change

The federal government has consistently supported port development, particularly in the case of public terminals, for almost two hundred years, and has provided various ancillary services to the ports without charge. A key factor in this federal approach to port development has been to prohibit discrimination among ports either by governmental or private actions. One result of this policy has been that federal port activities have had little or no effect on the competitive relationship among ports.

However, while both the port industry and the federal government have traditionally supported this situation, the increasing policy and economic impacts of federal activities and regulations will affect port competition in the future. Factors relating to both technology and ecology have complicated the traditional port development process by requiring new administrative procedures and regulatory actions. The Corps of Engineers, which has historically been able to maintain approximate competitive equality among ports with its national dredging program, will no longer be able to do so. Modern containerships and supertankers have increased requests by ports for deeper channels and harbors. However, the combination of environmental regulations and inflationary pressures on capital budgets will reduce the amount of dredging possible at constant funding levels. Therefore, with existing funds it will be impossible for the Corps to continue its dredging program without establishing priorities which have the effect of favoring some ports over others. Because a comprehensive national study of port needs has never been performed, it is not possible to determine all the long-range impacts of a decreased amount of federally-funded dredging on overall United States maritime commerce. Nevertheless, the major implication of federal activities which affect port competition is the disruption of the traditional role of federal agencies in port development.

Furthermore, the Federal Maritime Commission is in the process of deciding the fate of the "mini-landbridge" operations which cause an overland diversion of containerized cargo from one port to another with part of the cost allegedly being absorbed by the containership operator. The Department of Transportation will present testimony to influence this case. Since the decision may have a direct impact on ports, the DOT is being placed in a position of possibly influencing the disruption of current competitive port relationships.

Many Coast Guard regulations and activities also have an economic impact on ports, such as the handling of hazardous cargoes, vessel traffic control systems, icebreaking services, and operations of deepwater terminals. The Office of the Secretary within the Department of Transportation has not been substantively

involved in economic analysis affecting ports in the past, but it
is now facing several such issues: the Mini-Landbridge case, the
licensing of deepwater ports, user taxes on waterways, and the
formation of a proposed Inland Waterways Administration within the
Department.

Environmental agencies will also influence the competitive
status of ports by their review of the primary and secondary
impacts of port development. Furthermore, in applying criteria
which differentiate factors among ports such as wave height,
amount of foggy weather, existing traffic congestion, degree of
adjacent industrialization, and local population density, any
federal agency may implement policies or programs which have the
effect of favoring some ports over others.

Recognizing the Administrative Dilemma

Federal port policy is on the horns of an administrative
dilemma in that executive agencies can no longer provide services
to ports without potentially altering their competitive status.
However, in practice the federal government has avoided acknow-
ledging or confronting the disruptive implications of its actions
on the traditional port development process.

Recent legislative activities illustrate that Congress has
not focused its attention on formulating policies which consider
this dilemma. Pending port aid legislation* proposed by twenty
sponsors and co-sponsors reflects the intent of Congress to avoid
discrimination among ports. This legislation states that if the
Secretary of Commerce recommends that the federal government
assist public ports in obtaining adequate funding capability for
further development, that:

such recommendation may not propose any action which
would disrupt the existing competitive relationship
among public ports or in any manner discriminate
between such ports.

While this assertion is consistent with earlier Congressional
statements, it does not address the annual federal expenditures of
hundreds of millions of dollars to provide services to the port
industry. Furthermore, the proposed legislation avoids mentioning
that federal funds are already being used to finance public ports
through the Economic Development Administration.

Other aspects of recent Congressional actions are also consistent with past approaches to federal port policy. The pending
port aid legislation, in addition to those considerations mentioned
above, would provide financial assistance for public ports but not
for private ones. Further, the recently enacted Deepwater Port
Act of 1974 reaffirmed support for public ports in assigning

---

*Refer to Chapter 10 for more information.

priority for licensing to public facilities over private terminals.

Fragmentation of Power

One reason that Congress and executive agencies have not directly confronted this administrative dilemma is that there is no organization exercising distinct policy leadership in this area. Federal power related to port planning and development is fragmented among more than forty federal organizations. Fragmentation of power also exists among congressional committees and subcommittees. The legislative authorities of some federal agencies are paradoxical in nature; the Secretary of Defense is responsible for determining the commercial adequacy of ports, while the Secretary of Commerce is responsible for the mobilization of ports in time of war. No one organization is coordinating the federal activities related to port development.

Fragmentation of power can also result in agencies working at cross-purposes to each other. For example, while the Economic Development Administration has funded more than $100 million in port and port-related projects in the past decade, these projects were not predicated on the needs of the port industry, but rather were aimed at alleviating regional economic distress or high rates of unemployment. Consequently, the activities of one federal agency may be helping a port while another agency is taking action which will do economic damage to the same port.

Duplication of effort can also result from this administrative environment. Three federal agencies are presently spending funds to perform economic analyses of port development. The Corps of Engineers performs cost-benefit analyses for local dredging projects as well as other studies. The Maritime Administration is funding regional studies of port development in conjunction with local parties. Under the Deepwater Port Act of 1974, the Department of Transportation is charged with considering the economic effects of offshore terminals compared with dredged deepwater channels providing access to onshore facilities. There is no formal mechanism for coordinating the studies of these three agencies, eliminating duplication of effort, or facilitating exchange of information.

Lack of National Goals

Port development is a component of both national transportation and water resources policy. Therefore, an underlying problem concerning the federal role in port planning and development is the lack of a clearly defined national policy for either water resources or transportation. While the Water Resources Council and the Department of Transportation have been working to correct this situation, neither has been notably successful. In addition, the lack of a national energy policy also contributes to the problems of ocean port policy and development. While port interests are applying for licenses to construct offshore terminals, no distinct federal energy policy specifies the level of future oil imports.

Improving Federal Port-Related Expenses

The ability to improve federal spending in port-related activities depends on the administrative approach of federal port policy and the availability of adequate data to implement such a policy program. The formation of clearly defined national approaches to the policy areas of transportation, water resources, and energy will influence the elaboration of federal port policy. Since ports make up an integral part of both transportation and water systems, progress in port policy will always be limited as long as there are ambiguities and conflicts between national water policy and national transport policy.

As one analyst has pointed out:[1]

Unless investment criteria are rendered compatible between these two areas, the gap between objective evidence and optimal public investment patterns will continue to plague investment analysts who must calculate one set to comply with legislative mandate, and another set to satisfy their curiosity about how far such results actually are from economic investment optimality. Investments in water projects do not produce economic effects sufficiently different from investments in transport projects to justify disparate investment criteria, and the full effects of existing disparities must be quantitatively assessed to determine the net impact these procedures have on resource allocation patterns.

While the task is difficult, the quest for objective public expenditure analysis must proceed in pursuit of a common denominator for investment criteria. Whether this common denominator is based strictly on economic efficiency or includes a multi-dimensional criterion, there is much room for improvement in the way federal expenditures are made.

However, vested interests have traditionally opposed the setting of a common denominator for public investment, since this action would place in jeopardy their present system of obtaining federal subsidies and services. Nevertheless, the social benefits of improving the allocation of federal resources can be great.

In order to view federal investment in port-related activities in a national framework, adequate data are required concerning the capacity of present and planned terminals, the degree of overcapacity existing and anticipated in the future, and the impact of federal funds for port projects at local, state, and federal levels. Current research and data-gathering activities of the Corps of Engineers, MarAd and DOT* will provide basic inform-

*Questionnaires sent to port authorities by DOT in relation to the 1974 National Transportation Report should provide insight into how ports assess their current capacity.

ation in the area of cargo-handling capacity and perceived needs
of ports, but more emphasis in this area is needed.

Possibilities for Institutional Change

The institutional structure which has developed in the port
area is resistant to change or transfers of power among organizational actors. This resistance is emphasized by the failure of
administrative attempts over the past century to remove the responsibility for evaluating dredging projects from the Corps of Engineers. While in theory activities of the Corps, the Department of
Transportation, and the Maritime Administration could be placed
within a single agency to reduce the fragmentation of bureaucratic
power, this is unlikely to occur in that it represents a major
organizational change in an environment dominated by entrenched
vested interests. Consequently, in the short term more emphasis
must be placed on bringing about greater coordination of activities
among agencies.

Comprehensive National Port Study

Although the Corps of Engineers, MarAd, and DOT are performing
various port economic analyses, no formal mechanism exists to
coordinate these studies. In addition, no agency is attempting to
analyze the economic impact of all federal actions on the national
port structure. A comprehensive national port study could provide
the mechanism needed to coordinate existing economic analyses and
the information necessary to fully understand the economic impact
of federal actions on the competitive relationship among ports
nationwide.

The pending port aid legislation calls for a comprehensive
national port study that could fulfill the above objectives if so
directed. This legislation delegates the Secretary of Commerce
(apparently through the Maritime Administration) to direct the
analysis. It could be argued that either DOT or the Corps of
Engineers should be in charge of such a study. However, as long
as the Corps, MarAd, and DOT all perform different types of port
economic analyses which influence local and regional port development in varying ways, it is important that all three agencies be
substantively involved and committed to such a national study.
The effective coordination and cooperation among these three
agencies is of greater consequence than the choice of the director
of the study.

A key part of such a study should be the creation of a framework for port analyses which could apply to future port studies of
the three agencies. The conceptual definition of optimal national
port capacity and the means of determining such an objective
should be decided upon. A basic agreement on data bases and
methodology would provide a base for future studies on a local,
regional or national level. The use of a common framework would
also eliminate possible double counting of benefits for specific
projects, and would serve to coordinate the activities of the

three agencies. The difficulty in setting up a common framework
and performing a comprehensive national port study should not be
underestimated; it is a complex and formidable task. Nevertheless,
this should be performed to determine the full impact on ports of
spending federal funds in port-related activities.

Impacts of Executive Agencies

Even without Congress enacting new port-related legislation,
executive agencies may initiate actions which improve the federal
approach to port policy. The Environmental Protection Agency and
the Council on Environmental Quality should re-evaluate environmental regulations affecting port development, particularly the
criteria for dredged spoil disposal, to determine whether such
regulations represent a reasonable compromise in improving the
environment without unduly restricting port development. (A five-
year study under the Corps of Engineers will hopefully resolve the
issue of the disposal of dredged spoils.)

If legislation calling for a comprehensive national port
study is not enacted, MarAd should continue to sponsor regional
port studies and emphasize interagency coordination. Such studies
aid both the ports and the federal agencies to better perceive the
future needs of the industry.

The Corps of Engineers

A key factor in the future will be the allocation of federal
funds for dredging. Since environmental regulations and inflation
are increasing the costs of dredging and the use of larger vessels
requires deeper channels, the dredging activities of the federal
government will take on greater significance.

The Corps is in the position of influencing the allocation of
limited funds among many ports requesting dredging. Within budget
limitations set by Congress and OMB, the Corps may either distri-
bute its dredging efforts over a large number of competing ports
or establish priorities for dredging only a select number of
ports. This situation suggests the following implications:
first, a wide distribution of funds will limit the amount of
dredging for each maintenance and new project and ensure that a
large number of ports may have difficulty handling sailings of
existing vessels, much less those of future deeper-draft vessels.
Second, a more selective allocation of funds will facilitate
commerce through those ports dredged but disrupt traditional
competitive relationships among ports.

An alternative which should be considered is enlarging the
budget of the Corps of Engineers for dredging activities. Increases in funding levels would allow the Corps to more adequately
maintain the existing competitive relationship among ports.
Nevertheless, before such funding is increased, it is imperative
to analyze the future needs of the port industry, taking into
account such factors as trade patterns, the construction of deep-

water ports, mini-landbridge and rate-absorption case decisions,
environmental regulations, regional impacts of ports, labor union
agreements, and the possibility of new charges for waterway users.
Only by undertaking a comprehensive national port study can a
rational determination of funding requirements for federal dredging
activities be arrived at.

However, without the completion of such a study the Corps
would not have available information on the national and regional
needs of the port industry and, as a consequence, the agency would
be forced to consider dredging requests of competing ports without
the benefit of this analysis. Since port development has regional
as well as national impacts, the agency should develop at least a
regional approach in performing economic analyses of port dredging
projects. The Corps should calculate the benefits and costs of
placing a new investment at alternative locations within a region,
rather than its traditional emphasis on conducting only local
analyses.

However, if the Corps does not adopt a regional approach of
its own accord, environmental interests opposing a particular
dredging project may force the Corps through legal proceedings to
perform regional analyses to meet the intent of required Environmental Impact Statements.

The Department of Transportation

Both the Office of the Secretary and the Coast Guard within
DOT are being drawn into activities and roles which affect port
competition. The Coast Guard implements operational regulatory
programs which entail economic impacts on port development and, as
a consequence, greater concern should be placed on economic analysis within this agency. The Office of the Secretary is presently
involved in several strategic policy-making decisions that may
influence future port development. Since traditionally the Department has placed little emphasis in these areas, new legislative
and administrative responsibilities in the maritime area require
re-evaluation of agency resources.

DOT should formulate an explicit internal policy defining
what roles the Coast Guard and the Office of the Secretary will
play in economic analysis related to port development. The Department of Transportation should specifically place more resources in
both the Office of the Secretary and the Coast Guard to carry out
complementary roles and responsibilities.

The recently established Office of Deepwater Ports within OST
may be able to provide a focal point for coordination between the
Coast Guard and OST on maritime affairs. If the mandate of the
Office of Deepwater Ports is too narrow to permit such a function,
a new organization within OST could facilitate a more direct
implementation of program responsibilities. One possibility would
be the establishment of an "Office of Terminal Interface Systems"
within OST with responsibility to consider intermodal policy and

planning for all transport modes. This new organization might establish an ongoing research group to study related maritime issues (with the exception of those analyzed by the Office of Deepwater Ports). This group could be composed of a permanent Departmental planning staff plus a number of rotating Coast Guard personnel to aid coordination between the OST policy development and Coast Guard operational regulatory programs.

Role of States

In addition to these organizational considerations at the federal level, state governments will influence the formation and implementation of port policies and strategies for development. While not traditionally instrumental in the process of port operations, planning and development directed by private and public port authorities, state capitals will be increasingly drawn into this policy area. One example of this is that states now have veto power over offshore terminal development affecting their coasts under the recently enacted Deepwater Port Act of 1974.

Furthermore, most coastal states are now formulating plans pursuant to the Congressional passage of the Coastal Zone Management Act. Once these plans are completed and approved by the federal Office of Coastal Zone Management, new port development will have to take place in accordance with these plans. Consequently, the states will be providing a mechanism, in theory at least, whereby they can explicitly compare a proposed port development with alternative uses for parcels of coastal land.

In addition, most states have formed departments of transportation. In theory, the existence of these state DOTs will facilitate the comparison of costs and benefits of spending funds in port development versus other areas of transportation, a comparison presently not done at the federal level.

States should view their new role in port development as an opportunity to re-evaluate state subsidies to ports and to attempt to optimize their expenditures for port-related projects. In some states administrative action is already taking place to reduce intrastate port rivalry or to better coordinate all modes of transportation. In 1970, the Virginia Legislature reorganized the existing Virginia State Ports Authority for the purpose of unifying the state's competing ports.[2] Other states have placed formerly quasi-autonomous public port authorities within a state department of transportation. A recent Texas report calls for some degree of state participation in local port planning "in order for the state to enjoy optimal development of its port system."[3]

Furthermore, as a consequence of Congressional port-related legislation, the federal government must take into account the increasing role of state capitals in the port development process.

A New Federal Role

The traditional federal port policy in the United States has been one in which programs of federal agencies did not disturb the competitive relationship among ports. Modern technology, combined with other factors such as environmental regulations, has disrupted this policy approach. Federal agencies may affect port competition in three ways: (1) allocation of funds for dredging or port facilities; (2) implementation of existing regulations as they pertain to the siting and operation of terminal facilities and their vessel movements; or (3) formulation of new policies or programs which directly or indirectly affect ports. The federal government must acknowledge the administrative dilemma confronting the traditional approach to federal port policy, establish a unified governmental approach to port planning and development, and take the necessary steps to evaluate the future competitive impacts on ports of its actions.

APPENDIX A

STATUTORY AUTHORITY FOR FEDERAL ORGANIZATIONS
INVOLVED IN PORT POLICY AND DEVELOPMENT

Exhibit A.1

Principal Statutory Authorities for Federal
Organizations Involved in
Port Policy and Development

Agency	Authority
1. Atomic Energy Commission (AEC)	42 USC 2011, 2051 (Sections 1 and 31 of Atomic Energy Act of 1954 as amended)
	42 USC 2051, 2201 (Sections 31 and 161 of Atomic Energy Act of 1954 as amended)
2. Council on Environmental Quality (CEQ)	See Chapter 5
3. Department of Agriculture	21 USC 114b-c
- Bureau of Animal Husbandry	U.S. Dept. of Agriculture Act of 1862, 33 USC 610
- Bureau of Entomology and Plant Quarantine	Animal and Plant Health Inspection Service, 5 USC 301 and Reorganization Plan 2 of 1953
4. Department of the Army	10 USC 3012(b)
- Army Corps of Engineers	See Chapter 6
Board of Engineers for Rivers and Harbors	
5. Department of Commerce	
- Economic Development Administration	Public Works and Economic Development Act of 1965; 79 Stat. 552; 42 USC 3121
- Maritime Administration	See Chapter 7
- National Oceanographic and Atmospheric Administration (NOAA)	Reorganization Plan 4 of 1970
Office of Coastal Zone Management	Coastal Zone Management Act of 1972, 82 Stat. 1280; P.L. 92-583; Sec. (c)(610) of the Deepwater Port Act of 1974

Agency	Authority
NOAA (continued)	
National Ocean Survey	P.L. 91-144; 83 Stat. 326
National Marine Fisheries Service	50 CFR, Chs. I and II P.L. 86-359; 73 Stat. 642; 16 USC 760e to 760g
National Weather Service	15 USC 313; 33 USC 313; 44 USC 213
Sea Grant Program	80 Stat. 998; 33 USC 1121 et seq.
6. Department of Defense	See Dept. of Army, Navy
7. Department of Health, Education, and Welfare (HEW)	
- Public Health Service	42 USC 264-272
8. Department of Housing and Urban Development (HUD)	
- Housing and Home Finance Agency (Community Facilities Administration)(Urban Renewal Administration)	42 USC 3102; 74 USC 1491; 42 USC 3104-08; 42 USC 1450; 40 USC 461
9. Department of the Interior	
- Geological Survey	42 USC 1340; 42 USC 366; 43 USC 31; 76 Stat. 427
- Bureau of Land Management	OCS Lands Act of Aug. 7, 1953 (67 Stat. 462; 43 CFR 3380); 43 USC 1334, 1362
- Bureau of Sport Fisheries and Wildlife	Fish and Wildlife Act of 1956 as amended; 70 Stat. 1119; 16 USC 742(a)-742(e)
- Office of Land Use and Water Planning	See Chapter 4
- Office of Water Resources Research	78 Stat. 331; 42 USC 1961b
10. Department of Justice	
- Immigration and Naturalization Service	26 Stat. 1085; 8 USC 1304

Agency	Authority
11. Department of Labor	
- Occupational Safety and Health Administration	National Occupational Safety and Health Act of 1970, P.L. 91-596, Dec. 1970; 33 USC 929, 930, 941; 5 USC 22
12. Department of the Navy - Oceanographic Office	10 USC 5011-5012; 10 USC 7230; 10 USC 7391-7393; 14 USC 3; 33 USC 360; 33 USC 1051; 50 USC 191A; 50 USC 194
13. Department of State	22 USC 2656; Sec. 11 of the Deepwater Port Act of 1974
14. Department of Transportation (DOT)	See Chapter 9
- The United States Coast Guard	See Chapter 8
15. Department of the Treasury	
- Bureau of Customs	19 USC 2071; 19 USC 2; 19 CFR 1.2; Executive Order 10289, Sept. 17, 1951
- Internal Revenue Service	Act of July 1, 1862; 12 Stat. 432; 26 USC 3900
16. The Executive Offices of the President	
- Council of Economic Advisers	Employment Act of 1946; 60 Stat. 24; 15 USC 1023; Reorganization Plan 9 of 1953, August 1, 1953
- The Office of Management and Budget (OMB)	Reorganization Plan 2 of 1970, July 1, 1970; Executive Order 11541, July 1, 1970
17. Environmental Protection Agency	See Chapter 5
18. Federal Communications Commission (FCC)	48 Stat. 1064; 15 USC 21; 47 USC 35
19. Federal Energy Administration	FEA Act of 1974, P.L. 93-275

Agency	Authority
20. Federal Maritime Commission (FMC)	39 Stat. 733; Shipping Act of 1916; Merchant Marine Act of 1920; Intercoastal Shipping Act of 1933; Merchant Marine Act of 1936; Water Quality Improvement Act of 1970
21. Federal Power Commission (FPC)	41 Stat. 1063 as amended by 49 Stat. 863, 49 Stat. 838, 52 Stat. 821-833
22. Federal Trade Commission (FTC)	FTC Act of 1914, 38 Stat. 717, 15 USC 41-51; Clayton Act of 1914, 38 Stat. 730, 15 USC 12
23. General Services Administration (GSA)	Reorganization Plan 1 of 1973; Executive Order 11737, July 1, 1973; Executive Orders 11051, 11490, 11073
24. Interstate Commerce Commission (ICC)	24 Stat. 379, 383; 49 USC 1-22; Sec. 8 of the Deepwater Port Act of 1974
25. National Aeronautics and Space Administration (NASA)	42 USC 2451
26. Smithsonian Institution	20 USC 41
27. U.S. Postal Service	P.L. 86-682; 74 Stat. 587; 39 USC Sec. 904
28. Water Resources Council	Water Resources Planning Act of 1965, P.L. 89-90; Water Resources Development Act of 1974, P.L. 93-251

APPENDIX B

PRINCIPAL MANAGEMENT AND LABOR ORGANIZATIONS

Exhibit B.1

Principal Management and Labor Organizations

A.   Management Organizations

   1.   American Association of Port Authorities*

      This forum has representation from most of the port
authorities in the United States. Its purpose is to exchange
information between members to solve mutual port problems through
annual conventions, a monthly journal, and a continuing series
of special reports. The stated objectives of this organization
are:

   (1) the improvement of port facilities and cargo handling
        procedures.

   (2) increasing international trade.

   (3) economic expansion of existing ports and develop-
        ment of new port facilities.

   (4) the rapid and efficient movement of passengers
        and cargoes through seaports.

   This organization is the voice of individual port operators,
and because of its wide representation in this critical segment
of our economy, exercises substantial political influence in
maritime matters.

   2.   American Institute of Merchant Shipping

      AIMS came to existence on January 1, 1969, superseding
the American Merchant Marine Institute (AMMI), the Committee of
American Steamship Lines (CASL) and the Pacific American Steamship Association (PASA). The Institute represents the owners
of approximately 700 U.S.-flag ships: the subsidized operators,
tanker operators, and some unsubsidized dry cargo operators. It
negotiates agreements with the union manning the member's ships,
carries out policy research, and represents the interests of
members before concerned Congressional committees and agencies
of the Executive Branch.

   3.   American Maritime Association

      The AMA represents the owners of approximately 300 non-
subsidized dry cargo ships, many of which are primarily dependent
upon government-generated cargo. The Association's functions are
similar to those of AIMS.

----

*Unless otherwise noted, material has been taken from the United
States Coast Guard, Ports and Waterways Administration and Management, July 1971, Appendix B-4, pp. B-4-1 to B-4-8.

4.   Shipbuilders Council of America

        The Council is a national trade association composed of
private U.S. shipbuilders, ship repairers, and allied suppliers.
The Council represents its members before congressional committees and Executive Branch agencies.

5.   New York Shipping Association

        The Association is the primary agency of management
for negotiating agreements with the longshoremen working in ports
on the Atlantic and Gulf coasts. In addition, each port has its
own shipping association to negotiate the local provisions of
such agreements. On the West Coast the Pacific Maritime Association carries out a similar function.

6.   American Institute of Marine Underwriters

        The Institute of Marine Underwriters represents the
special managerial interests of the Insurance Industry underwriting commercial maritime activities. This organization is
active in the establishment of rates and premiums in various
marine endeavors and would exercise significant influence in public and industry acceptance of an expanded marine safety program.

7.   The American Petroleum Institute

        This organization represents the interests of the Petro-
leum Industry including offshore mining and marine transportation
of petroleum products. It is actively engaged in all aspects of
waterborne transportation of oil products including development
of construction and safety standards of tank vessels, manning
standards for vessels and all standards and procedures for offshore drilling. It is also a powerful lobbyist and exercises
substantial political influence in legislative matters dealing
with the transportation of petroleum.

8.   The Great Lakes Carrier Association

        This organization exercises similar functions to those
of the API in matters dealing with marine transportation of cargoes related to the Steel Industry. They are also active in promoting the interests of other major carriers of bulk cargo on
the Great Lakes such as wheat and other grains.

9.   The International Cargo Bureau

        This is a private organization certified by the Coast
Guard to conduct cargo loading inspections and cargo gear inspection for certain commodities such as grain. In the execution of
these responsibilities, the ICB can and does issue cargo loading
certificates and cargo gear certificates which certify that regulations regarding loading of certain cargoes have been complied
with.

10. American Bureau of Shipping

This highly technical, nonprofit organization is a sea-worthiness and marine plans classification society. Nearly all U.S. vessels in the world are classified by ABS. Certain certi-ficating responsibilities have been delegated to ABS by the Coast Guard such as certification of certain types of cargo gear. This organization is the exclusive agency issuing load line certificates.

11. American Waterway Operators

This organization is the spokesman for all major barge and towboat operators on the inland waterways. They are an in-fluential lobbyist group and exert considerable political influ-ence in marine legislation concerning inland waters.

12. The Marine Chemists' Association

This private corporation has been delegated the respon-sibility by the Coast Guard of inspecting tanks on vessels to certify they are gas-free and safe to enter before any work is done inside the tank by maintenance personnel.

13. American Pilots' Association

The APA is basically a lobbyist organization to promote the interests of port and river pilots. It is politically power-ful in matters of marine legislation and regulation.

14. United States Salvage

This private organization surveys and certifies sea-worthiness in small vessels such as oceangoing barges. It also conducts investigations which are supplemental to those conducted by the Coast Guard.

15. Water Resources Congress*

The WRC evolved through the merger of the National Rivers and Harbors Congress and the Water Resources Associated-Mississippi Valley Association. It is the oldest and the largest national organization dedicated to the best use of America's natural water resources.

B.   Labor Organizations

1. International Organization of Masters, Mates and Pilots

MMP represents licensed deck personnel operating U.S.-flag ships out of all coasts. It contracts for approximately 5,000 jobs.

---

*From the "1974 Platform, Water Resources Congress," Washington, D.C. 20036.

2.   National Marine Engineers' Beneficial Association

MEBA represents licensed engineer room personnel personnel operating U.S.-flag ships out of all coasts. Its contracts
cover approximately 600 jobs.

3.   American Radio Association

The ARA represents radio officers serving on ships
operating out of all coasts. Its contracts cover about 600 jobs.

4.   Radio Officers Union of the Commercial Telegraphers Union

ROU represents radio officers serving on ships operating
out of all coasts, providing coverage of about 400 jobs.

5.   Staff Officers Association of America

The SOA represents pursers on ships operating out of
the Atlantic and Gulf Coasts. Its contracts cover approximately
225 jobs.

6.   American Merchant Marine Staff Officers Association

AMMSOA represents pursers on ships operating out of
the Pacific Coast. Its contracts provide coverage of about 150
jobs.

7.   National Maritime Union

The NMU represents unlicensed deck, engine and stewards
department personnel on ships operating out of the Atlantic, Gulf
and Great Lakes. Its contracts cover approximately 25,000 jobs.

8.   Seafarers' International Union of North America

The SIU has two districts: the Atlantic-Gulf and the
Pacific. Under the Pacific District are the Sailors' Union of
the Pacific (SUP), covering unlicensed deck jobs on dry cargo
ships and all unlicensed jobs on tankers, the Marine Firemen,
Oilers, Watertenders and Wipers of the Pacific (MFOWW), and the
Marine Cooks and Stewards of the Pacific (MCSP). The SIU contracts cover approximately 20,000 jobs.

9.   International Longshoremen's Association

The ILA represents approximately 75,000 longshoremen
working in Atlantic, Great Lakes and Gulf ports.

10. International Longshoremen's and Warehousemen's Union

ILWU represents about 15,000 longshoremen working in
ports on the Pacific Coast.

11.   The International Brotherhood of Longshoremen

        IBL represents a few thousand longshoremen employed in
certain Gulf and Atlantic Coast ports.

12.   International Brotherhood of Boilermakers, Iron
        Shipbuilders, Blacksmiths, and Helpers

        This industrial union represents many of the workers
employed in private and governmental shipyards on all coasts.

13.   Labor Coordination

        There are two large groupings under the aegis of the
AFL-CIO: the Maritime Trades Department and the Maritime Committee. The latter, headed by Joseph Curran, consists of the ILA,
NMU, MEBA, MMP, and ARA. The MTD, headed by Paul Hall, represents the SIU, the shipbuilders, and a number of unions only
indirectly related to the maritime industry.

APPENDIX C

CHANNEL AND HARBOR PROJECTS WITH AUTHORIZED DEPTH

OF 25 FEET OR MORE

EXHIBIT C.1

CHANNEL AND HARBOR PROJECTS WITH AUTHORIZED DEPTH
OF 25 FEET OR MORE
Allotments (Thousands of Dollars)

	1970		1971		1972		1973	
	Construction	Maintenance	Construction	Maintenance	Construction	Maintenance	Construction	Maintenance
ALA.								
Mobile Harbor		1,355.3		1,472.3		1,789.7	50.0	2,255.0
ALASKA								
Iliuliuk Harbor								
Skyway Harbor		32.7						
CALIF.								
San Francisco Bay to Stockton	250.0	3,019.3	760.0	5,721.6	853.0	574.0	1,000.0	2,2000.0
Humboldt Harbor and Bay								
Los Angeles-Long Beach Harbors								
Napa River								
Oakland Harbor	100.0	172.2		725.6		4,451.9		250.0
Redwood City Harbor		140.1		200.0		196.3		150.0
Richmond Harbor		114.2		145.0		186.4		150.0
Sacramento R. Deep Water Ship Channel	20.9	1,061.9		1,605.7		1,433.5		1,250.0
San Diego Harbor				170.4	996.0		1,000.0	
San Francisco Harbor		284.5		474.0		222.5		350.0
San Joaquin River		51.5		93.1		494.5		440.0
San Pablo Bay and More Island Strait		425.9		602.0		491.6		650.0
Suisun Bay Channel		177.3		17.6		183.5		200.0
Port Hueneme Harbor					89.0		400.0	
CONN.								
Bridgeport Harbor								
New Haven Harbor		11.5		(-)70.0		740.8		900.0
New London Harbor								
Thames River								

Source: U.S. Army Corps of Engineers.

EXHIBIT C.1--Continued

	1970		1971		1972		1973	
	Construction	Maintenance	Construction	Maintenance	Construction	Maintenance	Construction	Maintenance
DEL.								
Delaware River, Phila. to Sea	4,867.0	4,059.3	8,913.0	5,655.0	4,292.0	5,700.9	7,500.0	7,000.0
Inland Waterway, Del. R. to Chesapeake Bay		1,044.2		3,320.0		3,409.8		2,250.0
Wilmington Harbor		482.2		613.0		43.1		550.0
FLA.								
Canaveral Harbor	150.0	838.2	430.8	357.9		546.5		684.0
Carrabelle Harbor				0.4				
Charlotte Harbor		75.4		158.9		161.9		192.0
Fernandina Harbor		113.2		25.0		295.3		94.0
Fort Pierce Harbor								
Hollywood Harbor	(-)545.0	648.9	3,325.0	793.3		515.0	6,300.0	600.0
Jacksonville Harbor				28.2				
Key West Harbor		6.7	150.0	(-)10.2			3,500.0	
Miami Harbor				6.4				
Palm Beach Harbor				82.1				87.0
Panama City Harbor		52.0		347.5		21.7		105.0
Pensacola Harbor				2.7				280.0
Port Everglades Harbor		189.1		(-)18.1		344.4		
Port St. Joe Harbor				190.2				
St. Augustine Harbor		30.4		115.3		867.3		
Tampa Harbor							1,500.0	
GA.								
Brunswick Harbor	85.0	578.1	3,015.0	829.0		913.7	1,200.0	950.0
Savannah Harbor		1,546.5		2,619.9		1,954.8		2,800.0
HAWAII								
Honolulu Harbor		0.8		19.6		52.4		233.0
Kahului Harbor								398.0
Kawaihae Harbor								
Nawiliwili Harbor								107.0
Port Allen Harbor								142.0
ILL.								
Calumet Harbor and River	(-)470.0	501.4	760.0	439.0		1,431.5		430.0
Chicago Harbor	(-)46.5			20.0		265.7		15.0

EXHIBIT C.1--Continued

	1970 Construction	1970 Maintenance	1971 Construction	1971 Maintenance	1972 Construction	1972 Maintenance	1973 Construction	1973 Maintenance
IND.								
Indiana Harbor		77.1		60.0		517.0		425.0
LA.								
Calcasieu River at Devil's Elbow	(-)4.2				20.0		130.0	
Calcasieu River and Pass		2,020.6		2,074.8		3,405.8		3,300.0
Mississippi River, Baton Rouge		6,325.0		4,626.1		6,057.3		6,000.0
Mississippi River-Gulf Outlet	800.0	8,814.0	1,800.0	1,915.5	793.0	3,373.5	900.0	3,500.0
Micloud Canal	15.0		35.0		99.0		1,000.0	
MAINE								
Kennebec River				130.2		11.8		
Kennebank River								
Portland Harbor		3.0						
Portsmouth Harbor and Piscataqua R.		107.0		7.4		7.9		
Searsport Harbor		158.6		155.7				
MD.								
Baltimore Harbor and Channels	(-)100.0	860.0		1,005.4		813.4		1,000.0
MASS.								
Boston Harbor								
Cape Cod Canal		21.3		27.1		23.5		40.0
Cross Rip Shoals		1,440.2		1,934.4		1,745.4		2,350.0
Fall River Harbor	100.0		125.0		650.0			385.0
Mystic River								
New Bedford and Fairhaven Harbor								
Pollock Rip Shoals								
Salem Harbor								
Town River	(-)415.0	3,640.0	3,640.0	342.0	4,565.0	133.4	5,900.0	
Weymouth Fore								
MICH.								
Great Lakes Connecting Channels	(-)6.0	647.2		549.0	592.0	2,473.3	4,900.0	600.0
Ludington Harbor		415.0		(-)5.1	40.0		60.0	
Detroit River		5.0		226.0		393.5		400.0
Grays Reef Passage								
Keweenaw Waterway		100.7		85.0		116.8		122.0
Mishegon Harbor								
Rouge River		425.0		471.0		1,377.5		355.0

EXHIBIT C.1--Continued

	1970		1971		1972		1973	
	Construction	Maintenance	Construction	Maintenance	Construction	Maintenance	Construction	Maintenance
Saginaw River	2,071.0	313.2	(-)275.0	261.2		1,278.4		250.0
St. Clair River	(-)19.0	529.?		514.5		449.4		285.0
Channels in Lake St. Clair		106.9		90.5		3,466.1		45.0
MINN.								
Minnesota River	(-)25.0	696.3	(-)5.4	456.3		1,768.2		870.0
	(-)47.8	125.1		22.0		142.3		150.0
MISS.								
Gulfport Harbor		1,339.4		399.5		418.0		750.0
Pascagoula Harbor		774.2		768.6		639.7		800.0
N.J.								
Del. R., Phila. to Trenton		260.7		430.9	4,071.0	1,069.7	4,676.0	1,250.0
Newark Bay, Hackensack and Passaic Rvs.	(-)540.0		3,284.0	370.0		462.8		1,800.0
Raritan River		147.2		600.0		138.4		300.0
N.Y.								
Buttermilk Channel		290.2	(-)14.5			481.5		
East River				215.7				
Gowanus Creek Channel		531.6		560.0		645.2		900.0
Hudson River		867.1		620.0		1,163.9		770.0
Hudson River Channel								

EXHIBIT C.1—Continued

	1970		1971		1972		1973	
	Construction	Maintenance	Construction	Maintenance	Construction	Maintenance	Construction	Maintenance
Jamaica Bay								
New York and New Jersey Channels	360.0	1,586.6	3,400.0	535.0	4,588.0	2,022.4	5,500.0	770.0
New York Harbor		346.7		510.0		1,225.7		1,100.0
Oswego Harbor		5.9		128.0		279.6		130.0
N.C.								
Cape Fear R. above Wilmington	351.0	13.8	(-)376.6	74.9				
Morehead City Harbor		649.7		535.0		673.1	100.0	1,161.0
Wilmington Harbor	1,265.0	451.6	376.6	1,064.6		926.0	390.0	1,400.0
OHIO								
Ashtabula Harbor	(-)151.0	200.2		256.0		293.4		200.0
Cleveland Harbor		1,662.6	371.0	2,155.3		9,003.7		1,665.0
Conneaut Harbor		76.8		235.0		1,153.9		180.0
Fairport Harbor		170.0		310.0		1,041.0		280.0
Huron Harbor		80.2		90.0		292.3		125.0
Lorain Harbor		283.2	20.0	164.0	1,589.0	1,188.3	3,300.0	220.0
Sandusky Harbor		260.4	840.6	65.0		1,256.9		270.0
Toledo Harbor		1,157.3		783.0		1,889.7		770.0
ORE.								
Columbia River bet. Vancouver and The Dalles		214.3		160.2		155.0		160.0
Columbia and Lower Willamette Rivers	1,440.0	2,230.1	1,520.0	3,391.7	445.0	3,510.6	3,800.0	3,800.0
Columbia River at Mouth	(-)2.0	670.5	(-)20.0	587.5		731.0		800.0
Coos Bay		1,467.9		1,209.3		440.5		500.0
Multnomah Channel								
Umpqua River	(-)55.0	73.5	1,855.0	166.0	3,443.0	105.9	1,947.0	225.0
Yaquina Bay and Harbor		385.1		489.0		458.3		480.0
PENNA.								
Erie Harbor		128.3		130.0		1,219.1		175.0
Schuylkill River		769.5		633.4		641.6		400.0
S.C.								

EXHIBIT C.1--Continued

	1970		1971		1972		1973	
	Construction	Maintenance	Construction	Maintenance	Construction	Maintenance	Construction	Maintenance
Port Royal Sound		235.0		290.0		157.0		185.0
Charleston Harbor		1,396.7		1,553.2		1,849.0		2,200.0
Georgetown Harbor		1,367.8		970.0		1,145.0		1,300.0
Shipyard River		196.6		200.0		215.8		245.0
TEX.								
Brazos Island Harbor	(-)14.0	571.0		464.2		519.0		475.0
Channel to Port Bolivar		1.8		19.0				20.0
Freeport Harbor		525.1		737.1		573.0		400.0
Galveston Harbor and Channel		530.1		1,137.0		1,503.2		1,225.0
Houston Ship Channel	(-)16.0	2,286.9	215.8	1,564.0		1,851.5		2,300.0
Matagorda Ship Channel		1,428.0	34.1	338.5		1,087.2		1,100.0
Port Aransas-Corpus Christi WW.	3,661.0	433.0	5,610.0	1,610.0	496.0	1,136.2	4,700.0	1,700.0
Sabine-Neches Waterway		1,840.0		2,794.0		2,617.9		2,700.0
Texas City Channel		523.0				693.7		
VA.								
Channel to Newport News	50.0	81.0	50.0	352.0	30.0	524.2		330.0
James River		507.0		601.4				823.0
Norfolk Harbor		1,906.5		1,749.3		1,176.0		1,350.0
Thimble Shoal Channel		284.0		709.0				700.0
WASH.								
Bellingham Garbor		25.0						
Grays Hbr. and Chehalis R.		1,459.9		1,495.0		1,858.2		1,800.0
Olympia Harbor	(-)1.3							
Port Gamble Harbor								
Port Orchard Bay								
Seattle Harbor						145.2		
Tacoma Harbor				224.9				

EXHIBIT C.1--Continued

	1970		1971		1972		1973	
	Construction	Maintenance	Construction	Maintenance	Construction	Maintenance	Construction	Maintenance
WIS.								
Ashland Harbor				20.0		707.4		22.0
Green Bay Harbor	1,000.0	69.3	1,200.0	260.0	1,272.0	246.2	1,500.0	300.0
Kenosha Harbor		40.2		45.0		89.3		45.0
Milwaukee Harbor		125.4		36.0		423.9		300.0
Sheboygan Harbor		60.1		15.0		74.5		45.0
P.R.								
Arecibo Harbor								
Mayaguez Harbor								
San Juan Harbor			(-)115.8	10.0				512.0
R.I.								
Providence River and Harbor	3,820.0	440.0	4,500.0	759.5				
TOTAL	17,948.1	75,034.1	45,438.1	79,555.6	28,923.0	109,832.9	59,753.0	89,399.0

APPENDIX D

LEGISLATION PERTAINING TO THE PORT ACTIVITIES
OF THE CORPS OF ENGINEERS

EXHIBIT D.1

LEGISLATION PERTAINING TO THE PORT ACTIVITIES
OF THE CORPS OF ENGINEERS
(Source: EP 1165-2-1)

1. 11 March 1779, Corps of Engineers. Resolved, "That the
engineers in the service of the United States shall be formed into
a corps and styled the 'Corps of Engineers,' that a commandant of
the Corps of Engineers shall be appointed by Congress."

2. 24 May 1824, Navigation. The first appropriation by Congress
for work in navigable waters was $75,000 for improving navigation
over sand bars in the Ohio River and for removing snags from the
Ohio and Mississippi Rivers (4 Stat. 32).

3. 14 June 1880 River and Harbor Act. Sunken Vessels. Section
4 authorized Secretary of the Army to require removal of sunken
vessels (amended 2 August 1882 and 3 March 1899).

4. 5 July 1884, River and Harbor Act
Navigation Obstructions. Section 2 called for a report on bridges,
causeways and piers obstructive to navigation and on best mode of
alteration.
Abolition of Tolls. Section 4 prohibits the collection or levy of
tolls or operating charges for passage through any canal or other
navigation works belonging to the United States. Amended by
Rivers and Harbor Act of 3 March 1909 (23 Stat. 147, 33 U.S.C. 5).
Operation and Repair. Section 4 also provided for operation and
repair of works for navigation.

5. 24 April 1888, Condemnation Proceedings and Donations.
Authorized the Secretary of the Army to initiate condemnation
proceedings for any lands, rights-of-way, or material needed to
maintain, operate, or prosecute works for the improvement of
rivers and harbors and to accept donations of lands or materials
required for the maintenance or prosecution of such works (24
Stat. 94, 33 U.S.C. 591).

6. 11 August 1888, River and Harbor Act.
Alteration of Bridges. Section 9 authorized Secretary of the Army
to require alteration of bridges obstructive to navigation (amended
by Section 4 of 19 Sept. 1890 Act to provide for hearings).
Fishway Construction. Section 11 authorized construction of
fishways whenever Federal river and harbor improvements obstruct
passage of fish (26 Stat. 426, 33 U.S.C. 608).
Harbor Lines. Section 12 authorized establishment of harbor lines
(penalties for violation provided in 1890 Act).

7. 19 September 1890, River and Harbor Act.
Refuse. Section 6 prohibited obstruction of navigation by deposits
of refuse, etc., in navigable waters (26 Stat. 453, 33 U.S.C.
625).
Construction in Navigable Waters. Section 7 declared it unlawful
to construct wharf, pier, or other structure in navigable waters
without permission of Secretary of Army. Construction of bridges
to require permission and approval of plans by the Secretary of
the Army.
Removal of Wrecks. Section 8 states that wrecks of vessels obstructive to navigation will be removed by the Secretary of the Army
without liability to owners.

8. 21 February 1891, Commercial Statistics. Requires owners,
agents, masters and clerks of vessels arriving or departing from
locations on waterway improvements to furnish statistics on vessels'
passengers, freight and tonnage (26 Stat. 766, 46 U.S.C. 48).

9. 13 July 1892, River and Harbor Act. Dredging Restrictions.
Section 5 prohibited the expenditure of money appropriated for the
improvement of rivers and harbors, for dredging inside of duly
established harbor lines (27 Stat. 111, U.S.C. 628).

10. 13 March 1899, River and Harbor Act.
Permits. Section 10 prohibited placing obstructions to navigation
outside established Federal harbor lines and excavating from or
depositing material in such waters, unless a permit for the works
has been authorized by the Secretary of the Army (30 Stat. 1151,
33 U.S.C. 403).
Harbor Lines. Section 11 authorized the Secretary of the Army to
establish harbor lines beyond which no piers, wharves, etc., shall
be extended without a permit (30 Stat. 1151, 33 U.S.C. 404).

11. 13 June 1902, Pub. Law 154, 57th Congress. River and Harbor
Act. BERH. Section 3 authorized the establishment of the Board
of Engineers for Rivers and Harbors with a primary function of
reviewing all survey reports authorized by Congress, except for
those under jurisdiction of the Mississippi River Commission. (32
Stat. 372, 33 U.S.C. 541).

12. 3 March 1905, Pub. Law 215, 58th Congress. River and Harbor
Act. Refuse Regulations. Section 4 authorized the Secretary of
the Army to prescribe regulations to govern the depositing of
refuse in navigable waters (33 Stat. 1147, 33 U.S.C. 419).

13. 4 March 1913, Pub. Law 429, 62nd Congress. River and Harbor
Act. Contents of Survey Reports. Section 3 required that additional information be included in reports on terminal and transfer
facilities, water power development, and other subjects that could
be properly connected with a project (37 Stat. 825, 33 U.S.C.
545).

14. 4 March 1915, Pub. Law 291, 64th Congress. Appropriation Act.
Contributed Funds. Section 4 authorized the Secretary of the Army
to receive contributions from private parties for expenditure with
Federal funds on authorized river and harbor improvements (38
Stat. 1053, 33 U.S.C. 560).
Bends. Section 5 provides that channel dimensions include in-
creases at entrances, bends, sidings, and turning places for free
movement of vessels.
Anchorages. Section 7 authorized the Secretary of the Army to
establish anchorage grounds for vessels in all harbors, rivers,
bays and other navigable waters (38 Stat. 1053, 33 U.S.C. 471).
NOTE: This function was transferred to the Secretary of Transpor-
tation by the Department of Transportation Act of 15 Oct. 1966,
Pub. Law 89-670.

15. 18 July 1918, Pub. Law 200, 65th Congress. River and Harbor
Act of 1918. Condemnation. Section 5 granted the Secretary of
the Army the right to take immediate possession of lands on which
he has instituted condemnation proceedings in the name of the
United States for the acquisition of dry lands, easements, or
rights-of-way needed for authorized river and harbor improvements
(40 Stat. 911, 33 U.S.C. 594).

16. 28 February 1920, Pub. Law 152, 66th Congress. Transportation
Act. Section 500 stated the policy of Congress to promote water
transportation. Duties of the Secretary of the Army with the
object of promoting water transportation were outlined (41 Stat.
499, 49 U.S.C. 142).

17. 22 September 1922, Pub. Law 362, 67th Congress. Commercial
Statistics. Section 11 provides for the principal program governing the collection and compilation of statistics on the waterborne
commerce of the United States (42 Stat. 1043, 33 U.S.C. 555).

18. 7 June 1924, Pub. Law 238, 68th Congress. Oil Pollution Act.
Prohibited the discharge of oil, except as permitted by the Secretary of the Army, from vessels into navigable waters of the United
States (43 Stat. 604, 33 U.S.C. 431). The Oil Pollution Act of
1924, as amended (80 Stat. 1246-1252), was repealed by Section 108
of Pub. Law 91-224 (84 Stat. 113).

19. 3 July 1930, Pub. Law 520, 71st Congress. Beach Erosion
Board Established. Section 2 established the Beach Erosion Board.
This Act of Congress provided for the Federal Government to make
shore and beach protection studies in cooperation with local
interests. The BEB was directed to furnish technical assistance
and review reports of the investigations (46 Stat. 945, 33 U.S.C.
426). NOTE: The Act of 7 November 1963 abolished BEB, transferred
review functions to BERH, and established the Coastal Engineering
Research Center.

20. <u>10 February 1932, Pub. Law 16, 72nd Congress. Recreational
Boating</u>. "The Fletcher Act" broadened the scope of Federal interest in navigation to include as "commerce" the use of waterways by
"seasonal passenger craft, yachts, houseboats, fishing boats,
motor boats, and other similar water craft, whether or not operated
for hire" (47 Stat. 42, 33 U.S.C. 541).

21. <u>30 August 1935, Pub. Law 409. River Harbor Act of 1935</u>.
<u>Content of Survey Reports</u>. Section 5 required that navigation
studies of inlets and harbor improvement contain information
concerning the configuration of the shoreline for at least 10
miles on either side regarding possible erosion effects of the
improvements (49 Stat. 1048, 33 U.S.C. 546a).

22. <u>26 June 1936, Pub. Law 834, 74th Congress. Shore Protection
Policy</u>. Stated the policy of the Congress for the improvement and
protection of beaches. Investigation, duties, reports, and expenses of the Beach Erosion Board were outlined (49 Stat. 1982).
NOTE: This Act was amended and restated 31 July 1945 (59 Stat.
508).

23. <u>19 July 1937, Pub. Law 208, 75th Congress. Contributed Funds.
Clearing and Snagging</u>. Section 2 authorized small clearing and
snagging projects for flood control, limited to $100,000 Federal
cost. This section amended 3 September 1954 (Pub. Law 780, 83rd
Congress) (50 Stat. 877, 33 U.S.C. 701g).

24. <u>20 June 1938, Pub. Law 685, 75th Congress. River and Harbor
Act of 1938. Land Exchange</u>. Section 2 authorized the Secretary
of the Army upon the recommendation of the Chief of Engineers to
exchange land or other property of the Government for private
lands or property which may be advisable in the execution of
authorized work of river and harbor improvement (52 Stat. 804, 33
U.S.C. 558b).

25. <u>21 June 1940, Pub. Law 647, 67th Congress. Bridge Alterations</u>.
The Bridge Alteration Act (Truman-Hobbs Act) provided for appor-
tionment between the United States and the owners of the cost of
altering or relocating railroad and combined railroad and highway
bridges, when found unreasonably obstructive to navigation. The
owner must bear that part of the costs attributable to benefits
involving the owner and the United States pays the balance including that attributable to the necessities of navigation (54 Stat.
479, 33 U.S.C. 511). NOTE: The Truman-Hobbs Act was amended 16
July 1952 to include public-owner highway bridges and applied to
other purposes. Corps activities were transferred to the Department of Transportation 15 Oct. 1966. Section 6 remains the basis
for sharing costs of bridge changes in navigation survey reports.

26. <u>2 March 1945, Pub. Law 14, 79th Congress. River and Harbor
Act of 1945. Clearing and Snagging</u>. Section 3 authorized small
clearing and snagging projects for navigation or flood control.
Annual expenditure for nation limited to $300,000 (59 Stat. 23, 33
U.S.C. 603a).

27. 31 July 1945, Pub. Law 166, 79th Congress. Shore Protection
Studies. This Act repealed the Act of June 26, 1936 (49 Stat.
1982) and established authority for the Beach Erosion Board to
pursue a program of general investigation and research and to
publish technical papers (59 Stat. 508, 33 U.S.C. 426a).

28. 13 August 1946, Pub. Law 727, 79th Congress. Shore Protection
Cost Sharing. Authorized Federal participation up to one-third of
the cost, but not the maintenance, of protecting shores of publicly-
owned property (amended by Acts dated 28 July 1956, 23 October
1962 and 31 December 1970 (60 Stat. 1056, 33 U.S.C. 426e)).

29. 17 May 1950, Pub. Law 516, Title I. River and Harbor Act of
1950.
Consultants. Section 105 authorized the Chief of Engineers to
procure temporary or intermittent services of experts or consultants or organizations in connection with civil functions of the
Corps of Engineers without regard to the Classification Act (64
Stat. 168, 33 U.S.C. 569a).
Transfer of Bridges. Section 109 authorized the Secretary of the
Army to transfer or convey to state authorities or political
subdivisions all rights, title and interest of the United States
in and to all bridges constructed or acquired in connection with
the improvement of canals, rivers, harbors or flood control works,
etc., if determined to be in the best interest of the United
States (64 Stat. 169, 33 U.S.C. 534).

30. 3 September 1954, Pub. Law 780, 83rd Congress. Flood Control
Act of 1954. Section 209 authorized recreational facilities in
reservoir areas open to the public and free of charge to the user.
Clearing and Snagging. Section 208 amended Section 2 of the Flood
Control Act of August 28, 1937, as amended, to authorize $2,000,000
for small clearing and snagging projects in any one year and each
project limited to $100,000 (68 Stat. 1266, 33 U.S.C. 701g).

31. 15 June 1955, Pub. Law 71, 84th Congress. Hurricane Studies.
Authorized studies of the coastal and tidal areas of the eastern
and southern United States with reference to areas where damages
had occurred from hurricanes (69 Stat. 132).

32. 11 July 1956, Pub. Law 685, 84th Congress. Small Projects.
Modified Section 205 of the 1948 Flood Control Act by increasing
the Federal expenditure limit on each project as well as the total
funds allotted per fiscal year (70 Stat. 522, 33 U.S.C. 701s).

33. 28 July 1956, Pub. Law 826, 84th Congress. Beach Nourishment.
Section 1 defines periodic beach nourishment as "construction" for
the protection of shores and provided for Federal assistance to
privately-owned shores if there is benefit from public use or from
protection of nearby public property (70 Stat. 702, 33 U.S.C.
426e).

34. 2 July 1958, Pub. Law 85-480. Publications. Authorized the
Chief of Engineers to publish and sell information pamphlets,
maps, brochures and other material on river and harbor, flood
control and other civil works activities (72 Stat. 279, 33 U.S.C.
557a-b).

35. 12 August 1958, Pub. Law 85-624. Fish and Wildlife Coordination Act. Provided that fish and wildlife conservation receive
equal consideration with other project purposes (74 Stat. 563, 13
U.S.C. 661nt).

36. 14 July 1960, Pub. Law 86-645. River and Harbor and Flood
Control Act of 1960. Small Navigation Projects. Section 107
established a new special continuing authority authorizing construction of small navigation projects. Latest amendment is Sec.
112 of Pub. Law 91-611 (74 Stat. 486, 33 U.S.C. 577).

37. 30 August 1961, Pub. Law 87-167. Oil Pollution Act of 1961.
Prevention of Oil Pollution. Implemented the provisions of the
International Convention of the Prevention of Pollution of the Sea
by Oil, 1954 (75 Stat. 402, 33 U.S.C. 1001). Administration of
this Act, as amended, was transferred from the Secretary of the
Army to the Secretary of Transportation by Pub. Law 89-670 (80
Stat. 931, 49 U.S.C. 1651).

38. 23 October 1962, Pub. Law 87-874. River and Harbor and Flood
Control Act of 1962.
Shore Protection. Section 103 amended the Act approved 13 August
1946, as amended by the Act approved 28 July 1956, and indicated
the extent of Federal participation in the cost of beach erosion
and shore protection (50 percent when the beaches are publicly-
owned or used, and 70 percent Federal participation for seashore
parks and conservation areas when certain conditions of ownership
and use of the beaches are met).
Small Beach Erosion Projects. Authority for the Secretary of the
Army to undertake construction of small beach and shore protection
projects was also established under Section 103 (76 Stat. 1178, 33
U.S.C. 426g).
Reimbursement. Section 103 also authorized reimbursement of local
interests for work done by them after initiation of survey studies
which form the basis for the projects (76 Stat. 1178, 33 U.S.C.
426e-nt).

39. 28 May 1963, Pub. Law 88-29. Outdoor Recreation Act. Gave
Congressional approval to major recommendations of the Outdoor
Recreation Resources Review Commission. Section 1 states: "That
the Congress finds and declares it to be desirable that all American people of present and future generations be assured adequate
outdoor recreation resources, and that it is desirable for all
levels of government and private interests to take prompt and
coordinated action...to conserve, develop, and utilize such resources for the benefit and enjoyment of the American people" (77
Stat. 49, 16 U.S.C. 4601).

40. 7 November 1963, Pub. Law 88-172. CERC Established. Section
1 abolished the Beach Erosion Board and established the Coastal
Engineering Research Center (77 Stat. 304, 33 U.S.C. 426-1nt).
BEC Functions Transferred. Section 3 transferred the review
functions of the Beach Erosion Board to BERH (77 Stat. 305, 33
U.S.C. 4263).

41. 22 July 1965, Pub. Law 89-90. Water Resources Planning Act.
Water Resources Council Established. Established a Water Resources
Council. Membership in 1972 included the Secretaries of Interior,
Agriculture, Army, Health, Education and Welfare, Transportation,
and the Chairman of the Federal Power Commission. Associate
members are the Secretaries of Commerce and of Housing and Urban
Development, and the Administrator of the Environmental Protection
Agency. Duties of the Council include formulation of policies to
be followed by Federal agencies in planning and developing water
and related land resources projects and review of plans developed
regionally for those purposes and periodic assessment of national
water needs. The Act establishes river basin commissions and
provides for financial assistance to the states (79 Stat. 244, 42
U.S.C. 1962).

42. 27 October 1965, Pub. Law 89-298. River and Harbor and
Flood Control Act. Administrative Authority. Section 201 permits
the Secretary of the Army to administratively authorize water
resources development projects where the estimated Federal cost is
less than $10 million. Approval by Public Works Committees is
required prior to appropriation of funds (79 Stat. 1073, 42 U.S.C.
1962d-5).

43. 4 July 1966, Pub. Law 89-487. Freedom of Information Act.
Provided guidelines for public availability of records of Federal
agencies. Pub. Law 90-23, approved 5 June 1967, codified the
provisions of Pub. Law 89-487 (80 Stat. 250 and 81 Stat. 54, 5
U.S.C. 552).

44. 1 September 1966, Pub. Law 89-551. Oil Pollution Act, 1961,
as amended. Amended the provisions of the Oil Pollution Act, 1961
(Pub. Law 87-167), implemented the provisions of the International
Convention for the Prevention of Pollution of the Sea by Oil,
1954, as amended, and for other purposes. Corps activities under
this Act, as noted below, were transferred to the Secretary of
Transportation by Pub. Law 89-670 (80 Stat. 372, 36 U.S.C. 45).

45. 15 October 1966, Pub. Law 89-670. The Department of Transportation Act. DOT Established. Established the Department of
Transportation (80 Stat. 931, 49 U.S.C. 1651nt).
Navigation Benefits Defined. Section 7(a) stated that standards
and criteria for economic evaluation of water resource projects
shall be developed by the Water Resources Council, defined "primary
direct navigation benefits," and expands the Council to include
the Secretary of Transportation on matters pertaining to navigation
features of water resource projects.

46. 13 August 1968, Pub. Law 90-483. River and Harbor and Flood Control Act of 1968.
Mitigation of Shore Damages. Section 111 authorized investigation and construction of projects to prevent or mitigate shore damages resulting from Federal navigation works (limited to $1 million per project) (82 Stat. 735, 33 U.S.C. 426i).
Excess Depths Maintenance. Section 117 authorized maintenance of excess depths required and constructed for defense purposes where the project also serves essential needs of general commerce (82 Stat. 737, 33 U.S.C. 562a).

47. 1 January 1970, Pub. Law 91-190. National Environmental Act Policy. Section 101 established a broad Federal Policy on Environmental Quality (83 Stat. 852, 42 U.S.C. 4331).
Agency Requirements. Section 102 directed that policies, regulations, and public laws will be interpreted and administered to the fullest extent possible in accordance with the policies of the Act, and imposes general and specific requirements on all Federal agencies (83 Stat. 853, 42 U.S.C. 4332).
Five Point Statement. Section 102(2)(c) required a five-point environmental impact statement (EIS) on proposed Federal actions affecting the environment (83 Stat. 853, 42 U.S.C. 4332).
CEQ Established. Section 202 established the Council on Environmental Quality (83 Stat. 854, 42 U.S.C. 4341). The duties and functions of the Council are outlined under Section 203 (83 Stat. 855, 42 U.S.C. 4343).

48. 31 December 1970, Pub. Law 91-611. River and Harbor and Flood Control Act of 1970.
Navigation Project Maintenance. Section 103 provided for Federal operation and maintenance of the general navigation features of small-boat harbor projects authorized during calendar year 1970 (84 Stat. 1819, 33 U.S.C. 426-2nt).
Land Acquisition Compensation Defined. Section 111 defined compensation for acquisition of real property taken in connection with any improvement of rivers, canals, or waterways of the United States (84 Stat. 1821, 33 U.S.C. 595a).
Project Cost Sharing for Charter Fishing Craft. Section 119 provided that charter fishing craft shall be considered as commercial vessels for the purpose of determining cost sharing in small-boat navigation projects (84 Stat. 1822, 33 U.S.C. 577a).
Economic, Social, Environmental Effects. Section 122 provided for submission of guidelines, not later than 1 July 1972, for considering possible adverse economic, social, and environmental effects of proposed projects.
Disposal Area Criteria. Section 123 authorized construction, operation, and maintenance of contained spoil disposal areas, subject to specific conditions of coordination with other agencies, local cooperation and applicability with water quality standards (84 Stat. 1823, 33 U.S.C. 1165a).
Hurricane Protection Cost Sharing. Section 208 authorized discretionary modifications in Federal participation in cost sharing for hurricane protection projects (84 Stat. 1829, 33 U.S.C. 426e).

Planning "Objectives." Section 209 expressed the intent of Congress that the objectives of enhancing regional economic development, the quality of the total environment, including its protection and improvement, the well-being of the people, and the
national economic development are the objectives to be included in
Federally-financed water resource projects (84 Stat. 1829, 42
U.S.C. 1962-2).
Completed Project Review. Section 216 authorized review and
report to Congress of the operation of completed projects when
found advisable due to significantly changed physical or economic
conditions.

49. 11 July 1972, Pub. Law 92-347. Golden Eagle Passbook and
Special Recreation User Fees. Each Federal agency developing,
administering, or providing specialized sites, facilities, equipment, or services related to outdoor recreation shall provide for
the collection of special recreation use fees for the use of
sites, facilities, equipment, or services furnished at Federal
expense (86 Stat. 459, 16 U.S.C. 460).

50. 18 October 1972, Pub. Law 92-500. The Federal Water Pollution
Control Act Amendments of 1972. Section 101 established a national
goal of eliminating all pollutant discharges into U.S. water by
1985 and an interim goal of making the waters safe for fish,
shellfish, wildlife and people by July 1, 1983 (86 Stat. 816).
Identification and Removal of In-Place Toxic Pollutants. Section
115 directs the Administrator of EPA to identify the location of
in-place pollutants with emphasis on toxic pollutants to harbors
and waterways and authorizes him, acting through the Secretary of
the Army, to make contracts for their removal and appropriate
disposal.
Areawide Waste Treatment Management. Section 208(h) authorizes
the Corps to provide assistance, in cooperation with EPA, in
planning areawide waste treatment programs.
Effluent Limitations. Section 301 prohibits the discharge of any
pollutant to waters of the United States, including the territorial
sea, unless such discharge is permitted under the provisions of a
new and comprehensive permit program established by the Act and
administered by EPA.
Toxic Standards. Section 307 provides for EPA establishment of
effluent limitations (or prohibitions) on toxic substances and
designation of the categories of sources to which such limitations
shall apply. Disposal of dredged material may be included in such
a category after consultation with the Secretary of the Army.
Oil and Hazardous Substance Liability. Section 311 prohibits the
discharge of oil or hazardous substances in harmful amounts and
provides that, if such discharges do occur, they may be the occa-
sion for clean-up requirements and civil penalties. It specifically excludes oil mixed with dredged spoil from coverage.

Federal Facilities Pollution Control. Section 313 provides that
each Federal agency shall comply with Federal, state, interstate,
and local requirements for control and abatement of pollution to
the same extent that any person is subject to such requirements.
The Refuse Act Permit Program. Sections 402 and 403 establish a
permit program in EPA which is to regulate (or prohibit) the
discharge of pollutants into the waters of the United States, to
include the territorial sea and which is to be in accord with the
EPA-established effluent limitations previously mentioned.
Section 402 replaces the Corps Refuse Act Permit Program under the
Act of 1899 without repealing that Act. All permits issued under
the Corps program are considered permits under the new EPA program.
Permits for Dredged or Fill Material. Section 404 authorizes a
separate permit program for the disposal of dredged or fill material in the nation's waters, to be administered by the Secretary of
the Army acting through the Chief of Engineers. Under this program,
permits are to be issued, after notice and opportunity for public
hearings, for disposal of such material at specified sites. These
sites are to be selected in compliance with guidelines developed
by EPA in conjunction with the Secretary of the Army. EPA is
authorized to forbid or restrict the use of specified areas whenever it determines that disposal of material at a specific site
would have an unacceptably adverse effect on municipal water
supplies, shellfish, and fishery areas, or recreational activities.
Authority to Maintain Navigation. Section 511(a) provides that
nothing in the Act is to be considered as affecting or impairing
the authority of the Secretary of the Army to maintain navigation
(86 Stat. 816).

51. 23 October 1972, Pub. Law 92-532. Marine Protection, Research
and Sanctuaries Act of 1972. Bans the unregulated dumping of
materials into the oceans, estuaries and Great Lakes (86 Stat.
1052).
Policy Statements. Section 2 states that unregulated ocean dumping is injurious to man and the environment and must be strictly
controlled.
Prohibited Acts. Section 101 exercises regulatory control over
any materials which are transported from the United States which
would be dumped in any ocean waters; over any materials which
would be dumped in the territorial sea or the contiguous zone of
the United States; and over any materials transported from any
location outside the United States which would be dumped in ocean
waters by any instrumentality of the United States government.
Environmental Protection Agency Permits. Section 102 provides
that the Administrator of the Environmental Protection Agency may
issue permits for the dumping of material (not to include dredged
material) if he determines that such dumping would not unreasonably
degrade or endanger human health, welfare or amenities, or the
marine environment, ecological systems, or economic potentialities.
The Administrator is permitted to establish and issue various
categories of permits including general permits (see Section 104),
and to designate dump and no-dump sites or times after consultation
with the Secretary of the Army.

Corps of Engineers Permits. Section 103 provides the Secretary of the Army with permit authority over the transportation of dredged material for the purpose of dumping in ocean waters. The Secretary may issue such permits where he determines that such dumping will not unreasonably degrade or endanger human health, welfare or amenities, or the marine environment, ecological systems, or economic potentialities.

Permit Conditions. Section 104 requires that permits granted by either the Administrator or the Secretary (Army) must set out a minimum, the amount, type and location of the material to be dumped, and the length of time for the dumping, and, after consultation with the Coast Guard, provide for any special monitoring and surveillance provisions.

52. 27 October 1972, Pub. Law 92-583. Coastal Zone Management Act of 1972.

National Policy. Section 302 declares a national interest in the effective management of the coastal zone, that present planning and regulation of land and water uses are inadequate, and that primary responsibility rests with state and local governments with Federal assistance (86 Stat. 1280).

Federal-State Coordination. Section 307 requires all Federal agencies with activities directly affecting the coastal zone, or with development projects within that zone, to assure that those activities or projects are consistent with the state program. Applicants for Federal licenses or permits are required to obtain state certification. Applicants for Federal assistance are required to indicate the views of the state management agency on the consistency of the proposal activities or project with the state program.

APPENDIX E

ORGANIZATION AND FUNCTIONS OF THE

OFFICE OF PORTS AND

INTERMODAL SYSTEMS

Exhibit E.1

Text of Administrative Order to the Office of Ports
and Intermodal Systems

U.S. Department of Commerce   Administrator's Order

Maritime Administration   Revokes   Order No.
                            AO-43 dated   97
MANUAL OF ORDERS   October 4, 1972 Effective Date
                                              June 25, 1973
Subject
          OFFICE OF PORTS AND INTERMODAL SYSTEMS
     ORGANIZATION, FUNCTIONS AND REDELEGATION OF AUTHORITY

Section 1. Organization:

1.01 The Office of Ports and Intermodal Systems is supervised by
a Chief who reports to the Assistant Administrator for Commercial
Development. The Office has the following elements:

     1 Office of the Chief
     2 Division of Ports
     3 Division of Intermodal Transport

Section 2. Redelegation of Authority:

2.01 The Chief, Office of Ports and Intermodal Systems is authorized to exercise all the authorities of the Assistant Administrator
for Commercial Development that are required to perform the functions set forth in Sections 3, 4, and 5 of this order.

2.02 The authorities may be redelegated in accordance with Administrator's Order 151.

Section 3. Office of the Chief:

3.01 The Chief of the Office, or his delegatee where appropriate,
is responsible for planning and directing the functions of all
component elements of the Office, and shall:

     1 Serve as program manager and principal advisor to the Assis-
        tant Administrator for Commercial Development in respect to
        port planning and development and the promotion of intermodal
        transport.

     2 Represent the Agency, and when designated, the Department or
        the Government, in matters related to port development or
        operations and intermodal transport involving maritime
        interests.

3   Coordinate and provide leadership in the Department of Com-
    merce overall effort and develop, manage and direct the
    Maritime Administration's activities to facilitate trade,
    travel and transport through the rationalization and simpli-
    fication of documents, procedures, requirements for data,
    information reporting and through removal of any other
    barriers to the efficient and orderly flow of commerce and
    transport.

Section 4.   The Division of Ports:

4.01   The Division of Ports shall:

1   Formulate national policies, objectives and plans, and conduct
    programs for the development and utilization of ports and
    port facilities, and provide technical guidance to the Region
    Directors in these areas.

2   Study, survey and investigate ocean and inland ports and
    territorial regions and zones tributary to ports; flow of
    commerce to and from the ports, marine terminals and facili-
    ties, and recommend improvements in their operation; recom-
    mend new locations and new types of terminal construction
    including offshore installations, and shore equipment required
    for modern ships, and to meet changing traffic conditions;
    develop estimates of national port needs and prepare long-
    range plans to assure that port facilities are adequate for
    foreign and domestic waterborne commerce of the United States;
    consult with and furnish information and advice to Government
    Agencies, Congress, private industries and state and local
    Governments.

3   Develop plans for more effective coordinated efforts with
    other Agencies of the Federal Government under normal peace-
    time operations, for the promotion, development and utiliza-
    tion of ports and port facilities.

4   Compile and publish information on the accomplishment of
    functions listed in 2 and 3 above, including the economic
    impact of United States ports; port development expenditures
    by United States ports; marine containerization and port
    development; and systems criteria for future terminal facili-
    ties reflecting advances in container, LASH, general cargo
    and bulk cargo operations.

5   Serve as port consultant to the Economic Development Adminis-
    tration providing comments and recommendations on applications
    for grants and loans for port technical assistance and public
    works projects received from economically distressed communi-
    ties.

6   Represent the Maritime Administration within the Federal
    Government with respect to port and navigation aspects of
    river basin studies, regional port studies, and programs for
    the study, use and development of the Nation's coasts and
    coastal resources.

7   Investigate the extent to which ports are involved with local
    environmental problems and the relationship of port organiza-
    tions with agencies concerned and make recommendations.

8   Formulate and recommend to the Assistant Administrator for
    Commercial Development research and development objectives
    for the promotion, development and utilization of ports and
    port facilities; propose research and development projects;
    participate in and review technical scopes of work for pro-
    jects, and upon request, comment on interim and final reports
    on research subjects in these areas.

9   Upon request represent the Department of Commerce and the
    United States in the international field of port activities;
    provide technical advice on ports to foreign countries and
    furnish foreign port data to other Government Agencies.

10 Prepare national emergency plans and develop preparedness
    programs for Federal operational control of ports and port
    facilities for emergency mobilization conditions.

Section 5.   The Division of Intermodal Transport

5.01   The Division of Intermodal Transport shall: ·

1   Formulate national policies, objectives and plans, and conduct
    programs for the promotion and development of integrated
    transportation systems, including containerization, pallet-
    ization and bulk transport, to obtain maximum benefits from
    the concept of intermodal transport; provide technical guid-
    ance to the Region Directors in these areas.

2   Survey, study, evaluate, and develop solutions to specific
    problems encountered in the technology of physical distribu-
    tion such as containerization and integrated transport tech-
    niques.

3   Develop plans and participate in arranging for pilot opera-
    tions, tests, and conferences concerned with improved tech-
    niques in intermodal transportation.

4   Promote coordination between the various modes of transport
    through utilization of intermodal equipment, simplified
    documentation, and the employment of advance management
    techniques, to broaden the range of benefits to be gained
    among shippers and carriers.

5 Maintain liaison with Federal agencies, commercial interests
   and international activities concerned with the coordination
   and development of intermodal transport systems, rendering
   information and technical advice.

6 Represent the Department of Commerce and the Federal Government in the field of intermodal transport as related to
   United States waterborne commerce as required.

7 Collect, analyze, and disseminate data relating to intermodal
   transportation systems.

MARVIN PITKIN
Assistant Administrator
for Commercial Development

Concurrence:

PHIL S. PEARCE
Deputy Assistant Administrator
for Administration and Finance

[Note: This exhibit was retyped at M.I.T. for greater legibility.]

APPENDIX F

LEGISLATION PERTINENT TO PORT AND WATERWAYS
ACTIVITIES OF THE U.S. COAST GUARD

Exhibit F.1

Legislation Pertinent to Port and Waterways
Activities of the U.S. Coast Guard

General

As discussed in Chapter 8, the general structure and organization of the U.S. Coast Guard was first arranged and codified under Title 14 of the U.S. Code, as recommended by House Report 887 in late 1949. General authority for all Coast Guard activities is derived from this authority; however, specific acts of Congress or statutory authority granted to the Coast Guard supplement the general authority outlined under Title 14. (Note: Headings correspond to those in the text.)

Activity	Authority
I. PORT SAFETY/SECURITY	
PORT SAFETY OPERATIONS:	
a. Supervise loading of dangerous cargoes.	46 USC 170
b. Inspect vessels carrying dangerous cargoes other than explosives.	46 USC 170 46 USC 391a
c. Supervise loading of radioactive cargo.	46 USC 170
d. Movement control of vessels carrying high-hazard or high-explosive cargo.	14 USC 89 46 USC 170
e. Escort vessels carrying Class "A" explosive cargoes.	14 USC 89 14 USC 170
f. Inspect and survey waterfront facilities.	46 USC 170 50 USC 191
g. Inspection of foreign vessels with dangerous cargoes.	46 USC 170 46 USC 391a

Activity	Authority
h. Development of standards and enforcement of regulations for all port facilities, particularly those concerned with hazardous or pollutant materials.	Port and Waterways Safety Act of 1971
i. Inspection of all port facilities and structures.	"
j. Investigation of casualties occurring in any port or waterway facility.	"
k. General statutory objectives-- statements.	Port and Waterways Safety Act of 1970
	Port and Waterways Safety Act of 1972
	Executive Order 10173

PORT SECURITY

| a. Port security operations including harbor patrols. | 50 USC 191 as amended |
| b. General statutory outline. | 14 USC 1 |

II. MERCHANT MARINE SAFETY

VESSEL INSPECTION AND SAFETY

a. Review plans and specifications for construction or alteration of merchant vessels.	46 USC 369
b. Inspect vessels under construction to assure compliance with approved plans.	46 USC 363, 362, 367, 391a, 395, 404
c. Conduct periodic inspections of merchant vessel hulls, machinery and equipment.	46 USC 362, 363, 367, 391a, 395, 404
d. Prepare Certificates of Inspection. Prepare certificates in accordance with international conventions.	46 USC 399, 400
e. Conduct stability tests, perform calculations, draft stability letters.	46 USC 369

Activity	Authority

f.   Develop standards, prescribe and approve safety equipment and devices. Conduct factory inspections of required safety items.

46 USC 369

g.   Administer load-line regulations, review load-line computations, conduct load-line inspections.

46 USC 369

h.   Participate with professional societies to develop safety codes and standards.

46 USC 369

i.   Conduct admeasurement and documentation of U.S. vessels and all ancillary functions.

46 USC 369
46 USC 71 et seq.
46 USC 11 et seq.

VESSEL MANNING AND PERSONNEL

a.   Prescribe manning of vessels necessary for safe navigation.

46 USC 222, 223, 224, 672, 673

b.   Develop Rules of the Road and establish traffic separation lanes for prevention of collision.

33 USC 154, 157, 353

c.   Investigate marine casualties, personal injuries and deaths.

46 USC 239
33 USC 361

d.   Maintain liaison with other Coast Guard divisions, other government agencies, vessel owners, and industry associations to improve safety standards.

e.   Make determinations as to navigability of inland waters.

33 USC 151

f.   Plan development and administration of standards and practices for regulation of Merchant Marine personnel.

46 USC 224, 224a

g.   Determine eligibility, conduct examinations, issue appropriate licenses and certificates.

46 USC 224

h.   Conduct shipment and discharge of seamen.

46 USC 563 et seq.

i.   Investigate violations of laws leading to determination of misconduct, negligence or incompetence.

46 USC 239

Activity	Authority
j. Conduct personnel action pro-ceedings leading to suspension and/or revocation of licenses and certifi-cates.	46 USC 239
k. Licensing towboat personnel.	H.R. 6479
HAZARDOUS MATERIALS TRANSPORT	
a. General authority	14 USC, Sections 2, 88. Water Quality Improvement Act of 1970
b. Issue and enforce regulations relative to procedures, methods and equipment for prevention and removal of discharges of hazardous materials other than oil.	Port and Waterways Safety Act of 1970 Port and Waterways Safety Act of 1972
c. Determine degree of hazard inherent in water transportation of dangerous substances, determine pre-cautions and devices necessary for safety.	46 USC 170, 369
FIRE FIGHTING AND FIRE PREVENTION	
a. Prescribe minimum standards for all port facilities to prevent fire, explosions, or other serious casualties.	14 USC 88(b), 42 USC 1856 Port and Waterways Safety Act of 1971
VESSEL TRAFFIC SYSTEMS	
a. Port and Waterway Traffic Control and Advisory Services	Port and Waterways Safety Act of 1971 Port and Waterways Safety Act of 1972
b. Enforcement of Bridge to Bridge Radio Act.	S. 699 H.R. 756

III. MARINE POLLUTION

The general authority vested in the Coast Guard in this area is derived from five major Acts or Conventions. They are:

1. The Refuse Act of 1899

2. The Oil Pollution Act of 1961

Activity   Authority

---

3. Federal Water Pollution
Control Act as amended by the Water
Quality Improvement Act of 1970.

4. The International Convention
for the Prevention of Pollution of
the Sea by Oil, 1954, as amended.

5. National Environmental
Policy Act of 1969.

The specific statutory authority is
as follows:

a. Enforcement of pollution   14 USC 2, 33 USC 407,
laws (regulatory powers).   33 USC 431 et seq.
                                       33 USC 1001 et seq.

b. Establish criteria for   Water Quality Improvement
removal of discharged oil.   Act of 1970
                                       P.L. 91-224

c. Develop and implement oil   As above
removal contingency plans.

d. Issue and enforce regula-   As above
tions relative to procedures, methods
and equipment for preventing discharges of oil.

e. Receive reports of pollution   As above
incidents with the potential for
polluting the navigable waters, or
actually polluting the navigable
waters.

f. Issue and enforce regula-   As above
tions relative to design and installation of marine sanitation devices
on vessels.

IV. OTHER AREAS

BRIDGE ADMINISTRATION

a. Establish location and clear-   33 USC 401, 491-507,
ances for bridges and causeways over   525-534
navigable waters.

b. Administer alteration of   33 USC 511-524
obstructive bridges.

Activity	Authority
c. Regulation of drawbridge operation.	33 USC 499
d. Regulation of bridge lighting.	14 USC 81
NAVIGATION AND NAVIGATIONAL AIDS	
a. Provide and maintain aids to navigation.	14 USC 81
b. Mark obstructions and wrecks.	14 USC 86
c. Enforcement of navigation laws.	33 USC 154, 241, 301, 1051
d. Establishment and enforcement of anchorage regulations.	33 USC 180, 258, 322, 471
e. Provide domestic icebreaking services.	14 USC 93
f. Administer Recreational Boating Safety Program.	46 USC 526-527
g. Conduct search and rescue activities and coordination.	14 USC 88
h. Enforcement of federal laws concerned with the orderly flow of seaborne commerce.	14 USC 2 14 USC 141-142
i. Emergency Preparedness.	Executive Order 11490 Dept. of Transportation Act, 80 Stat. 931 49 USC 1651

APPENDIX G

UNITED STATES COAST GUARD

PLANNING AND PROGRAMMING

PROCEDURES

APPENDIX G

UNITED STATES COAST GUARD PLANNING AND PROGRAMMING PROCEDURES

This discussion is based on the following five sources:

1)   United States Coast Guard, Planning and Programming Manual -
      1971, CG-411 (Washington, D.C.: U.S. Department of Trans-
      portation, January 1971).

      The following four sources are amendments to the above:

      a)   U.S.C.G., Planning and Programming Manual, CG-411,
            Amendment No. 1, Dec. 9, 1971.

      b)   U.S.C.G., Planning and Programming Manual, CG-411,
            Amendment No. 2, Oct. 4, 1972.

      c)   U.S.C.G., Planning and Programming Manual, CG-411,
            Amendment No. 3, Dec. 19, 1972.

      d)   U.S.C.G., Planning and Programming Manual, CG-411,
            Amendment No. 4, Aug. 30, 1973.

Introduction

This section traces in detail the planning and programming
process of the U.S. Coast Guard. Readers are advised to first
consult the text discussion on the subject, appearing in Chapter
8, before referring to the specific details discussed here.

Coast Guard Planning and Programming - General Characteristics

Plans and Program Classifications within the Coast Guard
are based on the Planning-Programming-Budgeting System (PPBS).
As explained in Chapter 8, the PPB system defines an input-out-
put system analysis which seeks generally to measure the efficiency of an organization by documenting objectives, plans,
criteria, and benefits set down and accomplished by the organization. The utilization of PPB as an analytic tool also facilitates measuring the structural efficiency of components within
an agency or organization. Coast Guard program structure has
evolved under this analytic constraint.

Program Structure

A.   Program Area Level - Coast Guard Headquarters

Management responsibility for an approved Coast Guard program rests with the Commandant at Headquarters. The Chief of
Staff carries out delegated responsibilities from the Commandant
and coordinates efforts through his Program Directors.

The Program Directors in turn give effect to proposed projects through designated Program Managers. The program director and manager level is responsible for the effective and efficient accomplishment of objectives generated from above.

B.   Support Area Level - Coast Guard Headquarters

Support Directors and Office Chiefs, acting in support of logistic capacities, are subject to the determinations of the program directors/managers relative to the overall objectives.

C.   Field Operations

The District Commander and District Division Chiefs stand in the same relation to the structure of Coast Guard programs at the field level as to that of Coast Guard Headquarters. Chiefs of Operations Divisions are the District Operating Program Managers for the same programs, and have the same responsibilities for facilities under the District Commander as has the Program Director under the Commandant at Headquarters.

A pictorial illustration of this program structure for Coast Guard Headquarters is given in Exhibit G.1. As noted, field operations are symmetrical in structure.

Programming Concepts

A.   General Staff Responsibilities

The Offices of the Commandant, the Chief of Staff, the Program Directors and the Program Managers are the principals in the planning systems of the Coast Guard. The responsibilities of the Commandant and Chief of Staff are oriented to the overall objectives of the Coast Guard, while the Program Directors and Managers are chiefly involved with the component parts (designated programs) of these objectives.

The Commandant is responsible to the Secretary of Transportation for the development and implementation of Coast Guard programs responsive to statutory and executive direction. The most direct policy guidance of the Commandant is his review of various long-range funding forecasts ("Forecast Stage Budget") and his annual approval of the Proposal/Program Data Summary package.

And, as the principal spokesman for the Coast Guard, the Commandant normally appears before Congressional committees during budgetary authorization hearings, as well as the Office of Management and Budget.

The responsibility of the Chief of Staff is to insure that Coast Guard program development is in accordance with guidance from the Commandant. Accordingly, the Chief of Staff is the focal point for policy and program review.

Exhibit G.1

Program Structure – U.S.C.G. Headquarters

Program Area	Program	Program Director	Program Manager
Search and Rescue	Search and Rescue	Chief, O	Chief, OSR
	Domestic Icebreaking	Chief, O	Chief, OSR
Aids to Navigation	Short Range Aids to Navigation	Chief, W	Chief, WAN
	Aids to Navigation (Loran A)	Chief, W	Chief, WAN
	Aids to Navigation (Loran C & Omega)	Chief, W	Chief, WAN
Bridges	Bridge Administration	Chief, W	Chief, WBR
Merchant Marine Safety	Commercial Vessel Safety	Chief, M	Deputy M
Law Enforcement	Port Safety and Security	Chief, W	Chief, WLE
	Enforcement of Maritime Laws and Treaties	Chief, O	Chief, OSR
	Maritime Environmental Protection	Chief, W	Chief, WEP
Recreational Boating Safety	Boating Safety	Chief, B	Deputy B
Oceanography, Meteorology and Polar Operations	Ocean Stations	Chief, O	Chief, OMS
	Polar Operations – Water	Chief, O	Chief, OMS
	Polar Operations – Science	Chief, O	Chief, OMS
	Marine Science Activities	Chief, O	Chief, OMS
Military Preparedness and Operations	Military Operations	Chief, O	Chief, OMR
	Military Preparedness	Chief, O	Chief, OMR
Reserve Training	Coast Guard Reserve Forces	Chief, R	Deputy R

Support Area	Support Director	Support Manager
General Administration	CCS	Chief, CPA
Command and Control (Communications)	Chief, O	Chief, OC
Personnel Support	Chief, P	P Staff Asst.
Engineering Support	Chief, E	Note 1
Fiscal and Supply Support	Compt.	Deputy F
Research & Development	Chief, D	Chief, DP
Medical Support	Chief, K	Chief, KMA
Legal Support	Chief, L	Deputy L
Inspector General	I.G.	Deputy I.G.
Civil Rights	Chief, H.	Asst. H
Public and International Affairs	Chief, A.	Deputy A
Retired Pay	Chief, P	P Staff Asst.

Note 1: Chief ECV, ENE, EEE, EOE, EAE as appropriate.

Source: U.S.C.G., Planning and Programming Manual, CG-411.

The Program Director acts for the Commandant in the management of his assigned program. As such, the director is at the point where major policy is translated into plans and program designs for the specific guidance of his Program Manager and subordinate units.

Involved in detailed planning, programming, budgeting, and program execution, the Program Manager assists the program director through continuous review and implementation of routine program policy. It is from this level that the majority of program documentation, studies and reports are staffed.

The responsibilities for the Program Directors/Managers are as follows:

1. Manage with a clear objective constantly in the forefront.

2. Develop and use measurable program benefits.

3. Develop and use measures of effectiveness to match against costs.

4. Identify policies under which the program is carried out (alternative policies permit alternative hardware, or mixes thereof).

5. Record and update the Plan Summaries.

6. Perform studies of impact of changes in demand, policy, criteria, and technology, developing feasible alternatives and proposing necessary legislation.

7. Develop appropriate data base (management information) for managing and evaluating the execution of the program.

8. Review and/or develop program resource change proposals and budgets for R&D, AC&I, and OE, and identify priorities for rapid dollar-level adjustments.

9. Request and give direction to major support from Personnel, Engineering, Comptroller, R&D.

B.   The Planning and Programming Process - Overview

Exhibit G.2 illustrates a general overview of the planning and programming process of the Coast Guard. The lines of demarcation between Planning, Programming, and Budgeting, as shown in the figure, cannot be clearly defined. An example of this is that Planning is normally associated with the years beyond the current budget year, while Programming is generally concerned with the existing budget year.

EXHIBIT G.2

RESOURCE PLANNING AND PROGRAMMING PROCEDURE

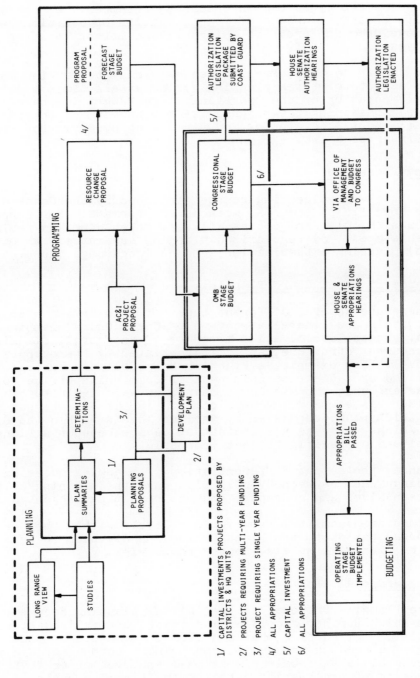

1/ CAPITAL INVESTMENTS PROJECTS PROPOSED BY DISTRICTS & HQ UNITS

2/ PROJECTS REQUIRING MULTI-YEAR FUNDING

3/ PROJECT REQUIRING SINGLE YEAR FUNDING

4/ ALL APPROPRIATIONS

5/ CAPITAL INVESTMENT

6/ ALL APPROPRIATIONS

Source: U.S. Coast Guard, Planning and Programming Manual, CG-411.

Any one PPB cycle commences about September 1 of the budget
year with an annual update of Plan Summaries or Position Papers
to be developed for programs which will be effective later in the
fiscal year.

To summarize then, Program Managers will be working on
various aspects of three planning cycles at all times: (1)
the implementation of the Operating Stage Budget in the current
year; (2) monitoring the progress of the budget for the following year; and (3) developing and firming up programs for the
current year plus two.

Planning Procedures

The task of allocating scarce resources by the Coast Guard
follows specific procedures, methods and formats. For purposes
of discussion, planning cycles will be broken down and reviewed
in three stages: a) regularized planning apparatus - an overview; b) planning authorization; and c) long-range views.

"Regularized" Coast Guard Planning

There are several different types of regularized planning
levels within the general structure of Coast Guard planning procedures. These levels, all components of an overall planning
and procedures structure, are differentiated by the _outputs_ of
each level. For example, a Planning Proposal is a vehicle to
be utilized by a district commander or Commanding Officer of a
Headquarters unit who wishes to change an existing situation or
plan under his command. A Development Plan is a multiyear phase
construction plan, submitted by various levels within the Coast
Guard, which serves as a coordination device between a Planning
Proposal and a specific Project Proposal.

Hence, the output differentiation of planning modes basically distinguishes between overall planning, the planning of specific alternatives and concepts, and the resulting project designs.

Plans are submitted from various levels within the Coast
Guard organization to the Plans Evaluation Division (CPE).
There the plan will be distributed for review.

Planning Proposal

The Planning Proposal is the initial planning document
through which further steps leading toward accomplishment will
be resolved. Filed by either a district commander or Commanding
Officer of a Headquarters unit, the primary purpose of a planning proposal is to obtain operational approval prior to the
introduction of engineering detail. Additional documents, such
as AC&I Project Proposals (acquisition, construction, and improvement) or Development Plans, may be required at later times, but
it is intended that these documents be used interdependently to
facilitate planning.

The Planning Proposal must:

a. Identify the problem.

b. Explain why a change is necessary.

c. Present feasible alternative solutions to the
    problem, and analyze each. Present cost data.

d. Recommend a solution and state why it is recom-
    mended.

e. State the impact if the proposal is not approved.

f. Contain assurances concerning displacement of
    persons from housing.

g. Discuss the environmental effects of the proposal
    if adopted.

General plans are handled, as mentioned previously, by the
Plans Evaluation Division. Planning necessary for resource requirements and utilization standards associated with Aviation
and Vessel Plans is centralized in the Commandant.

Development Plan

When a multiyear funding level is required for a shore facility program submitted under the planning proposal, a Development
Plan is submitted outlining the long-term course of the program.
As such, the development plan serves as a bridge between the capital investment Planning Proposal and a subsequent AC&I Project
Proposal, the latter being a specific funding and design proposal. The Plan will include a site development plan, general
design data, a financial plan, and a construction schedule based
on a "priority of needs and orderly construction flow." The
development plan need only refer to a planning proposal as authority.

Acquisition, Construction, and Improvements

(AC&I) Project Proposal Reports

AC&I Project Proposal Reports are submitted in support of
capital investment projects at Coast Guard shore facilities.
Filed by district commanders and Commanding Officers at Headquarters, the AC&I Reports follow the justification and approval
of operational concepts and project feasibility outlined in a
Planning Proposal. The Report then lays out the design and
engineering concepts, cost estimates, status of lands and other
pertinent project data, and includes engineering alternatives and
their considerations.

The criteria for inclusion of projects under AC&I are shown
in Exhibit G.3. Exhibit G.4 shows a flow chart description of the

Exhibit G.3

Criteria for Inclusion of Projects under A C & I (Acquisition, Construction, and Improvement)

	Aids to Navigation	Shore Facilities	Vessels	Aircraft
Acquisition Construction	Acquisition or establishment of new facility or structure over $1,000.[1]	Any family housing or land. Acquisition of new facility or structure over $50,000.	Any acquisition over 64' in length.	Any acquisition.
Rebuilding replacement alteration restoration	Complete or partial renewal of structure if: (a) cost exceeds $50,000 and (b) it is over 75% renewed.	Complete or partial renewal of structure if: (a) cost exceeds $50,000 and (b) it is over 75% renewed.	Complete or partial renewal of hull or machinery[3] if: (a) over $50,000 and (b) over 75% renewed.	Complete or partial renewal of aircraft if: (a) over $50,000 and (b) over 75% renewed.
Improvement[2] modification addition expansion	Betterment costing over $50,000 per single facility or structure.	Betterment costing over $50,000 per facility or structure.	Betterment costing over $50,000 per vessel.	Betterment costing over $50,000 per aircraft.

[1] Projects between $1,000 and $50,000 treated collectively under Waterways A/N Projects.

[2] Conversions, as a program, are OE unless each conversion of a single facility is over $50,000 (except LAMP).

[3] Machinery means entire plant and not individual equipments.

Source: U.S.C.G., Planning and Programming Manual, CG-411.

EXHIBIT G.4

Resource Change Proposal Procedure

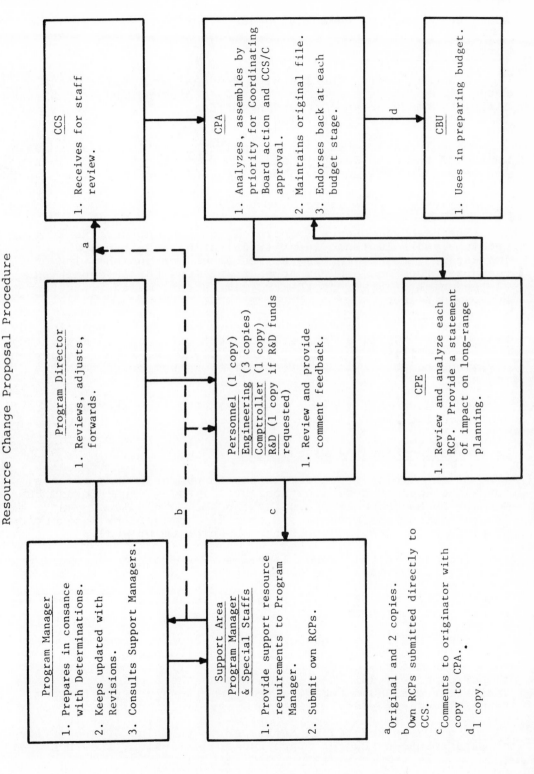

Source: U.S.C.G., Planning and Programming Manual, CG-411.

AC&I Report review process at Headquarters.

AC&I Priorities

Associated with the Planning Proposal and AC&I Project Proposal Report is a program priority statement prepared by each district commander and Commanding Officer of headquarters units. This priority listing is filed as of November 1 of each year.

Closely associated with the priority listing is an annual update of the Plan Summary, filed on September 1 of each year, and representing a condensed outlining of program plans.

Resource Change Proposal

The Resource Change Proposal is a document used to analyze problems and solutions, identify criteria, and then argue for increases/decreases in program resources, or the shifting of resources from one program to another. The RCP is submitted to the Chief of Staff by the Program/Support Manager via the Program Director.

Since it is used for several purposes after submission to the OCS, the RCP is a complete document which can be evaluated by several Divisions (e.g., Programs Division, Plans Evaluation Division, Budget Division) for analyzing budget and resource requests.

RCPs cover a five-year span beginning with the Budget Year and extending the following four years.

Determinations for the Fiscal Year

As an ongoing procedure in the annual budgetary process, formalized budget determinations are filed by each Program/Support Manager by November 15 preceding the following fiscal year. These determinations are general statements of conditions, assumptions, or plans which are the basis for the problem or goal.

Included in this general process are Program Proposals which, submitted annually to the Department about May 1 of the current fiscal year, are the basis for the Coast Guard's Forecast Stage Budget. The appropriations format of this document is program-rather than budget-oriented.

Submitted in conjunction with the Program Proposal on May 1 is the Program Data Summary (PDS). The PDS presents data for each program subcategory on outputs, benefits, and their costs in personnel and dollars, and maintains the continuity of the various program subcategories from year to year (the Program Proposal generally deals with one-year decisions).

The PDS is updated in September at the time of the Office of Management and Budget Stage Budget submission, and then again in February to assure conformity with the President's budget submission to Congress.

At the time of submission in May, the PDS would contain data for the Budget Year under consideration by the Program Proposal, the four following years, and the two previous years.

Development of Programs for the OMB Stage Budget

The Department of Transportation is organized such that the Commandant of the Coast Guard reports directly to the Secretary. Matters of major significance move from the Chief of Staff/Office of the Assistant Secretary working levels to the Office of the Secretary for proper functioning.

The main contact point for most matters of resource planning and programming is the Office of Planning and Program Review under the Deputy Under Secretary of Transportation. Within this office, the Deputy Under Secretary holds hearings each spring to discuss Coast Guard programs, and to hear from selected Program/Support Managers and Directors on their recommendations. Based on this spring preview, the DOT specifies budget levels for submission to the Office of Management and Budget Stage Budget. These levels will normally require eliminating certain line item requests contained in the spring preview.

A Coordinating Board is set up between DOT and the Coast Guard to facilitate decisions on line request eliminations, and to forward their recommendations to the Chief of Staff. After obtaining Commandant approval, the Budget Division builds the OMB Stage Budget around the approved lists.

Planning Authorization Process

The capital investment AC&I projects of the Coast Guard must be authorized by Congressional action each year before funds may be appropriated for those purposes. The Programs Division coordinates the various actions that are required by this task.

Initially, the budget document submitted to OMB in the fall and the revised budget document submitted to Congress in the winter have a separate justification sheet for each capital investment line item under AC&I. These sheets describe the item and its relationship to existing conditions, long-range planning, cost estimates, and so on.

Selected draft sheets are further refined within the Program and Budget Divisions and incorporated within budget documentation in September. After final OMB hearings in the fall, and the completion of any later adjustments required by the Coast Guard, the sheets are then submitted to the Budget Division for incorporation into the budget materials for Congress.

Planning Factors for Field Budget Submission

A letter of transmittal containing several enclosures is distributed by the Programs Division in February to each allotment unit for use in preparing field budgets. The letter and its distribution is derived from inputs by Program/Support Managers and Subhead Administrators, and is a compilation of information to assist and inform field commanders in drawing up their budget requests. The scope of the material varies with the recipient command, but typically a district receives:

1) A listing of the Operating Expense changes and the AC&I projects included in the Congressional Stage Budget just submitted,

2) A similar listing of those Operating Expense items expected to be included in the budget for the year following,

3) A vessel maintenance plan listing major jobs to be funded by headquarters,

4) An electronics installation plan, and

5) Information on Reserve Training levels.

Exhibit G.5 illustrates the Planning Factors Development and Distribution Process.

Other Budgetary Functions and Policies

Oftentimes, after funds have been appropriated, it is desired to use them for reasons other than for which they have been appropriated. Reprogramming procedures have been established to allow the moving of resources with a minimum of confusion and delay.

Generally, the reprogramming of Operating Expenses is broken down in two fashions: a) by subheads, or ledger accounts which cut across program lines (i.e., military pay); or b) by program (i.e., Port Safety and Security). Generally, reprogramming by subhead results from the need to reallocate funds from lower- to higher-priority requirements, while reprogramming between programs results when a new mission is started, or an existing mission is expanded without funding by additional appropriations.

Supplementing AC&I funds is often accomplished through a surplus account or from a funded project. If such a situation is not feasible, limited reprogramming of funds can be accomplished by the Commandant, who has authority to construct needed public works under $200,000 each from any construction funds available without Congressional clearance (for projects which have not been through authorization procedures). Similarly, the Commandant has authority to replace any operating facility damaged or destroyed, using any available construction funds without

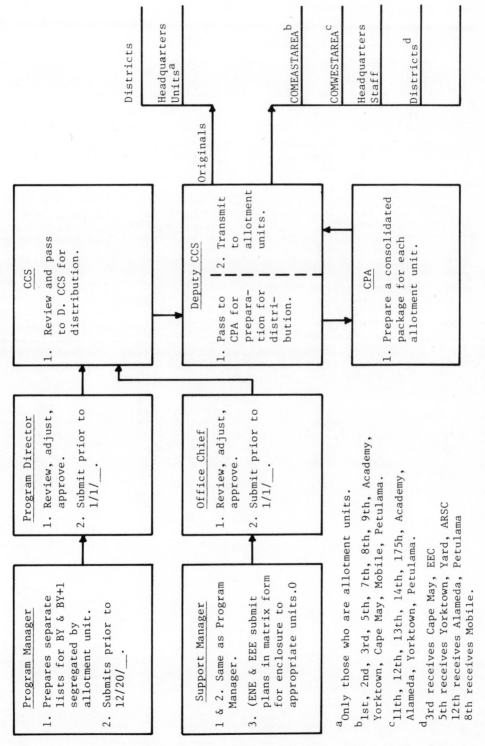

EXHIBIT G.5

PLANNING FACTORS DEVELOPMENT AND DISTRIBUTION

Program Manager

1. Prepares separate lists for BY & BY+1 segregated by allotment unit.

2. Submits prior to 12/20/___.

Support Manager

1 & 2. Same as Program Manager.

3. (ENE & EEE submit plans in matrix form for enclosure to appropriate units.0

Program Director

1. Review, adjust, approve.

2. Submit prior to 1/1/___.

Office Chief

1. Review, adjust, approve.

2. Submit prior to 1/1/___.

CCS

1. Review and pass to D. CCS for distribution.

Deputy CCS

1. Pass to CPA for preparation for distribution.

2. Transmit to allotment units.

CPA

1. Prepare a consolidated package for each allotment unit.

Districts

Headquarters Units[a]

Originals

COMEASTAREA[b]

COMWESTAREA[c]

Headquarters Staff

Districts[d]

[a]Only those who are allotment units.

[b]1st, 2nd, 3rd, 5th, 7th, 8th, 9th, Academy, Yorktown, Cape May, Mobile, Petulama.

[c]11th, 12th, 13th, 14th, 175h, Academy, Alameda, Yorktown, Petulama.

[d]3rd receives Cape May, EEC
5th receives Yorktown, Yard, ARSC
12th receives Alameda, Petulama
8th receives Mobile.

Source: U.S.C.G., Planning and Programming Manual, CG-411.

approval of Congress.

Special Analytic Studies

Implicit in the PPBS policy process is a continuous reexamination of fundamental operating techniques and assumptions. Accordingly, the Coast Guard participates in an ongoing study effort which is centralized at the Chief of Staff level to avoid duplications.

Studies directed by the Department of Transportation are subject to planning procedures within the Coast Guard. Guidelines are set by the Chief of Staff to govern the manner and scope of Departmental liaison.

In addition to generating and participating on study efforts, the Chief of Staff of the Coast Guard endeavors to keep abreast of analytical investigations which may affect the Coast Guard or its programs.

Long-Range View

The Long-Range View is a broad policy statement which attempts to place where the Coast Guard will be in 10 years. Accordingly, in this view are embedded the basic assumptions which are being made at present operational levels. Its objective is to provide an orientation and basis for concurrent and intermediate decisions and actions.

APPENDIX H

DEEPWATER PORT SUBJECT AREAS AND LICENSING PROCEDURES

UNDER S.1751

Exhibit H.1

Deepwater Port Subject Areas

Topic	Department	Agencies Involved
Geology	DOI	Geological Survey
Ocean Currents	DOC	National Oceanic and Atmospheric Administration
	DOD	Navy Corps of Engineers
Salinity/temperature	DOC	National Oceanic and Atmospheric Administration
	DOD	Navy Corps of Engineers
Climate	DOC	National Oceanic and Atmospheric Administration
Biologic Life	DOI	Bureau of Sport Fisheries and Wildlife
	DOC	National Oceanic and Atmospheric Administration
Navigation	DOT	U.S. Coast Guard
	DOD	Corps of Engineers
Commercial Fishing	DOC	National Oceanic and Atmospheric Administration
Outdoor Recreation	DOI	Bureau of Outdoor Recreation National Park Service
Effects on Shoreline	DOD	Corps of Engineers
	DOI	Land Use Planning
	DOC	National Oceanic and Atmospheric Administration

Topic	Department	Agencies Involved
Wave Size (continued)	DOD	Navy Corps of Engineers
Pipeline Construction	DOT	Office of Pipeline Safety
	DOI	Geological Survey Bureau of Land Management
	DOD	Corps of Engineers
Dredging/Filling	DOD	Corps of Engineers
	DOI	Bureau of Sport Fisheries and Wildlife
	DOC	National Oceanic and Atmospheric Administration
Pipeline Safety	DOT	Office of Pipeline Safety
	DOI	Geological Survey
Platform Safety	DOI	Geological Survey
	DOT	U.S. Coast Guard
Vessel Operations Safety	DOT	U.S. Coast Guard
Platform Design and Construction	DOI	Geological Survey
	DOD	Corps of Engineers
	DOC	Maritime Administration
Deepwater Port Operations	DOT	U.S. Coast Guard
	DOI	Geological Survey
	DOD	Corps of Engineers
Navigation Aids	DOT	U.S. Coast Guard
Navigation Operations	DOT	U.S. Coast Guard
	DOD	Corps of Engineers

Topic	Department	Agencies Involved
Pipeline Construction (Land)	DOD	Corps of Engineers
	DOI	Geological Survey Land Use and Water Planning
Siting	DOI	Bureau of Land Management Geological Survey
	DOD	Corps of Engineers
Zoning for Land Installations	DOI	Office of Land Use and Water Planning
	DOC	National Oceanic and Atmospheric Administration
Pollution (Air and Water)		Environmental Protection Agency
	DOT	U.S. Coast Guard
	DOI	Geological Survey
Ocean Dumping	DOD	Corps of Engineers
	DOI	Bureau of Sport Fisheries and Wildlife
	DOC	National Oceanic and Atmospheric Administration
Law Enforcement (Civil/ Criminal)	DOI	Geological Survey Bureau of Land Management
	DOD	Corps of Engineers
	DOT	U.S. Coast Guard
		Environmental Protection Agency
Tariff-User Rates	ICC	
Fee Schedule	DOI	Bureau of Land Management
	DOD	Corps of Engineers
	DOT	U.S. Coast Guard
		Environmental Protection Agency

Topic	Department	Agencies Involved
Maritime Technology	DOC	Maritime Administration
	DOI	Geological Survey
	DOT	U.S. Coast Guard
Bonding	DOI	Geological Survey
	DOD	Corps of Engineers
International Careers	DOS	
	DOD	
National Security	DOD	
Economic Analysis	DOI	Bureau of Land Management
	DOC	Maritime Administration
	DOD	Corps of Engineers
Environmental Concerns		Council of Environmental Quality Environmental Protection Agency
	DOC	National Oceanic and Atmospheric Administration
	DOI	Geological Survey Bureau of Land Management Bureau of Sport Fisheries and Wildlife

EXHIBIT H.2

DEPARTMENT OF THE INTERIOR: DEEPWATER PORT COORDINATION CHART
OF FEDERAL AGENCY INVOLVEMENT

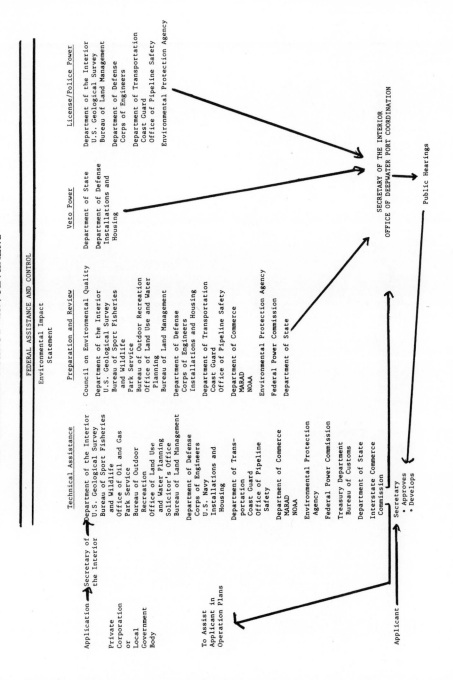

APPENDIX I

FEDERAL EXPENDITURES IN THE WATER RESOURCES AREA

EXHIBIT I.1

Federal outlays by category and agency for water resources and related developments
(in millions of dollars)

Program and Agency	1971 Actual	1972 Actual	1973 Estimate	1974 Estimate
Flood control works:				
Agriculture: Soil Conservation Service (mostly grants)	65.5	71.2	90.7	75.3
Defense–Civil: Corps of Engineers	404.1	457.1	562.6	497.9
Interior: Bureau of Reclamation	2.4	1.8	2.5	2.4
State: International Boundary and Water Commission	1.8	2.9	7.8	12.3
Tennessee Valley Authority	0.4	.1	.9	.9
Total flood control works	474.2	533.1	664.5	588.8
Beach erosion control: Defense – Civil: Corps of Engineers	1.7	3.0	4.2	2.8
Irrigation and water conservation works:				
Agriculture: Soil Conservation Service (grants	10.9	12.1	15.4	14.0
Interior:				
Bureau of Indian Affairs	6.9	11.7	13.0	15.0
Bureau of Reclamation (includes grants and loans)	64.6	84.3	147.6	122.5
Total irrigation works	82.4	108.1	176.0	151.5
Navigation facilities:				
Commerce: Economic Development Administration (mostly grants)		15.0	14.5	12.5
Defense–Civil:				
Corps of Engineers	220.0	233.3	259.3	218.7
Panama Canal Company		.1	1.8	1.0
Transportation: Saint Lawrence Seaway Corporation	0.1	.5	.6	1.7
Tennessee Valley Authority	0.3	2.2	4.9	.6
Total navigation facilities	220.4	251.1	281.1	234.5
Multiple-purpose dams and reservoirs with hydroelectric power facilities:				
Defense–Civil: Corps of Engineers	326.3	380.9	312.4	306.3
Interior: Bureau of Reclamation	119.2	144.7	181.3	149.5
Tennessee Valley Authority[1]	31.9	39.9	57.7	74.7
Total multiple-purpose facilities	477.4	565.5	551.4	530.5

EXHIBIT I.1--continued

Powerplants:				
Defense-Civil: Panama Canal Company	2.8		4.0	.3
Interior: Territorial Affairs (grants)		1.9	2.2	1.1
Tennessee Valley Authority	364.6	452.7	333.7	351.4
Total powerplants	367.4	454.6	339.9	352.8
Power transmission facilities:				
Defense-Civil: Panama Canal Company		1.2	.8	.2
Interior:				
Territorial Affairs (grants)	10.8	1.0	.8	.2
Bureau of Reclamation	101.9	6.9	8.8	16.9
Bonneville Power Administration		90.2	82.3	89.8
Southwestern Power Administration	2.4	2.6	1.7	.6
Tennessee Valley Authority	72.9	75.3	84.6	75.8
Total power transmission facilities	188.0	177.2	179.0	183.5
Water supply and waste disposal facilities:				
Agriculture:				
Farmers Home Administration (grants)	20.4	25.6	46.5	46.6
Forest Service	8.1	11.9	29.7	31.7
Commerce: Economic Development Administration and Regional Action Planning Commissions (primarily grants)	69.5	102.2	106.2	96.5
Health, Education, and Welfare: Health Services and Mental Health Administration	15.6	21.3	31.5	36.9
Housing and Urban Development: grants and loans	163.4	148.2	145.2	144.1
Interior:				
National Park Service	5.6	24.3	20.0	22.1
Bureau of Reclamation	29.2	16.4	29.4	25.5
Environmental Protection Agency (grants)	478.4	413.4	727.0	1,600.0
Other agencies (mostly grants)	16.6	15.8	15.6	12.0
Total water supply and waste disposal	806.8	779.1	1,151.1	2,015.4
Total water resources and related developments	2,618.3	2,871.7	3,347.2	4,059.8

1. Includes outlays for Raccoon Mountain Pumped Storage Power Project (a single-purpose project) as follows: 1971, $16.2; 1972, $25.9; 1973 est., $40.0; 1974 est., $53.8.

Source: Water Policies for the Future, Final Report to the President and to the Congress by the National Water Commission, June 1973, p. 502.

EXHIBIT I.2

Comparison of Federal outlays for water resources with those for other Federal civil public works and the total U.S. budget (billions of dollars)

| Year | Federal Civil Public Works | | | | Federal Water Resources Expenditures | | |
	Direct Civil Construction	Grants	Net Lending	Total	Total Civil Works	% of Total Civil Works	% of Total Budget
1964	2.7	4.2	0.1	7.0	1.5	21	1.3
1965	2.8	4.6	0.2	7.6	1.5	20	1.3
1966	3.0	4.4	0.3	7.7	1.7	22	1.3
1967	2.8	4.7	0.4	7.9	1.7	22	1.1
1968	2.5	5.3	0.3	8.1	1.8	22	1.0
1969	2.2	5.5	0.3	8.0	1.8	22	1.0
1970	2.2	5.8	0.3	8.3	1.9	23	0.9
1971	2.6	6.4	0.2	9.2	2.6	28	1.2
1972	3.3	6.5	0.2	10.0	2.9	29	1.2
1973 est.	3.8	7.2	0.3	11.3	3.3	29	1.3
1974 est.	3.3	8.1	0.3	11.7	4.1	35	1.5

Source: Water Policies for the Future, Final Report to the President and to the Congress by the National Water Commission, June 1973, p. 503.

EXHIBIT I.3

ESTIMATED HISTORICAL FEDERAL EXPENDITURES FOR
WATER RESOURCES AND RELATED ACTIVITIES

	Indexing Factor	Navigation	Flood Control	Irrigation	Power	Water Supply & Pollution Control	Watershed Protection	Fisheries & Wildlife	Multiple Purpose	Total
1900	18.7	.35	—	—	—	—	—	—	—	.35
1905	18.6	.43	—	.09	—	—	—	—	—	.52
1910	17.5	.55	—	.14	—	—	—	—	—	.69
1915	18.2	.85	—	.18	—	—	—	—	—	1.03
1920	6.8	.28	.06	.04	—	—	—	—	—	.38
1925	8.1	.53	.12	.07	—	—	—	—	—	.72
1930	8.3	.66	.35	.07	.04	—	—	—	—	1.12
1935	8.6	1.48	.38	.18	.11	—	—	—	—	2.15
1940	7.0	1.02	.74	.24	.23	.01	—	—	.11	2.35
1945	5.5	.28	.40	.08	.14	—	—	—	.07	.97
1950	3.3	.44	.90	.48	.53	.03	.01	—	.84	3.23
1955	2.55	.29	.38	.19	.44	.02	.02	.01	.66	2.01
1960	2.03	.59	.69	.17	.46	.15	.03	.02	1.07	3.18
1965	1.73	.70	.92	.16	.61	.23	.06	.02	.49	3.19
1970	1.22	.23	.36	.11	.55	.56	.08	.02	.40	2.31

Note: Totals—without indexing factor—do not agree with amounts shown in Figure 16-1 due to differences in accounting procedures. The indexing factor is the multiplier used to convert current dollars to 1972 constant dollars.

EXHIBIT I.4

Total historical expenditures for water resources development

	Period of Estimate	Cumulative Expenditures (billions of 1972 dollars)			
		Federal Ownership or Financed	State & Local Ownership and Financed	Private Ownership and Financed	Total
Instream Uses					
Hydro Power	Total to 1968	9.3	3.2	6.2	18.7
Flood Control	Total to 1969	25.3	2.0	1.3	28.6
Navigation	Total to 1969	16.8	1.6	-	18.4
Recreation	Total 1956-65	1.1	1.9	3.3	6.3
Fish & Wildlife				-	
Waste Treatment	Total to 1971	11.3[1]	62.8	no est.	78.7
Sanitary Sewers	Total to 1971			4.6[2]	
Storm & Combined Sewers	Total to 1971	-	36.3	3.2[2]	39.5
Out-of-Stream Uses					
Municipal Water	Total to 1971	6.6	78.5	9.3[2]	94.4
Industrial (except cooling water)	Total to 1965	6.6	4.6	13.3	24.5
Cooling Water	Total to 1969	0.1	0.1	1.4	1.6
Irrigation	Total to 1968	10.6	3.4	13.9	27.9
Total		87.7	194.4	56.5	338.6

[1] Includes $6.6 billion at Federal facilities.
[2] To 1966 only.

Source: Water Policies for the Future, Final Report to the President and to the Congress by the National Water Commission, June 1973, p. 506.

EXHIBIT I.5

Projection of capital investment costs based on extrapolation of "needs" in Framework Studies of WRC

(billions of 1972 dollars)

Category	1970-1980				1980-2020			
	Federal	Non-Federal	Total	Percent of Total	Federal	Non-Federal	Total	Percent of Total
Municipal and Industrial Water Supply	0.4	13.7	14.1	7	6.7	32.2	38.9	7
Irrigation and Drainage	3.0	12.0	15.0	7	9.6	27.8	37.4	7
Power[1]	6.9	12.9	19.8	10	6.7	35.1	41.8	8
Flood Control	8.5	10.4	18.9	9	22.3	25.0	47.3	9
Recreation	9.4	9.3	18.7	9	24.4	24.4	48.8	9
Fish and Wildlife	2.4	1.8	4.2	2	6.9	5.2	12.1	2
Water Quality	31.0	50.5	81.5	40	116.0	111.0	227.0	42
Land Management	6.7	6.7	13.4	6	15.3	15.3	30.6	6
Navigation	10.8	3.1	13.9	6	25.5	7.6	33.1	6
Shoreline Protection and Development	2.8	2.8	5.6	3	7.8	7.9	15.7	3
Other	1.3	1.3	2.6	1	2.6	2.7	5.3	1
	83.2	124.5	207.7	100	243.8	294.2	538.0	100

[1] Primarily hydroelectric although cooling water facilities were included in some studies.

Source: Water Policies for the Future, Final Report to the President and to the Congress by the National Water Commission, June 1973, p. 507.

Chapter 1

1. For additional information on port development, management
   and operations, refer to Roy S. MacElwee, Port Development
   (New York: McGraw-Hill Book Company, 1926); Marvin L. Fair,
   Port Administration in the United States (Cambridge, Md.:
   Cornell Maritime Press, 1954); T. Arthur Smith, A Function-
   al Analysis of the Ocean Port (Silver Spring, Md.: Operations
   Research, Inc., 1964); Martin J. Schwimmer and Paul A.
   Amundsen, Management of a Seaport (Kings Point, N.Y.:
   National Maritime Research Center, 1973).

2. Remarks by Howard F. Casey, Deputy Assistant Secretary of
   Commerce for Maritime Affairs, at Conference on Port Planning and Development, Milwaukee, Wisconsin, November 29,
   1973, p. 5.

3. U.S. Secretary of Transportation, "A Progress Report on
   National Transportation Policy" (Washington, D.C.: Department of Transportation, May 1974), p. 24.

Chapter 2

1. This section of the report makes use of the following
   source: U.S. Maritime Administration, Division of Ports,
   Office of Ports and Intermodal Systems, Public Port Financing in the United States (Washington, D.C.: U.S. Department
   of Commerce, June 1974).

2. Albert T. Rosselli, "Economic Rationalization of Port
   Investment" (Milwaukee, Wisconsin: paper presented at
   the Conference on Port Planning and Development, Nov. 27-30,
   1973), pp. 6-7.

3. Ibid., p. 6.

4. Port of Seattle Commission, "Seattle Maritime Commerce and
   Its Impact on the Economy of King County (Seattle, Washington, 1971), p. 2.

5. John Miloy and Anthony E. Copp, Economic Analysis of Texas
   Marine Resources and Industries (College Station, Texas:
   Texas A & M University Sea Grant Program, June 1970),
   pp. 58-60.

6. Wayne E. Etter and Robert C. Graham, Financial Planning
   for the Texas Port System (College Station, Texas: Texas
   A & M University Sea Grant Program, March 1974), pp. 53-54.

7. For additional information on containerization, see Henry S. Marcus, _Planning Ship Replacement in the Containerization Era_ (Lexington, Mass.: Lexington Books, D. C. Heath and Company, 1974).

8. _Public Port Financing in the United States_, _op._ _cit._, p. 14.

9. Remarks by Howard F. Casey, Deputy Assistant Secretary of Commerce for Maritime Affairs, at the Conference on Port Planning and Development, Milwaukee, Wisconsin, November 29, 1973, p. 5.

10. Etter and Graham, _op._ _cit._, p. 77.

11. Donald A. Walsh, "Master Planning Considerations for the Port of Los Angeles" (Los Angeles Metropolitan Section: The Society of Naval Architects and Marine Engineers, September 13, 1973), p. 26.

12. Remarks of J. Eldon Opheim at the Conference on Port Planning and Development, Milwaukee, Wisconsin, November 27-30, 1973, p. 4.

13. _Public Port Financing in the United States_, _op._ _cit._, pp. 38-39.

14. Dan M. Bragg and James R. Bradley, "Work Plan for a Study of the Feasibility of an Offshore Terminal in the Texas Gulf Coast Region" (College Station, Texas: Texas A & M University Sea Grant Program, June 1971), p. 17.

15. "Tex. Superport Victory Feared," _New Orleans Times-Picayune_, as published in _Todd Daily Maritime_ (New York: Todd Shipyards Corporation, March 29, 1972), p. 4.

16. Paul J. Garfield and Wallace F. Lovejoy, _Public Utility Economics_ (Englewood Cliffs, New Jersey: Prentice-Hall, Inc., 1964), pp. 15-17.

Chapter 3

1. Daniel Bell, _The Coming of Post-Industrial Society_ (New York: Basic Books, Inc., 1969), p. 189.

2. Theodore Lowi, _The End of Liberalism_ (New York: W. W. Norton and Company, 1969), p. 31.

3. Francis E. Rourke, ed., _Bureaucratic Power in National Politics_ (Boston: Little, Brown and Company, 1972), p. 1.

4. Dudley Pegrum, Transportation Economics and Public Policy
    Irwin Series in Economics, Third Edition (Homewood, Illinois:
    Richard D. Irwin, Inc., 1973), Chapter 3, p. 46. Also see
    William J. Hull and Robert W. Hull, The Origin and Develop-
    ment of the Waterways Policy of the United States (Washing-
    ton, D.C.: National Waterways Conference, Inc., 1967).

5. Constitution, Article 1, Section 9.

6. James P. Morris and Robert F. Steeves, "Federal Policy for
    United States Ports" (Silver Spring, Maryland: Operations
    Research, Inc., August 25, 1964), p. v.

7. 24 May 1824, Navigation, 4 Stat. 32.

8. William J. Hull and Robert W. Hull, The Origin and Develop-
    ment of the Waterways Policy of the United States (Washing-
    ton, D.C.: National Waterways Conference, Inc., 1967).

9. Supra, p. 9.

10. Supra, p. 16.

11. Supra, pp. 16-22.

12. Interstate Commerce Act, 24 Stat. 379, 49, U.S.C.A., 1887.
    Also see Act of Sept. 18, 1940, Ch. 722; 54 Stat. 899; note
    preceding 49 U.S.C. Sec. 1 (1958).

13. U.S. Senate, Committee on Government Operations, "S. 3010,
    A Bill to Establish a Department of Transportation," Hear-
    ings, 89th Congress, 2nd Session (Washington, D.C.: Govern-
    ment Printing Office, 1966), pp. 213-218.

14. See U.S. Congressional Record, House Report 902, 49th
    Congress, 1st Session (Washington, D.C.: Government Printing
    Office, 1926), pp. 432, 2196. Also U.S. House of Represen-
    tatives, Committee on Interstate and Foreign Commerce,
    "National Transportation Inquiry Hearings," Hearings, 80th
    Congress, 2nd Session (Washington, D.C.: Government Printing
    Office, 1957), pp. 14-21. Also see John D. Costello,
    "Public Law 89-670, A Comparative Analysis," unpublished
    M.A. thesis completed at the School of Government and Busi-
    ness Administration, George Washington University, August
    1969.

15. Supra, note 8, p. 64.

16. Act of Sept. 7, 1916, Ch. 451; 39 Stat. 728; 46 U.S.C.
    Sec. 801 to 842 (1958).

17. Supra, note 6, p. 8.

18. Act of March 2, 1919, Ch. 95, Sec. 1; 40 Stat. 1286; 33 U.S.C.
    Sec. 551 (1958).

19. Act of June 5, 1920, Ch. 250; 41 Stat. 988; 46 U.S.C. Sec.
     861-89 (1958).

20. Grant Miller Davis, The Department of Transportation
     (Lexington, Mass.: Heath Lexington Books, 1970), Chap. 2.

21. Ibid.

22. P.L. 255-722, 76th Congress, 1st Sess., 1940.

23. U.S. House of Representatives, Report on Practices and Pro-
     cedures of Government Control, H. Doc. 678, 78th Congress
     (Washington, D.C.: Government Printing Office, 1944),
     p. 144.

24. U.S. House of Representatives, National Resources Planning
     Board, Transportation and National Policy, H. Doc. 883,
     77th Congress (Washington, D.C.: Government Printing Office,
     1942), p. 158.

25. Ibid.

26. Ibid., p. 276.

27. Supra, note 20.

28. Ibid.

29. National Water Commission Act, 82 Stat. 868, September 26,
     1968.

30. Theodore M. Schad, "Findings of the National Water Commis-
     sion" (Washington, D.C.: American Society of Civil Engi-
     neers' National Water Resources Conference, January 31,
     1973).

31. Senator William Proxmire, Uncle Sam - the Last of the Big-
     time Spenders (New York: Simon and Schuster, 1972), p. 142.

32. National Water Commission, Water Policies for the Future,
     Final Report to the President and to the Congress of the
     United States by the National Water Commission (Washington,
     D.C.: Government Printing Office, June 1973), pp. 120-121.

33. Supra, note 31. Also see Arthur A. Maass, "Congress and
     Water Resources," in Francis E. Rourke, Bureaucratic Power
     in National Politics (Boston: Little, Brown and Company,
     1972).

34. American Waterways Operators, Inc., "Big Load Afloat: U.S.
     Domestic Water Transportation Resources" (Washington, D.C.:
     American Waterways Operators, Inc., 1973), p. 111.

35. Ibid.

36. See "If Not, Why Not, AWO President Asks on Inflation Im-
     pact Statements," in American Waterways Operators, Inc.,
     "Weekly Letter," Vol. XXXII, Number 13 (Washington, D.C.:
     American Waterways Operators, Inc., March 13, 1975).

37. Harley H. Hinrichs and Graeme M. Taylor, Program Budgeting
     and Benefit-Cost Analysis (Pacific Palisades, California:
     Goodyear Publishing Co., Inc., 1969).

38. National Water Commission, Water Policies for the Future,
     Final Report to the President and to the Congress of the
     United States by the National Water Commission (Washington,
     D.C.: Government Printing Office, June 1973), pp. 383-387.
     Also see U.S. Water Resource Council, Summary and Analysis
     of Public Response to the Proposed Principles and Standards
     for Related Land Resources and Draft Environmental Statement
     (Washington, D.C.: Government Printing Office, August 1972),
     pp. 89-107.

39. Ibid., National Water Commission Report, p. 384.

40. Water Resources Development Act of 1974, P.L. 93-251,
     88 Stat. 12, March 7, 1974: See House Reports 93-541, 93-
     796, Senate Report 93-615.

41. Federal Register, Vol. 39, Number 158, August 14, 1974,
     p. 29242. Also National Waterways Conference, "Criteria
     News," Issue No. 58 (Washington, D.C.: National Waterways
     Conference, Inc., March 28, 1974), p. 1.

42. General Services Administration, National Archives and
     Records Service, Office of the Federal Register, "Notices:
     United States Water Resources Council," Federal Register,
     Vol. 39, No. 158 (Washington, D.C.: U.S. Government Print-
     ing Office, August 14, 1974), p. 29242.

43. National Waterways Conference, "Criteria News," Issue No.
     60 (Washington, D.C.: National Waterways Conference, Inc.,
     January 15, 1975).

44. Ibid.

45. David C. Major, "Multiobjective Water Resource Planning,"
     Review Draft, American Geophysical Union Water Resources
     Monograph No. 4 (Cambridge, Mass., 1973).

46. James P. Morris and Robert F. Steeves, "Federal Policy for
     United States Ports," supra, note 6, p. 5.

47. Merchant Marine Act of 1920, Act of March 2, 1919, Ch. 95,
     Sec. 1; 40 Stat. 1286; 33 U.S.C. Sec. 551 (1958).

48. U.S. House of Representatives, Merchant Marine and Fisher-
     ies Committee, "Ports and Waterways Safety Act of 1971,"
     H.R. 867, House Report 92-563 (Washington, D.C.: U.S. Govern-
     ment Printing Office, September 1971). Also see U.S.
     Senate, Committee on Commerce, "Navigable Waters Safety
     and Environmental Quality Act of 1971," S. 2074, Hearings,
     Senate Report 92-724 (Washington, D.C.: U.S. Government
     Printing Office, Sept. 22-24, 1971).

49. See story by Robert F. Morison, "Offshore Ports Bill Battle
     Shaping Up," The Journal of Commerce, May 16, 1974.

50. "Panels Fail to Combine House Superport Bills," The Baltimore
     Sun, May 9, 1974. Reprinted in the Todd Daily Maritime,
     No. 74-89 (New York, New York: Todd Shipyards Corporation,
     May 9, 1974), p. 2.

51. John Burby, The Great American Motion Sickness (Boston,
     Mass.: Little, Brown and Co., 1971), p. 247.

52. U.S. House of Representatives, Select Committee on Commit-
     tees, Staff Summary Report, "Committee Reform Amendments
     of 1974," H. Res. 988, 93rd Congress, 2nd Session (Washing-
     ton, D.C.: U.S. Government Printing Office, March 21, 1974).

53. Ibid.

54. U.S. House of Representatives, Select Committee on Commit-
     tees, "Committee Organization in the House," Hearings,
     93rd Congress, 1st Session (Washington, D.C.: U.S. Govern-
     ment Printing Office, Oct. 11, 1973), Vol. 3 of 3, Part 2
     of 2, p. 380.

55. Supra, note 51, p. 248.

56. United States Senate, Committee on Commerce, "Authorizing
     a National Oceans Policy Study," Report 93-685, 93rd Con-
     gress, 2nd Session (Washington, D.C.: U.S. Government
     Printing Office, Feb. 8, 1974).

57. United States Senate, Committee on Commerce, "Senate Reso-
     lution 222," Background Report, 93rd Congress, 2nd Session
     (Washington, D.C.: U.S. Government Printing Office, Janu-
     ary 31, 1974). Ibid.

Chapter 4

1. 42 U.S.C. 2011, 2051.

2. 42 U.S.C. 2051, 2201.

3. 42 U.S.C. 2451.

4. This authority is contained in 10 U.S.C. 7391-7393.

5. Martin J. Schwimmer and Paul A. Amundsen, _Management of a
    Seaport_ (Kings Point, N.Y.: National Maritime Research
    Center, 1973), p. 36.

6. 10 U.S.C. 5012.

7. 20 U.S.C. 41.

8. See the Public Works and Economic Development Act of 1965;
    79 Stat. 552; 42 U.S.C. 3121.

9. Criteria for EDA approval is contained in Title 13, Chapter
    3, Part 302 of the CFR.

10. U.S. Department of Commerce, _1973 Annual Report of the EDA_
    (Washington, D.C.: U.S. Government Printing Office, 1974),
    p. 4.

11. Some assistance was also provided under the EDA's _Technical
    Assistance Projects_ program; see _Ibid._, _1973 Annual Report_,
    p. 12.

12. _Supra_, note 9.

13. U.S. Department of Commerce, Maritime Administration, Divi-
    sion of Ports, Office of Ports and Intermodal Systems,
    Public Port Financing in the United States (Washington, D.C.:
    Government Printing Office, June 1974), p. 50.

14. _Ibid._ Also see note 8.

15. _Ibid._, p. 51.

16. _Ibid._, p. 41.

17. Act of September 27, 1974, P.L. 93-423, HR 14883.

18. 42 U.S.C. 1450; 40 U.S.C. 461; 42 U.S.C. 1491, 1487.

19. Federal Energy Administration Act of 1974, P.L. 93-275,
    May 7, 1974.

20. U.S. Senate, Committees on Commerce, Interior and Insular
    Affairs, and Public Works, Special Joint Subcommittee on
    Deepwater Ports Legislation, "Deepwater Port Act of 1973,"
    Hearings, 93rd Congress, 1st sess., Part II (Washington,
    D.C.: Government Printing Office, 1974), p. 706.

21. Deepwater Port Act of 1974, HR 10701, January 4, 1975.
    See the _Congressional Record--House_, Conference Report on
    HR 10701, December 16, 1974, p. HR 12036.

22. Supra, note 20; also see Ibid., pp. 706-707.

23. 26 Stat. 1085; 8 U.S.C. 1304.

24. 33 U.S.C. 929, 930, 941; 5 U.S.C. 22; also see the National
    Occupational Safety and Health Act of 1970, P.L. 91-596,
    Dec. 1970.

25. Federal Trade Commission Act of 1914, 38 Stat. 717, 15 U.S.C.
    41-51; Clayton Act of 1914, 38 Stat. 730; 15 U.S.C. 12.

26. Deepwater Port Act of 1974, HR 10701, January 4, 1975; See
    Supra, note 21. Also see "Statement of the FTC on S. 1751,
    Deepwater Port Facilities Act of 1973," presented by James T.
    Halverson, Director, Bureau of Competition, before Special
    Joint Subcommittee of the Senate Committees on Commerce,
    Interior and Insular Affairs, and Public Works, Deepwater Port
    Act of 1973, U.S. Senate, 93rd, First Session, October 3,
    1973, Part 1, p. 634.

27. Ibid.

28. The FCC was created by the Communications Act of 1934
    (48 Stat. 1064; 15 U.S.C. 21; 47 U.S.C. 35, 151-609) to
    "regulate interstate and foreign communications by wire and
    radio in the public interest." It was assigned additional
    regulating jurisdiction under the provisions of the Commu-
    nications Satellite Act of 1962, 76 Stat. 419; 47 U.S.C.
    701-744.

29. The FPC was created under the Federal Water Power Act of
    1920, 41 Stat. 1063, June 10, 1920, as amended by the Federal
    Power Act, 49 Stat. 863, August 26, 1935. Further amendments
    were contained in the Public Utility Act of 1935, 49 Stat.
    838, August 26, 1935, and the Natural Gas Act of 1938,
    52 Stat. 821-833, 15 U.S.C. 717-717W, June 21, 1938. Addi-
    tional responsibilities have been assigned by other legisla-
    tion and by Executive Orders.

30. National Environmental Policy Act of 1969, Public Law 91-190,
    42 U.S.C. 4321 et seq., January 1, 1970.

31. 19 U.S.C. 2071.

32. Supra.

33. 19 U.S.C. 2071, 2072.

34. Department of the Treasury, Bureau of Customs Circular
    MAN-9-0:I:PA, June 15, 1973.

35. 19 U.S.C. 2; 19 CFR 1.2; Executive Order 10289, September 17,
    1951.

36. See Martin J. Schwimmer and Paul A. Amundsen, _Management of a Seaport_ (Kings Point, N.Y.: National Maritime Research Center, 1973), p. 37.

37. Executive Order 11735, July 1, 1973.

38. See Executive Orders 11051, 11490. Executive Order 11073, the OEP statutory mandate, remains in force.

39. _Supra_, note 36, pp. 34-35.

40. _Ibid_. Also see Animal and Plant Health Inspection Service, established April 2, 1972, pursuant to 5 U.S.C. 301 and Reorganization Plan 2 of 1953.

41. 33 U.S.C. 610.

42. 21 U.S.C. 114 b-c.

43. 42 U.S.C. 264-272.

44. P.L. 86-682; 74 Stat. 587; 39 U.S.C. Sec. 904; reorganized by the Act of Aug. 12, 1970, effective July 1, 1971; 84 Stat. 719, 39 U.S.C. Prec. 101 note, as the U.S. Postal Service.

45. 43 U.S.C. 31; 76 Stat. 427; 43 U.S.C. 1340.

46. 43 U.S.C. 366.

47. 43 U.S.C. 31.

48. Reorganization Plan 3 of 1946, Sections 402, 403; 5 U.S.C. 133-1-16. Also see Dept. of Interior responses to Senate Subcommittee questionnaire on "Deepwater Port Act of 1973," Joint Hearings before the Special Subcommittee on Deepwater Ports Legislation of the Committees on Commerce, Interior and Insular Affairs, and Public Works, _supra_, note 20, p. 719.

49. _Ibid_., p. 720.

50. Fish and Wildlife Act of 1956 as amended; 70 Stat. 1119; 16 U.S.C. 742(a)-742(1). Also see "Deepwater Port Act of 1973," Dept. of Interior questionnaire, _supra_, note 20.

51. _Supra_, note 46. General Services Administration, National Archives and Record Service, _U.S. Government Manual 1973/74_ (Washington, D.C.: U.S. Government Printing Office, 1974), p. 268.

52. _Ibid_., p. 267.

53. Deepwater Port Act of 1974, HR 10701, January 4, 1975; see _supra_, note 21.

54. *Ibid*, Section 4(e)(3) of the Act.

55. 78 Stat. 331; 42 U.S.C. 1961b.

56. Testimony of Dr. William Johnson, Energy Adviser to the
     Deputy Secretary of the Department of the Interior, before
     the United States Senate, Committees on Commerce; Interior
     and Insular Affairs; and Public Works; Special Joint Sub-
     committee on Deepwater Ports Legislation, "Deepwater Port
     Act of 1973," Hearings, 93rd Congress, 1st Session (Washing-
     ton, D.C.: U.S. Government Printing Office, July 23, 1973,
     Part I, p. 149.

57. *Ibid*., pp. 149-156.

58. General Services Administration, National Archives and
     Records Service, U.S. Government Manual, 1973/74 (Washington,
     D.C.: U.S. Government Printing Office, 1973), p. 80.

59. BOB was created by the Act of June 10, 1921 (42 Stat. 20;
     31 U.S.C. 11-16).

60. Joel Havemann, "White House Report/OMB's Legislative Role
     Is Growing More Powerful and More Political," National
     Journal Reports (Washington, D.C.: National Journal, Oct. 27,
     1973), p. 1589.

61. *Ibid*., p. 1594.

62. *Ibid*. Also see *supra*, note 56, Part I, p. 286.

63. Richard Neustadt, "Presidency and Legislation, the Growth
     of Central Clearance," The American Political Science Review,
     Vol. XLVII, September 1954.

64. David J. Allee and Helen M. Ingram, Authorization and
     Appropriation Processes for Water Resources Development,
     National Water Commission Report NWC-71-023 (Ithaca, New
     York: Cornell University Press, 1972), pp. 3-14.

65. *Supra*, note 60.

66. National Waterways Conference, "National Waterways Confer-
     ence Newsletter" (Washington, D.C.: National Waterways Con-
     ference Inc., April 19, 1974), pp. 1-2.

67. *Ibid*.

68. Interviews with officials from OMB and the Corps of Engi-
     neers. Also see *supra*, note 66.

69. *Supra*, note 60.

70. *Ibid*., p. 1590.

71. General Services Administration, National Archives and
     Records Service, "Water Resources Council," The Federal
     Register (Washington, D.C.: U.S. Government Printing Office,
     September 10, 1973), p. 24778 et seq.

72. U.S. Senate, Select Committee on National Water Resources,
     Senate Report 29, 87th Congress, 1st Session (Washington,
     D.C.: U.S. Government Printing Office, 1960).

73. Water Resources Planning Act of 1965, Public Law 89-90,
     42 U.S.C. 1962a, July 22, 1965.

74. U.S. Water Resources Council, Summary and Analysis of Pub-
     lic Response to the Proposed Principles and Standards for
     Related Land Resources and Draft Environmental Statement
     (Washington, D.C.: U.S. Government Printing Office, August
     1972). Also see Supra, note 71.

75. Supra, note 71.

76. Ibid.

77. Water Resources Development Act of 1974, P.L. 93-251,
     88 Stat. 12, March 7, 1974.

78. Ibid. Also see National Waterways Conference, Inc., "Water
     Resources Development Act Becomes Law: More Confusion Than
     'Compromise?'" Criteria News (Washington, D.C.: National
     Waterways Conference, Inc.), Issue No. 58, March 28, 1974.

79. National Waterways Conference, Inc., "C.O.M.A.'s Guidance
     Seen As Assuring More Responsive Policy Recommendations."
     Criteria News (Washington, D.C.: National Waterways Confer-
     ence, Inc.), Issue No. 60, January 15, 1975.

80. Arthur Krock, The Consent of the Governed (Boston: Little,
     Brown and Co., 1971), Chapter 7.

81. 39 Stat. 728, Chapter 451, Sept. 7, 1916.

82. 41 Stat. 988, Chapter 250, June 15, 1920.

83. Intercoastal Shipping Act of 1933, P.L. 415, March 3, 1933.

84. 49 Stat. 1985, June 29, 1936.

85. 84 Stat. 91; 33 U.S.C. 1101.

86. Sec. 11(p)(1), 84 Stat. 91.

87. FMC Agreement #10,000, North Atlantic Pool, Docket 72-17.

88. CONASA vs. American Mail Line et al., FMC Docket 70-19.

89. _Intermodal Service to Portland, Oregon_, FMC Docket 70-19.

90. See "Initial Decision of C. W. Robinson, Chief Administrative Law Judge," FMC Docket 72-17, December 10, 1973.

91. Henry S. Marcus, "The Need for a Unified Governmental Approach to Port Planning," paper presented before the 1973 Annual Transportation Research Forum Meeting, Cleveland, Ohio, Oct. 15-17, 1973, p. 12.

92. _Delaware River Port Authority v. Sea-Land Service, Inc._, FMC Docket 71-65.

93. _Intermodal Service at Philadelphia_, FMC Docket 73-35.

94. _Supra_, note 88. Also see _Far East Conference vs. Seatrain_, FMC Docket 73-8.

95. _Board of Commissioners of the Port of New Orleans, et al. vs. Seatrain International S.A._, FMC Dockets 73-42, 73-61, 73-69, 74-4.

96. 24 Stat. 379, 383; 49 U.S.C. 1-22.

97. _U.S. Government Manual_, _op. cit._, p. 496.

98. _Ibid_.

99. Deepwater Port Act of 1974, HR 10701, January 4, 1975; see _Supra_, note 21.

100. See "FMC-ICC Jurisdictional Battle Flares," _Journal of Commerce_, October 10, 1974.

101. _Ibid_.

102. "Two Ship Lines See Need for Rulemaking Proceeding to Solve Intermodal Problems," Late News, _Traffic World_ (Washington, D.C.: Traffic Service Corporation, September 17, 1973), pp. 7-10.

103. The criteria for ICC decisions are contained in 49 U.S.C. 1-22 and 24 Stat. 379 as amended.

104. Reorganization Plan No. 4 of 1970, Oct. 3, 1970.

105. _Report of the Commission on Marine Science, Engineering and Resources_ (Washington, D.C.: U.S. Government Printing Office, January 1969).

106. _U.S. Government Manual_, _op. cit._ p. 135.

107. Coastal Zone Management Act of 1972, Public Law 92-583, 86 Stat. 1280, Oct. 27, 1972.

108. Marine Mammals Protection Act of 1972, P.L. 92-522, June 15, 1972.

109. Marine Protection, Research and Sanctuaries Act of 1972, Public Law 92-532, Oct. 23, 1972.

110. Weather Modification Reporting Act of 1972, P.L. 92-205, HR 6893, Dec. 18, 1971.

111. P.L. 91-144, 83 Stat. 326.

112. 33 U.S.C. 833.

113. 15 U.S.C. 313.

114. 16 U.S.C. 760; P.L. 86-359; 50 C.F.R., Chs. I and II.

115. U.S. Government Manual, op. cit., p. 136.

116. P.L. 92-583, 86 Stat. 1280.

117. Ibid., Section 303, p. 2.

118. Robert W. Knecht, "Coastal Zone Management: the Federal Role," paper presented before the Ninth Annual Conference of the Marine Technology Society, Washington, D.C., September 10-12, 1973. See Marine Technology Society, Proceedings, Ninth Annual Conference (Washington, D.C.: Marine Technology Society, September 10-12, 1973).

119. Martin J. Schwimmer and Paul A. Amundsen, Management of a Seaport (Kings Point, New York: National Maritime Research Center, 1973), pp. 82-83.

120. U.S. Department of Commerce, National Oceanographic and Atmospheric Administration, Office of Coastal Zone Management, "State Coastal Zone Management Activities--1974" (Washington, D.C.: U.S. Department of Commerce, Oct. 1974).

121. Testimony by Dr. Robert Knecht, National Oceanographic and Atmospheric Administration, in supra, note 20, p. 285.

122. Ibid., p. 288. Also see supra, note 60.

123. Deepwater Port Act of 1974, HR 10701, January 4, 1975; see supra, note 21.

124. Ibid., Section 4 of the Act.

125. United States Coast Guard, Ports and Waterways Administration and Management (Washington, D.C.: U.S. Coast Guard, July 1971), Appendix B-3.

126. U.S. Department of Commerce, NOAA, "State Coastal Zone Management Activities--1974," supra, note 120.

127. Transportation Development Division, Highway Users Federa-
     tion for Safety and Mobility, "A Status Report of State
     Departments of Transportation" (Washington, D.C.: Highway
     Users Federation for Safety and Mobility, December 1970)
     p. 1.

128. Wayne M. Pecknold, "Methodology for Systems Planning and
     Programming: Passenger," resource paper for the Joint M.I.T.
     Center for Transportation Studies and the Civil Engineering
     Department Workshop No. III, February 24-27, 1974 (Cambridge:
     M.I.T.), p. 7. Paper revised March 31, 1974.

129. "A Status Report of State Departments of Transportation,"
     op. cit., p. 2.

130. "Public Port Financing in the United States," supra, note 13,
     p. 36.

131. Ibid.

132. Ibid.

Chapter 5

1. National Environmental Policy Act of 1969, Public Law 91-
    190, 42 U.S.C. 4321 et seq., 83 Stat. 852, January 1, 1970.

2. Ibid., Section 102(2)(c).

3. Ibid.

4. National Waterways Conference, "Criteria News," Issue No.
    60 (Washington, D.C.: National Waterways Conference, Inc.,
    January 15, 1975), p. 10.

5. See "Court Grants Delay in Locks and Dam 26 Lawsuit" in
    American Waterways Operators, "Weekly Letter" (Washington,
    D.C.: American Waterways Operators, Inc., February 22, 1975).
    Also see "Trial Postponed in Controversial Locks 26 Case
    Until Congress Acts on Army Secretary's Request for Reaffir-
    mation" in National Waterways Conference, "Newsletter"
    (Washington, D.C.: National Waterways Conference, Inc.,
    March 7, 1975), p. 7.

6. See "Cross-Florida Barge Canal Economic Restudy Report Sub-
    mitted" in American Waterways Operators, "Weekly Letter,"
    Vol. 32, Number 15 (Washington, D.C.: American Waterways
    Operators, Inc., April 12, 1975), p. 4.

7. See "Ports Decide to Appeal Minibridge Decision" in The
    Journal of Commerce, Friday, April 11, 1975.

8. Office of the Chief of Engineers, U.S. Army Corps of Engineers, <u>Disposal of Dredge Spoil</u>, Technical Report H-72-8 (Washington, D.C.: U.S. Department of the Army, November 1972), p. 32.

9. <u>Ibid</u>.

10. <u>Ibid</u>., see pages 49-53.

11. See "Environmental Analysis Alters One-Third of Current Corps of Engineers Projects" in American Waterways Operators, "Weekly Letter" (Washington, D.C.: American Waterways Operators, Inc., March 29, 1975), p. 5.

12. "Texas Urged to Assume the Financial Burden for Intercoastal Canal," <u>The Journal of Commerce</u>, Thursday, April 17, 1975.

13. These disequilibriums are implied in the resolutions concerning federal funding assistance to ports enacted at the 1973 AAPA Annual Meeting. See Resolutions E-17, E-18, and E-19, AAPA Annual Meeting, San Diego, California, October 18, 1973. See also Walter C. Boyer, "A Discussion of Environmental Problems Looming Ahead," in Eric Schenker and Harry C. Brockel, eds., <u>Port Planning and Development as Related to Problems of U.S. Ports and the U.S. Coastal Environment</u> (Cambridge, Maryland: Cornell Maritime Press, Inc., 1974), p. 188.

14. <u>Ibid</u>. See AAPA Annual Resolutions.

15. <u>Ibid</u>.

16. The National Environmental Policy Act of 1969; P.L. 91-190, 42 U.S.C. 4321 et seq.; 83 Stat. 852, January 1, 1970.

17. <u>Ibid</u>.

18. 42 U.S.C. 4372;84 Stat. 114.

19. National Environmental Policy Act of 1969, P.L. 91-190, <u>op</u>. <u>cit</u>.

20. Water Quality Improvement Act of 1970, P.L. 91-224, 3 April 1970.

21. <u>Ibid</u>., P.L. 91-224. The procedures under this plan were published pursuant to Section 11 of the FWPCA of 1961, P.L. 87-88.

22. See testimony by Russell B. Train, Chairman, Council on Envi-
     ronmental Quality, before the United States Senate, Commit-
     tees on Commerce, Interior and Insular Affairs, and Public
     Works, Special Joint Subcommittee on Deepwater Ports Legis-
     lation, "Deepwater Port Act of 1973," Hearings, 93rd Con-
     gress, First Session (Washington, D.C.: U.S. Government
     Printing Office, July 23, 1973), p. 80.

23. Ibid.

24. General Services Administration, National Archives and
     Records Service, U.S. Government Manual 1973/74 (Washington,
     D.C.: U.S. Government Printing Office, 1973), p. 430.

25. P.L. 80-845, 50 U.S.C. 191, as amended, including the FWPCA
     of 1961 (P.L. 87-88); Water Quality Act of 1965 (P.L. 89-
     234); Clean Water Restoration Act of 1966 (P.L. 89-753);
     the Water Quality Improvement Act of 1970 (P.L. 91-224), and
     the 1972 Amendments thereto (P.L. 92-340).

26. P.L. 91-604, 42 U.S.C. 1857.

27. See supra, notes 25 and 26.

28. National Environmental Policy Act of 1969, P.L. 91-190,
     42 U.S.C. 4321, op. cit.

29. 1972 Amendments to the Water Quality Improvement Act of
     1970, P.L. 92340.

30. United States Environmental Protection Agency, Office of
     Enforcement and General Counsel, "The National Water Permit
     Program" (Washington, D.C.: U.S. Government Printing Office,
     June 1, 1973).

31. Ibid., pp. 7-12.

32. Ibid., p. 20.

33. Ibid., p. 22.

34. 33 U.S.C. 431, 33 U.S.C. 466. See United States Coast
     Guard, Ports and Waterways Administration and Management
     (Washington, D.C.: U.S. Coast Guard, July 1971), Appendix,
     p. 13-2-10.

35. United States Senate, Joint Report of the Committees on
     Commerce; Interior and Insular Affairs; and Public Works,
     "Deepwater Port Act of 1974," Report No. 93-1217, 93rd Con-
     gress, 2nd Session (Washington, D.C.: U.S. Government Print-
     ing Office, October 2, 1974).

36. Henry S. Marcus, "The U.S. Superport Controversy," Techno-
     logy Review (Cambridge, Mass.: M.I.T. Press, March/April
     1973), p. 49.

37. _Supra_, note 22.

38. Arthur D. Little Co., Report to the Council on Environmental Quality, _Potential Onshore Effects of Deepwater Oil Terminal-Related Industrial Development_ (Cambridge, Mass.: Arthur D. Little, Inc., 1970). Also _supra_, note 35, Appendix D.

39. _Ibid_.

40. Stephen Moore, Robert Dwyer and Arthur Katz, "A Preliminary Assessment of the Environmental Vulnerability of Machias Bay, Maine, to Oil Supertankers," Report No. 162 (Cambridge, Mass.: Dept. of Civil Engineering, M.I.T., January 1973).

41. _Ibid_. Also see Marcus, _supra_, note 36, p. 56.

42. _Supra_, note 22.

Chapter 6

1. U.S. House of Representatives, Subcommittee of the Committee on Appropriations, "Public Works for Water and Power Development and Atomic Energy Commission Appropriation Bill, 1974," Hearings, 93rd Congress, 1st Session (Washington, D.C.: Government Printing Office, 1973), pp. 26 and 31.

2. _Ibid_., p. 87.

3. U.S. Army Corps of Engineers, _Digest of Water Resources Policies and Activities_, EP 1165-2-1 (Washington, D.C.: Government Printing Office, Dec. 1972), pp. A-34 to A-35. Excerpts of this material are used for explanation of the Corps' role in port development.

4. U.S. House of Representatives, Appropriations Subcommittee, "Public Works," _op. cit_., p. 46.

5. _Ibid_., pp. 55-56.

6. _Ibid_., p. 61 (see General Morris's comments).

7. Corps of Engineers, EP 1165-2-1, _op. cit_., 28 Dec. 1972, p. A-62.

8. _Ibid_., p. A-27.

9. _Ibid_., p. A-86.

10. Federal Water Pollution Control Act, Public Law 92-500, 86 Stat. 816, October 18, 1972.

11. Corps of Engineers, EP 1165-2-1, _op. cit_., 28 Dec. 1972, p. A-34.

12. Ibid., p. A-94.

13. Ibid., p. A-39.

14. Ibid., p. A-41.

15. Ibid., pp. A-43-44.

16. Ibid., p. A-46.

17. Ibid., p. A-57.

18. River and Harbor and Flood Control Act, Public Law 89-298, 79 Stat. 1073, October 27, 1965.

19. David Allee and Helen Ingram, Authorization and Appropriation Processes for Water Resource Development, prepared under National Water Commission Contract NWC-72-023 (New York: Cornell University Press, 1972), p. 6-30.

20. River and Harbor Act of 1899, 30 Stat. 1151, 33 U.S.C. 403, March 13, 1899.

21. Corps of Engineers Regulation ER 1145-2-303, see supra, note 3, p. A-139, "Regulatory Functions to Protect/Preserve Navigable Waters and Environment."

22. U.S. House of Representatives, Subcommittee on Investigations and Oversight of the Public Works Committee, Statement by General Koisch (Washington, D.C.: Government Printing Office, 1971).

23. Supra, note 1, "Public Works," p. 125.

24. Allee and Ingram, Authorization, op. cit., p. 6-33.

25. Ibid., p. 6-30.

26. Supra, note 1, "Public Works."

27. Corps of Engineers, EP 1165-2-1, op. cit., 28 Dec. 1972, p. A-91.

28. Ibid. Also see supra, note 1, "Public Works."

29. Ibid., EP 1165-2-1, p. A-91.

30. Corps of Engineers, ER 1145-2-303, p. A-141; see supra, note 21.

31. Ibid., ER 1145-2-303, p. A-139.

32. River and Harbor and Flood Control Act of 1968, Public Law 90-483, 82 Stat. 735, August 13, 1968.

33. Corps of Engineers, EP 1165-2-1, op. cit., 28 Dec. 1972, p. A-32.

34. Ibid., p. A-17.

35. Department of Transportation Act, Public Law 89-670, 49 U.S.C. 1651, October 15, 1966.

36. Corps of Engineers, EP 1165-2-1, op. cit., 28 Dec. 1972, p. A-18.

37. See Corps of Engineers Studies: Tampa Harbor, Florida, Report to Congress, House Document 91-401 (Washington, D.C.: Government Printing Office, Oct. 12, 1970); Port Everglades Harbor, Florida, Report to Congress, House Document 93-144 (Washington, D.C.: Government Printing Office, Sept. 5, 1973).

38. Robert R. Nathan Associates, Inc., Foreign Deepwater Port Development, Department of the Army, Institute for Water Resources, Corps of Engineers (Washington, D.C.: Government Printing Office, 1971), Vol. 1, p. 541.

39. Robert R. Nathan Associates, Inc., U.S. Deepwater Port Study, Department of the Army, Institute for Water Resources, Corps of Engineers (Washington, D.C.: Government Printing Office, 1972), Vol. I, p. IV.

40. U.S. Bureau of the Census, Domestic and Intermodal Transportation of U.S. Foreign Trade: 1970 (Washington, D.C.: Government Printing Office, 1972), p. 1.

41. U.S. Department of Commerce, Bureau of the Census, Domestic Movement of Selected Commodities in United States Waterborne Foreign Trade: 1956 (Washington, D.C.: U.S. Bureau of the Census, 1959).

42. This study has not been performed to date due to lack of funds.

43. Supra, note 1, "Public Works," p. 35.

44. U.S. Senate, Special Joint Subcommittee on Deepwater Ports Legislation composed of the Committees on Commerce, Interior and Insular Affairs, and Public Works, "Deepwater Port Act of 1973," Hearings, 93rd Congress, First Session, Part I (Washington, D.C.: Government Printing Office, July 25, 1973), p. 488.

45. Ibid. Also see statement by Rep. John Young, p. 71.

46. Ibid, p. 62.

47. National Environmental Policy Act of 1969, P.L. 91-190, 42 U.S.C. 4321 et seq., and Exec. Order 11514, 35 F.R. 4247.

48. Federal Register, Vol. 38, Number 147, Part II, August 1,
     1973.

49. Ibid., p. 20550, Section 1500-2, p. 20554.

50. Corps of Engineers, EP 1165-2-1, op. cit., 28 Dec. 1972,
     pp. A-34 to A-35.

51. R. Keith Adams, "Today's Port and Harbor Planning," paper
     presented at the Conference on Port Planning and Development,
     Milwaukee, Wisconsin, Nov. 27-30, 1973, p. 12.

52. Ibid., p. 14.

53. Ibid.

54. U.S. Army Corps of Engineers, Interim Review Report--Los
     Angeles, Long Beach Harbors (Washington, D.C.: Government
     Printing Office, 1972).

55. Supra, note 1, "Public Works," pp. 102-103.

56. American Waterways Operators, "Environmental Analysis
     Alters One-Third of Current Corps of Engineers Projects"
     (Washington, D.C.: American Waterways Operators, Inc.,
     March 29, 1975), p. 5. Also see U.S. Army Corps of Engi-
     neers, Directorate of Civil Works, "Environmental Program,"
     EP 1105-2-500 (Washington, D.C.: U.S. Dept. of the Army,
     June 1973).

57. Ibid. Also see U.S. Army Corps of Engineers, Directorate
     of Civil Works, "Dredged Material Research Program,"
     EC 1130-2-122 (Washington, D.C.: U.S. Department of the
     Army, April 20, 1973), p. 5.

58. See statement by Dr. Joel F. Gustafsen in Walter C. Boyer,
     Deputy Administrator, Maryland Port Administration, "A Dis-
     cussion of Environmental Problems Looming Ahead," paper
     presented at the Conference on Port Planning and Develop-
     ment, Milwaukee, Wisconsin, November 19, 1973, p. 5.

59. David C. Major, "Multiobjective Water Resource Planning,"
     review draft, American Geophysical Union Water Resources
     Monograph 4 (Cambridge, Mass., 1973), p. 5.

60. National Waterways Conference, "Criteria News," Issue No.
     60 (Washington, D.C.: National Waterways Conference, Inc.,
     January 15, 1975), p. 8.

61. Alan A. Altshuler, The Politics of the Federal Bureaucracy
     (New York: Harper and Row, 1968).

62. Ibid., p. 281.

63. William Proxmire, Uncle Sam - The Last of the Bigtime Spenders (New York: Simon and Schuster, 1972), p. 142.

64. Ibid., p. 144.

65. Eric Schenker and Michael Bunamo, "A Study of the Corps of Engineers' Regional Pattern of Investments," The Southern Economic Journal, Vol. XXXIX, No. 4, April 1973, p. 548.

66. Ibid., p. 557.

67. See U.S. Water Resources Council, Summary and Analysis of Public Response to the Proposed Principles and Standards for Related Land Resources and Draft Environmental Statement (Washington, D.C.: Government Printing Office, August 1972), p. 42.

Chapter 7

1. National Archives and Records Service, General Services Administration, U.S. Government Manual, 1973/74 (Washington, D.C.: Government Printing Office, 1973), p. 132.

2. Merchant Marine Act of 1936; Act of June 29, 1936, Ch. 858; 49 Stat. 1985; 46 U.S.C. Sec. 1101 (1958).

3. Executive Office of the President, The Budget of the United States Government, FY 1975 (Washington, D.C.: Government Printing Office, 1974), pp. 183-184.

4. 39 Stat. 728, Chapter 451, Sept. 7, 1916. The Shipping Act was repealed by the Transportation Act of 1940, 54 Stat. 898, 950, Sept. 18, 1940.

5. Ibid., Preamble to the Act.

6. James P. Morris and Robert F. Steeves, "Federal Policy for United States Ports" (Silver Spring, Maryland: Operations Research Inc., 1964), p. V.

7. Merchant Marine Act of 1920, 41 Stat. 988, Chapter 250, June 15, 1920; Section 8: 46 U.S.C. 867, 41 Stat. 992.

8. Grant Miller Davis, The Department of Transportation (Lexington, Mass.: Heath Lexington, 1970), Chapter 3.

9. Supra, note 2, 49 Stat. 1985, June 29, 1936.

10. Supra, note 2, Preamble to the Act.

11. Sec. 212(a), supra, note 2; 46 U.S.C. 1122, 49 Stat. 1990.

12. Title I, supra, note 2; 46 U.S.C. 1101, P.L. 91-469.

13. See note 6.

14. _Supra_, note 6, Section 5.60, pp. 41-42.

15. Reorganization Plan 21 of 1950; 64 Stat. 1273, May 24, 1950.

16. Section 104 of the Plan, _supra_.

17. Reorganization Plan 7 of 1961; 75 Stat. 840 as amended by P.L. 91-469, 84 Stat. 1036.

18. _Supra_, notes 15, 17. Also see note 6, p. 36.

19. _Supra_, note 6, p. 36.

20. Ernest T. Bauer, Chief, Division of Ports, Office of Ports and Intermodal Systems, Maritime Administration, "Needful Steps for Improved Future MarAd-Port Industry Relationships," paper presented before the North Atlantic Ports Association, Washington, D.C., December 7, 1972.

21. _Ibid_.

22. Interstate Commerce Commission Delegation TM-1, April 4, 1957. Executive Order 11490.

23. U.S. Maritime Administration, _Manual of Orders_, AO-27 (Washington, D.C.: U.S. Department of Commerce, Maritime Administration).

24. U.S. Dept. of Commerce, Maritime Administration, Office of Ports and Intermodal Systems, "Highlights of MarAd Port Activities," October 1973, No. II (Washington, D.C.: Government Printing Office), p. 1.

25. U.S. Maritime Administration, _Manual of Orders_, AO-97 (Washington, D.C.: U.S. Dept. of Commerce, Maritime Administration, June 1973).

26. _Ibid_., Section 4.01(4).

27. _Ibid_., Section 4.01(5).

28. Soros Associates Inc., _Offshore Terminal Systems Concepts_ (Washington, D.C.: U.S. Department of Commerce, Sept. 1972).

29. Ernest T. Bauer, Chief, Division of Ports, Office of Ports and Intermodal Systems, Maritime Administration, "Needful Steps for Improved Future MarAd-Port Industry Relationships," paper presented before the North Atlantic Ports Association, Washington, D.C., December 7, 1972. Also see Howard F. Casey, Deputy Assistant Secretary of Commerce for Maritime Affairs, Maritime Administration, _U.S. Dept. of Commerce News_, MarAd, MA SP 74-10, May 23, 1974. Remarks presented before the Society of Naval Architects and Marine Engineers, Chicago, May 23, 1974, pp. 5-7.

30. Robert Blackwell, Assistant Secretary of Commerce for Maritime Affairs, U.S. Dept. of Commerce News, MarAd, MA SP 74-7, April 3, 1974. Remarks presented before the Radio Technology Commission for Marine Services and the Propeller Club of St. Petersburg, St. Petersburg, Florida, April 3, 1974, p. 3.

31. Supra, note 29, remarks by Howard Casey, p. 6.

32. U.S. Maritime Administration, U.S. Dept. of Commerce News, MarAd, MA NR 74-15, "MarAd Releases Hazardous Substances Transportation Study" (Washington, D.C.: U.S. Department of Commerce, June 17, 1974).

33. Federal Water Pollution Control Act, Public Law 92-500, 86 Stat. 816, October 18, 1972.

34. U.S. Department of Commerce, Maritime Administration, A Modal Economic and Safety Analysis of the Transportation of Hazardous Substances in Bulk (revised edition)(Washington, D.C.: U.S. Department of Commerce, 1974).

35. Supra, note 32, p. 2.

36. Supra, note 29, remarks by Howard Casey, pp. 6-7.

37. Supra, note 30, remarks by Robert Blackwell, p. 5.

38. U.S. Maritime Administration, U.S. Department of Commerce News, MarAd, MA NR 74-12, "MarAd Announces Second Phase of Satellite Program" (Washington, D.C.: U.S. Department of Commerce, May 30, 1974).

39. Horst Nowacki, Harry Benford, and Anthony Atkins, Economics of Great Lakes Shipping in an Extended Season (Ann Arbor, Michigan: University of Michigan, Report No. 139, January 1973), Maritime Administration Contract No. 1-35487.

40. U.S. Department of Commerce, Maritime Administration, Domestic Waterborne Shipping - Market Analysis (Chicago, Illinois: Kearney Management Consultants, February 1974).

41. Ibid. See Executive Summary, pp. 10-16.

42. U.S. Maritime Administration, U.S. Department of Commerce News, MarAd, MA NR 74-11, "North American Ports' Futures Surveyed by MarAd" (Washington, D.C.: U.S. Department of Commerce, May 28, 1974).

43. U.S. Department of Commerce, Maritime Administration, Division of Ports, Office of Ports and Intermodal Systems, Public Port Financing in the United States (Washington, D.C.: U.S. Department of Commerce, June 1974).

44. Ibid., p. iv.

45. Ibid.

46. U.S. Department of Commerce, Maritime Administration,
     "Neobulk Cargo Study" (Boston, Mass.: Harbridge House
     Inc., August 1974).

47. U.S. Department of Commerce, Maritime Administration,
     Office of Ports and Intermodal Systems, "Highlights of
     MarAd Port Activities," October 1973, No. II (Washington,
     D.C.: Government Printing Office), p. 6.

48. Supra, note 29, remarks by Howard Casey, p. 7.

49. Ibid., p. 7.

50. Supra, note 29, p. 1, remarks by Ernest T. Bauer.

51. Manalytics Inc., The Impact of Maritime Containerization
     on the United States Transportation System (Washington,
     D.C.: U.S. Department of Commerce, February 1972).

Chapter 8

 1. H. R. Kaplan and LCDR James Hunt, USCG, This is the Coast
     Guard, Cambridge, Md.: Cornell Maritime Press, Inc.,
     © 1972, pp. 3-7.

 2. Ibid., p. 2.

 3. June 18, 1878, Ch. 265, Sec. 4, Stat. 163.

 4. Kaplan, op. cit., p. 10.

 5. Ibid., pp. 10-15. See also 33 U.S.C. 711.

 6. Ibid., p. 40.

 7. Jan. 28, 1915, Ch. 20, Sec. 1, 38 Stat. 800.

 8. 14 U.S.C. 1.

 9. Supra, note 6.

10. A codification of these transfers is contained in 14 U.S.C.
     1; also see Title 49, U.S.C., Chapter 23, Transportation.

11. 50 U.S.C. 191. Also see Kaplan, op. cit., p. 45.

12. Ibid.

13. Kaplan, op. cit., p. 65.

14. Act of 1799, see 14 U.S.C. 1.

15. 14 U.S.C. 1; Aug. 4, 1949, Ch. 393, 63 Stat. 496.

16. P.L. 89-670, 80 Stat. 931, Oct. 15, 1966.

17. U.S. House of Representatives, House Report 557, 81st Con-
     gress (Washington, D.C.: U.S. Government Printing Office,
     1949).

18. Aug. 4, 1969, Ch. 393, 63 Stat. 496; Oct. 5, 1961, P.L. 87-
     396, Sec. 1, 75 Stat. 827; June 12, 1970, P.L. 91-278,
     Section 1(1) 84 Stat. 304.

19. 14 U.S.C. 1 et seq.

20. 14 U.S.C. 3.

21. United States Coast Guard, Ports and Waterways Administra-
     tion and Management (Washington, D.C.: U.S. Coast Guard,
     July 1971), p. 6.

22. Ibid., pp. 6-10.

23. Ibid., p. 6.

24. Ibid., p. 10.

25. Rivers and Harbors Act of 1915, Ch. 142, Sec. 4; 38 Stat.
     1049, 1053; 33 U.S.C. Sec. 565 (1958); March 4, 1915.

26. U.S. House of Representatives, Merchant Marine and Fish-
     eries Committee, "Ports and Waterways Safety Act of 1970,"
     Hearings, H.R. 17830 (Washington, D.C.: U.S. Government
     Printing Office, July 22-24, 30; August 10, 11; Sept. 15,
     16, 26, 1970).

27. U.S.C.G., Ports and Waterways, op. cit., p. 112.

28. Executive Order 10173, June 1950.

29. U.S.C.G., Ports and Waterways, op. cit., pp. 113-114; the statutory citings for these duties are as follows (as numbered in the text):

   1)   50 U.S.C. 191 - E.O. 10173 as amended; 33 CFR parts 3.6, 121-126.
   2)   46 U.S.C. 170; 46 CFR 146.
   3)   46 U.S.C. 391a; 46 CFR parts 30-39.
   4)   46 U.S.C. 362, 319a, 170, 882, 390b; 46 CFR part 2, 201-213.
   5)   33 U.S.C. 471, 180, 258, 322; 33 CFR part 110.
   6)   33 U.S.C. 474; 33 CFR part 92.
   7)   46 U.S.C. 9.
   8)   46 U.S.C. 85, 88; 46 CFR parts 42-46.
   9)   33 U.S.C. 431-437; 33 U.S.C. 1001-1015; 33 CFR part 151.
  10)   33 CFR 407.
  11)   14 U.S.C. 89.
  12)   14 U.S.C. 141.
  13)   14 U.S.C. 88.

30. Ibid., p. 114.

31. Ibid., pp. 114-118.

32. 33 CFR 6.

33. U.S.C.G., Ports and Waterways, op. cit., p. 115.

34. The basic federal legal mandate is included in 33 CFR 126; supplementary Coast Guard regulations, issued by the Commandant, are outlined in 33 CFR 6.12 and 6.14.

35. 46 CFR 146-149.

36. U.S.C.G., Ports and Waterways, op. cit., p. 117.

37. 46 CFR 30-40.

38. United States Coast Guard, Planning and Programming Manual, CG-411 (Washington, D.C.: U.S. Department of Transportation, July 1971), p. V-16.

39. This authority is derived generally from Title 14, U.S.C. Under 14 U.S.C. 141, Chapter 7, "Cooperation with Other Agencies," the Coast Guard may "utilize its personnel and facilities to assist any Federal agency, State, Territory, possession, or political subdivision thereof, or the District of Columbia, to perform any activity for which such personnel and facilities are especially qualified" (author's stress). Additionally, the Coast Guard "may avail itself of such officers and employees, advice, information, and facilities of any Federal agency, State, Territory, possession or political subdivision thereof, or the District of Columbia as may be helpful in the performance of its duties."

40. A survey of FY 1974 budget requests and marine environmental protection appropriations to the Coast Guard shows the area received 4% of the total operating allocations to the Service. This compares with 33% appropriated for Search and Rescue, traditionally the Coast Guard's highest budget percentage request annually.

41. U.S.C.G., Ports and Waterways, op. cit., p. 118.

42. 33 CFR 109-110.

43. The duties of the program reflect Coast Guard sentiment on fulfilling their charge to "render aid to distressed persons, vessels,..." under 14 U.S.C. 88 and others. The program is the preventative aspects of this charge.

44. U.S.C.G., Ports and Waterways, op. cit., p. 120.

45. Ibid., pp. 120-121.

46. See Exhibit 8.3.

47. Ibid.

48. U.S.C.G., Ports and Waterways, op. cit., p. 120.

49. Ibid., p. 121.

50. Ibid., pp. 120-121.

51. Ibid., pp. 121-127.

52. Ibid., p. 127.

53. On Monday, June 22, 1970, a freight train derailment caused the evacuation of Crescent City, Illinois, as compressed propane gas explosions raged, destroying one-third to one-half of the entire city. The Washington Post, June 22, 1970, A-3. And there have been several serious incidents involving waterways carriers (see U.S.C.G., Ports and Waterways, op. cit., p. 55).

54. See U.S.C.G., Ports and Waterways Administration and Management, op. cit., pp. 64-65.

55. Ibid.

56. U.S. House of Representatives, Merchant Marine and Fisheries Committee, "Ports and Waterways Safety Act of 1971," H.R. 867, House Report 92-563 (Washington, D.C.: U.S. Government Printing Office, September 1971). Also see U.S. Senate, Committee on Commerce, "Navigable Waters Safety and Environmental Quality Act of 1971," S. 2074, Hearings, Senate Report 92-724 (Washington, D.C.: U.S. Government Printing Office, September 22-24, 1971).

57. Water Quality Improvement Act of 1970, Public Law 91-224, April 3, 1970.

58. Ibid., Sections 12(a) and 12(d).

59. 14 U.S.C., Sections 2 and 88.

60. The Act is a general statement of policy and has been implemented by DOT in a variety of programs.

61. Office of the Secretary, Department of Transportation, Sixth Annual Report, FY 1972 (Washington, D.C.: U.S. Government Printing Office, 1972), p. 45.

62. Ibid.

63. Ibid., p. 123.

64. Some few, and partial, systems have been devised. Long Beach pilots have used radar in their operations since 1949, and Los Angeles pilots followed suit in 1951. The Port of New York instigated a "Harbor Radar Experiment" in 1951 and 1952, but the technique was not continued. The New York Port Authority tried a three-year experiment, beginning in 1962, using radar in conjunction with T.V., the "RATAN" (radio and television aid to navigation) system. Again the project was not continued. In 1969 the Coast Guard began another experimental project using shore-based radar in San Francisco Bay. An experimental Harbor Advisory Radar (HAR) was added in January of 1970. Unfortunately, the pilot system was not extensive enough to prevent in January 1971 a major collision between two oil tankers in San Francisco Bay which spilled 800,000 gallons of oil, and renewed emphasis on attaining quickly an efficient traffic control system in congested ports. An exception to this general pattern was the establishment of traffic control systems in the St. Mary's River in Michigan under 33 CFR 92. See DOT, Sixth Annual Report, FY 1972, op. cit., p. 123.

65. U.S.C.G., Ports and Waterways Administration and Management, op. cit., p. 91.

66. Ibid., pp. 90-91.

67. Ibid., p. 90.

68. Ports and Waterways Safety Act of 1972, P.L. 92-340, July 10, 1972.

69. Ibid.

70. See Exhibit 8.3.

71. United States Coast Guard, <u>Vessel Traffic Systems Study -
     Final Report</u>, Volume 1, Executive Summary (Washington, D.C.:
     U.S. Department of Transportation, March 1973), p. 1.

72. Ibid., pp. 2-3.

73. <u>Ibid</u>., p. 3.

74. <u>Ibid</u>., p. 3.

75. <u>Ibid</u>.

76. <u>Ibid</u>., pp. 4-5.

77. <u>Ibid</u>., p. 21.

78. U.S.C.G., Summary: VTS Report, <u>op</u>. <u>cit</u>., p. 8. The three
     additional systems, together with their dates of anticipated
     operation, are: Houston/Galveston, 1974; New Orleans, 1975;
     New York, 1976.

79. <u>Ibid</u>., p. 8. These systems are as follows: one on the Ohio
     River near Louisville, Ky.; the Atchafalaya River near
     Morgan City, Louisiana; and a planned system for the St. Clair
     River between Lake St. Clair and Lake Huron in Michigan.

80. <u>Ibid</u>., pp. 8-9.

81. <u>Ibid</u>., p. 18. Present operating systems in San Francisco
     and Puget Sound were built with federal funds and are oper-
     ated by Coast Guard personnel.

82. <u>Ibid</u>., p. 19.

83. U.S.C.G., <u>Ports and Waterways Administration and Management</u>,
     <u>op</u>. <u>cit</u>., p. 95.

84. <u>Ibid</u>., p. 99. The other ports included Miami, Florida;
     Sabine, Texas; Galveston, Texas; Willapa Bay, Washington;
     and Ketchikan, Alaska.

85. <u>Ibid</u>., pp. 95-100.

86. <u>Ibid</u>., pp. 95-96.

87. 14 U.S.C. 88(b).

88. 42 U.S.C. 1856-1856d.

89. <u>Supra</u>, note 56.

90. 33 CFR 6.14-1. Also see James P. Morris and Robert F.
     Steeves, "Federal Policy for United States Ports" (Silver
     Spring, Maryland: Operations Research Inc., 1964), p. 31.

91. See Exhibit 8.3.

92. The citings for these Acts are as follows: a) 33 U.S.C.
    407; b) 33 U.S.C. 1001 *et seq*.; c) W.Q.I.A. - P.L. 91-224.

93. National Environmental Policy Act of 1969, P.L. 91-190,
    42 U.S.C. 4321, 83 Stat. 852, January 1, 1970.

94. Water Quality Improvement Act of 1970, P.L. 91-224,
    April 3, 1970.

95. *Ibid*. The procedures under this plan were published pursu-
    ant to Section 11 of the F.W.P.C.A.

96. *Ibid*., P.L. 91-224.

97. U.S.C.G., *Ports and Waterways Administration and Management*,
    op. cit., p. 49.

98. *Ibid*., p. 49.

99. United States Coast Guard, *Planning and Programming Manual*,
    op. cit., p. V-55.

100. U.S.C.G., *Ports and Waterways Administration and Management*,
    op. cit., p. 43.

101. *Ibid*., p. 43.

102. United States Coast Guard, *Planning and Programming Manual*,
    op. cit., p. V-54.

103. *Ibid*., p. V-55.

104. See Exhibit 8.3.

105. U.S.C.G., *Ports and Waterways Administration and Management*,
    op. cit., p. 45.

106. *Ibid*., p. 45.

107. *Ibid*.

108. William E. Lehr, "Marine Oil Pollution Control," *Technology
    Review* (Cambridge, Mass.: M.I.T. Press, February 1973), p. 18.

109. *Ibid*., p. 18.

110. *Ibid*., p. 18.

111. *Ibid*., p. 22.

112. Executive Order 11490, October 30, 1969.

113. U.S.C.G., <u>Planning and Programming Manual</u>, CG-411, <u>op</u>. <u>cit</u>., p. V-12.

114. 80 Stat. 931; 49 U.S.C. 1651.

115. The duties and functions were transferred under 49 U.S.C. 1655, Section (g).

116. U.S.C.G., <u>Planning and Programming Manual</u>, CG-411, <u>op</u>. <u>cit</u>., p. V-12.

117. Grant Miller Davis, <u>The Department of Transportation</u> (Lexington, Mass.: Heath Lexington Books, 1970).

118. <u>Ibid</u>., p. 107.

119. U.S.C.G., <u>Planning and Programming Manual</u>, CG-411, <u>op</u>. <u>cit</u>., p. I-1.

120. Davis, <u>The Department of Transportation</u>, <u>op</u>. <u>cit</u>., p. 107.

121. This section is condensed from U.S.C.G., <u>Planning and Programming Manual</u>, CG-411, <u>op</u>. <u>cit</u>., with amendments. See Appendix 8.3.

122. See "Admiral Says Coast Guard Must Expand," <u>Houston Chronicle</u>, August 2, 1974; reprinted in <u>Todd Daily Maritime</u> (New York, New York: Todd Shipyards Corporation, August 7, 1974).

123. National Advisory Committee on Oceans and Atmosphere, "Third Annual Report to the President and the Congress" (Washington, D.C.: U.S. Government Printing Office, June 28, 1974), p. 37.

124. The Deepwater Port Act of 1974, HR 10701, January 4, 1975; see <u>Congressional Record - House</u>, Conference Report on HR 10701, December 16, 1974, p. HR 12036 et cet.

125. Interviews with USCG personnel on project.

126. Ports and Waterways Safety Act of 1972, P.L. 92-340, July 10, 1972.

127. See "LNG Site Role Urged for the Coast Guard," <u>The Baltimore Sun</u>, December 18, 1974; reprinted in <u>Todd Daily Maritime</u>, No. 74-239 (New York: Todd Shipyards Corp., December 18, 1974), p. 2.

Chapter 9

1. Dudley F. Pegrum, <u>Transportation, Economics and Public Policy</u> (Homewood, Illinois: Richard D. Irwin Inc., 1973), p. 47.

2. Herman Mertins, <u>National Transportation Policy in Transi-</u>
    tion (Lexington, Mass.: Heath Lexington Books, 1972),
    p. 3.

3. Wilfred Owen, <u>Strategy for Mobility</u> (Washington, D.C.:
    The Brookings Institution, 1939), p. 192.

4. Mertins, <u>op</u>. <u>cit</u>., p. 3; also see Grant Miller Davis, <u>The</u>
    <u>Department of Transportation</u> (Lexington, Mass.: Heath
    Lexington Books, 1970), p. 16.

5. The Department of Transportation Act, 80 Stat. 931, 49 U.S.C.
    1651. See Davis, <u>op</u>. <u>cit</u>., pp. 88-101; and Pegrum, <u>op</u>. <u>cit</u>.,
    p. 22.

6. Some of those agencies included the U.S. Coast Guard, the
    Federal Railroad Administration, the Federal Aviation Ad-
    ministration, the Saint Lawrence Seaway Development Corpora-
    tion, among others.

7. Mertins, <u>op</u>. <u>cit</u>., p. 24. Also see Pegrum, <u>op</u>. <u>cit</u>. p. 67.

8. Mertins, <u>op</u>. <u>cit</u>., pp. 24-25.

9. Pegrum, <u>op</u>. <u>cit</u>., p. 67; Mertins, <u>op</u>. <u>cit</u>., p. 25.

10. Mertins, <u>op</u>. <u>cit</u>., p. 5.

11. The Act has been superseded by the River and Harbor Act of
    1892 (33 C.F.R., Sec. 209.385(b)); and the River and Harbor
    Act of 1899 (30 Stat. 1151).

12. <u>Ibid</u>.

13. See the discussion on the Cullom Committee Report, and
    others in Pegrum, <u>op</u>. <u>cit</u>., p. 275.

14. Interstate Commerce Act, ch. 722; 54 Stat. 899, 929; 49 U.S.C.,
    Sec. 901-23 (1958).

15. Davis, <u>op</u>. <u>cit</u>., p. 8.

16. The Department of Transportation Act, 80 Stat. 931; 49 U.S.C.
    1651. See U.S. Senate, Committee on Government Operations,
    "S. 3010, A Bill to Establish a Department of Transporta-
    tion." Hearings, 89th Congress, 2nd Session (Washington,
    D.C.: U.S. Government Printing Office, 1966). Also see
    Davis, <u>The Department of Transportation</u>, <u>op</u>. <u>cit</u>., Chapter 2.

17. Mertins, <u>op</u>. <u>cit</u>., p. 13.

18. U.S. House of Representatives, Committee on Interstate and
    Foreign Commerce, "Return of the Railroads to Private Control,"
    Hearings on H.R. 4378, 66th Congress, 1st Session (Washing-
    ton, D.C.: U.S. Government Printing Office, 1919), p. 3315.

19. Transportation Act of 1920, P.L. 152-91, 66th Congress, 1st Session, 1920.

20. Ibid.

21. Davis, op. cit., p. 16.

22. Transportation Act of 1940, P.L. 255-722, 76th Congress, 1st Session, 1940.

23. Ibid.

24. Pegrum, op. cit., p. 302.

25. Ibid.

26. Ibid., p. 303.

27. U.S. House of Representatives, National Resources Planning Board - Transportation and National Policy, H. Doc. 883, 77th Congress, 2nd Session (Washington, D.C.: U.S. Government Printing Office, 1942), p. 158.

28. Ibid. Also see Chapter 3.

29. U.S. Department of Commerce, A Report to the Congress by the Commission on Organization of the Executive Branch of Government (Washington: U.S. Government Printing Office, March 1949), p. 14.

30. Ibid.

31. Charles Dearing and Wilfred Owen, National Transportation Policy (Washington, D.C.: The Brookings Institution, 1949), p. 353.

32. Ibid.

33. U.S. Senate, Committee on Interstate and Foreign Commerce, National Transportation Policy, 87th Congress, 1st Session (Washington, D.C.: U.S. Government Printing Office, 1961), p. 94.

34. U.S. House of Representatives, Message from the President of the United States Transmitting a Proposal for a Cabinet-Level Department of Transportation Consolidating Various Existing Transportation Agencies, H. Doc. 399, 89th Congress, 2nd Session (Washington, D.C.: U.S. Government Printing Office, 1966), pp. 38-39.

35. The two bills were S. 3010 and H.R. 13200.

36. Department of Transportation Act, P.L. 89-670, 89th Congress, 2nd Sess., October 15, 1966.

37. U.S. Department of Transportation, Office of the Secretary, Regulations of the Office of the Secretary (Washington, D.C.: U.S. Department of Transportation), Section 1.3, p. 2.

38. Ibid.

39. John Burby, The Great American Motion Sickness (Boston: Little, Brown and Company, 1971), p. 42. Also see Davis, op. cit., p. 193.

40. Supra, note 37. Also see Davis, op. cit., p. 154.

41. U.S. Senate, Committee on Government Operations, "Creating a Department of Transportation," Hearings on S. 3010, 89th Congress, 2nd Session (Washington, D.C.: U.S. Government Printing Office, 1966), pp. 529-553.

42. Ibid.

43. DOT, Regulations, op. cit., Part 1.

44. Ibid.

45. DOT, Regulations, op. cit., Part 1; Davis, op. cit., pp. 155-165; Mertins, op. cit., Chapter 4.

46. National Environmental Policy Act of 1969, 83 Stat. 852; P.L. 91-190.

47. 49 U.S.C. 1671, et seq.

48. 18 U.S.C. 831-835.

49. 49 U.S.C. 1651, et seq.

50. DOT responsibility in this area would not be confined solely to pipeline safety.

51. The Water Pollution Control Act of 1972, P.L. 92-500, October 18, 1972.

52. DOT, Regulations, op. cit., Part 1; also see Davis, op. cit., p. 155.

53. 10 U.S.C. 47; supra, note 52.

54. Supra, note 52.

55. See Davis, op. cit., p. 154.

56. 14 U.S.C. 1651 et seq.

57. Department of Transportation Act, 80 Stat. 931, 49 U.S.C. 1651, Oct. 15, 1966.

58. See Mertins, op. cit., Chapters 7 and 8.

59. Davis, op. cit., pp. 157-158.

60. Formally, the PPB system has been replaced by MBO, or Manage-
     ment by Objective. Presumably a new system will be insti-
     tuted with the Ford Administration, MBO being initiated by
     his predecessor. However, the genesis of these input-output,
     system analysis methods is the PPB system. A great deal
     of literature has been published on PPBS. Some of these
     are the following: Charles J. Hitch and Roland N. McKean,
     The Economics of Defense in the Nuclear Age (Cambridge,
     Mass.: Harvard University Press, 1960); Harley H. Hindrichs
     and Graeme M. Taylor, Program Budgeting and Benefit-Cost
     Analysis (Pacific Palisades, California: Goodyear Publishing
     Co., 1969); and U.S. Senate Subcommittee on National Secu-
     rity and International Operations of the Committee on Govern-
     ment Operations, Planning-Programming-Budgeting, 90th Con-
     gress, 1st Session (Washington, D.C.: U.S. Government
     Printing Office, 1970).

61. Davis, op. cit., p. 158.

62. See "Railroad Spokesman Hits 'Inadequate Role' of DOT in
     Planning Waterway Projects" in National Waterways Confer-
     ence, "Criteria News" (Washington, D.C.: National Waterways
     Conference, Inc., April 11, 1975), p. 12.

63. Robert Binder, Assistant Secretary Designate for Policy,
     Plans and International Affairs, Department of Transporta-
     tion, remarks before the Conference on Port Planning and
     Development, Milwaukee, Wisconsin, Nov. 27, 1973. Also
     see Pegrum, op. cit., Chapters 21-22.

64. Ibid. Also see Office of the Secretary, Department of
     Transportation, Sixth Annual Report, FY 1972 (Washington,
     D.C.: U.S. Government Printing Office, 1972), p. 61.

65. Ibid.

66. Ibid.

67. DOT, Sixth Annual Report, FY 1972, op. cit., p. 62.

68. Ibid.

69. Intermodal Service to Portland, Oregon, FMC Docket 70-19.

70. CONASA vs. American Mail Line et al. FMC Docket 73-38.

71. Supra, note 69. Also see Chapter 4 of this report.

72. The argument that a port, or other facility, is "naturally tributary" has been used in previous cases before regulatory bodies. See Pegrum, op. cit., Chapter 17, "Competition and Regulation in Transportation."

73. Supra, note 70.

74. See Chapter 4 of this report for a further discussion on this issue.

75. The Deepwater Port Act of 1974, HR 10701, January 4, 1975; see Congressional Record - House, Conference Report on HR 10701, December 16, 1974, p. H.R. 12036 et seq.

76. Ibid.

77. Section 4(d)(3) of the Act, Ibid.

78. U.S. Department of Transportation, Office of the Assistant Secretary for Policy, Plans and International Affairs, Economic Aspects of Refinery and Deep-Water Port Location in the United States (Washington, D.C.: U.S. Department of Transportation, May 1974).

79. Ibid.

80. Ibid.

81. See "Gov't Moves on Deep Port Licensing" in The Journal of Commerce, January 9, 1975; reprinted in Todd Daily Maritime, No. 75-5 (New York: Todd Shipyards Corporation, January 9, 1975), p. 1.

82. 18 U.S.C. 831-835.

83. 49 U.S.C. 1651 et seq.

84. 49 U.S.C. 1671 et seq.

85. Such laws and regulations include hazardous cargo movements, regulation of land-based transportation media, and so on. See 14 U.S.C. 1651 et seq.

86. Supra, note 34.

87. See "New Inland Waterway Unit Urged" in The Journal of Commerce, August 21, 1974; reprinted in Todd Daily Maritime, No. 74-162, op. cit., August 22, 1974, p. 2. Also see National Waterways Conference, "Newsletter" (Washington, D.C.: National Waterways Conference, Inc., April 19, 1974), p. 7.

88. Department of Transportation Act, 80 Stat. 931, 49 U.S.C. 1651, October 15, 1966.

89. Section 7(a) of the Act, <u>Ibid</u>.

90. Ports and Waterways Safety Act of 1972, P.L. 92-340,
     July 10, 1972.

91. Mertins, <u>op</u>. <u>cit</u>., p. 181.

92. <u>Ibid</u>.

93. <u>Ibid</u>., p. 190.

94. <u>Ibid</u>., p. 193.

95. The integration of future transportation systems in the
     structure of American life is a prominent concern in the
     literature. See Daniel Bell, <u>The Coming of Post-Industrial</u>
     <u>Society</u> (New York: Basic Books Inc., 1969), Chapter 3;
     Wilfred Owen, <u>Strategy for Mobility</u> (Washington, D.C.:
     The Brookings Institution, 1939); and Mertins, <u>National</u>
     <u>Transportation Policy in Transition</u>, <u>op</u>. <u>cit</u>., Chapters
     7 and 8.

Chapter 10

1.   U.S. Department of Commerce, Maritime Administration, Divi-
     sion of Ports, Office of Ports and Intermodal Systems,
     <u>Public Port Financing in the United States</u> (Washington,
     D.C.: U.S. Department of Commerce, June 1974), p. 53.

2.   Appendix C.

3.   Port-related services of the Coast Guard in 1972 included:
     (a) $4,722,010 for replacement of lightships and lighthouse
     automation; (b) approximately $12 million for altering or
     removing bridge obstructions to harbor navigation; (c)
     project allocation for shore facilities and navigational
     aids, totaling $4,029,816; and (d) a vessel traffic system
     in Puget Sound, entailing $929,500. In addition, in 1973,
     research concerning traffic systems will approach $1.5
     million. Source: <u>Public Port Financing in the United</u>
     <u>States</u>, <u>op</u>. <u>cit</u>., p. 52.

4.   For more information on conferences, see Daniel Marx, Jr.,
     <u>International Shipping Cartels</u> (Princeton, New Jersey:
     Princeton University Press, 1953); and Allen R. Ferguson,
     Eugene M. Lerner, John S. McGee, Walter Y. Oi, Leonard A.
     Rapping, and Stephen P. Sobotka, <u>The Economic Value of the</u>
     <u>United States Merchant Marine</u> (Evanston, Illinois:
     Transportation Center, Northwestern University, 1961).

5.   The case of a U.S. shipper diverting his cargo from a
     foreign-flag conference operator to a non-conference
     foreign-flag operator with lower rates easily shows the
     point.

6.   William Proxmire, <u>Uncle Sam - The Last of the Bigtime
      Spenders</u> (New York: Simon and Schuster, 1972), p. 143.

7.   U.S. Army Corps of Engineers, Los Angeles District, <u>Los
      Angeles-Long Beach Harbors - Interim Review Report</u>
      (Washington, D.C.: U.S. Army Corps of Engineers, July 1972).

8.   <u>Public Port Financing in the United States</u>, <u>op</u>. <u>cit</u>., p. 61.

Chapter 11

1.   Dwight M. Blood, <u>Inland Waterway Transport Policy in the
      U.S.</u>, prepared for the National Water Commission (University
      Station, Laramie, Wyoming: January 1972), pp. VI-26 and
      VI-27.

2.   Wayne E. Etter and Robert C. Graham, <u>Financial Planning for
      the Texas Port System</u> (College Station, Texas: Texas A&M
      University, March 1974), p. 73.

3.   <u>Ibid</u>., p. 78.

BIBLIOGRAPHY

Adams, R. Keith, "Today's Port and Harbor Planning." Paper pre-
    presented at the Conference of Port Planning and Develop-
    ment, Milwaukee, Wisconsin, Nov. 27-30, 1973.

Allee, David and Helen Ingram, Authorization and Appropriation
    Processes for Water Resource Development. New York:
    Cornell University Press, 1972. (Prepared under National
    Water Commission Contract NWC-72-023).
Allison, Graham, Essence of Decision: Explaining the Cuban
    Missile Crisis. Boston: Little, Brown and Company, 1967.

Altshuler, Alan A., The Politics of the Federal Bureaucracy.
    New York: Dodd, Mead and Company, 1968.

American Waterways Operators, "Big Load Afloat: U.S. Domestic
    Water Transportation Resources." Washington, D.C.: American
    Waterways Operators, Inc., 1973.
Arthur D. Little, Inc., Foreign Deep Water Developments. Cam-
    bridge, Mass.: Arthur D. Little, Inc., December 1971.

Arthur D. Little, Inc., Report to the Council on Environmental
    Quality, Potential Onshore Effects of Deepwater Oil Terminal-
    Related Industrial Development. Cambridge, Mass.: Arthur D.
    Little, Inc., 1970.

Bauer, Ernest T., Chief, Division of Ports, Office of Ports and
    Intermodal Systems, Maritime Administration, "Needful Steps
    for Improved Future MarAd-Port Industry Relationships."
    Paper presented before the North Atlantic Ports Association,
    Washington, D.C., December 7, 1972.

Bell, Daniel, The Coming of Post-Industrial Society. New York:
    Basic Books, Inc., 1969.

Binder, Robert, Assistant Secretary Designate for Policy, Plans
    and International Affairs, Department of Transportation.
    Remarks before the Conference on Port Planning and Develop-
    ment, Milwaukee, Wisconsin, Nov. 27, 1973.

Blackwell, Robert, Assistant Secretary of Commerce for Maritime
    Affairs, U.S. Department of Commerce News, MarAd, MA SP 74-7,
    April 3, 1974. Remarks presented before the Radio Techno-
    logy Commission for Marine Services and the Propeller Club
    of St. Petersburg, St. Petersburg, Florida, April 3, 1974.

Blood, Dwight M., Inland Waterway Transport Policy in the U.S.,
    University Station, Laramie, Wyoming: University of
    Wyoming, January 1972.

Board of Commissioners of the Port of New Orleans, et al. vs.
     Seatrain International S.A., FMC Dockets 73-42, 73-61,
     73-69, 74-4.

Bonafede, Dom, "White House Report/Ehrlichman Acts as Policy
     Broker in Nixon's Formalized Domestic Council." National
     Journal Reports, Vol. 3, Number 24, Washington, D.C.:
     National Journal, June 12, 1971.

Bonafede, Dom, "White House Report/President Nixon's Executive
     Reorganization Plans Prompt Praise and Criticism."
     National Journal Reports, Vol. 5, Number 10, Washington,
     D.C.: National Journal, March 10, 1973.

Boyer, Walter C., Deputy Administrator, Maryland Port Adminis-
     tration, "A Discussion of Environmental Problems Looming
     Ahead." Paper presented at the Conference on Port Planning
     and Development, Milwaukee, Wisconsin, November 19, 1973.

Bragg, Daniel and James Bradley, "Work Plan for a Study of the
     Feasibility of an Offshore Terminal in the Texas Gulf
     Coast Region." Texas: Industrial Economics Research Divi-
     sion, Texas Engineering Experiment Station, Texas A&M
     University, June 1971.

Burby, John, The Great American Motion Sickness. Boston:
     Little, Brown and Company, 1971.

Casey, Howard F., Deputy Assistant Secretary of Commerce for
     Maritime Affairs. Remarks before the Conference on Port
     Planning and Development, Milwaukee, Wisconsin, Nov. 29,
     1973.

Casey, Howard F., Deputy Assistant Secretary of Commerce for
     Maritime Affairs, MarAd, U.S. Department of Commerce News,
     MarAd, MA SP 74-10, May 23, 1974. Remarks presented before
     the Society of Naval Architects and Marine Engineers,
     Chicago, May 23, 1974.

Commodity Transportation and Economic Development Laboratory,
     M.I.T., "Regulation and Jurisdiction in Offshore Port
     Development." Cambridge, Mass.: M.I.T., June 1973.

Costello, John D., "Public Law 89-670, A Comparative Analysis."
     Unpublished M.A. thesis, School of Government and Business
     Administration, George Washington University, August 1969.

Davis, Grant Miller, The Department of Transportation. Lexing-
     ton, Mass.: Heath Lexington Books, 1970.

Dearing, Charles and Wilfred Owen, National Transportation
     Policy. Washington, D.C.: The Brookings Institution, 1949.

Downs, Anthony, Inside Bureaucracy. Boston: Little, Brown and
     Company, 1967.

Etter, Wayne E. and Robert C. Graham, Financial Planning for the
    Texas Port System. College Station, Texas: Texas A&M
    University Sea Grant Program, March 1974.

Executive Office of the President, Papers Relating to the Presi-
    dent's Departmental Reorganization Program - A Reference
    Compilation. Washington, D.C.: U.S. Government Printing
    Office, January 1972.

Executive Office of the President, The Budget of the United States
    Government, FY 1975. Washington, D.C.: Government Printing
    Office, 1974.

Fair, Marvin L., Port Administration in the United States.
    Cambridge, Maryland: Cornell Maritime Press, 1954.

Far East Conference vs. Seatrain, FMC Docket 73-8.

Federal Register, Vol. 38, Number 147, Part II, August 1, 1973.

Federal Register, Vol. 39, Number 158, August 14, 1974.

Ferguson, Allen R., Eugene M. Lerner, John S. McGee, Walter S.
    Oi, Leonard A. Rapping and Stephen R. Sobotka, The Economic
    Value of the United States Merchant Marine. Evanston,
    Illinois: Transportation Center, Northwestern University,
    1961.

Garfield, Paul J. and Wallace F. Lovejoy, Public Utility Econ-
    omics. Englewood Cliffs, New Jersey: Prentice-Hall, Inc.,
    1964.

General Services Administration, National Archives and Records
    Service, U.S. Government Manual, 1973/74. Washington, D.C.:
    U.S. Government Printing Office, 1973.

General Services Administration, National Archives and Records
    Service, Office of the Federal Register, Federal Register.
    Washington, D.C.: U.S. Government Printing Office (various
    volumes).

Havemann, Joel, "White House Report/OMB's Legislative Role Is
    Growing More Powerful and More Political." National Jour-
    nal Reports, Washington, D.C.: National Journal, Oct. 27,
    1973.

Hedden, Walter P., Mission: Port Development. Washington, D.C.:
    The American Association of Port Authorities, 1967.

Hindrichs, Harley H. and Graeme M. Taylor, Program Budgeting and
    Benefit-Cost Analysis. Pacific Palisades, California:
    Goodyear Publishing Co., 1969.

Hitch, Charles J. and Roland N. McKean, The Economics of Defense
    in the Nuclear Age. Cambridge, Mass.: Harvard University
    Press, 1960.

Hull, William J. and Robert W. Hull, The Origin and Development of the Waterways Policy of the United States. Washington, D.C.: National Waterways Conference, Inc., 1967.

Iglehart, John K., William Lilley III and Timothy B. Clark, "New Federalism Report/Budget Strains Alliance Between Nixon and State-Local Officials." National Journal Reports, Vol. 5, Number 7. Washington, D.C.: National Journal, February 17, 1973.

Johnson, Dr. William, Energy Adviser to the Deputy Secretary of the Department of the Interior. Testimony before the United States Senate, Special Joint Subcommittee on Deepwater Ports Legislation, "Deepwater Port Act of 1974." Report No. 93-1217, 93rd Congress, 2nd Session. Washington, D.C.: U.S. Government Printing Office, October 2, 1974.

Kaplan, H. R. and LCDR James Hunt, This Is The Coast Guard. Cambridge, Maryland: Cornell Maritime Press, 1972.

Krock, Arthur, The Consent of the Governed. Boston: Little, Brown and Co., 1971.

Lawrence, Samuel A., United States Shipping Policies and Politics. Washington, D.C.: The Brookings Institution, 1966.

Lehr, William E., "Marine Oil Pollution Control." Technology Review. Cambridge, Mass.: M.I.T. Press, February 1973.

Lowi, Theodore, The End of Liberalism. New York: W. W. Norton and Company, 1969.

MacElwee, Roy S., Port Development. New York: McGraw-Hill, 1926.

Major, David C., "Multiobjective Water Resource Planning." Review Draft, American Geophysical Union Water Resources Monograph 4, Cambridge, Mass., 1973.

Manalytics, Inc., The Impact of Maritime Containerization on the United States Transportation System. Washington, D.C.: U.S. Department of Commerce, February, 1972.

Marcus, Henry S., Planning Ship Replacement in the Containerization Era. Lexington, Mass.: Lexington Books, D. C. Heath and Company, 1974.

Marcus, Henry S., "The Need for a Unified Governmental Approach to Port Planning." Paper presented before the 1973 Annual Transportation Research Forum Meeting, Cleveland, Ohio, October 15-17, 1973.

Marcus, Henry S., "The U.S. Superport Controversy." Technology Review, Cambridge, Mass.: M.I.T. Press, March/April 1973.

Marine Technology Society, Proceedings, Ninth Annual Conference. Washington, D.C.: Marine Technology Society, September 10-12, 1973.

Marx, Daniel Jr., International Shipping Cartels. Princeton,
    New Jersey: Princeton University Press, 1953.

Mertins, Herman, National Transportation Policy in Transition.
    Lexington, Mass.: Heath Lexington Books, 1972.

Miloy, John and Anthony E. Copp, Economic Analysis of Texas
    Marine Resources and Industries. College Station, Texas:
    Texas A&M University Sea Grant Program, June 1970.

Moore, Stephen, Robert Dwyer and Arthur Katz, "A Preliminary
    Assessment of the Environmental Vulnerability of Machias
    Bay, Maine, to Oil Supertankers," Report No. 162. Cambridge,
    Mass.: Dept. of Civil Engineering, M.I.T., January 1973.

Morison, Robert F., "Offshore Ports Bill Battle Shaping Up,"
    The Journal of Commerce, May 16, 1974.

Morris, James P. and Robert F. Steeves, "Federal Policy for
    United States Ports." Silver Spring, Maryland: Operations
    Research, Inc., 1964.

National Advisory Committee on Oceans and Atmosphere, "Third
    Annual Report to the President and the Congress." Washing-
    ton, D.C.: U.S. Government Printing Office, June 28, 1974.

National Journal Reports. Washington, D.C.: National Journal,
    various issues.

National Water Commission, New Directions in U.S. Water Policy -
    Summary, Conclusions and Recommendations from the Final
    Report of the National Water Commission. Washington, D.C.:
    U.S. Government Printing Office, June 28, 1973.

National Water Commission, Water Policies for the Future, Final
    Report to the President and to the Congress of the United
    States by the National Water Commission. Washington, D.C.:
    Government Printing Office, 1973.

National Waterways Conference, Criteria News. Washington, D.C.:
    National Waterways Conference, Inc. (various issues).

National Waterways Conference, "National Waterways Conference
    Newsletter." Washington, D.C.: National Waterways Confer-
    ence, Inc. (various issues).

Nelson, James R., "Policy Analysis in Transportation Programs."
    Included in United States Congress, Joint Economic Commit-
    tee, "The Analysis and Evaluation of Public Expenditures:
    The PPB System." 91st Congress, 1st Session. Washington,
    D.C.: U.S. Government Printing Office, 1969.

Nowacki, Horst, Harry Benford and Anthony Atkins, Economics of
    Great Lakes Shipping in an Extended Season. Ann Arbor,
    Michigan: University of Michigan, Report No. 139, January
    1973, MarAd Contract No. 1-35487.

Opheim, J. Eldon, General Manager, Port of Seattle, Wash.
    Remarks before the Conference on Port Planning and Develop-
    ment, Milwaukee, Wisconsin, Nov. 27-30, 1973.

Owen, Wilfred, Strategy for Mobility. Washington, D.C.: The
    Brookings Institution, 1939.

Padelford, Norman J. and Jerry E. Cook, New Dimensions of U.S.
    Marine Policy. M.I.T. Sea Grant Program, Project MITSG 71-5.
    Cambridge, Mass.: M.I.T. Press, 1971.

Pecknold, Wayne M. "Methodology for Systems Planning and Program-
    ming: Passenger." Resource paper for the Joint M.I.T.
    Center for Transportation Studies and the Civil Engineering
    Department Workshop No. III, February 24-27, 1974, Cambridge,
    M.I.T.

Pegrum, Dudley, Transportation Economics and Public Policy.
    Homewood, Illinois: Richard D. Irwin, Inc., 1973.

Pressman, Jeffrey, L. and Aaron Wildavsky, Implementation.
    Berkeley, Calif.: University of California Press, 1973.

Port of Seattle Commission, "Seattle Maritime Commerce and Its
    Impact on the Economy of King County." Seattle, Wash.:
    Port of Seattle, 1971.

Proxmire, William, Uncle Sam - The Last of the Bigtime Spenders.
    New York: Simon and Schuster, 1972.

Quade, Quentin L. and Thomas J. Bennett, American Politics,
    Effective and Responsible? New York: American Book Company,
    1969.

Report of the Commission on Marine Science, Engineering and
    Resources. Washington, D.C.: U.S. Government Printing
    Office, January 1969.

Robert R. Nathan Associates, Inc., Foreign Deepwater Port Develop-
    ment. Department of the Army, Institute for Water Resources,
    Corps of Engineers. Washington, D.C.: Government Printing
    Office, 1971.

Robert R. Nathan Associates, Inc., U.S. Deepwater Port Study.
    Department of the Army, Institute for Water Resources,
    Corps of Engineers, Washington, D.C.: Government Printing
    Office, 1972.

Rosselli, Albert T., "Economic Rationalization of Port Invest-
    ment." Milwaukee, Wisconsin: Paper presented at the Con-
    ference on Port Planning and Development, Nov. 27-30, 1973.

Rourke, Francis E., Bureaucratic Power in National Politics.
    Boston: Little, Brown and Company, 1972.

Schad, Theodore M., "Findings of the National Water Commission."
    Washington, D.C.: American Society of Civil Engineers'
    National Water Resources Conference, January 1973.

Schenker, Eric and Michael Bunamo, "A Study of the Corps of
    Engineers' Regional Pattern of Investments." The Southern
    Economic Journal, Vol. XXXIX, No. 4, April 1973.

Schmid, A. Alan, Federal Decisionmaking for Water Resource Develop-
    ment. National Water Commission Report Number PB 211 441.
    Springfield, Virginia: National Technical Information Ser-
    vice, 1972.

Schwimmer, Martin J. and Paul A. Amundsen, Management of a Seaport.
    Kings Point, N.Y.: National Maritime Research Center, 1973.

Simon, Herbert, Administrative Behavior. New York: The Free
    Press, 1957.

Smith, T. Arthur, A Functional Analysis of the Ocean Port.
    Silver Spring, Maryland: Operations Research, Inc., 1964.

Soros Associates, Inc., Offshore Terminal Systems Concepts.
    Washington, D.C.: U.S. Department of Commerce, September
    1972.

Thompson, James D., Organizations in Action: Social Science
    Bases of Administrative Theory. New York: McGraw-Hill, 1967.

Todd Daily Maritime. New York, New York: Todd Shipyards Corpora-
    tion (various issues).

Transportation Development Division, Highway Users Federation for
    Safety and Mobility, "A Status Report of State Departments
    of Transportation." Washington, D.C.: Highway Users Fed-
    eration for Safety and Mobility, December 1970.

"Two Ship Lines See Need for Rulemaking Proceeding to Solve Inter-
    modal Problems," Late News, Traffic World. Washington, D.C.:
    Traffic Service Corporation, September 17, 1973.

U.S. Army Corps of Engineers, Digest of Water Resources Policies
    and Activities, EP 1165-2-1. Washington, D.C.: Government
    Printing Office, 1972.

U.S. Army Corps of Engineers, Directorate of Civil Works, "Dredged
    Material Research Program." EC 1130-2-122. Washington, D.C.:
    U.S. Department of the Army, April 20, 1973.

U.S. Army Corps of Engineers, Directorate of Civil Works, "Environ-
    mental Program." EP 1105-2-500. Washington, D.C.: U.S.
    Department of the Army, June 1973.

U.S. Army Corps of Engineers, Interim Review Report--Los Angeles, Long Beach Harbors. Washington, D.C.: Government Printing Office, 1972.

U.S. Army Corps of Engineers, Office of the Chief of Engineers, Disposal of Dredge Spoil, Technical Report H-72-8. Washington, D.C.: U.S. Department of the Army, November 1972.

U.S. Army Corps of Engineers, Port Everglades Harbor, Florida. Study Report to Congress, House Document 93-144. Washington, D.C.: Government Printing Office, 1973.

U.S. Army Corps of Engineers, Tampa Harbor, Florida. Study Report to Congress, House Document 91-401. Washington, D.C.: Government Printing Office, 1970.

U.S. Bureau of the Census, Domestic and Intermodal Transportation of U.S. Foreign Trade: 1970. Washington, D.C.: Government Printing Office, 1972.

United States Coast Guard, Planning and Programming Manual, CG-411. Washington, D.C.: U.S. Department of Transportation, July 1971.

United States Coast Guard, Ports and Waterways Administration and Management. Washington, D.C.: U.S. Coast Guard, July 1971.

United States Coast Guard, Vessel Traffic Systems Study - Final Report, Vol. 1, Executive Summary. Washington, D.C.: U.S. Department of Transportation, March 1973.

United States Code, Congressional and Administrative News. 89th Congress, Second Session, Volume 3. Washington, D.C.: U.S. Government Printing Office, 1966.

U.S. Congressional Record, House Report 902, 49th Congress, 1st Session. Washington, D.C.: Government Printing Office, 1926.

United States Constitution.

U.S. Department of Commerce, A Report to the Congress by the Commission on Organization of the Executive Branch of Government. Washington, D.C.: U.S. Government Printing Office, March 1949.

U.S. Department of Commerce, 1973 Annual Report of the EDA. Washington, D.C.: U.S. Government Printing Office, 1974.

U.S. Department of Commerce, Bureau of the Census, Domestic Movement of Selected Commodities in United States Waterborne Foreign Trade: 1956. Washington, D.C.: U.S. Bureau of the Census, 1959.

U.S. Department of Commerce, Maritime Administration, A Modal
     Economic and Safety Analysis of the Transportation of
     Hazardous Substances in Bulk (revised edition). Washington,
     D.C.: U.S. Department of Commerce, 1974.

U.S. Department of Commerce, Maritime Administration, Environ-
     mental Impact Statement--U.S. Tanker Construction Program.
     Washington, D.C.: U.S. Dept. of Commerce, 1972.

U.S. Department of Commerce, Maritime Administration, Office of
     Ports and Intermodal Systems, "Highlights of MarAd Ports
     Activities," October 1973, No. II. Washington, D.C.:
     Government Printing Office.

U.S. Department of Commerce, Maritime Administration, Domestic
     Waterborne Shipping--Market Analysis. Chicago, Illinois:
     Kearney Management Consultants, February 1974.

U.S. Department of Commerce, Maritime Administration, "Neobulk
     Cargo Study." Boston, Mass.: Harbridge House, Inc.,
     August 1974.

U.S. Department of Commerce, Maritime Administration, Division
     of Ports, Office of Ports and Intermodal Systems, Public
     Port Financing in the United States. Washington, D.C.:
     U.S. Department of Commerce, June 1974.

U.S. Department of Commerce, National Oceanographic and Atmo-
     spheric Administration, Coastal Zone Management Task Force,
     "Status of State Coastal Zone Management Efforts." Washing-
     ton, D.C.: U.S. Department of Commerce, NOAA, May 1973.

U.S. Department of Commerce, National Oceanographic and Atmo-
     spheric Administration, Office of Coastal Zone Management,
     "State Coastal Zone Management Activities 1974." Washington,
     D.C.: U.S. Department of Commerce, NOAA, October 1974.

U.S. Department of the Interior, Draft Environmental Impact
     Statement on Deepwater Ports. Washington, D.C.: U.S.
     Department of the Interior, June 1973.

U.S. Department of Transportation, "1974 National Transportation
     Study, Manual 1: General Information." Washington, D.C.:
     U.S. Department of Transportation, May 1972.

U.S. Department of Transportation, Transportation Information.
     A Report to the Committee on Appropriations of the House
     of Representatives. Washington, D.C.: U.S. Department of
     Transportation, May 1969.

U.S. Department of Transportation, Office of the Secretary,
     "A Progress Report on National Transportation Policy."
     Washington, D.C.: U.S. Department of Transportation, May
     1974.

U.S. Department of Transportation, Office of the Secretary, A Statement on National Transportation Policy. Washington, D.C.: U.S. Department of Transportation, 1971.

U.S. Department of Transportation, Office of the Secretary, "DOT News." 63-DOT-73. Washington, D.C.: U.S. Department of Transportation, Nov. 27, 1973.

U.S. Department of Transportation, Office of the Secretary, 1974 National Transportation Report--Current Performance and Future Prospects. Washington, D.C.: U.S. Department of Transportation, December 1974.

U.S. Department of Transportation, Office of the Secretary, Regulations of the Office of the Secretary. Washington, D.C.: U.S. Department of Transportation, 1970.

U.S. Department of Transportation, Office of the Secretary, Sixth Annual Report FY 1972. Washington, D.C.: U.S. Government Printing Office, 1972.

U.S. Department of Transportation, Office of the Assistant Secretary for Policy, Plans and International Affairs, Economic Aspects of Refinery and Deep-Water Port Location in the United States. Washington, D.C.: U.S. Department of Transportation, May 1974.

U.S. Department of the Treasury, Statement of Appropriations and Expenditures for Public Buildings, Rivers and Harbors, Forts, Arsenals, Armories, and Other Public Works, from March 4, 1789, to June 30, 1882. Washington, D.C.: U.S. Government Printing Office, 1882.

U.S. Environmental Protection Agency, Office of Enforcement and General Counsel, "The National Water Permit Program." Washington, D.C.: U.S. Government Printing Office, June 1, 1973.

U.S. House of Representatives, Committee on Interstate and Foreign Commerce, "National Transportation Inquiry Hearings." Hearings, 80th Congress, 2nd Session. Washington, D.C.: Government Printing Office, 1957.

U.S. House of Representatives, Committee on Interstate and Foreign Commerce, "Return of the Railroads to Private Control." Hearings on H.R. 4378, 66th Congress, 1st Session. Washington, D.C.: U.S. Government Printing Office, 1919.

U.S. House of Representatives, House Report 557, 81st Congress. Washington, D.C.: U.S. Government Printing Office, 1949.

U.S. House of Representatives, Merchant Marine and Fisheries Committee, "Ports and Waterways Safety Act of 1970." Hearings, H.R. 17830. Washington, D.C.: U.S. Government Printing Office, July 22-24, 30, 1970; August 10, 11, 1970; September 15, 16, 26, 1970.

U.S. House of Representatives, Merchant Marine and Fisheries
    Committee, "Ports and Waterways Safety Act of 1971."
    H.R. 867, House Report 92-563. Washington, D.C.: U.S.
    Government Printing Office, September 1971.

U.S. House of Representatives, Message from the President of the
    United States Transmitting a Proposal for a Cabinet-Level
    Department of Transportation Consolidating Various Existing
    Transportation Agencies. H. Doc. 399, 89th Congress, 2nd
    Session. Washington, D.C.: U.S. Government Printing Office,
    1966.

U.S. House of Representatives, National Resources Planning
    Board - Transportation and National Policy. H. Doc. 883,
    77th Congress, 2nd Session. Washington, D.C.: U.S. Govern-
    ment Printing Office, 1942.

U.S. House of Representatives, Report on Practices and Procedures
    of Government Control. H. Doc. 678, 78th Congress. Wash-
    ington, D.C.: Government Printing Office, 1944.

U.S. House of Representatives, Select Committee on Committees,
    "Committee Organizations in the House." Hearings, 93rd
    Congress, 1st Session. Washington, D.C.: U.S. Government
    Printing Office, Oct. 11, 1973.

U.S. House of Representatives, Select Committee on Committees,
    Staff Summary Report, "Committee Reform Amendments of 1974."
    H. Res. 988, 93rd Congress, 2nd Session. Washington, D.C.:
    U.S. Government Printing Office, March 21, 1974.

U.S. House of Representatives, Subcommittee on Investigations
    and Oversight of the Public Works Committee. Statement by
    General Koisch. Washington, D.C.: Government Printing
    Office, 1971.

U.S. House of Representatives, Subcommittee of the Committee on
    Appropriations, "Public Works for Water and Power Develop-
    ment and Atomic Energy Commission Appropriation Bill, 1974."
    Hearings, 93rd Congress, 1st Session. Washington, D.C.:
    Government Printing Office, 1973.

U.S. Maritime Administration, Economics of Deepwater Terminals.
    Washington, D.C.: U.S. Department of Commerce, 1972.

U.S. Maritime Administration, Manual of Orders, AO-27. Washing-
    ton, D.C.: U.S. Department of Commerce, Maritime Adminis-
    tration.

U.S. Maritime Administration, Manual of Orders, AO-97. Washing-
    ton, D.C.: U.S. Department of Commerce, Maritime Adminis-
    tration, June 1973.

U.S. Maritime Administration, U.S. Department of Commerce News,
     MarAd, MA NR 74-11, "North American Ports Futures Surveyed
     by MarAd." Washington, D.C.: U.S. Department of Commerce,
     May 28, 1974.

U.S. Maritime Administration, U.S. Department of Commerce News,
     MarAd, MA NR 74-12, "MarAd Announces Second Phase of Satel-
     lite Program." Washington, D.C.: U.S. Department of Com-
     merce, May 30, 1974.

U.S. Maritime Administration, U.S. Department of Commerce News,
     MarAd, MA NR 74-15, "MarAd Releases Hazardous Substances
     Transportation Study." Washington, D.C.: U.S. Department
     of Commerce, June 17, 1974.

U.S. Senate, Committee on Commerce, "Authorizing a National
     Oceans Policy Study." Report 93-685, 93rd Congress, 2nd
     Session. Washington, D.C.: U.S. Government Printing
     Office, Feb. 8, 1974.

U.S. Senate, Committee on Commerce, "Energy Policy Act of 1973 -
     Report on S. 70 to Promote Commerce and Establish a Council
     on Energy Policy, and for Other Purposes." Senate Report
     93-114. Washington, D.C.: U.S. Government Printing Office,
     April 10, 1972.

U.S. Senate, Committee on Commerce, "Navigable Waters Safety
     and Environmental Quality Act of 1971." S. 2074, Hearings,
     Senate Report 92-724. Washington, D.C.: U.S. Government
     Printing Office, September 22-24, 1971.

U.S. Senate, Committee on Commerce, "Senate Resolution 222."
     Background Report, 93rd Congress, 2nd Session. Washington,
     D.C.: U.S. Government Printing Office, January 31, 1974.

U.S. Senate, Committee on Government Operations, "Creating a
     Department of Transportation." Hearings on S.3010, 89th
     Congress, 2nd Session. Washington, D.C.: U.S. Government
     Printing Office, 1966.

U.S. Senate, Committee on Government Operations. "S. 3010, A
     Bill to Establish a Department of Transportation." Hearings,
     89th Congress, 2nd Session. Washington, D.C.: U.S. Govern-
     ment Printing Office, 1966.

U.S. Senate, Committee on Interstate and Foreign Commerce,
     National Transportation Policy. 87th Congress, 1st Session.
     Washington, D.C.: U.S. Government Printing Office, 1961.

U.S. Senate, Joint Report of the Committees on Commerce; Interior
     and Insular Affairs; and Public Works, "Deepwater Port Act
     of 1974." Report No. 93-1217, 93rd Congress, 2nd Session.
     Washington, D.C: U.S. Government Printing Office, Octo-
     ber 2, 1974.

U.S. Senate, Select Committee on National Water Resources,
    Senate Report 29. 87th Congress, 1st Session. Washington,
    D.C.: U.S. Government Printing Office, 1960.

U.S. Senate, Special Joint Subcommittee on Deepwater Ports Legis-
    lation composed of the Committees on Commerce, Interior and
    Insular Affairs, and Public Works, "Deepwater Port Act of
    1973." Hearings, 93rd Congress, First Session, Parts I and
    II. Washington, D.C.: Government Printing Office, 1973.

U.S. Senate, Subcommittee on National Security and International
    Operations of the Committee on Government Operations,
    Planning-Programming-Budgeting. 90th Congress, 1st Session.
    Washington, D.C.: U.S. Government Printing Office, 1970.

U.S. Water Resources Council, Summary and Analysis of Public
    Response to the Proposed Principles and Standards for
    Related Land Resources and Draft Environmental Statement.
    Washington, D.C.: Government Printing Office, August, 1972.

Walsh, Donald A., "Master Planning Considerations for the Port
    of Los Angeles." Los Angeles Metropolitan Section: The
    Society of Naval Architects and Marine Engineers, Septem-
    ber 13, 1973.

LEGISLATIVE ACTS

24 May 1824, Navigation, 4 Stat. 32.

Act of March 2, 1919, Ch. 95, Sec. 1; 40 Stat. 1286; 33 U.S.C.
    Sec. 551, 1958.

Act of June 5, 1920, Ch. 250; 41 Stat. 988; 46 U.S.C. Sec. 861-
    889, 1958.

Act of Sept. 7, 1916, Ch. 451; 39 Stat. 728; 46 U.S.C. Sec. 801
    to 842, 1958.

Act of September 18, 1940, Ch. 722; 54 Stat. 899.

Bureau of the Budget, Act of June 10, 1921, 42 Stat. 20,
    31 U.S.C. 11-16.

Clayton Act of 1914, 38 Stat. 730, 15 U.S.C. 12, 1914.

Coastal Zone Management Act of 1972, P.L. 92-583, 86 Stat. 1280,
    October 27, 1972.

Communications Act of 1934, 48 Stat. 1064, 15 U.S.C. 21,
    47 U.S.C. 35, 151-609, 1934.

Communications Satellite Act of 1962, 76 Stat. 419, 47 U.S.C. 701-
    744, 1962.

CONASA vs. American Mail Line et al., FMC Docket 73-38.

Deepwater Port Act of 1974, HR 10701, January 4, 1975; see
    Congressional Record - House, Conference Report on HR 10701,
    December 16, 1974.

Delaware River Port Authority v. Sea-Land Service, Inc., FMC
    Docket 71-65.

Department of Transportation Act, Public Law 89-670, 49 U.S.C.
    1651, October 15, 1966.

Economic Opportunity Act of 1964, Public Law 88-452, 78 Stat.
    508, 42 U.S.C. 2701, August 20, 1964.

Exec. Order 11514, 35 F.R. 4247 (Chapter 5, footnote #77).

Federal Energy Administration Act of 1974, P.L. 93-275, May 7,
    1974.

Federal Trade Commission Act of 1914, 38 Stat. 717, 15 U.S.C. 41-
    51, 1914.

Federal Water Pollution Control Act, Public Law 92-500, 86 Stat.
    816, October 18, 1972.

Federal Water Power Act of 1920, 41 Stat. 1063, June 10, 1920;
    as amended by the Federal Power Act, 49 Stat. 863, August 26,
    1935.

Fish and Wildlife Act of 1956, 70 Stat. 1119, 16 U.S.C. 742(a)-
    742(1), 1956.

FMC Agreement #10,000, North Atlantic Pool, FMC Docket 72-17.

Intercoastal Shipping Act of 1933, P.L. 415, March 3, 1933.

Intermodal Service at Philadelphia, FMC Docket 73-35.

Intermodal Service to Portland, Oregon, FMC Docket 70-19.

Interstate Commerce Act, 24 Stat. 379, 49 U.S.C.A., 1887.

Interstate Commerce Commission Delegation TM-1, April 4, 1957.

Marine Mammals Protection Act of 1972, P.L. 92-522, June 15, 1972.

Marine Protection, Research and Sanctuaries Act of 1972, P.L. 92-
    532, Oct. 23, 1972.

Marine Resources and Engineering Development Act, P.L. 89-454,
    June 17, 1966.

Merchant Marine Act of 1920, Act of March 2, 1919, Ch. 95,
    Sec. 1; 40 Stat. 1286; 33 U.S.C. Sec. 551 (1958).

Merchant Marine Act of 1936; Act of June 29, 1936, Ch. 858;
    49 Stat. 1985; 46 U.S.C. Sec. 1101 (1958).

National Environmental Policy Act of 1969, Public Law 91-190,
    42 U.S.C. 4321 et seq., 83 Stat. 852, January 1, 1970.

National Occupational Safety and Health Act of 1970, P.L. 91-
    596, December 1970.

National Water Commission Act, 82 Stat. 868, Sept. 26, 1968.

Natural Gas Act of 1938, 52 Stat. 821-833, 15 U.S.C. 717-717W,
    June 21, 1938.

Ports and Waterways Safety Act of 1972, P.L. 92-340, July 10,
    1972.

Public Law 255-722, 76th Congress, 1st Session, 1940.

Public Utility Act of 1935, 49 Stat. 838, August 26, 1935.

Public Works and Economic Development Act of 1965; 79 Stat. 552,
    42 U.S.C. 3121, 1965.

Reorganization Plan 7 of 1961; 75 Stat. 840 as amended by Public
    Law 91-469, 84 Stat. 1036.

Reorganization Plan 21 of 1950; 64 Stat. 1273, May 24, 1950.

River and Harbor Act of 1899, 30 Stat. 1151, 33 U.S.C. 403,
    March 13, 1899.

Rivers and Harbors Act of 1915, Ch. 142, Sec. 4; 38 Stat. 1049,
    1053; 33 U.S.C. Sec. 565 (1958); March 4, 1915.

River and Harbor and Flood Control Act, Public Law 89-298,
    79 Stat. 1073, October 27, 1965.

River and Harbor and Flood Control Act of 1968, Public Law 90-
    483, 82 Stat. 735, August 13, 1968.

Shipping Act of 1916, 39 Stat. 728, Chapter 451, Sept. 7,
    1916. (Shipping Act repealed by Transportation Act of
    1940.)

Transportation Act of 1920, P.L. 152-91, 66th Congress, 1st
    Session, 1920.

Transportation Act of 1940, P.L. 255-722, 54 Stat. 898, 950,
    Sept. 18, 1940.

U.S. v. Appalachian Electric Power Company, 311 U.S. 377 (1940).

U.S. v. California, 332 U.S. 19, March 13-14, 1947.

U.S. v. Louisiana, 363 U.S. 1, May 31, 1960.

U.S. v. Ray, 423 Fed. Rep. 2nd 16, Jan. 22, 1970.

Weather Modification Reporting Act of 1972, P.L. 92-205, H.R. 6893,
    Dec. 18, 1971.

Water Pollution Control Act of 1972, P.L. 92-500, Oct. 18, 1972.

Water Quality Improvement Act of 1970, P.L. 91-224, April 3, 1970.

Water Resources Development Act of 1974, P.L. 93-251, 88 Stat. 12,
    March 7, 1974.

Water Resources Planning Act of 1965, P.L. 89-80, July 22, 1965.

Accounting Procedures Act of 1950, 112

Act of 1799, 139, 141

Aeronautics Board, Civil (CAB), 189

Agriculture, Department of, 49, 51-52
  Secretary of, 56

Air-Delivered Anti-Pollution Transfer System (ADAPTS), 164

Aliens, regulations for, 50

"Alphabetocracy," 21

Animal disease regulations, 51

Animal Husbandry, Bureau of, 49, 51

Animal and Plant Inspection Service, 51

Antitrust laws, and deepwater ports, 192

Applications Technology Satellite-F, 135

Army, Department of the, 88, 97, 211. See also Corps of Engineers, U.S. Army
  Secretary of, 56, 95, 98, 111, 150, 166

Arthur D. Little, Inc., 112, 115, 135

"Assigning Emergency Preparedness Functions to Federal Departments and Agencies," 165

Atomic Energy Commission (AEC), 46

Attorney General, U.S., 50, 192

Authorization and Appropriation Processes for Water Resource Development, 104-108

Aviation Administration, Federal, 180

Baltimore, Port of, 80

Barges, domestic movement of, 62

Bell, Daniel, 21

Black, W. B., 176

Bolling Committee Report, 38, 211

Bonds regulations, 51, 71

Bridge Administration Program, 143, 166

Brooks, E., 116

Budget, Bureau of the, 54

Budget and Accounting Act of 1921, 55

Budgets, federal, 18, 37-39, 175, 211-214, 215-223. See also Economics
  of the Corps of Engineers, 3, 56, 77, 87, 88, 95-98, 104-109, 116, 193, 202-203
  of the Department of Transportation, 136, 185
  of the Economic Development Administration, 3, 46-49, 134, 136, 203, 216
  of the Internal Revenue Service, 51
  of the Maritime Administration, 18, 47, 126, 135-136, 137
  of the National Oceanographic and Atmospheric Administration, 64, 70, 136
  of the Office of Management and Budget, 54-56, 205
  of the U.S. Coast Guard, 151, 163, 168, 202

Budgets, state, 18, 64, 70, 71, 80-81, 222

Bunamo, Michael, 124-125

Buoy system, 63

Cargo
  bulk, 9-10, 19
  general, 10, 19
  hazardous, 82, 149-150, 154-156, 164, 170, 183-184, 194
  neobulk, 136

Cargo and Hazardous Materials Division, 153, 154

Cargo Promotion, Division of, 132

Chart operations, 63

Chemical Data Guide, 156

Chemical Transportation Industry Advisory Committee, 156

Civil Works Directorate, 98

Civil Works Investment Program, 94

Clean Air Act, 83, 85

Coast Guard, U.S. (USCG), 5, 39, 139-171
  budget of, 151, 163, 168, 202
  and the Department of Transportation, 40, 139, 141, 151, 154-155, 165-167, 172, 180, 183-184, 195-196
  organization of, 142-146
  and pollution, 85, 161-165, 171

Coast Guard (continued)
 and port development, 99, 204,
  215-216, 221-222
 regulations by, 109, 139-142,
  147-157, 161-166, 168-171, 190,
  195-196
Coastal Engineering Research Center
 (CERC), 93
Coastal Environment, Office of, 65
Coastal Zone, Committee on Multiple
 Use of the, 119
Coastal Zone Management, Office of
 (OCZM), 65, 205
Coastal Zone Management Act of
 1972, 35, 54, 63-64, 65, 70, 222
Coming of Post-Industrial Society,
 The (Bell), 21
Commerce, Department of, 56, 113, 178
 and the Economic Development Adminis-
 tration, 46
 and the Maritime Administration,
 126-127, 132, 180
 Secretary of, 213, 214, 217, 219
Commerce Committee, Senate, 39, 190
Commercial Fisheries, Bureau of, 62
Commercial Vessel Safety, 146, 153
Committee of Six, 27
Committee of Three, 27
Common Carrier Bureau, 50
Common carriers, regulation of, 59,
 61-62
Communications regulations, 50
Community Facilities Administration,
 49
Competition, port, 10-16, 18-19, 20,
 207
 and environmental regulations, 81,
 216
 and federal policy, 22, 41, 189,
 215-223
 and offshore terminals, 50, 217,
 222
Congress, port policies of, 35-39,
 210-214, 216-217. See also
 Legislation
 and the Corps of Engineers, 95-96,
 99, 110, 124
 and the Department of Transportation,
 176-178, 185, 197-199
 and economics, 197-199
Congressional and Intergovernmental
 Affairs, Office of the Assistant
 Secretary for, 184
Constitution (U.S.), 1, 22
Construction Engineering Research
 Lab (CERL), 93

Containerization, 1-3, 10-14, 59-60,
 116, 137, 206-208
Corps of Engineers, U.S. Army, 4-5,
 22, 39, 40, 87-125, 175, 211
 budget of, 3, 56, 77, 87, 88, 95-98,
 104-109, 116, 193, 202-203
 Chief of Engineers of, 98, 109, 110,
 123
 dredging by, 76-80, 87-88, 99, 115-116,
 119, 120-122, 203, 208-209, 215, 219,
 220-221
 and the Maritime Administration, 126,
 128
 organization of, 90-94
 and the U.S. Coast Guard, 166
Corpus Christi, Port of, 116
"Criteria for Determining Acceptability
 of Dredged Spoil Disposal to the
 Nation's Waters," 77
Cross-Florida Barge Canal, 76
Customs, Bureau of, 49, 50-51, 212

Dangerous Cargo Act of 1970, 149
Dearing, Charles, 178
Deepwater Port Act of 1974, 35, 37,
 49
 and the Department of Transportation,
 190-193, 196, 199, 217
 and offshore terminals, 49, 50, 53,
 61, 65, 70, 170, 172, 222
 and public ports, 216-217
Deepwater Port Liability Fund, 192
Deepwater ports. See also Offshore
 terminals
 and competition, 50
 and environmental policy, 19, 82,
 85-86, 192, 196
 legislation on, 55, 82. See also
 Deepwater Port Act of 1974
 regulation of, 170, 190-193, 216
 studies on, 54, 113, 114, 116, 134,
 193, 199
Deepwater Ports, Office of (ODP), 194,
 197, 221
Deepwater Ports Project, 170
Defense, Department of, 166
 Secretary of, 217
Defense policy, 22, 126, 141, 165-166
Delaware River Port Authority case,
 60
Department of Transportation Act of
 1966, 111-112, 141, 166, 183, 185,
 186, 194
Departmental Emergency Transportation
 Preparedness, 165

Digest of Water Resources Policies and
  Activities, 117
Discount rate, 31, 33-35, 58, 88, 123
Domestic and International Transporta-
  tion of U.S. Foreign Trade for 1970,
  113-114
DOT. See Transportation, Department
  of
Doyle, Thomas, 178
Doyle Report, 178
Dredged Material Study Program, 115
Dredging
  evaluation of, 115-116, 219
  finance of, 56, 104, 108, 116, 119,
    203, 208-209, 215, 220-221
  regulations of, 76-80, 87-88, 99,
    115-116, 120-122
Dredging Study, National, 115

Economic Advisers, Council of (CEA),
  54
"Economic Aspects of Refinery and
  Deep-Water Port Location in the
  United States," 193
Economic Development Administration
  (EDA), 3, 46-47, 134, 203, 216, 217
"Economic Rationalization of Port
  Investments," 9
Economics. See also Budgets, federal
  and the Corps of Engineers, 94-98,
    119, 124
  of deepwater ports, 19, 54, 193,
    199
  of oil transport, 170
  of port investments, 1, 9-10, 18,
    111, 122-123, 207-209, 216, 219
  and technology, 87
  of transportation, 173-174, 186,
    197-199
"Economics of Great Lakes Shipping
  in an Extended Season," 135
Electric power regulation, 50
Emergencies, 51, 165-166, 207
Emergency Preparedness, Office of
  (OEP), 51
End of Liberalism, The (Lowi), 21
Energy Administration, Federal (FEA),
  49, 204
Energy policies, 49, 85, 204
Engineers. See Corps of Engineers,
  U.S. Army
Entomology and Plant Quarantine,
  Bureau of, 49, 51
Environment, Safety and Consumer
  Affairs, Office of the Assistant
  Secretary for, 183, 188, 194, 196
Environmental Data Service, 63

Environmental Impact Statements (EIS),
  3, 53, 74-76, 83, 117, 162, 221
Environmental policy, 4-5, 112, 117,
  220
  and competition, 81, 216
  and deepwater ports, 19, 82, 85-86,
    192, 196
  and the Department of Transportation,
    187
  on dredging, 76-80, 87-88, 99, 104,
    120-122, 220-221
  legislation for, 1, 3, 4, 50, 53,
    73, 82, 88, 120, 171
  organizations for, 73-86
  and the U.S. Coast Guard, 85,
    161-165, 171
Environmental Protection Agency (EPA),
  56, 81, 82-85, 164, 184
  and deepwater ports, 192
  and dredging, 77, 99, 120, 121
  and port development, 52, 204, 220
Environmental Quality, Council on
  (CEQ), 56, 81-82, 83, 85, 117,
  162
  and port development, 52, 203, 220
Environmental Quality, Office of,
  81-82
Environmental Quality Improvement
  Act of 1970, 82
Environmental research, 46, 53, 63,
  120, 135
Environmental Research Labs, 63
Environmental Science Services
  Administration, 62
Espionage Act of 1917, 141, 147
Executive reorganization plans,
  51, 54, 58, 62, 82, 128
Explosive Loading Details (ELD), 149

Facilitation, Office of, 188
Federal, Communications Commission
  (FCC), 49, 50
Federal Energy Administration Act of
  1974, 49
Federal port policy. See Port policy
Federal Register, 64, 83, 117
Federal Reports Act of 1942, 112
Federal Water Pollution Control Act
  (FWPCA), 83, 85, 96, 120, 121,
  134, 162
Finance. See Budgets, federal; Budgets,
  state; Economics
Fire prevention and fighting, 160-161
Flood Control Acts
  of 1937, 110
  of 1954, 110
  of 1965, 110
  of 1970, 111, 112

FMC. See Maritime Commission,
  Federal
"Foreign Deep Water Port Develop-
  ments," 112-113
Functional rationality, 21

Gallatin, Albert, 175
Gallatin Plan, 175
Gas regulation, 50
General Services Administration
  (GSA), 49, 51, 136
General Survey Act of 1824, 22, 23
Geological Survey, 52-53
Great Lakes shipping operations, 135

Hamilton, Alexander, 139
Hamilton, Lee, 38
Hazardous cargo, 82, 149-150,
  154-156, 164, 170, 183-184, 194
Hazardous Materials, Office of, 183
Hazardous Materials Transportation
  Control Act of 1970, 155
Health, Education and Welfare,
  Department of, 49
  Secretary of, 56
High Water Mark ownership, 66
Highways Administration, Federal, 180
Highways Trust Fund, 212
Hinterland of the port, 10, 11-16
Hoover, Herbert, 178
Hoover Commission, 178
Housing and Home Finance Agency, 46
Housing and Urban Development,
  Department of (HUD), 49, 51, 56
Humphrey, Hubert, 197, 210

Immigration and Naturalization
  Service, 49, 50, 51
Impact of Maritime Containerization
  on the United States Transportation
  System, The, 206
Inland Waterways Administration, 172,
  197, 211, 216
Inland Waterways Commission, 25
Inter-Agency Committee, National, 162
Intercoastal Shipping Act of 1933, 59
Inter-Governmental Maritime Consultative
  Organization (IMCO), 156
"Interim Review Report on Los Angeles-
  Long Beach Harbors," 119
Interior, Department of the (DOI), 39,
  52-53, 98, 204
  Secretary of, 53, 56, 190
Interior Committee, Senate, 55
Interior and Insular Affairs Committee,
  37
Intermodal Service at Philadelphia

case, 60
Intermodal Service to Portland, Oregon
  case, 59-60, 189
Intermodal Transport, Division of, 132
Internal Revenue Service (IRS), 49, 51
International Convention for the
  Prevention of Pollution of the Sea
  by Oil, 162
International law, and offshore
  terminals, 49
Interstate Commerce Act of 1887, 23,
  61, 136
Interstate Commerce Commission (ICC),
  23, 58, 61-62, 176, 177, 189, 204,
  211
Interstate and Foreign Commerce
  Committee, 136, 176, 178
Investigation and Research, Board of,
  27-28

Johnson, Lyndon B., 178
Jones, James R., 56
Justice, Department of, 49, 50

Kennedy, John F., 57
Kerr, Robert, 56-57
Koisch, Frank, 104
Knecht, Robert, 65

Labor, Department of, 49, 50
Labor and Public Welfare Committee,
  Senate, 56
Lake Survey, U.S., 63
Land Management, Bureau of (BLM), 53
Land resources, 53, 56, 57
Land Use and Water Planning, Office
  of, 53
LASH (Lighter Aboard SHip), 14
Law enforcement. See Regulations
Law Enforcement Division, 162
Legislation, 211-212. See also Congress;
  individual acts
  and competition, 22
  and the Corps of Engineers, 110-112
  on deepwater ports, 55, 65, 70,
    190-193
  environmental, 1, 3, 4, 50, 53, 73,
    82, 88, 120, 171
  for port finance, 47, 110, 212-214,
    216
  and promotion, 36-37
  on transportation, 23-29, 184
  on the U.S. Coast Guard, 143
Licensing, of deepwater ports, 53,
  170, 172, 190-193, 196, 216
Lifesaving Service, 140
Lighthouse Establishment, 140

Liquefied natural gas (LNG),
50, 156, 170, 194
Liquid petroleum gas (LPG), 154,
170
Little, Arthur D., Inc., 112, 115,
134
Local port policy, 3, 6, 23,
143-146
Locks and Dam 26, 76, 190
Long Beach, Port of, 10
Longshoring unions, 210
Los Angeles, Port of, 10, 119, 208
 Director of Planning and Research,
16
Louisiana Offshore Oil Port, Inc.
(LOOP), 18-19
Lowi, Theodore, 21

Mail regulations, 52
Management and Budget, Office of
(OMB), 52, 54-56, 95, 98, 109,
168, 185
 and dredging, 56, 220
 and port development, 205, 211
 and user charges, 30-31, 56
Manalytics Inc., 137
Manual of Orders, 132, 133
Marine Council, 119
Marine Environment and Systems,
Office of, 143, 160, 163
Marine Environmental Protection
Program, 162
Marine Fisheries Service, National,
63
Marine Inspection, Officer in Charge
(OCMI), 143, 146, 153
Marine Inspection and Navigation,
Bureau of, 141
Marine Inspection Zones, 146
Marine Mammals Protection Act of
1972, 63
Marine Mineral Technology Center,
62
"Marine Oil Pollution Control," 164
Marine Protection, Research, and
Sanctuaries Act of 1972, 63, 99,
120
Marine Resources and Engineering
Development Act of 1966, 29
Marine Sport Fisheries Program, 62
Marine Studies, Engineering and
Resources, Commission on, 29
Marine Traffic Management Branch, 160

Maritime Administration (Mar Ad),
5, 6, 25, 51, 126-138, 180, 193
budget of, 18, 47, 126, 135-136, 137
and container terminals, 11-14
organization of, 130
and port development, 40, 210-211,
219
research by, 204, 217
Maritime Board, 127, 128
Maritime Commission, 127-128
Maritime Commission, Federal (FMC),
52, 58-61, 128, 211
and mini-landbridges, 59, 60-61, 62,
76, 172, 196, 215
regulations by, 189, 204
Maritime Pollution Control Branch,
162, 163
Maritime Subsidy Board, 126
Maryland, Department of Transportation
of, 71
Mean Low Water Mark ownership, 66
Memorandum of Understanding between
the Economic Development Administration
and the Maritime Administration, 47
Merchant Marine, U.S., 46, 126
Merchant Marine Act of 1920, 25, 59,
126-127, 132, 134, 136-137, 138
Merchant Marine Act of 1936, 59, 127
Merchant Marine Act of 1970, 211
Merchant Marine and Fisheries
Committee, 37, 211
Merchant Marine Safety, 142, 146,
151-161
Office of, 151, 153-154, 156,
183-184, 196
Michigan, University of, shipping
studies of, 135
Military readiness. See Defense
policy
Mines, Bureau of, 62
Mini-landbridge cases
and the Federal Maritime Commission,
59, 60-61, 62, 76, 172, 196, 215
and the Secretary of Transportation,
189, 216

Nathan, Robert R., Associates, 113
National Aeronautics and Space
Administration (NASA), 46, 135
National Data Buoy Project, 63
National Environmental Policy Act of
1969 (NEPA), 50, 81-82, 97, 112,
121, 183

National Environmental Policy Act
of 1969 (continued)
and Environmental Impact Statements,
3, 53, 74, 83, 117, 162
National Journal Reports (NJR), 55-56
National Resources Planning Board, 27,
177-178
National Response Team, 162
Natural Gas Pipeline Safety Act of
1968, 183, 194
Navigable waters of the United States,
96, 99, 120
Navigational Aids, 142
Navy, U.S. 46, 140-141
"Neobulk Shipping Study," 136
New Hampshire Office of Comprehensive
Planning, 65
New Orleans, Port of, 61
New York City Department of Ports and
Terminals, 10
NOAA. See Oceanographic and Atmospheric
Administration, National
"North American Port Development
Expenditure Survey," 135
North Atlantic Container Pool Agreement
case, 59
North Atlantic Ports Association, 136

Occupational Safety and Health
Administration (OSHA), 49, 50
Ocean Survey, National, 63
Oceanographic and Atmospheric Adminis-
tration, National (NOAA), 53-54, 55,
62-66, 70, 192
Oceanographic Data Center, National, 63
Oceanographic Instrumental Center,
National, 63
Oceanographic Office, 46
Oceans Agency, Federal, 39
Oceans Policy Study, National, 39
"Offshore Terminal Systems Concepts,"
134
Offshore terminals, 49, 53, 61, 65,
70, 183. See also Deepwater ports
and competition, 18-19, 50
development of, 116, 134, 197
and dredging, 217
economics of, 19, 193, 199
and environmental policy, 19, 85-86
licensing of, 170, 172, 190-193, 196
ownership of, 66
state policy on, 70, 222
Oil and Hazardous Materials Pollution
Control, National Contingency Plan
for, 82, 162

Oil Pollution Act of 1961, 162
Oil transport, 1, 85-86, 162-165,
170, 184
OMB. See Management and Budget,
Office of
Operations Research, Inc., 22, 128
Ordinary High Tide Mark ownership, 66
Organization-sets, 40
Outer Continental Shelf Lands Act,
53
Outer Continental Shelf Mineral
Leasing Program, 53
Overcapacity, of container terminals,
206-208
Owen, Wilfred, 178
Ownership, port. See Private ports;
Public ports

Permit authority, 99, 104, 120-121
Pipeline Safety, Office of, 183, 194
Planning and development, 46-49, 54-58
by the Corps of Engineers, 94, 122-123
by the Maritime Administration,
130-134
of transportation, 22, 174, 175,
185-187, 199-201
in the U.S. Coast Guard, 166-168
Planning-Programming-Budgeting-System
(PPBS), 167, 187
Plant pests regulation, 51-52
Policy. See Port policy
Policy, Plans and International
Affairs, Office of Assistant
Secretary for (TPI), 193
Politics, and port policies, 35-39,
123-125, 197, 211-212
Pollutant Discharge Elimination
System, National (NPDES), 83
Pollution. See also Environmental
policy
control of, 83, 134, 150, 151,
161-165, 171
detection of, 46
legislation about, 3, 192
Pooling, of carrier services, 59
Port, Captain of the (COTP), 143, 146,
147-151, 153, 155, 161
Port Authorities, American Association
of (AAPA), 72, 81, 214
Port Finance Committee of, 16
Port Authority of New York and New
Jersey, 10
Port development, 6-14, 22, 202-214,
215-223. See also Planning and
development

Port development (continued)
  budgets for, 3, 37-39, 46-49,
    64, 202-203, 208-209
  and the Corps of Engineers, 94,
    122-123, 202-203
  and the Maritime Administration,
    126-127, 130-134
  and states, 205
  and the U.S. Coast Guard, 99, 204,
    215-216, 221-222
Port of entry, 51
Port policy, 40, 46-66, 126, 132-134,
  203-204, 215-223. See also Local
  port policy; Regional port policy;
  State port policy
  of Congress, 35-39, 210-214, 216-217
  and the Department of Transportation,
    185-199, 203
  history of, 1-5, 21-39
  impact of, 41-42
Port Safety/Security, 147, 156, 160,
  163
Port study, national, 219-222
Portland, Port of, 59, 189
Ports. See Deepwater ports; Offshore
  terminals; Private ports; Public
  ports
Ports, Division of, 132
Ports and Intermodal Systems, Office
  of (OPIS), 132, 133, 134
Ports and Systems, Division of, 132,
  133
Ports and Waterways Planning Staff,
  143, 146
Ports and Waterways Safety Act of 1970,
  146-147
Ports and Waterways Safety Act of 1971,
  35, 36, 150, 161
Ports and Waterways Safety Act of 1972,
  109, 151, 154, 155, 157, 170, 198
Postal Service, U.S., 49, 52
"Potential Onshore Effects of Deepwater
  Oil Terminal-Related Industrial
  Development," 85
Power Commission, Federal (FPC), 49, 50,
  98
  Chairman of, 56
Prevention and Detection of Illegal
  Entry (PADIE), 151
Principles and Standards for Planning,
  of the Water Resources Council, 57,
  122, 123
Private ports, 6-7, 19
Promotion
  in legislation, 36-37
  in the Maritime Administration, 137

Proxmire, William, 124, 208
Public Health Service, U.S., 49, 51,
  52
"Public Port Financing in the United
  States," 135
Public ports, 6, 7-20, 66, 216-217
  and environmental regulations, 81
  facilities for, 202, 213-214
  finance of, 136, 213-214
Public Works Committee, 37, 98, 104,
  110, 114
Public Works Impact Program (PWIP), 47
Public works programs, 175. See also
  Corps of Engineers, U.S. Army

Quarantines, 51, 52

Radioactive waste, 46
Railroad Administration, Federal, 180
Railroad War Board, 176
Railroads, 173, 175, 176
  regulation of, 23, 27, 62, 112, 136
Railroads, Association of American,
  125
Rate absorption cases, 59-60, 62, 172,
  195-196
Rates
  discount, 31, 33-35, 58, 88, 123
  regulation of, 59-62
Rationality, functional, 21
Recreation projects, 121
Refuse Act of 1899, 162
Regional port policy, 3, 119-120,
  143-146
Regional Representatives, 185
Regulations
  by the Department of Transportation,
    183
  on dredging, 76-80, 87-88, 99,
    115-116, 120-122
  organizations for, 49-52, 58-66
  power of, 22, 223
  by the U.S. Coast Guard, 109, 139-142,
    147-157, 161-166, 168-171, 190,
    195-196
Reorganization plans. See Executive
  reorganization plans
"Replacement of Alton Locks and Dam
  26, An Advisory Report of the
  Department of Transportation to the
  Senate Commerce Committee," 190
Report of the Commission on Marine
  Science, Engineering and Resources, 62
Research organizations, 46, 52-54, 63,
  93, 164-165
Revenue Cutter Service, 139-141

River Basin Commissions, 56
River and Harbor Acts, 90
  of 1823, 175
  of 1899, 99
  of 1902, 114
  of 1915, 146
  of 1917, 109
  of 1918, 110
  of 1945, 110
  of 1960, 109, 110
  of 1968, 109
  of 1970, 109, 110, 111, 112
Rivers and Harbors, Board of
  Engineers for (BERH), 94, 98
Robert R. Nathan Associates, 113
Robinson, C. W., 59
Roosevelt, Franklin D., 27, 177
Roosevelt, Theodore, 25

Safety
  and the Department of Transportation,
    183, 187, 192, 194
  and the U.S. Coast Guard, 146-161, 192
Saint Lawrence Seaway Development
  Corporation, 180
San Francisco Bay Area In-Depth
  Study, 114
Schenker, Eric, 124-125
Science Foundation, National, 63
Sea Grant Programs, Office of, 63
Seadock, 19
Search and Rescue, 142
Sea-Train, Inc., 61
Seattle, Port of, 10, 16, 189
Secretaries. See individual departments
Security, of ports, 141, 147
Senate Select Committee on Committees, 38
Senate Select Committee on National
  Water Resources, 56-57
Shipping Act of 1916, 25, 59, 126
Shipping Board, 25, 126
Smithsonian Institution, 46
Smuggling, 139
Soros Associates, 134
Space vehicle transport, 46
Sport Fisheries and Wildlife, Bureau
  of, 53, 62
State, Department of, 49
"State Coastal Zone Management
  Activities," 65
State port policy, 3, 23, 66-71, 80-81,
  205, 222
Stratton Commission, 29
"Study of the Corps of Engineers'
  Regional Pattern of Investments,"
  124-125

Subcommittee on Investigations and
  Oversight, 104
Superports. See Offshore terminals
Systems Analysis and Information,
  Office of, 113
Systems Development and Technology,
  Office of, 184

Taft, William H., 140
Tank vessel regulations, 150
Technology, 1, 87, 115-120, 164-165,
  170, 184, 200
Technology Review, 164
Tennessee Valley Authority, 211
Terminal facilities. See
  Containerization; Offshore terminals
Texas, superport of, 18, 116
Texas General Land Office, 65
Texas Intercoastal Canal case, 80-81
Three Marine Leagues ownership, 66
Three Mile ownership, 66
Trade Commission, Federal (FTC), 49,
  50, 192
Trade Studies, Division of, 132
Traffic systems, 156-160
Transportation, 173-184
  and economics, 37-39, 173-174,
    186, 197-199
  history of, 173-180
  policy on, 174, 177, 185-197
  and port policy, 22-29, 53, 58,
    61-62, 126, 185-199
  in states, 70, 71, 222
  and water resources, 32, 197-199
Transportation, Department of (DOT),
  5, 32, 52, 71, 74, 172-201, 211,
  219
  and the Corps of Engineers, 113
  and deepwater ports, 190-193, 196,
    199, 217
  and the future, 199-201
  history of, 23, 27-29, 175-180
  and the Maritime Administration, 210
  and mini-landbridges, 215
  organization of, 180-185
  policies of, 185-199, 203
  and port competition, 221-222
  Secretary of. See Transportation,
    Office of the Secretary of
  and the U.S. Coast Guard, 40, 139,
    141, 151, 165-167, 172, 180, 183-184,
    195-196
Transportation, Office of the Secretary
  of (OST), 56, 180, 183, 185
  and economics, 198, 215-216
  licensing by, 53, 170, 172
  and port competition, 221-222

Transportation, Office of the
  Secretary of (continued)
 and the U.S. Coast Guard, 154-155,
  161, 166
Transportation Act of 1920, 176
Transportation Act of 1940, 27, 177
Transportation Authority, Federal, 27
Transportation Board, Federal, 27
Transportation of Explosives Act, 183,
  194
Transportation Safety Board, National,
  180
Transportation Studies, National, 188-189,
  200
Treasury, Department of the, 49, 50,
  51, 139, 140
 Secretary of, 51, 139, 141, 175

Uncle Sam--The Last of the Big Time
  Spenders (Proxmire), 124
Uniform Code of Military Justice, 184
Uniform Intermodal Interchange Agreement,
  188
Urban Renewal Administration, 49
U.S. Code, 63
User charges, for inland waterways,
  30-33, 56, 88, 172, 212, 216

Very Large Crude Carriers (VLCCs), 85
Vessel Traffic System (VTS) Study,
  158-160
Virginia State Ports Authority, 222

Washington Public Ports Association, 136
Water Commission, National, 29-31, 34,
  104, 210, 212
Water Pollution Control Act of 1972, 184
Water Quality Improvement Act (WQIA) of
  1970, 59, 82, 150, 154, 155, 162, 163
Water resources
 and economics, 32, 197-199
 policy on, 29-30, 34, 39, 88, 93-94,
  110, 111
 protection of, 56-57, 83-85
 research on, 52-53, 93-94
Water Resources, Institute of (IWR),
  93-94, 112-113
Water Resources Council (WRC), 53, 54,
  56-58, 97, 98, 111
 and the Department of Transportation,
  187, 198, 217
 and discount rates, 34, 123
 and dredging, 108, 203, 210
 and user charges, 30-31

Water Resources Development Act of
  1974, 34, 58, 123
Water Resources Planning Act of
  1965, 56, 57
Water Resources Research, Office
  of, 53
Waterways, Assistant Secretary
  for, 197
Waterways Conference Newsletter,
  National, 56
Waterways Experiment Station (WES),
  93, 112, 115
Waterways Operators, American (AWO),
  32, 72
Weather Modification Reporting Act
  of 1972, 63
Weather Service, National, 63
Woodworth, Lourin, 176
"Work Plan for a Study of the
  Feasibility of an Offshore Terminal
  in the Texas Coast Region," 18